PHR®/SPHR®
Professional in Human Resources Certification Practice Exams

PHR®/SPHR®
Professional in Human Resources Certification Practice Exams

Tresha Moreland, MBA, MS, SPHR
Gabriella Parente-Neubert, MLHR, PHR
Joanne Simon-Walters, MBA, PHR

New York • Chicago • San Francisco
Athens • London • Madrid • Mexico City
Milan • New Delhi • Singapore • Sydney • Toronto

Cataloging-in-Publication Data is on file with the Library of Congress

McGraw-Hill Education books are available at special quantity discounts to use as premiums and sales promotions, or for use in corporate training programs. To contact a representative, please visit the Contact Us pages at www.mhprofessional.com.

PHR®/SPHR® Professional in Human Resources Certification Practice Exams

Copyright © 2014 by McGraw-Hill Education. All rights reserved. Printed in the United States of America. Except as permitted under the Copyright Act of 1976, no part of this publication may be reproduced or distributed in any form or by any means, or stored in a database or retrieval system, without the prior written permission of publisher, with the exception that the program listings may be entered, stored, and executed in a computer system, but they may not be reproduced for publication.

All trademarks or copyrights mentioned herein are the possession of their respective owners and McGraw-Hill Education makes no claim of ownership by the mention of products that contain these marks.

1 2 3 4 5 6 7 8 9 0   DOC DOC   1 0 9 8 7 6 5 4

ISBN: Book p/n 978-0-07-184088-0 and CD p/n 978-0-07-184089-7
of set 978-0-07-184091-0

MHID: Book p/n 0-07-184088-5 and CD p/n 0-07-184089-3
of set 0-07-184091-5

Sponsoring Editor	**Acquisitions Coordinator**	**Proofreader**	**Illustration**
Stephanie Evans	Mary Demery	Susie Elkind	Cenveo Publisher Services
Editorial Supervisor	**Technical & Developmental Editor**	**Production Supervisor**	**Art Director, Cover**
Patty Mon	Bill Kelly	Jean Bodeaux	Jeff Weeks
Project Manager	**Copy Editor**	**Composition**	
Harleen Chopra, Cenveo® Publisher Services	Nancy Rapoport	Cenveo Publisher Services	

Information has been obtained by McGraw-Hill Education from sources believed to be reliable. However, because of the possibility of human or mechanical error by our sources, McGraw-Hill Education, or others, McGraw-Hill Education does not guarantee the accuracy, adequacy, or completeness of any information and is not responsible for any errors or omissions or the results obtained from the use of such information.

McGraw-Hill Education is an independent entity from HR Certification Institute™ and is not affiliated with HR Certification Institute in any manner. This publication and CD-ROM are not sponsored by, endorsed by, or affiliated with HR Certification Institute in any manner. This publication and CD-ROM may be used in assisting students to prepare for the Professional in Human Resources (PHR®) and Senior Professional in Human Resources (SPHR®) exams. Neither HR Certification Institute nor McGraw-Hill Education warrant that use of this publication and CD-ROM will ensure passing any exam. PHR and SPHR are registered trademarks of HR Certification Institute in the United States and certain other countries. All other trademarks are trademarks of their respective owners.

I would like to dedicate this book to human resource professionals who wish to propel their careers forward. In the words of Aristotle, "We are what we repeatedly do. Excellence, therefore, is not an act but a habit." May excellence be your habit.

—*Tresha*

I would like to dedicate this book to my daughter, Grace. You are my inspiration, the light in my eyes, and the smile on my face every day. Having you as my daughter has been my greatest accomplishment and my most cherished gift. I love you.

—*Gabriella*

I would like to dedicate this book to my husband, Steven Walters; my five-year-old son, Steven Drake Walters II; and my one-year-old daughter, Farai Chase Walters. The three of you are my constant source of inspiration.

—*Joanne*

ABOUT THE AUTHORS

Tresha Moreland, MBA, MS, SPHR, is an executive leader in Human Resources. She has held key human resource leadership roles for over 20 years in multiple industries, such as manufacturing, distribution, retail, hospitality, and healthcare. She has developed a business philosophy of integrating human resources with business strategy, creating a hybrid HR leadership approach. This approach enables the leveraging of human resources to achieve business results.

Tresha is the founder and publisher of HR C-Suite (www.hrcsuite.com). HR C-Suite is a first-of-its-kind resource that organizes HR strategy based on desired business result. She has received a master's degree in human resource management (MS) and a master's degree in business administration (MBA). She has also earned a certification as a Senior Professional in Human Resources (SPHR).

Gabriella Parente-Neubert, MLHR, PHR, has more than 12 years of progressive HR experience maximizing a company's human capital potential in multiple industries, including manufacturing, nonprofit, insurance, and consulting fields. Gabriella has unique insights into what makes people successful in their careers and how that impacts the bottom line of an organization.

Gabriella also works to transform lives and careers as a certified life/career coach and as an adjunct professor. Gabriella holds her Professional in Human Resources and received her BS in Psychology from Heidelberg University and an MS in Labor and Human Resources from The Ohio State University.

Joanne Simon-Walters, MBA, PHR, has over 15 years of progressive management experience in multiple industries: educational services, K–12 and higher education, information technology, financial services, and nonprofit organizations. Joanne is an experienced HR Director for a nonprofit school network and teaches HR and technology workshops at a community college.

Joanne is Professional in Human Resources (PHR)–certified, holds an MBA with a concentration in technology management and a BBA with a concentration in finance. Joanne is a trained paralegal specializing in employment law and blogs at http://hrvista.wordpress.com/. She is also a member of multiple professional organizations including the Society for Human Resources Management and the National Association for African-Americans in Human Resources.

About the Technical and Developmental Editor

Bill Kelly, SPHR-CA, is the owner of Kelly HR, an HR consulting services firm specializing in providing generalist HR consulting services and support for small business enterprises. Bill's experience includes over 40 years of professional-level HR responsibilities that include 22 years within the industry at Bechtel in San Francisco California, and, later, at Brown and Caldwell Environmental Engineers in Pleasant Hill, California. His credentials include experience in employee relations, state and federal legal compliance, staffing and recruitment, equal employment opportunity and affirmative action, compensation, benefits, training and development, health and safety, and government contract management. Bill also has 18 years of HR consulting experience, which includes providing HR services, support, and advice to a wide range of Northern California clients. For 17 years, he has served as an instructor for the University of California Extension Program teaching Management of Human Resources; Recruiting, Selection, and Placement; and California Employment Law, as well as professional HR Certification Preparation courses for U.C. Berkeley. Bill has taught Professional PHR/SPHR Certification Preparation for 15 years and California HR Certification Preparation for 7 years for the Society for Human Resource Management (SHRM) and the Northern California HR Association (NCHRA). He played a key role in the development of California's HR certification credential; also, he was the project manager for the team of California HR professionals who developed SHRM's first California Learning System in support of California certification. Bill's professional leadership also includes roles on the Board of Directors and National Vice President for the Society for Human Resource Management (SHRM); the Board of Directors and President for the HR Certification Institute (HRCI); State Director, California State Council of SHRM; the Board of Directors and President for the Northern California HR Association (NCHRA); and Commissioner and Chair, Marin County Personnel Commission. Bill received his BS in political science from Spring Hill College in Mobile, Alabama, and undertook post-graduate studies in Organizational Management at the College of William and Mary in Williamsburg, Virginia, and the University of Virginia in Richmond, Virginia. Prior to HR, Bill had a military career, achieving the rank of Major in the United States Army with tours of duty in the United States, Germany, Thailand, and Vietnam.

CONTENTS

Preface xi

Acknowledgments xxi

Introduction xxiii

Chapter 1 Pre-Assessment Test: PHR and SPHR 1

Questions 3

Quick Answer Key 20

Answers 22

Chapter 2 Business Management and Strategy 39

Questions 42

Quick Answer Key 78

Answers 79

Chapter 3 Workforce Planning and Employment 109

Questions 111

Quick Answer Key 142

Answers 143

Chapter 4 Human Resource Development 167

Questions 169

Quick Answer Key 194

Answers 195

Chapter 5 Compensation and Benefits 215

Questions 217

Quick Answer Key 237

Answers 238

Chapter 6 Employee and Labor Relations 253

Questions 255

Quick Answer Key 277

Answers 278

Chapter 7   Risk Management   297

Questions   299

Quick Answer Key   315

Answers   316

Appendix   About the CD-ROM   329

System Requirements   329

Total Tester Premium Practice Exam Software   329

PDF Copy of the Book   330

Technical Support   330

Contents

PREFACE

The objective of this book is to prepare you for the PHR and SPHR exams by familiarizing you with the functional areas of the PHR and SPHR Bodies of Knowledge as well as the style, format, and difficulty of the exam questions. The questions in this book explore the more complex topics of the PHR and SPHR Bodies of Knowledge you may be faced with when you take the PHR or SPHR exam.

The best approach to prepare for either the PHR or the SPHR exam using this book is to:

1. Take the pre-assessment exam in Chapter 1.

2. Determine your strengths and weaknesses based on the results of the pre-assessment exam. Decide on first-, second-, and third-priority areas for study so that you can budget your study time effectively. Consider whether you may need an additional self-study resource, such as the *PHR®/SPHR® Professional in Human Resources Certification All-in-One Exam Guide*.

3. Review the questions and in-depth answers to ensure you understand not only why an answer is correct, but also why the other answers were wrong.

4. Remember that all of the questions and in-depth answer explanations in the print book are included in the test engine on the companion CD-ROM, allowing you to practice questions in both print and electronic format. If you are interested in full-length practice exams, rather than studying by specific functional area, we recommend you go straight to the CD-ROM and select Practice Exam for the PHR or SPHR exam.

Because the primary focus of this book is to help you pass the exams, we cover all functional areas of both the PHR and SPHR exam. Each question in the book features a detailed explanation of why one answer choice is the correct answer and why each of the other answer choices is incorrect. Because of this, we believe this book will also serve as a valuable professional resource after your exam.

Inside This Book

We've organized this book so that each chapter consists of a battery of practice exam questions representing one of the functional areas, with the answer explanations providing the emphasis on the "why" as well as the "how-to" of working with and supporting human resource concepts.

The Human Resources Certification Institute PHR and SPHR Body of Knowledge divides objectives into "Responsibilities" and "Knowledge of" objectives. The Knowledge objectives indicate the scope of the information you need to know, whereas the Responsibilities objectives indicate the ways in which you should know how to apply that knowledge in a professional setting. If you do not have the required knowledge outlined in the Knowledge objectives, it is unlikely you will know how to properly apply that knowledge outlined in the Responsibilities objectives. The majority of questions in this book ask you to apply your knowledge in an HR setting, rather than simply to recall or identify information.

In Every Chapter

We've created a set of chapter features that will guide you through the study and review process, and provide helpful exam-taking hints. Take a look at what you'll find in every chapter:

- Every chapter focuses on one **functional area** with questions specific to that area.

- The **practice exam questions** are similar to those found on the actual exams, and are meant to present you with some of the most common and confusing problems that you may encounter when taking the actual exams. The questions are designed to help you anticipate what the exam will emphasize and to help ensure you know what you need to know to pass the exams.

- The **Quick Answer Key** provides the question number with the corresponding letter for the correct answer. This allows you to score your answers quickly before you begin your review of the explanations.

- Each question is accompanied by an **in-depth answer explanation—** explanations are provided for both the correct and incorrect answers, and can be found at the end of each chapter. By reading the answer explanations, you'll reinforce what you learned when answering the questions, while also becoming familiar with the structure of the exam questions.

Pre-Assessment Test

This book features a pre-assessment test as its first chapter. The pre-assessment test will help you gauge whether you're ready to start with practice exams, or whether you may need to spend more time reviewing a PHR/SPHR self-study guide beforehand. It will also help you assess your areas of strength and weakness and allow you to tailor your studies based on your needs. We recommend you stake this pre-assessment before beginning Chapter 2.

Exam Objective Map

Following the introduction, you will find an Exam Objective Map. This map has been constructed in the form of a table to allow you to reference the official certification exam objective, the chapter in which each objective is covered, and the specific questions pertaining to each objective.

On the CD-ROM

Included on the CD-ROM, you will find all of the practice exam questions included in this print book in a customizable Total Tester Premium Edition Test Engine. The test engine allows you to select all PHR or SPHR questions. You can choose to take full-length practice exams that simulate the actual exam environment, or to build custom practice exams that focus on particular functional areas.

For more information on the CD-ROM, please see the Appendix.

How to Use This Book

While this book is designed as a stand-alone practice exams book, you may find that you need additional study before you are ready to start answering practice exam questions. This book serves as an excellent companion to McGraw-Hill Education's *PHR®/SPHR® Professional in Human Resources Certification All-in-One Exam Guide*. These books can work together as a comprehensive program for self-study, but both books are discrete and complete test prep guides.

Strategies for Use

There are a variety of ways in which this book can be used, whether in tandem with the *All-in-One Exam Guide* or on its own.

With the All-in-One Exam Guide   If you opt for this approach, you can begin by taking the pre-assessment test included as Chapter 1 in this practice exams book. This pre-assessment test will help you gauge your level of competency in each of the different functional areas and highlight those areas in which you excel and those in which you would benefit from additional review. Knowing this information at the outset of your studies will allow you to check your progress and allot your study time based on your needs.

Taking a chapter-by-chapter approach, you can opt to read an All-in-One Exam Guide chapter, then practice what you have learned with the questions in the corresponding Practice Exams chapter, alternating between books throughout your course of study. You can work through the chapter of questions in the practice exams book, or select that functional area as a custom exam on the CD-ROM. Each question in the Total Tester maps to a chapter in the All-in-One Exam Guide. Both books cover one functional area per chapter and work together well as companion study resources.

Alternately, you can work through the entire All-in-One Exam Guide, then use the two practice exams included with the All-in-One Exam Guide's CD-ROM, and the more than 600 practice exam questions in the Practice Exams book's CD-ROM for a battery of full practice exams to build your exam-taking confidence and stamina.

The Practice Exams Book on Its Own   Whether you are using this book after you have read the All-in-One Exam Guide or you're using it on its own, one course of study is to begin with the pre-assessment test in Chapter 1. Armed with the knowledge of your levels of expertise by functional area, you can use the Exam Objective Map to tailor the order in which you review the objectives and practice exam questions.

Or, if you are simply looking for practice exams, you can skip straight to the Total Tester Premium Edition test engine and begin taking full-length, timed, electronic practice exams. The exams can also be customized by functional area, so you can focus your studies on one or two functional areas at a time, or all of them at once. You can also customize your exams to be shorter to build up your exam-taking stamina, or start with the full 175-question practice exams. The Total Tester has a pool of more than 600 practice exam questions to draw from to create randomized exams that are designed to represent the kinds of questions—and number of questions in each functional area—that you'll see on the actual PHR or SPHR exam.

The Professional in Human Resources (PHR) and Senior Professional in Human Resources (SPHR) Exams

A common question that many HR professionals ask themselves is which credential should they pursue and what is the difference?

Professional in Human Resources (PHR)

The Professional in Human Resources (PHR) certification focuses on the technical and operational aspects of Human Resources. This focus includes HR practices and U.S. laws and regulations. According to HRCI, the PHR certification is ideal for those HR professionals whose focus is on program implementation and has a tactical orientation. Generally, it is for the individual who may report to another HR professional and has responsibilities that are focused on tasks versus organizational strategies.

The PHR certification is recommended for those professionals who are exempt and have at least two years of experience. Exempt status is defined by the Fair Labor Standards Act (FLSA). Incidentally, what is exempt versus non-exempt and the FLSA are good topics to know for the exam. While two years of experience are recommended, the formal eligibility requirements are

- A minimum of one year of experience in an exempt-level HR position with a master's degree or higher, OR

- A minimum of two years of experience in an exempt-level HR position with a bachelor's degree, OR

- A minimum of four years of experience in an exempt-level HR position with a high school diploma

Senior Professional in Human Resources (SPHR)

The Senior Professional Human Resources (SPHR) certification is ideal for HR professionals who focus on organizational strategy and policy making. According to HRCI, the ideal candidate for this exam is one who plans, versus one who implements, programs or policies. The SPHR level candidate focuses on the "big picture" and is accountable for HR outcomes and how those outcomes impact the organization as a whole. An SPHR-level candidate possesses a breadth and depth of knowledge in all HR disciplines and understands the business beyond the HR function.

Like PHR candidates, SPHR candidates must also be exempt, but they are required to have at least four years of experience. The formal eligibility requirements are

- A minimum of four years of experience in an exempt-level HR position with a master's degree or higher, OR
- A minimum of five years of experience in an exempt-level HR position with a bachelor's degree, OR
- A minimum of seven years of experience in an exempt-level HR position with a high school diploma

Registering for the PHR or SPHR exam

To register for the PHR or SPHR exam, you will need to go to the HR Certification Institute's (HRCI) web site. HRCI provides an online application process. You can go directly to the application page by visiting www.hrci.org/apply. The HRCI application page will take you through these application steps:

1. **Set up an online account**   Click the Log In tab and select Create an Account. If you already have an account but forgot your password, follow the instructions to reset your password.
2. **Complete the application**   The site will walk you through the process of completing your application. The site will ask for your full name, address, demographic information, and your HR experience.
3. **Affirmation**   You will be asked to attest that the information you provided is true and accurate.
4. **Application fee payment**   The site will direct you to submit your payment for the exam fee.
5. **Schedule your exam**   Both exams are administered through HRCI's partner, Prometric. Prometric operates testing centers throughout the United States and in over 160 countries.

Taking the Exam Again?

We applaud your decision to take the exam again. The latest pass rate (December 2013–January 2014) of the SPHR exam was 62 percent, and the pass rate of the PHR exam was 59 percent. So if you are taking the exam again, you are among many.

Here are some steps to take to get ready to re-take the exam:

- Reapply. You will have to reapply and pay the same fee in order to retake the exam; unfortunately, there are no discounts. You will follow the same registration process as before. Don't wait to re-take the exam. You can re-take the exam in the next testing period (in six months). Use what you learned the first time around as a foundation and build on it for the second exam. If you wait to retake the exam, not only will you lose the information you studied, but you will also lose the momentum and courage you built up to take the exam in the first place.

- Shake off the first exam and resist feeling sorry for yourself. Anyone who passes on the second try demonstrates a spirit of determination, which is a commendable characteristic.

- Arrest the negative self-talk. Thoughts like "I can't do this" or "I don't have what it takes" should be shown the door. You do have what it takes. Muster up that determination and get it done!

Preparation and "Day of" Strategies

Whether you are studying for the PHR or SPHR exam for the first or second time, remember that all of the exam questions are based on HR best practices; federal law, which may differ from state law; and how federal laws are applied in specific situations. Don't fall into the trap of answering the questions in the way you are used to doing things in your company. Your company's practices may differ from best practices and federal law.

To prepare for the exam, you will want to:

- Find a study partner or study group. As a self-study candidate, you can utilize online study groups through shrm.org, workforce.com, and hr.com.

- Develop a study plan to determine how much time you need to spend on each section to master your weak areas and reinforce your strong areas.

- Review the PHR and SPHR Bodies of Knowledge and HRCI standards.

- Thoroughly read the HRCI.org web site.

- Start self-studying four months before the test.

- Don't rely on a single source of study materials. The *PHR/SPHR Professional in Human Resources Certification All-in-One Exam Guide* is a great additional resource.

- Keep taking assessments until you master the content and feel confident about the results. Also, take assessments under the same testing conditions as the test. No distractions: three hours of uninterrupted time.

- Take the test within two weeks of completing the study of all materials.

Mental and Physical Preparedness Strategies

Keeping yourself in stellar physical health is crucial for excelling on the PHR and SPHR exams. Both exams are a marathon in itself and your physical preparedness will play an important role in your success or failure on the exam.

Sleep

Sleep is of utmost importance, not only on exam day but also in the weeks and months leading up to the exam. Getting at least 7–8 hours of sleep will help the mind work as efficiently as possible. You will also need the extra stamina during your study time as well, not just on exam day.

Exercise

Exercise has been proven to relieve stress while providing an outlet for the extra amount of work you have taken on to prepare for the exam. To keep your physical health in tip-top shape, it is advisable to remain with your current exercise regimen.

Eating Habits

To be physically in the best shape to excel on the exam, consider your eating habits as well. Food will provide you with the energy you need to take on the challenge of studying and passing the exam.

Mental Preparedness

Getting into the right state of mind is critical to doing your very best on each question. One of the most important things you can do to mentally prepare is to study in advance for the exam. Successful candidates study months in advance of the actual test date.

Strategies to Employ the Day of the Exam

Exam day approaches quickly, and if you're using this book you've been working hard at preparing and studying. However, knowing what to expect in the exam environment is helpful too.

What You Should Bring

Expect the testing center of your choice to be secured. You will be required to produce identification that ideally includes both your photo and signature.

Examples of government-issued identification that includes both photo and signature are

- Valid driver's license
- Valid military identification card
- Valid passport
- Valid national identification card
- Voter's registration card (Puerto Rico test sites only)

What if you do not have identification that includes both photo and signature? You will be required to provide a secondary identification that would provide a photo or signature. Acceptable examples include:

- Valid employer identification card
- Valid credit card with signature
- Valid bank card with photo

Your social security card, birth certificate, and library card are not acceptable, so leave those at home.

You may store the following items in the locker during the exam to increase physical comforts:

- Watch
- Outerwear/sweater (unless being worn for the entire exam)
- Mobile device
- Medical supplies (such as inhalers, tissues, eye drops, cough drops)
- Food or drink
- Purse/bag
- Hat

The testing center security may require that you empty your pockets and place items such as a purse, wallet, and mobile devices in the locker as well. You may also be scanned for items as well as videotaped during the exam.

You cannot leave the test center or use a mobile device during the test or during a break. (You cannot smoke or take a smoke break during the exam.) Your exam will not count if you leave the test center or use a mobile device.

Before the Exam Starts

Exam day is not a day to be late. Most testing centers are strict on the exam start time and most likely will not permit late entries after the exam has started. Get directions to the testing center in advance and allow more than enough time to accommodate any traffic delays.

Once you are sitting in the room waiting for the exam to start, expect the proctor to spend about 15 minutes providing instructions, including a tutorial on how to use the computer technology. Take this time to take deep breaths and be seated comfortably.

The Exam Room Environment

The exam room temperatures will vary. There have been reports in years past that some testing centers lost the ability to heat the room during the December testing month. However, test takers were required to continue on with the exam. The lesson learned here is to be sure to wear comfortable clothes and a jacket in case the room is uncomfortably cold.

Dealing with noises is a fact of life when sharing a room with others. If hearing other people cough or sneeze is distracting for you, learn how to block it out and focus on the exam. Consider taking practice assessments in an environment where there are other people around. If you can't easily block out noises, there are reports of testing centers permitting disposable earplugs.

Keeping Your Mind Focused During a Long Test

In the workplace, it is not uncommon to get up and walk around if you feel you need air or to refocus on a tedious project. But in the testing environment, you do not have the ability to just get up and walk around if the desire comes over you. Utilize breaks when they are available. Stretch your legs and take deep breaths when you can. These little actions will go a long way and help you keep your focus.

Exam Tips: The Best Way to Approach the Questions

Whether you are taking the PHR or the SPHR exam, you can expect to see the following types of questions on the exam:

- Questions that require that you understand the purpose of a particular law
- Questions that require that you know the order of a particular process
- Questions that require that you understand why a particular law is being applied incorrectly
- Questions that require that you understand the cause and effect of a particular HR best practice
- Questions that require that you know the definition of a particular term

Regardless of the type of question, as you work through the exam, consider the following approaches and strategies to answering the questions.

Take a High-Level View

Be sure to identify what the question is asking. Resist the temptation of thinking how you handled a relevant situation in the workplace. It is helpful to take a high-level view and ask yourself how you would answer the question if you were the CEO of the company.

 NOTE When writing the questions in this book, we often thought of how to best handle a situation that would deliver on overall organizational objectives and not just how to avoid a lawsuit.

Eliminate Choices

Of the four choices, there is likely one obviously wrong answer, one that may be somewhat wrong, and two reasonably similar answer choices. Eliminate the wrong choices using the cross-out option to help you keep track of what you eliminated.

Use the Mark Feature

Use the mark feature to come back to questions you are unsure of so as not to waste valuable time (especially at the beginning of the test). In order to finish a question, you will need to unmark it.

Do Not Look for Patterns

Don't look for patterns in the answer choices. Contrary to popular belief, C is not always the most common answer.

 NOTE When we wrote the questions in this book, we intentionally mixed up the answer choices so there would be no patterns. If we did that in this book, rest assured you can expect the same on the exam.

Read the Entire Question

Some questions begin with a brief narrative before the question itself. Resist the temptation to assume what the question is asking and jump to the multiple-choice answer choices. Read each question fully and understand what it is asking in its entirety.

Many examinees get questions wrong by assuming what the question is asking. If you slow down and read the question in its entirety, you will be so much closer to answering the question correctly.

Learn How to Pace Yourself

You will have three hours to answer 175 questions. This means you will have just about a minute to spend on each question. Three hours seems like a long time, but three hours will not seem long enough if you spend too much time on each question. Also, it's not a race. Be sure to use all three hours.

As you are taking the practice exam questions in this book, learn to develop a sense of timing and pace yourself. Taking multiple practice exams will help you get a feel for how much time you could, and should, spend on each question.

ACKNOWLEDGMENTS

For my former workplace inspirers, Sandi Calvo, Terry Gray, and Gaylia Bond, who motivated me to pursue my SPHR certification and education, and to chase my professional dreams. For my family and friends who cheer me on, instilling an undercurrent of determination, resilience, and faith, which directs the wind in my sails.

—Tresha

I would like to thank my parents, David Simon and Ruthella Christian-Simon, for providing me with the solid foundation needed to pursue my dreams with courage.

—Joanne

I would like to thank my parents, Nick and Maryanne Parente, who taught me a strong work ethic and unrestrained persistence in the face of uncertainty.

—Gabriella

INTRODUCTION

Over time, the role of human resources has taken on greater importance and has become a larger part of an organization's strategy for success. The quest to leverage the workforce to achieve business objectives has become critical for organizations today. Understanding how to engage the workforce within the risk and legal constraints has become a balancing act that the human resource professional must master in today's complex workplace.

There is no dispute that the biggest line item on any budget's profit and loss statement is labor costs. However, an uncertain economy, tightening resources, and increasing regulations force organizations to think differently about how to achieve their objectives efficiently and effectively. This is the human resource professional's golden moment to step up to a plate not previously available.

The achievement of a PHR or SPHR certification can really only *begin* through proper education and understanding, and must continue with the dedicated execution of this knowledge. This book is written to provide a foundation in the many different functional areas that make up effective and strategic human resources.

We wish you the best of luck on your exam.

Exam Objective Map

The Exam Objective Map allows you to reference the official certification exam objective, the chapter in which each objective is covered, and the specific questions pertaining to each objective.

Official Exam Objective	Chapter Number	Question Number
1.0 Business Management and Strategy (Responsibilities)	2	1–102
1.1 Interpret and apply information related to the organization's operations from internal sources, including finance, accounting, business development, marketing, sales, operations, and information technology, in order to contribute to the development of the organization's strategic plan.	2	1–7
1.2 Interpret information from external sources related to the general business environment, industry practices and developments, technological advances, economic environment, labor force, and the legal and regulatory environment, in order to contribute to the development of the organization's strategic plan.	2	8–14

Official Exam Objective	Chapter Number	Question Number
1.3 Participate as a contributing partner in the organization's strategic planning process (for example: provide and lead workforce planning discussion with management, develop and present long-term forecast of human capital needs at the organizational level). *SPHR only.*	2	15–17
1.4 Establish strategic relationships with key individuals in the organization to influence organizational decision-making.	2	18–24
1.5 Establish relationships/alliances with key individuals and outside organizations to assist in achieving the organization's strategic goals and objectives (for example: corporate social responsibility and community partnership).	2	25–31
1.6 Develop and utilize business metrics to measure the achievement of the organization's strategic goals and objectives (for example: key performance indicators, balanced scorecard). *SPHR only.*	2	32–34
1.7 Develop, influence, and execute strategies for managing organizational change that balance the expectations and needs of the organization, its employees, and other stakeholders.	2	35–41
1.8 Develop and align the human resource strategic plan with the organization's strategic plan. *SPHR only.*	2	42–44
1.9 Facilitate the development and communication of the organization's core values, vision, mission, and ethical behaviors.	2	45–51
1.10 Reinforce the organization's core values and behavioral expectations through modeling, communication, and coaching.	2	52–58
1.11 Provide data such as human capital projections and costs that support the organization's overall budget.	2	59–65
1.12 Develop and execute business plans (i.e., annual goals and objectives) that correlate with the organization's strategic plan's performance expectations to include growth targets, new programs/services, and net income expectations. *SPHR only.*	2	66–68

Official Exam Objective	Chapter Number	Question Number
1.13 Perform cost/benefit analyses on proposed projects. *SPHR only.*	2	69–71
1.14 Develop and manage an HR budget that supports the organization's strategic goals, objectives, and values. *SPHR only.*	2	72–74
1.15 Monitor the legislative and regulatory environment for proposed changes and their potential impact to the organization, taking appropriate proactive steps to support, modify, or oppose the proposed changes.	2	75–81
1.16 Develop policies and procedures to support corporate governance initiatives (for example: whistleblower protection, code of ethics). *SPHR only.*	2	82–84
1.17 Participate in enterprise risk management by ensuring that policies contribute to protecting the organization from potential risks.	2	85–90
1.18 Identify and evaluate alternatives and recommend strategies for vendor selection and/or outsourcing. *SPHR only.*	2	91–93
1.19 Oversee or lead the transition and/or implementation of new systems, service centers, and outsourcing. *SPHR only.*	2	94–96
1.20 Participate in strategic decision-making and due diligence activities related to organizational structure and design (for example: corporate restructuring, mergers and acquisitions [M&A], divestitures). *SPHR only.*	2	97–99
1.21 Determine strategic application of integrated technical tools and systems (for example: new enterprise software, performance management tools, self-service technologies). *SPHR only.*	2	100–102
1.0 Business Management and Strategy (Knowledge)	2	103–130
1.1 The organization's mission, vision, values, business goals, objectives, plans, and processes.	2	103–105
1.2 Legislative and regulatory processes.	2	106–109
1.3 Strategic planning process, design, implementation, and evaluation.	2	110–112
1.4 Management functions, including planning, organizing, directing, and controlling.	2	113–115

Official Exam Objective	Chapter Number	Question Number
1.5 Corporate governance procedures and compliance (for example: Sarbanes-Oxley Act).	2	116–118
1.6 Due diligence processes (for example: M & A, divestitures). *SPHR only.*	2	119–121
1.7 Transition techniques for corporate restructuring, M & A, offshoring, and divestitures. *SPHR only.*	2	122–124
1.8 Elements of a cost-benefit analysis during the life cycle of the business (such as scenarios for growth, including expected, economic stressed, and worst case conditions) and the impact to net worth/earnings for short-, mid-, and long-term horizons.	2	125–127
1.9 Business concepts (for example: competitive advantage, organizational branding, business case development, corporate responsibility).	2	128–130
2.0 Workforce Planning and Employment (Responsibilities)	3	1–73
2.1 Ensure that workforce planning and employment activities are compliant with applicable federal laws and regulations.	3	1–4
2.2 Identify workforce requirements to achieve the organization's short- and long-term goals and objectives (for example: corporate restructuring, workforce expansion or reduction).	3	5–8
2.3 Conduct job analyses to create and/or update job descriptions and identify job competencies.	3	9–12
2.4 Identify, review, document, and update essential job functions for positions.	3	13–16
2.5 Influence and establish criteria for hiring, retaining, and promoting based on job descriptions and required competencies.	3	17–20
2.6 Analyze labor market for trends that impact the ability to meet workforce requirements (for example: federal/state data reports).	3	21–22
2.7 Assess skill sets of internal workforce and external labor market to determine the availability of qualified candidates, utilizing third-party vendors or agencies as appropriate.	3	23–26

Official Exam Objective	Chapter Number	Question Number
2.8 Identify internal and external recruitment sources (for example: employee referrals, diversity groups, social media) and implement selected recruitment methods.	3	27–30
2.9 Establish metrics for workforce planning (for example: recruitment and turnover statistics costs).	3	31–34
2.10 Brand and market the organization to potential qualified applicants.	3	35–36
2.11 Develop and implement selection procedures (for example: applicant tracking, interviewing, reference and background checking).	3	37–42
2.12 Develop and extend employment offers and conduct negotiations as necessary.	3	43–46
2.13 Administer post-offer employment activities (for example: execute employment agreements, complete I-9/e-Verify process, coordinate relocations, and immigration).	3	47–50
2.14 Develop, implement, and evaluate orientation and onboarding processes for new hires, rehires, and transfers.	3	51–54
2.15 Develop, implement, and evaluate employee retention strategies and practices.	3	55–58
2.16 Develop, implement, and evaluate the succession planning process. *SPHR only.*	3	59–61
2.17 Develop and implement the organizational exit/off-boarding process for both voluntary and involuntary terminations, including planning for reductions in force (RIF).	3	62–65
2.18 Develop, implement, and evaluate an affirmative action plan (AAP) as required.	3	66–69
2.19 Develop and implement a record retention process for handling documents and employee files (for example: pre-employment files, medical files, and benefits files).	3	70–73
2.0 Workforce Planning and Employment (Knowledge)	3	74–104
2.11 Applicable federal laws and regulations related to workforce planning and employment activities (for example: Title VII, ADA, EEOC Uniform Guidelines on Employee Selection Procedures, Immigration Reform and Control Act).	3	74

Official Exam Objective	Chapter Number	Question Number
2.12 Methods to assess past and future staffing effectiveness (for example: costs per hire, selection ratios, adverse impact).	3	75–76
2.13 Recruitment sources (for example: employee referral, social networking/social media) for targeting passive, semi-active, and active candidates.	3	77–78
2.14 Recruitment strategies.	3	79–80
2.15 Staffing alternatives (for example: outsourcing, job sharing, phased retirement).	3	81–82
2.16 Planning techniques (for example: succession planning, forecasting).	3	83
2.17 Reliability and validity of selection tests/tools/ methods.	3	84–85
2.18 Use and interpretation of selection tests (for example: psychological/personality, cognitive, motor/physical assessments, performance, assessment center).	3	86–89
2.19 Interviewing techniques (for example: behavioral, situational, panel).	3	90–91
2.20 Impact of compensation and benefits on recruitment and retention.	3	92–93
2.21 International HR and implications of global workforce for workforce planning and employment. *SPHR only.*	3	94
2.22 Voluntary and involuntary terminations, downsizing, restructuring, and outplacement strategies and practices.	3	95–96
2.23 Internal workforce assessment techniques (for example: skills testing, skills inventory, workforce demographic analysis).	3	97–98
2.24 Employment policies, practices, and procedures (for example: orientation, on-boarding, and retention).	3	99–100
2.25 Employer marketing and branding techniques.	3	101–102
2.26 Negotiation skills and techniques.	3	103–104

Official Exam Objective	Chapter Number	Question Number
3.0 Human Resource Workforce Development (Responsibilities)	4	1–56
3.1 Ensure that human resources development activities are compliant with all applicable federal laws and regulations.	4	1–6
3.2 Conduct a needs assessment to identify and establish priorities regarding human resource development activities.	4	7–12
3.3 Develop/select and implement employee training programs (for example: leadership skills, harassment prevention, computer skills) to increase individual and organizational effectiveness.	4	13–25
3.4 Evaluate effectiveness of employee training programs through the use of metrics (for example: participant surveys, pre- and post-testing). *SPHR only.*	4	26–28
3.5 Develop, implement, and evaluate talent management programs that include assessing talent, developing career paths, and managing the placement of high-potential employees.	4	29–35
3.6 Develop, select, and evaluate performance appraisal processes (for example: instruments, ranking and rating scales) to increase individual and organizational effectiveness.	4	36–41
3.7 Develop, implement, and evaluate performance management programs and procedures (includes training for evaluators).	4	42–47
3.8 Develop/select, implement, and evaluate programs (for example: telecommuting, diversity initiatives, repatriation) to meet the changing needs of employees and the organization. *SPHR only.*	4	48–50
3.9 Provide coaching to managers and executives regarding effectively managing organizational talent.	4	51–56
3.0 Human Resource Development (Knowledge)	4	57–92
3.27 Applicable federal laws and regulations related to human resources development activities (for example: Title VII, ADA, Title 17 [Copyright law]).	4	57–59

Official Exam Objective	Chapter Number	Question Number
3.28 Career development and leadership development theories and applications (for example: succession planning, dual career ladders).	4	60–62
3.29 Organizational development (OD) theories and applications.	4	63–65
3.30 Training program development techniques to create general and specialized training programs.	4	66–71
3.31 Facilitation techniques, instructional methods, and program delivery mechanisms.	4	72–74
3.32 Task/process analysis.	4	75–77
3.33 Performance appraisal methods (for example: instruments, ranking and rating scales).	4	78–80
3.34 Performance management methods (for example: goal setting, relationship to compensation, job placements/promotions).	4	81–83
3.35 Applicable global issues (for example: international law, culture, local management approaches/practices, societal norms). *SPHR only.*	4	84–87
3.36 Techniques to assess training program effectiveness, including use of applicable metrics (for example: participant surveys, pre- and post-testing).	4	88–90
3.37 Mentoring and executive coaching.	4	91–92
4.0 Compensation and Benefits (Responsibilities)	5	1–43
4.1 Ensure that compensation and benefits programs are compliant with applicable federal laws and regulations.	5	1–6
4.2 Develop, implement, and evaluate compensation policies/programs (for example: pay structures, performance-based pay, internal and external equity).	5	7–12
4.3 Manage payroll-related information (for example: new hires, adjustments, terminations).	5	13–18
4.4 Manage outsourced compensation and benefits components (for example: payroll vendors, COBRA administration, employee recognition vendors). *PHR only.*	5	19–23

Official Exam Objective	Chapter Number	Question Number
4.5 Conduct compensation and benefits programs needs assessments (for example: benchmarking, employee surveys, trend analysis).	5	24–25
4.6 Develop/select, implement/administer, update and evaluate benefit programs (for example: health and welfare, wellness, retirement, stock purchase).	5	26–31
4.7 Communicate and train the workforce in the compensation and benefits programs, policies, and processes (for example: self-service technologies).	5	32–37
4.8 Develop/select, implement/administer, update, and evaluate an ethically sound executive compensation program (for example: stock options, bonuses, supplemental retirement plans). SPHR only.	5	38–40
4.9 Develop, implement/administer, and evaluate expatriate and foreign national compensation and benefits programs. SPHR only.	5	41–43
4.0 Compensation and Benefits (Knowledge)	5	44–79
4.38 Applicable federal laws and regulations related to compensation, benefits, and tax (for example: FLSA, ERISA, FMLA, USERRA).	5	44–46
4.39 Compensation and benefits strategies.	5	47–49
4.40 Budgeting and accounting practices related to compensation and benefits.	5	50–52
4.41 Job evaluation methods.	5	53–54
4.42 Job pricing and pay structures.	5	55–57
4.43 External labor markets and/or economic factors.	5	58–59
4.44 Pay programs (for example: variable, merit).	5	60–61
4.45 Executive compensation methods. SPHR only.	5	62–64
4.46 Noncash compensation methods (for example: equity programs, noncash rewards).	5	65–67
4.47 Benefits programs (for example: health and welfare, retirement, Employee Assistance Programs [EAPs]).	5	68–74
4.48 International compensation laws and practices (for example: expatriate compensation, entitlements, choice of law codes). SPHR only.	5	75–77
4.49 Fiduciary responsibilities related to compensation and benefits.	5	78–79

Official Exam Objective	Chapter Number	Question Number
5.0 Employee and Labor Relations (Responsibilities)	6	1–48
5.1 Ensure that employee and labor relations activities are compliant with applicable federal laws and regulations.	6	1–5
5.2 Assess organizational climate by obtaining employee input (for example: focus groups, employee surveys, staff meetings).	6	6–10
5.3 Develop and implement employee relations programs (for example: recognition, special events, diversity programs) that promote a positive organizational culture.	6	11–15
5.4 Evaluate effectiveness of employee relations programs through the use of metrics (for example: exit interviews, employee surveys, turnover rates).	6	16–20
5.5 Establish, update, and communicate workplace policies and procedures (for example: employee handbook, reference guides, or standard operating procedures) and monitor their application and enforcement to ensure consistency.	6	21–24
5.6 Develop and implement a discipline policy based on organizational code of conduct/ethics, ensuring that no disparate impact or other legal issues arise.	6	25–27
5.7 Create and administer a termination process (for example: reductions in force [RIF], policy violations, poor performance), ensuring that no disparate impact or other legal issues arise.	6	28–30
5.8 Develop, administer, and evaluate grievance/dispute resolution and performance improvement policies and procedures.	6	31–35
5.9 Investigate and resolve employee complaints filed with federal agencies involving employment practices or working conditions, utilizing professional resources as necessary (for example: legal counsel, mediation/arbitration specialists, investigators).	6	36–40
5.10 Develop and direct proactive employee relations strategies for remaining union-free in non-organized locations. *SPHR only.*	6	41–43
5.11 Direct and/or participate in collective bargaining activities, including contract negotiation, costing, and administration.	6	44–48

Official Exam Objective	Chapter Number	Question Number
5.0 Employee and Labor Relations (Knowledge)	6	49–80
5.50 Applicable federal laws affecting employment in union and nonunion environments, such as laws regarding antidiscrimination policies, sexual harassment, labor relations, and privacy (for example: WARN Act, Title VII, NLRA).	6	49–51
5.51 Techniques and tools for facilitating positive employee relations (for example: employee surveys, dispute/conflict resolution, labor/management cooperative strategies).	6	52–54
5.52 Employee involvement strategies (for example: employee management committees, self-directed work teams, staff meetings).	6	55–57
5.53 Individual employment rights issues and practices (for example: employment at will, negligent hiring, defamation).	6	58–60
5.54 Workplace behavior issues/practices (for example: absenteeism and performance improvement).	6	61–63
5.55 Unfair labor practices.	6	64–66
5.56 The collective bargaining process, strategies, and concepts (for example: contract negotiation, costing, and administration).	6	67–69
5.57 Legal disciplinary procedures.	6	70–72
5.58 Positive employee relations strategies and non-monetary rewards.	6	73–75
5.59 Techniques for conducting unbiased investigations.	6	76–78
5.60 Legal termination procedures.	6	79–80
6.0 Risk Management (Responsibilities)	7	1–35
6.1 Ensure that workplace health, safety, security, and privacy activities are compliant with applicable federal laws and regulations.	7	1–5
6.2 Conduct a needs analysis to identify the organization's safety requirements.	7	6–9
6.3 Develop/select and implement/administer occupational injury and illness prevention programs (i.e., OSHA, workers' compensation). *PHR only.*	7	10–12

Official Exam Objective	Chapter Number	Question Number
6.4 Establish and administer a return-to-work process after illness or injury to ensure a safe workplace (for example: modified duty assignment, reasonable accommodations, independent medical exam).	7	13–16
6.5 Develop/select, implement, and evaluate plans and policies to protect employees and other individuals, and to minimize the organization's loss and liability (for example: emergency response, workplace violence, substance abuse).	7	17–20
6.6 Communicate and train the workforce on security plans and policies.	7	21–23
6.7 Develop, monitor, and test business continuity and disaster recovery plans.	7	24–26
6.8 Communicate and train the workforce on the business continuity and disaster recovery plans.	7	27–29
6.9 Develop policies and procedures to direct the appropriate use of electronic media and hardware (for example: e-mail, social media, and appropriate web site access).	7	30–32
6.10 Develop and administer internal and external privacy policies (for example: identity theft, data protection, workplace monitoring).	7	33–35
6.0 Risk Management (Knowledge)	7	36–50
6.61 Applicable federal laws and regulations related to workplace health, safety, security, and privacy (for example: OSHA, Drug-Free Workplace Act, ADA, HIPAA, Sarbanes-Oxley Act).	7	36
6.62 Occupational injury and illness prevention (safety) and compensation programs.	7	37
6.63 Investigation procedures of workplace safety, health and security enforcement agencies.	7	38
6.64 Return to work procedures (for example: interactive dialog, job modification, accommodations).	7	39
6.65 Workplace safety risks (for example: trip hazards, blood-borne pathogens).	7	40
6.66 Workplace security risks (for example: theft, corporate espionage, sabotage).	7	41
6.67 Potential violent behavior and workplace violence conditions.	7	42

Official Exam Objective	Chapter Number	Question Number
6.68 General health and safety practices (for example: evacuation, hazard communication, ergonomic evaluations).	7	43
6.69 Organizational incident and emergency response plans.	7	44
6.70 Internal investigation, monitoring, and surveillance techniques.	7	45
6.71 Employer/employee rights related to substance abuse.	7	46
6.72 Business continuity and disaster recovery plans (for example: data storage and backup, alternative work locations, procedures).	7	47
6.73 Data integrity techniques and technology (for example: data sharing, password usage, social engineering).	7	48
6.74 Technology and applications (for example: social media, monitoring software, biometrics).	7	49
6.75 Financial management practices (for example: procurement policies, credit card policies and guidelines, expense policies).	7	50

Pre-Assessment Test: PHR and SPHR

Instructions

This pre-assessment test is designed to help you prepare to study for the HRCI Professional in Human Resources or Senior Professional in Human Resources certification exams. You should take this test to identify your current level of readiness to sit for the exam, and the areas where you should focus your study and preparation.

This pre-assessment test is broken into two parts:

- **Part I** PHR Pre-Assessment: 60 questions in 60 minutes
- **Part II** SPHR Pre-Assessment: An additional 15 questions in 15 minutes, for a total of 75 questions in 75 minutes

The first part is for both PHR and SPHR candidates. It includes 60 questions that are similar in style and format to the questions you will see on the actual PHR exam. PHR candidates should complete Part I and consider the Part II option. The second part is an additional batch of 15 SPHR-specific questions. They take into account the additional focus on the application/problem solving and synthesis/evaluation cognitive capabilities found in the SPHR exams. SPHR candidates should complete both Part I and Part II.

As you prepare to take this pre-assessment test, you should try to simulate the actual exam conditions as closely as possible. Go to a quiet place and be sure that you will not be interrupted for the full length of time it will take to complete the test. Do not use any reference materials or other assistance while taking the pre-assessment—remember, the idea is to help you determine what areas you need to focus on during your preparation for the actual exam.

The pre-assessment test contains questions divided in proportion to the PHR and SPHR exams. The next sections provide a breakdown of the exam content.

PHR

For this 60-question pre-assessment, the question breakdown is as follows:

Functional Area	Exam Weight	Number of Pre-Assessment Questions
1.0 Business Management and Strategy	11%	7
2.0 Workforce Planning and Employment	24%	14
3.0 Human Resource Development	18%	11
4.0 Compensation and Benefits	19%	11
5.0 Employee and Labor Relations	20%	12
6.0 Risk Management	8%	5

SPHR

For this 75-question pre-assessment (including the 60 questions in Part I and 15 questions in Part II), the question breakdown is as follows:

Functional	Exam Weight	Number of Pre-Assessment Questions
1.0 Business Management and Strategy	30%	20
2.0 Workforce Planning and Employment	17%	14
3.0 Human Resource Development	19%	13
4.0 Compensation and Benefits	13%	11
5.0 Employee and Labor Relations	14%	12
6.0 Risk Management	7%	5

Complete the entire pre-assessment test before checking your results. Once you have finished, use both the Quick Answer Key and the "In-Depth Answers" section to score your pre-assessment test. You can use the table in the "Analyzing Your Results" section to determine how well you performed on the test.

If you are a PHR candidate, answer all 60 questions in 60 minutes, and then move on to scoring your exam. If you are an SPHR candidate, or considering it, answer all 60 questions in 60 minutes in Part I, and then immediately move on to the additional set of 15 SPHR-specific questions in Part II. You will have an additional 15 minutes to answer them, for a total of 75 minutes. Once you have answered all 75 questions in the allotted 1 hour and 15 minutes, you will then move on to scoring your entire exam.

Are you ready? Go ahead and set your clock for 60 minutes and begin!

Part I: PHR

1. You have been asked to facilitate a session with leadership with the objective of creating the organization's mission statement. What key features of an effective mission statement should most likely be included?

   A. Inspirational, description of an overarching goal, long-term, focused

   B. Company description, what it does, and how it will accomplish overall goals

   C. Describes the unique ability a company possesses that cannot be easily duplicated

   D. Clearly describes position requirements, responsibilities, and qualifications

2. A new idea that is assigned a number and referred to a public committee is the first step to which of the following?

   A. Legislative process

   B. Regulatory process

   C. Rule-making process

   D. Objective process

3. Which of the following assesses information about political, economic, social, and technological trends that may influence the success of an organization?

   A. Mission statement planning

   B. Values statement planning

   C. Environmental scanning

   D. Core competency scanning

4. An organization struggles in achieving its objectives. Managers appear to be confused and inconsistent in reaching quality and service expectations. You want to develop leadership to overcome this challenge but must examine the matter closer. Which of the following management functions will most likely be examined closer?

   A. Controlling

   B. Directing

   C. Planning

   D. Organizing

5. You have started in a new HR leadership position with a publically traded organization. You want to ensure that the organization is compliant with the Sarbanes-Oxley Act of 2002. Which of the following is required by the Sarbanes-Oxley Act?

A. Implement a plan to keep employees safe from workplace-related injuries and illnesses.

B. Implement a plan that gives instruction in how to ensure business operations in an emergency.

C. Ensure bargaining in good faith with the representative of unionized employees.

D. Ensure a code of ethics that applies to key officers, such as the CEO, has been adopted.

6. Which of the following include key elements of an effective cost/benefit analysis?

A. Balance sheet, income statement, cash flow statement, financial statement ratios

B. Intangible and tangible costs, benefits, and forecast of impact to the bottom line

C. Assets, liabilities, shareholder's equity, earnings per share, cash flow, footnotes

D. Metrics, balanced scorecard, HRIS system, reports, spreadsheets, and footnotes

7. The CEO has announced a new competitor has moved into the market. All senior leaders are expected to present ideas on how to respond to this new threat. Which of the following strategies would contribute significantly to the organization's objectives?

A. Building a strong budget and reports, communicating with and training managers to spend within budget expectations

B. Creating a strong leadership development program and requiring every supervisor and manager to attend

C. Recruiting, developing, and rewarding skilled employees in alignment with organizational objectives

D. Developing metrics and a balanced scorecard, reporting numbers and their meaning to leadership on a regular basis

8. A Catholic seminary states in a job posting for a teaching faculty member that an active member of the Catholic Church is preferred. A Jewish person is interviewed and not awarded the position due to religious affiliation. Is this legal?

A. No, this is not legal. The posting should have never included a preference for any religious affiliation.

B. Yes, it is legal but the employer opened itself up to liability by interviewing non-Catholics.

C. No, this is not legal. Title VII identifies religious affiliation as a protected class.

D. Yes, it is legal. This is a bona-fide occupational qualification (BFOQ) exception of Title VII.

9. Which of the following established adverse impact as unlawful?

   A. *United States v. Commonwealth of Virginia*

   B. *Washington v. Davis*

   C. *Griggs v. Duke Power Company*

   D. *Abermale Paper v. Moody*

10. In the case of a reduction in force (RIF), under the Age Discrimination in Employment Act (ADEA) can an employee revoke a waiver after it is signed and accepted?

    A. Yes, the employee has 7 days to revoke a signed waiver.

    B. Yes, the employee has 45 days to reconsider a signed waiver.

    C. No, the employee has 45 days to consider a waiver. If the employee then chooses to sign that waiver, it can't be revoked.

    D. Yes, the employee has 180 days to consider a waiver and file with the EEOC.

11. Which of the following is a standard of the Uniform Guidelines on Employee Selection Procedures (UGESP)?

    A. If a pre-employment test causes disparate impact then it is not lawful.

    B. Each position within a company must utilize a standardized application.

    C. A pre-employment test or other selection tool must be a valid predictor of job success.

    D. If a company adopts an electronic application process, any paper-based process must be eliminated.

12. Which of the following is a lawful interview question?

    A. Are you a U.S. citizen?

    B. Do you have access to reliable transportation?

    C. Do you have children?

    D. Would you be willing to undergo a drug screen prior to an offer of employment?

13. A Dean's Assistant at a high school physically assaults a problem student. The investigation reveals that she was previously convicted of battery. What is this an example of?

    A. Negligent hiring

    B. Slander

    C. Defamation

    D. Insubordination

14. Which of the following staffing strategies involve filling all key positions with expatriates?

A. Regiocentric

B. Polycentric

C. Geocentric

D. Ethnocentric

15. When is an Employment Eligibility Verification form (I-9) required to be completed?

A. Within three days of the offer of employment being made

B. Prior to the first day of employment

C. The day the offer of employment is made

D. Within three business days of the employee's start date

16. A type of interview where the questions are designed to use past behavior to measure the likelihood of future behavior is known as _____.

A. Structured

B. Behavioral

C. Patterned

D. Directive

17. Which of the following is not considered an employment test by the Equal Employment Opportunity Commission (EEOC)?

A. Job application

B. Assessment centers

C. Performance evaluation

D. Personality assessment

18. When an interviewer disproportionately evaluates a candidate positively based on one characteristic, this is known as _____.

A. Halo effect

B. Leniency effect

C. First impression

D. Similar-to-Me

19. Which of the following requires that affirmative action steps be taken in advertising jobs and when recruiting, employing, training, promoting, compensating, and terminating employees?

A. Title VII

B. Executive Order 11246

C. Civil Rights Act of 1964

D. Rehabilitation Act of 1973

20. The Pregnancy Discrimination Act of 1978 established which of the following?

   A. A pregnant employee must receive at least 12 weeks of maternity leave.

   B. An employer must provide reasonable accommodations for pregnant employees.

   C. A pregnant employee should be afforded the same rights and benefits as any other employee with a short-term disability.

   D. A pregnant employee must be provided with 12 weeks of paid maternity leave.

21. Your company has decided to move to electronic personnel files. Which of the following is the most important legal issue?

   A. Compatibility with the HRIS system

   B. Complete files available on demand

   C. Easily accessible for employees and supervisors

   D. Controls to prevent unauthorized access

22. What is the first step in the intervention design stage when choosing an organizational development initiative?

   A. Determine readiness of staff involved to accept change.

   B. Measure results and evaluate process.

   C. Implement plan.

   D. Identify specific target variables.

23. An organization that develops software for service organizations is experiencing a new change in corporate culture, including the outsourcing of development positions to India. According to the Change Process Theory, which of the following would be indicative of the refreezing stage?

   A. Employees are accepting of the idea of development going to India.

   B. Employees work in conjunction with employees in India on a regular basis.

   C. Employees know a change is on the horizon.

   D. Employees stop complaining about the change.

24. What is the main benefit of Total Quality Management?

   A. Increase quality among staff.

   B. Managers are trained on effective workplace management.

   C. Deal with employee issues as they arise.

   D. Find and eliminate problems that interfere with quality.

25. What is an example of self actualization on Maslow's Hierarchy of Needs?

   A. Opportunities for growth and development

   B. Training and recognition

   C. Work groups and client

   D. Working conditions

26. Based on adult learning principles, what is the best way to train an adult learner to focus on "real world" issues?

   A. Uncover participants' expectations at the beginning of training.

   B. Show how participants can immediately bring the learning back to their jobs.

   C. Explain the "What's in it for me?" concept.

   D. Allow for planning between instructor and the group.

27. An employee has experienced negative training experiences in the past, including being reprimanded for not scoring 100 percent on the post-test and having non-relevant training in the past. The company is rolling out a new training program for products that are coming to market. What is the best way the organization can combat this obstacle to learning?

   A. Understand why there is resistance to training.

   B. See why negative attitudes have traveled between different departments.

   C. Discover why employees perceive training to be inconsequential.

   D. Show employees the connection between the mission and vision and the training.

28. A participant in a training program who prefers to sit in the front of the class and learns best from diagrams, illustrated textbooks, videos, and computer-based training programs is mostly likely a _____ type of learner?

   A. Visual

   B. Auditory

   C. Kinesthetic

   D. Hands-on

29. According to B. F. Skinner's theory of behavioral reinforcement, which best describes negative reinforcement?

   A. Behavior is not reinforced because no response is given.

   B. Decrease in the undesirable behavior response causes something negative to occur.

C. Avoid an undesirable consequence by giving the person a reward when the desired response is given.

D. Behavior will diminish and eventually become nonexistent because no response is given.

30. What is the first step of the ADDIE model?

A. Program design

B. Needs assessment

C. Implementation of programs

D. Program development

31. What is a main advantage to using a survey/questionnaire for a needs assessment?

A. Generate real-life data.

B. Minimize interruption of work flow.

C. Can reach a large number of people in a short period of time.

D. Allows for research to take place during work hours.

32. What is the strength in using a subject matter expert in selecting a facilitator for training?

A. Relates practical experience

B. Enhances learning through observing, describing, and coaching

C. Versed in adult learning and motivation concepts

D. Expertise in systems, processes, and information technology

33. In order for an employee to qualify for unemployment insurance benefits, an unemployed worker must meet which of the following qualification?

A. Must not have been terminated for gross misconduct

B. Must have worked the proceeding 26 weeks

C. Must not turn down a position with a 45-minute commute

D. Must not turn down a position with a 25-percent pay decrease

34. The HR department of a 100-person gym is looking for ways to reduce the gym's high unemployment costs. They have had a high turnover rate at 25 percent for the last year and an unemployment experience rating of 9 percent. What would be the best action for HR to take to reduce high unemployment costs?

A. Conduct surveys of incoming applicants to determine their reward preference.

B. Utilize hiring tools such as behavioral interviews and pre-employment assessment to ensure the best fit for the organization.

C. Hire an attorney to fight all unemployment claims.

D. Hire additional staff to make up for the staff who has left the organization.

35. Which of the following statements is true regarding workers' compensation?

    A. Employer assumes all costs of worker-related injuries unless a drug test shows there were illegal substances in the employee's body at the time of the accident.

    B. Employer assumes all costs of worker-related injury if an investigation shows that it is the company's fault.

    C. Employer assumes all costs of worker-related injuries only if the employer is held negligent.

    D. Employer assumes all costs of worker-related injuries regardless of who is at fault.

36. What is the best method that employers can use to manage workers' compensation costs?

    A. Implement preventive injury programs.

    B. Drug and alcohol test after every injury.

    C. Have all managers attend training on workers' compensation claims processes.

    D. Have all employees attend training on workers' compensation claims processes.

37. Which of the following is a main factor for a company that is trying to determine if a worker is an employee or an independent contractor?

    A. The nature of the work performed

    B. How much the employee is paid

    C. The nature and degree of control exercised by the company

    D. How long the worker has worked with the company

38. Employees covered by the Federal Labor Standards Act (FLSA) must receive overtime for any hours worked:

    A. Over 32 hours in a week

    B. Over 16 hours in a weekend

    C. Over 40 hours in a week

    D. Over 10 hours in a weekend

39. What does the HR department need to be aware of regarding FLSA child labor laws?

    A. If employees are 14–15 years old, they may not work more than three hours a day during school hours.

    B. If employees are 16–17 years old, they may not work more than three hours a day.

C. All people under the age of 16 are prohibited from most nonfarm work.

D. Only certain jobs are permitted for people 18 years and older, such as actors, newspaper carriers, and so on.

40. When would an employer choose to lag the market in terms of compensation?

    A. When the employer strategy is to be equal with the internal colleagues

    B. When the employer strategy is to be externally competitive

    C. When talent demand is higher than the supply

    D. When supply of talent is greater than demand

41. What is the main reason why an employer would choose to not continue providing COLA increases?

    A. Inflation has not grown as fast as wages have risen.

    B. Concern for losing control of wages.

    C. Job duties have not increased.

    D. Incentive pay is easily obtained by employees.

42. What is the main advantage for using group performance incentives?

    A. Can help equalize pay between employees on the same level.

    B. Can help with fears of employees losing their jobs.

    C. Everyone is treated equal.

    D. Employees have higher morale at companies that utilize group performance incentives.

43. A large, hierarchical organization is looking to flatten their organization and remove levels of management. What would be the best choice to accomplish this in terms of compensation pay structures?

    A. Pay grade equalization

    B. Compa-ratios

    C. Broadbanding

    D. Range spreads

44. A union hires a person to apply for a job at a company that has been targeted for organizing. What is this an example of?

    A. Salting

    B. Inside organizing

    C. Leafleting

    D. Organizational picketing

45. Which of the following is a union security clause that requires all employees to be union members?

   A. Agency shop clause

   B. Continuity of membership clause

   C. Closed shop clause

   D. Union shop clause

46. Which of the following established that employees have the right to form unions for the purpose of collective bargaining?

   A. National Labor Relations Act (NLRA)

   B. Labor Management Relations Act (LMRA)

   C. Norris-LaGuardia Act

   D. Taft-Hartley Act

47. What is the HR significance of *Faragher v. City of Boca Raton* as it relates to a workplace sexual harassment issue?

   A. Established that a hostile work environment must be proven before a plaintiff can win on a sexual harassment claim.

   B. Established that quid pro quo harassment is the only actionable form of sexual harassment.

   C. Established that an employer can be held vicariously liable for the acts of a supervisor.

   D. Established that an employer can only be held liable for the actions of a supervisor if the plaintiff reported the harassment to the employer.

48. Which of the following is an example of an unfair labor practice (ULP)?

   A. Yellow-Dog Contract

   B. Hot-Cargo Agreement

   C. Iron-Clad Oath

   D. Fixed-Term Contract

49. John's supervisor finds out that he has been meeting with union representatives during his break. The manufacturing plant where John works is currently non-union. John's supervisor writes him up for engaging in non–work-related activities on company premises. What advice would you give to the supervisor?

   A. The write-up is lawful. It is management's right in a non-union shop to discourage union organization on the company's premises per the Labor Management Relations Act (LMRA).

   B. The employee's actions are lawful and protected by the provisions of the National Labor Relations Act (NLRA).

C. This write-up is lawful. Any discussion of organizing must happen off the employer's premises.

D. The employee's actions are unlawful because he used his company paid break period to discuss union organization.

50. A non-union employee requests that a coworker be present during an investigatory interview meeting with her supervisor. The supervisor denies this request. Have the employee's Weingarten rights been violated?

A. Yes, any employee has the right to request a representative be present at a disciplinary meeting, and the employer is obligated to honor that request.

B. No, a coworker is not a union representative. The supervisor should offer that a union representative be present during the meeting.

C. Yes, the courts have been consistent in their finding that Weingarten rights should be extended to all employees.

D. No, Weingarten rights are a right available by law only to union employees.

51. An employee is returning from leave, but his doctor has specified that he work part-time hours only. Another employee has had a change in his personal life that allows him to work only part-time hours as well. Both employees are graphic designers. Which of the following alternative work programs would best accommodate both employees and the company?

A. Compressed work week

B. Flextime

C. Telecommuting

D. Job sharing

52. A supervisor says to an employee during a performance evaluation, "You are doing a wonderful job. You can count on having a job here for life!" In terms of the employment-at-will doctrine, what is this an example of?

A. Public-policy exception

B. Fraudulent misrepresentation

C. Promissory estoppel

D. Express contract exception

53. A production manager directly talks with workers two reporting levels below him to try to determine their job satisfaction. This feedback mechanism is known as a _____.

A. Focus group

B. Survey

C. Exit interview

D. Skip-level interview

54. Two companies have a common owner but one is a union shop and one isn't, and the non-union workers are sometimes chosen for a job in place of the higher paid union workers. This is known as _____.

A. Alter ego

B. Double breasting

C. Secondary boycott

D. Ally doctrine

55. Requiring that an employer keep an employee on staff even though the company has replaced that employee's function with updated technology is which kind of an unfair labor practice?

A. Common situs

B. Hot-cargo

C. Featherbedding

D. Yellow-dog

56. According to the Occupational Safety and Health Administration (OSHA), which of the following best fits the general recording criteria?

A. An injury that results in medical treatment beyond first aid

B. A cut that results in receiving a small bandage

C. Flu symptoms that result in calling in sick

D. Cold symptoms that result in going home early

57. Which of the following is (are) key element(s) of an effective Occupational Injury and Illness Prevention Program?

A. A zero tolerance policy for workplace illness and injuries

B. A map of where all the first-aid kits are located in the building

C. Hazard identification, assessment, prevention, and control

D. A plan for the business to continue operations in the event of an incident

58. The Occupational Health and Safety Administration (OSHA) received a safety-related complaint from an anonymous source at a manufacturing plant. Which of the following is most likely an action that OSHA will take first?

A. Fine the manufacturing plant for safety violations.

B. Try to determine if the anonymous complaint is valid.

C. Inspect the manufacturing plant for safety violations.

D. Send notices to all employees requesting information.

59. An employee badly injures his ankles in a workplace accident. The employee's injury is partially healed after six months. There is sufficient evidence that the employee's position poses a direct threat of harm to his ankles' health. Which of the following is the best step to take?

    A. Terminate the employee because he can't perform the essential functions of the job.

    B. Keep the employee off of work indefinitely or until the ankles are 100 percent healed.

    C. Conduct an interactive dialogue with the employee and treating physician to see what other jobs can be performed.

    D. Create a new position and job description that works around the employee's physical restrictions.

60. Because of the nature of their work, healthcare employees are sometimes exposed to potential blood-borne pathogens through the handling of needles. According to OSHA, which of the following is a requirement for the employer?

    A. Train employees on culture, values, and safety protocols.

    B. Report the number of needle stick incidents to leadership.

    C. Identify some other tool that will replace the needles.

    D. Provide personal protective equipment such as gloves.

If you are a PHR candidate, you're all done! Time to score yourself and analyze your results. Please review the PHR Quick Answer Key, total your score, review the answer explanations for any questions you answered incorrectly or were unsure of, and then review the section "Analyzing Your Results."

If you are an SPHR candidate, continue on to the next section of questions before scoring your Part I questions.

Part II: SPHR

Give yourself an additional 15 minutes to answer these 15 questions.

61. An organization, in its mature life cycle, has many long-tenured, skilled staff. The CEO has asked all senior leaders to present long-term strategies to ensure future growth of the organization. Which of the following would contribute significantly to the organization's objectives?

    A. Information on job classes to be impacted by retirement and recommendations to address skilled shortages

    B. Metrics and a balanced scorecard that show how fast the organization can recruit skilled talent.

C. A report that shows all the mandatory training classes throughout the year and leadership attendance

D. Turnover information for each department and a recommendation to improve organizational retention

62. You have been asked to participate in a leadership objective alignment committee. The purpose of the committee is to establish and communicate a uniform way of how the organization is achieving its overall objectives. Which of the following is a strategic planning and performance management tool that would contribute significantly to accomplishing this initiative?

A. Job description

B. Code of conduct

C. Performance evaluation

D. Balanced scorecard

63. What are the key elements of an effective organizational balanced scorecard?

A. Strengths, weaknesses, opportunities, and threats

B. Recruitment, employee relations, benefits, and compensation

C. Talent, performance, change, and crisis management

D. Financial, customers, internal business processes, and learning

64. An organization will be developing a business plan that would expand one of the service lines generating additional revenue for the organization. You will be expected to participate and provide recommendations about workforce planning, staffing, and forecasting for the new service line. Which of the following would most likely be included in the business plan?

A. Compensation survey data, employee satisfaction data, customer satisfaction data, market survey data

B. Executive summary, objectives, management responsibilities, product information, and market, financial, and operations plan

C. Regulatory restrictions, potential fines, lawsuit risks, attorney fees, cost of employee resistance to change

D. Turnover metrics, exit interview information, applicant pool information, number of employees successfully hired the previous year

65. Which of the following decision-making needs would best be answered using a cost/benefit analysis?

A. Which metrics to use in the development of a balanced scorecard

B. How to improve turnover metrics and employee engagement

C. If a new HRIS system will yield positive results after the expense

D. If management responds positively to the leadership development program

66. An organization's CFO has announced that the budget process will be a zero-based budgetary approach. Which of the following actions will most likely be a part of the development of the HR budget?

    A. Start new each budget cycle by building every budgetary line item from scratch.

    B. Adjust every line item based on last year's performance.

    C. Obtain approval from the supervisor before spending money.

    D. The budget is frozen and no spending will be approved.

67. As an organization's HR leader, you see a need to implement a whistleblower protection policy. However, you must provide the senior leadership team with solid rationale for the policy to ensure buy-in. Which of the following reflects a strategic reason for implementing a whistleblower protection policy?

    A. To avoid public embarrassment and scrutiny if issues arise

    B. To encourage employees to report internally any wrongdoing

    C. To avoid SEC audits, violation findings, and fines

    D. To prevent employee-related lawsuits and grievances

68. What are the key elements of a request for proposal (RFP)?

    A. Strengths, weaknesses, opportunities, and threats

    B. Summary, expected deliverables, process, and costs

    C. Recruitment, benefits, compensation, and employee relations

    D. Identify, develop, execute, and monitor performance

69. Which of the following represents the first step of an effective project management process?

    A. Monitoring (controlling)

    B. Planning (resources)

    C. Executing (implementation)

    D. Defining (scoping)

70. An organization has chosen to purchase control of another company as a strategy to improve market share. Which of the following represents this action?

    A. Acquisition

    B. Merger

    C. Downsizing

    D. Restructuring

71. An organization has decided to implement a new technology system that links multiple functional departments together so that independent databases and redundant processes become minimized. Which of the following represents this type of system?

    A. Enterprise resource planning

    B. Human resource information system

    C. Performance management system

    D. Employee self-service system

72. Your organization is merging with another company, and you are asked to participate in the due diligence committee. Which of the following will contribute significantly to the due diligence investigation and overall business objectives?

    A. Cost-per-hire metrics of both organizations

    B. The number of applicants available to work

    C. Culture strengths and weaknesses of both companies

    D. Leadership development programs

73. An organization is moving to a shared service business model, which requires restructuring most of the support departments. Which of the following strategies would contribute significantly to an effective transition?

    A. Career transition

    B. Change management

    C. System implementation

    D. Project management

74. When discussing human resources development in a global economy, which of the following most accurately describes the employee development focus?

    A. Skill and knowledge gaps

    B. Power of relationships, awareness, and personal networks

    C. Mentor programs

    D. Developing emotional intelligence

75. Which of the following steps would assess individual contributors when completing a needs assessment for human resources development activities?

    A. During the annual performance review, a skill gap is revealed and a performance improvement plan is developed.

    B. Data entry training is needed for new computerized record-keeping systems.

    C. Departments with high turnover are identified.

    D. A SWOT analysis is conducted.

Congratulations, you're all done! Time to score yourself and analyze your results. Please review both the PHR and SPHR Quick Answer Key, total your score, review the answer explanations for any questions you answered incorrectly or were unsure of, and then review the section "Analyzing your Results."

Part I: PHR

1. B	3. C	5. D	7. C
2. A	4. A	6. B	

Business Management and Strategy score: _____

8. D	12. B	16. B	20. C
9. C	13. A	17. C	21. D
10. A	14. D	18. A	
11. C	15. D	19. B	

Workforce Planning and Employment score: _____

22. A	25. A	28. A	31. C
23. B	26. B	29. C	32. A
24. D	27. D	30. B	

Human Resource Development score: _____

33. A	36. A	39. A	42. A
34. B	37. C	40. D	43. C
35. D	38. C	41. B	

Compensation and Benefits score: _____

44. A	47. C	50. D	53. D
45. C	48. B	51. D	54. B
46. A	49. B	52. D	55. C

Employee and Labor Relations score: _____

56. A	58. B	60. D
57. C	59. C	

Risk Management score: _____

Total PHR score (out of 60): _____

Part II: SPHR

61. A	65. C	69. D	73. B
62. D	66. A	70. A	
63. D	67. B	71. A	
64. B	68. B	72. C	

Business Management and Strategy Score _____

74. B   75. A

Human Resource Development score: _____

Total SPHR score (out of 75): _____

Part I: PHR

1. ☑ **B.** Defining the organization's vision, mission, and values is all part of the strategy formulation process. An organization's mission statement describes the company and specifically how it will accomplish its vision or overall objective.
☒ **A, C,** and **D** are incorrect. **A** is incorrect because a vision statement is an inspirational statement that describes the organization's overall objective. **C** is incorrect because core competencies describe what product or service an organization excels in producing. **D** is incorrect because an objective statement falls under the mission statement and describes specific goals to be attained.

2. ☑ **A.** There are two different processes, regulatory and legislative. The legislative process starts when an idea is assigned a number and referred to a public committee in the House or Senate. This is the first of several steps by which a bill becomes a law. Additional steps include committee action, subcommittee review, scheduling of floor action, debate, voting, and a potential veto action.
☒ **B, C,** and **D** are incorrect. **B** is incorrect because the first step of a regulatory (also called rule-making) process is that a rule is proposed. **C** is incorrect because the "rule-making" process is the same thing as the regulatory process. **D** is incorrect because an objective process is not a term used for the legislative or regulatory process.

3. ☑ **C.** Environmental scanning is an essential part of the strategic planning process because it enables an organization to evaluate trends that can influence its success. Those trends include political, economic, social, and technological factors.
☒ **A, B,** and **D** are incorrect. **A** is incorrect because the mission statement is what defines what the organization does and how it intends to accomplish its vision. **B** is incorrect because the values statement defines the ethics and conduct that an organization adopted to accomplish its objectives. **D** is incorrect because the core competency of an organization is products or services that it excels in producing.

4. ☑ **A.** Of the four generally accepted functions of the manager role, the controlling function ensures that tactics, plans, and objectives are implemented according to quality and service expectations.
☒ **B, C,** and **D** are incorrect. **B** is incorrect because the directing function establishes relationships and supports a team in its ability to accomplish overall objectives. **C** is incorrect because the planning function establishes the objectives to be attained. **D** is incorrect because the organizing function determines the level of staff and materials needed to accomplish objectives.

5. ☑ **D.** Section 406 of the Sarbanes-Oxley Act requires employers to disclose whether or not the company has adopted a code of ethics that applies to key officers. Key officers include the Chief Executive Officer, Chief Finance Officer, and Controller, or people of similar duties.

   ☒ **A, B,** and **C** are incorrect. **A** is incorrect because a plan that ensures the safety of employees applies to the Occupational Safety and Health Administration (OSHA). **B** is incorrect because a plan to ensure the continuing of business operations in the event of a crisis or emergency is a business continuity plan and not required by the Sarbanes-Oxley Act. **C** is incorrect because it is the National Labor Relations Act (NLRA) that requires employers to bargain in good faith with the representative of unionized employees.

6. ☑ **B.** The key elements of an effective cost/benefit analysis is knowing all costs (intangible and tangible), monetary benefits as a result of the investment, and how this will impact the financial bottom line. A cost/benefit analysis is typically used to develop a business case for a purchase or to use in decision-making processes.

   ☒ **A, C,** and **D** are incorrect. **A** is incorrect because a balance sheet, income statement, cash flow statement, and financial statement ratios are all elements for financial reports and not necessarily for a cost/benefit analysis. **C** is incorrect because assets, liabilities, shareholder's equity, earnings per share, cash flow, and footnotes are elements of the financial reports listed in answer C. **D** is incorrect because metrics, a balanced scorecard, the HRIS system, reports, spreadsheets, and footnotes are all information items that may provide information for a cost-benefit analysis, but they are not the key elements of a cost/benefit analysis itself.

7. ☑ **C.** Many reports indicate that an organization's best competitive advantage lies within the people it recruits, develops, rewards, and retains. Recruiting, developing, and rewarding skilled employees in alignment with organizational objectives is the best option for enabling an organization to obtain a competitive advantage.

   ☒ **A, B,** and **D** are incorrect. **A** is incorrect because while a strong budget is important for financial viability and long-term planning, it alone is not what makes an organization competitive. **B** is incorrect because while leadership development programs are a good practice, unless they are aligned with overall organizational objectives, the effort will not yield a competitive advantage. **D** is incorrect because developing metrics is a good practice but unless it is aligned with organizational objectives or there is corrective action planning in place, the effort will not yield a competitive advantage.

8. ☑ **D.** Yes, this is legal. Title VII of the Civil Rights Act of 1964 provides a bona-fide occupational qualification (BFOQ) exception that allows religious organizations to give preference to members of that religion.

   ☒ **A, B,** and **C** are incorrect. **A** and **C** are incorrect because this is legal, and even though religious affiliation is a protected class, the scenario presented qualifies as a BFOQ. **B** is incorrect because it is okay to interview candidates who are not members of the preferred religious group.

9. ☑ **C.** The Supreme Court ruling in *Griggs v. Duke Power Company* was unanimous in establishing the concept now known as disparate (or "adverse") impact. The ruling in the case clarified that discrimination does not have to be intentional to exist. It is the employer's responsibility to show that the requirements they establish are job related.

☒ **A, B, and D are incorrect. A** is incorrect because *United States v. Commonwealth of Virginia* is a case in which the Supreme Court required the Virginia Military Institute to admit women. **B** is incorrect because *Washington v. Davis* established that if a test is a valid predictor of success on the job, then it is lawful even if it has an adverse impact on a protected class. **D** is incorrect because *Abermale Paper v. Moody* established that pre-employment tests must reflect the job requirements in order to be valid.

10. ☑ **A.** Under the Age Discrimination in Employment Act (ADEA), in the case of a reduction in force (RIF), an employee who signs a waiver may revoke that waiver within 7 days.

☒ **B, C, and D are incorrect.** An employee has 21 days to decide whether or not to sign a waiver when the action affects a single person and 45 days to decide whether or not to sign a waiver when a group of employees is affected. In either case, an employee has 7 days after agreeing to such a waiver to revoke his or her decision.

11. ☑ **C.** A pre-employment test or other selection tool must be a valid predictor of job success.

☒ **A, B, and D are incorrect. A** is incorrect because a pre-employment test that causes disparate impact may still be lawful if it is a valid predictor of success on the job. The landmark case on this topic is *Washington v. Davis*. **B** and **D** are incorrect because a standardized application is not a requirement. The same application process should be used for the same positions but not necessarily for all positions in a company.

12. ☑ **B.** The only lawful question is, "Do you have access to reliable transportation?" Alternately, it would be unlawful to ask a candidate, "Do you have a car?"

☒ **A, C, and D are incorrect.** It is illegal to ask about a person's citizenship status or family status during the selection process. In addition, any sort of medical screening can only happen after an offer of employment is made.

13. ☑ **A.** Negligent hiring occurs when the employer knew or should have known that a candidate's background may indicate that they are dangerous or untrustworthy.

☒ **B, C, and D are incorrect.** None of these choices define what is taking place in this scenario.

14. ☑ **D.** An ethnocentric approach is, in effect, when all key management positions are filled by people from the home country. The benefit is that the expat will be familiar with the company culture and business practices so communication with the home office is easier.

☒ **A, B,** and **C** are incorrect. **A** is incorrect because regiocentric refers to a staffing approach where HR policies and strategies reflect a particular geographic region. **B** is incorrect because a polycentric approach refers to a staffing method in which key positions in the home country are filled with expats but in the host country they are filled by host country nationals. **C** is incorrect because a geocentric approach places the best qualified people in key positions regardless of their home country.

15. ☑ **D.** Form I-9 must be completed by the end of the third business day following the employee's start date.
☒ **A, B,** and **C** are incorrect. There is only one time frame that the I-9 form must be complete and that is by the end of the third business day following the employee's start day. Therefore, all other answers are incorrect.

16. ☑ **B.** A behavioral interview is the type that contains questions that are designed to solicit from the candidate how they have responded to similar situations in the past. The way the situation was handled in the past is used as a predictor of future behavior.
☒ **A, C,** and **D** are incorrect. **A** and **D** are incorrect because structured and directive interviews are controlled by the interviewer. The same predetermined questions are asked of every candidate. **C** is incorrect because a patterned interview is one where there are groupings of questions that are designed to cover various areas related to the job requirement. The interviewer may not ask the same questions of all candidates but will ask questions from specific areas related to the job requirements.

17. ☑ **C.** A performance evaluation is not considered a pre-employment test.
☒ **A, B,** and **D** are incorrect. Job applications, assessment centers, and personality tests are all considered pre-employment tests by the EEOC. Therefore, the questions asked and the activities engaged in must be accurate predictors of job performance.

18. ☑ **A.** The halo effect occurs when an interviewer evaluates a candidate in a positive light based on one characteristic.
☒ **B, C,** and **D** are incorrect. **B** is incorrect because the leniency effect occurs when the interviewer goes easy on a candidate and justifies the candidate's negative behaviors. **C** is incorrect because a first impression is when the interviewer evaluates the candidate based on the first impression only, whether negative or positive. **D** is incorrect because similar-to-me occurs when the interviewer evaluates the candidate positively because the candidate has characteristics the interviewer identifies with.

19. ☑ **B.** Executive Order 11246 requires Government contractors to take affirmative action to ensure that equal opportunity is provided in all aspects of their employment.
☒ **A, C,** and **D** are incorrect. **A** and **C** are incorrect because Title VII of the Civil Rights Act of 1964 was enacted to outlaw all major forms of discrimination.

The Act included granting the ability to the U.S. District Courts to provide injunctive relief against any discrimination in public places, public education, and employment. **D** is incorrect because the Rehabilitation Act of 1973 was the first major piece of legislation to ensure a level playing field for individuals with disabilities.

20. ☑ **C.** The Pregnancy Discrimination Act of 1978 mandated that pregnant women be afforded the same rights and benefits as other employees with short-term disabilities.

    ☒ **A, B,** and **D** are incorrect. Paid maternity leave is not mandated at the federal level. Most companies have to offer up to 12 weeks of unpaid Family Medical Leave (FMLA) for qualifying conditions and qualifying employees.

21. ☑ **D.** The most important legal issue here is privacy of personnel records.

    ☒ **A, B,** and **C** are incorrect. These all have bearing on the decision to move to electronic files, but the most important legal issue of the choices presented is privacy.

22. ☑ **A.** The first step in choosing an organizational development initiative is to determine the readiness of the staff that is involved and see if they are ready to accept change.

    ☒ **B, C,** and **D** are incorrect. These are all later stages in the intervention design.

23. ☑ **B.** During the refreezing stage, the new ideal is a regular part of the organization.

    ☒ **A, C,** and **D** are incorrect. **A** is incorrect because this is an example of the moving stage. **C** and **D** are incorrect because they are examples of the unfreezing stage.

24. ☑ **D.** The main benefit of TQM is to find and eliminate problems that interfere with quality.

    ☒ **A, B,** and **C** are incorrect. These choices are not benefits of TQM.

25. ☑ **A.** Recognizing opportunities for growth development is an example of actualization.

    ☒ **B, C,** and **D** are incorrect. **B** is incorrect as this is an example of self-esteem. **C** is correct as this is an example of belonging and love. **D** is incorrect as this is an example of safety and security.

26. ☑ **B.** The best way to apply training to real-world issues for an adult learner is to show participants how they can immediately transfer the learning back to the job.

    ☒ **A, C,** and **D** are incorrect because although they may be factors in applying training, they are not the best options to apply training to adult learning principles.

27. ☑ **D.** To combat the lack of trust in training programs, the organization must help employees understand the connection between the organization's mission and how the training fits into that overall plan.

☒ A, B, and C are incorrect. Because these are examples of combating the obstacle of learning and peer group pressure, they are not the best techniques in combating a lack of trust in training programs.

28. ☑ A. This type of participant is a visual learner.
☒ B, C, and D are incorrect. B is incorrect as an auditory learner would learn best through audio formatted information, which may include reading text aloud, talking out loud, and listening to what people have to say. C and D are incorrect as a kinesthetic learner and a hands-on learner would learn best by actively exploring the physical world around them.

29. ☑ C. Negative reinforcement involves avoiding an undesirable consequence by giving the participant a reward when the desired response is exhibited.
☒ A, B, and D are incorrect. A and D are incorrect because these choices describe extinction. B is incorrect as this describes punishment.

30. ☑ B. The needs assessment is the first step in the ADDIE model.
☒ A, C, and D are incorrect because these choices are later steps in the ADDIE model.

31. ☑ C. A survey or a questionnaire can reach a large number of people in a short period of time.
☒ A, B, and D are incorrect because these choices are examples of advantages of the observation method to conducting a needs assessment.

32. ☑ A. A subject matter expert is able to relate practical experiences to the training.
☒ B, C, and D are incorrect. B is incorrect because this is a strength of a consultant. C is incorrect because this is a strength of a training expert. D is incorrect as this is a strength of a technical expert.

33. ☑ A. To qualify for unemployment benefits, an employee must not have been terminated for gross misconduct.
☒ B, C, and D are incorrect because they are not necessary qualifications for an employee to meet to qualify for unemployment benefits.

34. ☑ B. The best way this company can reduce unemployment costs is to hire the right people. That can be accomplished through behavioral interviews and pre-assessment screenings.
☒ A, C, and D are incorrect because these are not the best way to help reduce unemployment costs moving forward because they are not proactive or effective.

35. ☑ D. The employer assumes all costs of worker-related injuries regardless of who is at fault. This reduces the number of court cases, improves safety on the job, and helps speed the process for treatment.
☒ A, B, and C are incorrect because these are not correct statements about the workers' compensation and employer costs because they are not proactive or the most effective approaches.

36. ☑ **A.** Employers can dramatically manage their workers' compensation costs by implementing preventive injury programs.

☒ **B, C,** and **D** are incorrect. These are not correct statements about workers' compensation cost-saving strategies because they are not proactive techniques.

37. ☑ **C.** The nature and degree of control exercised by the employer are major factors in determining whether a worker is an independent contractor or an employee.

☒ **A, B,** and **D** are incorrect. These are these statements are not adequate in determining if a person is an independent contractor or an employee.

38. ☑ **C.** Employees who are eligible for overtime pay under the FLSA must work 40 or more hours in a workweek.

☒ **A, B,** and **D** are incorrect. Hours worked over 40 hours in a workweek qualify for overtime pay. Thirty two hours in a workweek or 10 or 16 hours in a weekend alone do not qualify for overtime pay.

39. ☑ **A.** Children ages 14–15 are permitted to work only three hours per day during school hours.

☒ **B, C,** and **D** are incorrect. **B** is incorrect as this choice does not accurately describe FLSA child labor provisions. **C** and **D** are incorrect as these choices reflect FLSA regulations for children under the age of 14.

40. ☑ **D.** When supply exceeds demand for talent, a company may choose to lag the market in terms of compensation.

☒ **A, B,** and **C** are incorrect. These are incorrect options because these will be better suited if a company chooses to lead or stay the same in the market place in compensation to attract talent.

41. ☑ **B.** An employer may choose to discontinue the practice of COLA increases if it feared that they may lose control of wages.

☒ **A, C,** and **D** are incorrect because a company would not choose to discontinue the COLA increases for any of these reasons. These reasons are not necessarily relevant to the practice of giving COLA increases.

42. ☑ **A.** The CEO may choose to use group performance incentives to equalize pay between employees on the same level.

☒ **B, C,** and **D** are incorrect because a company would not choose to offer group performance incentives for any of these reasons. These reasons are not necessarily true or relevant to the overall group performance incentive strategy.

43. ☑ **C.** Broadbanding salary grades is an effective way to widen the salary ranges and eliminate excess manager levels.

☒ **A, B,** and **D** are incorrect. These answers are incorrect because they are not effective solutions to lessening salary grades. These options neither evaluate the competitiveness of the employees wages nor do they refer to the structure of pay ranges.

44. ☑ **A.** Salting is when a union hires someone to apply for a job at a company that has been targeted for organizing. Once this person is hired, he or she works from the inside to begin organization efforts.

☒ **B, C,** and **D** are incorrect. **B** is incorrect because inside organizing is similar to salting in that an employee does work to organize workers from inside the company. However, the employee is not a person hired by the union specifically for this purpose. **C** and **D** are incorrect because leafleting and organizational picketing are methods unions use to get the word out to workers about the benefits of collective bargaining.

45. ☑ **C.** In a closed shop, the employer agrees to hire only union members. With the passage of the Taft-Hartley Act, closed shops became unlawful except in the construction industry.

☒ **A, B,** and **D** are incorrect. **A** is incorrect because an agency shop is one where union or non-union members may be hired but all non-union members are required to pay an agency fee or fair-share to cover collective bargaining costs. **B** is incorrect because "continuity of membership" is not a term associated with unions. **D** is incorrect because a union shop is one where the employer hires both union and non-union members but non-union employees must join the union within a specified period of time or lose their jobs.

46. ☑ **A.** The National Labor Relations Act (NLRA) was passed to protect the rights of employees to organize and collectively bargain.

☒ **B, C,** and **D** are incorrect. **B** and **D** are incorrect because neither the Labor Management Relations Act nor Taft-Hartley Act defines the relationship between unions and management and limits the activities of unions. **C** is incorrect because the Norris-LaGuardia Act made yellow-dog contracts where a person agrees not to join a union as a condition of employment.

47. ☑ **C.** *Faragher v. City of Boca Raton* is a landmark sexual harassment case that established that an employer can be held vicariously liable for the actions of its supervisory employees.

☒ **A, B,** and **D** are incorrect because the *Faragher v. City of Boca Raton* case refers to the employer's liability with respect to its supervisor's conduct and not about a hostile work environment, quid pro quo, or reporting requirements.

48. ☑ **B.** It is unlawful for a union to require that an employer stop doing business with another employer. This is called a "hot-cargo agreement" and is an unfair labor practice (ULP).

☒ **A, C,** and **D** are incorrect. **A** and **C** are incorrect because a yellow-dog or iron-clad contract is an unlawful contract between an employee and employer where the employee agrees, as a condition of employment, not to join a union. **D** is incorrect because a fixed-term contract is simply a contract entered into by two entities that has a definite end date.

49. ☑ **B.** Under the National Labor Relations Act (NLRA), it is unlawful for an employer to prohibit an employee from discussing union organization during non-work times, such as a break, and in non-work areas, such as a break room or parking lot.

☒ **A, C,** and **D** are incorrect because each of these options suggest that it is lawful that the employer can take actions against employees who discuss union organization during non-work times. The NLRA protects the employees' right to discuss union organization during non-work times even if they are on the employer's premises.

50. ☑ **D.** Weingarten rights are specifically available by law to union employees. It is a union employee's right to have union representation present during any investigative interview meeting.

☒ **A, B,** and **C** are incorrect. The courts have granted and revoked Weingarten rights to non-union employees several times since the Weingarten case was decided in 1975. It is a best practice for an employer to allow an employee to have someone else (must be a union representative) present during a disciplinary meeting if the employee requests this, but the employer is under no obligation to offer this option and, in the case of non-union employees, is under no obligation to grant the request.

51. ☑ **D.** Job share would work best because both employees have the exact same job and would complement each other's part-time schedules.

☒ **A, B,** and **C** are incorrect. **A** is incorrect because a compressed work week is when more hours are worked over fewer days (for example, four ten-hour days). This would not accommodate their need for part-time work. **B** is incorrect because flextime is when start and end times vary (for example, a start time of between 7 a.m. and 9 a.m. and an end time of between 4 p.m. and 6 p.m.). **C** is incorrect because telecommuting may or may not accommodate the need for the employees to work part time. It simply means working away from the home office but may still require that an employee work full-time hours.

52. ☑ **D.** This is an example of an express contract exception. An express contract can be created by an employer's verbal statements, in this case "…having a job for life."

☒ **A, B,** and **C** are incorrect. **A** is incorrect because a public-policy exception is made when the employer's conduct goes against public policy—for example, an employer terminates a person's employment shortly after the employee testifies in a whistleblower case where the employer is the defendant. **B** and **C** are incorrect because fraudulent misrepresentation and promissory estoppel are similar in that they both occur when an employee relies on a promise made by an employer to their detriment when the employer knew or should have known that the information was incorrect. For example, an employee is promised a promotion when the supervisor knows that the company is about to merge with another company and the affected employee's position is likely to be eliminated.

53. ☑ **D.** A skip-level interview occurs when a manager spends time with employees two levels below him in order to gauge job satisfaction and the employee's goals.

☒ **A, B,** and **C** are incorrect. **A** is incorrect because a focus group is a group of employees representing different functions in the company that come together to make decisions regarding specific company issues. **B** is incorrect because a survey is used to gather information on a number of issues in a company and may be anonymous. **C** is incorrect because an exit interview is usually conducted by HR and happens when a person decides definitively to leave the organization. This is usually the best way to get the "real" reason why someone leaves a position.

54. ☑ **B.** Double breasting occurs when workers in a non-union company are used to supplement or replace the work of higher paid workers in a unionized company.

☒ **A, C,** and **D** are incorrect. **A** is incorrect because alter ego doctrine establishes that a union represents both the main business and the alter ego if there exists an interrelation of operations, centralized labor relations, common management, and ownership. **C** is incorrect because a secondary boycott is an unfair labor practice whereby a union tries to convince a vendor of the employer not to do business with the employer. **D** is incorrect because the ally doctrine establishes that if the struck employer asks a neutral employer to produce work that would normally be produced by striking employees, the neutral employer becomes an ally and is also subject to being struck.

55. ☑ **C.** Featherbedding is an unfair labor practice on the part of the union. It occurs when a union requires an employer to continue to pay for services the employer no longer uses.

☒ **A, B,** and **D** are incorrect. **A** is incorrect because common situs refers to picketing that occurs in an area shared by more than one business. The union is required to clearly identify which business is being picketed and, where possible, restrict picketing only to the entrance of the employer being picketed. **B** is incorrect because hot-cargo refers to a union requiring an employer to refrain from doing business with an employer that the union has an issue with. **D** is incorrect because a yellow-dog contract is where an employer, as a condition of employment, requires an employee to promise not to join a union.

56. ☑ **A.** An injury that results in medical treatment is a required recordable event according to OSHA, section 1904.7(b)(1). OSHA further defines a medical treatment in section 1904.7(b)(5)(i) as a visit to a physician or another licensed healthcare professional.

☒ **B, C,** and **D** are incorrect. **B** is incorrect because a cut that results in the use of a band aid is considered first aid and not a medical treatment in OSHA section 1904.7(b)(5)(ii)(D). **C** and **D** are incorrect because flu or cold symptoms are not considered a workplace-related injury or illness.

57. ☑ **C.** An injury and illness prevention program is a proactive and systematic approach to finding and fixing workplace hazards before workers are injured or become ill. A key element of an injury and illness prevention program has hazard identification, assessment, prevention, and controls in place.

☒ **A, B, and D are incorrect. A** is incorrect because a zero tolerance policy for injury and illness is not practical. Accidents will inevitably occur in any organization. **B** is incorrect because while it is important to know where the first-aid kits are in an organization in case of an emergency, it is not an overarching effective key element. **D** is incorrect because a plan for a business to continue in the event of an incident is a business continuity plan and not an injury and illness prevention program.

58. ☑ **B.** First, OSHA will try to determine if the complaint is valid. If an employer is aware of the situation and has investigated and put into place preventive measures, OSHA may not necessarily take further action. It depends on the severity and the circumstances.

☒ **A, C, and D are incorrect. A** is incorrect because OSHA first needs to assess if the complaint is valid before deciding on any actions. **C** is incorrect because OSHA will not necessarily inspect an employer if it feels the complaint is not valid or the employer has taken care of any potential issues. **D** is incorrect because typically OSHA will not send all employees a notice.

59. ☑ **C.** If there is evidence that the employee's existing job poses a threat to the employee's health and wellness, the employer is not obligated to return the employee to that job. However, if the employee can no longer perform the essential functions of the job, the employer is obligated to reassign the employee to a position that does not pose a risk to the employee. The best step is to conduct an interactive dialogue with the employee and treating physician to explore what other positions will accommodate the employee.

☒ **A, B, and D are incorrect. A** is incorrect because terminating an employee outright is in violation of an employer's accommodation requirements under the Americans with Disabilities Act (ADA) and Equal Employment Opportunity Act (EEOC). **B** is incorrect because keeping an employee off work indefinitely may be unnecessary and not practical. There is a better alternative that will comply with requirements and uphold organizational productivity objectives. **D** is incorrect because creating a new job particularly in a tight economy is not practical as well as not required.

60. ☑ **D.** According to OSHA section 1910.1030(d)(3)(i), when there is occupational exposure, the employer is required to provide personal protective equipment. Examples of personal protective equipment are gloves, lab coats, facemasks, and eye guards.

☒ **A, B, and C are incorrect. A** is incorrect because while training employees on culture, values, and safety protocols is a good practice, it is not required by OSHA. **B** is incorrect because while reporting to leadership on incidents such as needlesticks may be required by the organization, it is not required by OSHA. **C** is incorrect because OSHA does not require the replacement of needles with other tools.

Part II: SPHR

61. ☑ **A.** A surge in retirement continues to be a chief concern for many employers. Some call the anticipated baby boomer retirements the "great brain drain" of an organization. An organization with long-tenured and skilled staff would benefit greatly from a proactive strategy that addresses anticipated retirements of skilled employees.

    ☒ **B, C,** and **D** are incorrect. **B** is incorrect because unless metrics are aligned with organizational objectives, it becomes a meaningless activity. **C** is incorrect because tracking mandatory training really has no relevance to the long-term organizational picture and needs. **D** is incorrect because while tracking turnover is a good practice, it alone is not a proactive approach to addressing the void in skill level that may affect an organization through anticipated retirement.

62. ☑ **D.** It is not unusual for an HR leader to be asked to participate in providing strategic information for a business plan in an organization. How to staff a new service line, where to find skilled talent, and which cost projections are crucial to a successful business plan. A business plan typically includes an executive summary, objectives, management responsibilities, product information, and a market, financial, and an operations plan.

    ☒ **A, B,** and **C** are incorrect. **A** is incorrect because a job description is a document that describes responsibilities and required qualifications of a job. **B** is incorrect because a code of conduct is an agreed upon manner by which each employee and manager will perform their functions in the workplace (behaviors, teamwork, and ethics). **C** is incorrect because a performance evaluation is a documented approach to assessing how an employee has performed over the previous year.

63. ☑ **D.** A balanced scorecard approach to performance management involved perspectives across the organization. These perspectives are typically financial, customers, internal business processes, and learning or growth.

    ☒ **A, B,** and **C** are incorrect. **A** is incorrect because strengths, weaknesses, opportunities, and threats represent the SWOT analysis for strategic planning purposes. **B** is incorrect because recruitment, employee relations, and benefits and compensation are functions within an HR department and alone are not related to the balanced scorecard. **C** is incorrect because talent, performance, change, and crisis management are strategies that may result from balanced scorecard findings or trends.

64. ☑ **B.** The purpose of a business plan is to help stakeholders such as investors assess the viability of a project or initiative. A business plan typically includes an executive summary, objectives, management responsibilities, product information, and a market, financial, and operations plan.

    ☒ **A, C,** and **D** are incorrect because while compensation data, metrics, and regulatory information are helpful in running a business at large, these items are not typically included in a business plan.

Chapter 1: Pre-Assessment Test: PHR and SPHR

65. ☑ **C.** The purpose of a cost/benefit analysis is to help determine if the benefit of a new project, system, or initiative outweighs the costs. In this question, the best answer is that a cost/benefit analysis can determine if the benefits of a new HRIS system outweigh the cost of purchasing a new system.

☒ **A, B, and D are incorrect. A** is incorrect because a cost/benefit analysis wouldn't necessarily help determine which metric to use. **B** is incorrect because a cost/benefit analysis doesn't shed light on turnover issues within an organization. **D** is incorrect because measuring management response to a development program is an evaluation method but not a cost/benefit analysis.

66. ☑ **A.** A zero-based budgeting process involves starting from scratch on every line item of the budget. It is starting over or building the budget from zero.

☒ **B, C, and D are incorrect. B** is incorrect because adjusting the budget based on the previous year's performance is called "incremental budgeting" as opposed to zero-based budgeting. **C and D** are incorrect because they both do not adequately define a zero-based budgeting concept.

67. ☑ **B.** One of the chief strategic reasons for implementing a whistleblower protection policy is to encourage employees to internally report wrongdoing. This will enable an organization to understand and correct issues.

☒ **A, C, and D are incorrect.** While implementing a whistleblower protection policy is a good practice in encouraging employees to internally report issues, there are no guarantees that it will prevent an issue from getting to the media or encourage lawsuits and fines. It does create a culture of transparency if the policy is implemented and carried out in the spirit it is intended.

68. ☑ **B.** A request for proposal (RFP) process varies from one company to another. However, there are common elements to an effective RFP. Those key elements include an executive summary, expected deliverables, the anticipated process, and costs.

☒ **A, C, and D are incorrect. A** is incorrect because strengths, weaknesses, opportunities, and threats represent the SWOT analysis and are unrelated to the RFP process. **C** is incorrect because recruitment, benefits, compensation, and employee relations represent the functions of the human resource department. **D** is incorrect because identifying, developing, executing, and monitoring performance represent steps to problem solving.

69. ☑ **D.** The basic process of an effective project management initiative includes the following steps in this order: defining (scoping), planning (who and what resources to use), executing (implementation), monitoring (controlling), and closing.

☒ **A, B, and C are incorrect** because, while these are part of the project management process, they are not the first step. Defining or scoping out the project identifies key objectives. All other steps fall in line after that key step.

70. ☑ **A.** An acquisition is when an organization purchases the control of another company. This includes the rights to its production of goods or services, resources, and existing customer relations.

☒ **B, C,** and **D** are incorrect. **B** is incorrect because a merger occurs when two organizations mutually join together to form a bigger entity. **C** is incorrect because downsizing refers to the reduction of an organization's headcount. **D** is incorrect because restructuring refers to the changing of internal divisions, leadership, and responsibilities to better align with overall organization objectives.

71. ☑ **A.** A technological solution that links together multiple functions with the intention of reducing redundant databases and processes is called enterprise resource planning (ERP). This enables departments to communicate electronically, which allows for a more efficient workflow.

☒ **B, C,** and **D** are incorrect because a human resource information, performance (HRIS), performance management, or employee self-service system are HR-specific driven solutions. These solutions have no linkage to business functions such as supply chain or customer service management.

72. ☑ **C.** Studies indicate that many companies may overlook culture compatibility and regret it later on. In many cases, merger and acquisition failures can be linked to culture incompatibilities. The key to a successful due diligence effort is having the ability to assess a separate company.

☒ **A, B,** and **D** are incorrect because information such as cost-per-hire, applicant pool, and leadership development programs are superficial information as they relate to a due diligence investigation.

73. ☑ **B.** Change management is a crucial transition technique that supports an organization's shift in direction. This includes restructuring, mergers and acquisitions, and even new system implementations. An effective change management technique systematically leverages knowledge, tools, and resources to support organizational change.

☒ **A, C,** and **D** are incorrect. **A** is incorrect because a career transition technique supports an employee who may be changing jobs or whose job is being downsized. **C** and **D** are incorrect because a system implementation and project management are actions or processes, which are narrowly focused on an initiative or project and do not necessarily address change management.

74. ☑ **B.** In a global economy, the employee development focus centers around power of relationships, awareness, mindsets, and personal networks.

☒ **A, C,** and **D** are incorrect. **A** is incorrect because this choice reflects an employee development focus in western cultures. **C** and **D** are incorrect because these choices do not reflect an employee development focus in a global economy.

75. ☑ **A.** When a performance review indicates a performance, skill, or knowledge gap, and a development plan is created, this is an example of an individual assessment.

☒ **B, C,** and **D** are incorrect. **B** is incorrect because this choice reflects an example of a task assessment. **C** is incorrect because this example is reflective of an organizational assessment. **D** is incorrect because this is not an example of an individual assessment.

Analyzing Your Results

Congratulations on completing the pre-assessment. You should now take the time to analyze your results with two objectives in mind:

- Identifying the resources you should use to prepare for the HRCI exam
- Identifying the specific topics that you should focus on in your preparation

First, use the table in the following section to help you gauge your overall readiness for the PHR or SPHR examination.

PHR

Total your score from both the PHR questions for an overall score out of 60.

Number of Answers Correct	Recommended Course of Study
1–30	We recommend that you spend a significant amount of time reviewing the material in the *PHR®/SPHR® Professional in Human Resources All-in-One Exam Guide* before using this book.
31–44	We recommend that you review your scores in the specific functional areas to identify the particular areas that require your focused attention and use the *PHR®/SPHR® Professional in Human Resources All-in-One Exam Guide* to review that material. Once you have done so, you should proceed to work through the questions in this book.
45–60	We recommend that you use this book to refresh your knowledge and prepare yourself mentally for the actual exam.

SPHR

Total your score from both the PHR and SPHR questions for an overall score out of 75.

Number of Answers Correct	Recommended Course of Study
0–38	We recommend that you spend a significant amount of time reviewing the material in the *PHR®/SPHR® Professional in Human Resources All-in-One Exam Guide* before using this book.
39–55	We recommend that you review your scores in the specific functional areas in the section that follows to identify the particular areas that require your focused attention and use the *PHR®/SPHR® Professional in Human Resources All-in-One Exam Guide* to review that material. Once you have done so, you should proceed to work through the questions in this book.
56–75	We recommend that you use this book to refresh your knowledge and prepare yourself mentally for the actual exam.

Once you have identified your readiness for the PHR or SPHR exam, you may use this table to identify the specific functional areas that require your focus as you continue your preparation.

PHR Rating Guide

Domain	Weight	Question Numbers in Pretest	High priority for Additional Study	Medium Priority for Additional Study	Low Priority for Additional Study
1.0 Business Management and Strategy	11%	1, 2, 3, 4, 5, 6, 7, and 8	0–3 correct	4 correct	5–7 correct
2.0 Workforce Planning and Employment	24%	8, 9, 10, 11, 12, 13, 14, 15, 16, 17, 18, 19, 20, and 21	0–7 correct	8–10 correct	11–14 correct
3.0 Human Resource Development	18%	22, 23, 24, 25, 26, 27, 28, 29, 30, 31, and 32	0–5 correct	6–7 correct	8–11 correct
4.0 Compensation and Benefits	19%	33, 34, 35, 36, 37, 38, 39, 40, 41, 42, and 43	0–5 correct	6–7 correct	8–11 correct
5.0 Employee and Labor Relations	20%	44, 45, 46, 47, 48, 49, 50, 51, 52, 53, 54, and 55	0–6 correct	7–8 correct	9–12 correct
6.0 Risk Management	8%	56, 57, 58, 59, and 60	0–2 correct	3 correct	4–5 correct

SPHR Rating Guide

Domain	Weight	Question Numbers in Pretest	High priority for Additional Study	Medium Priority for Additional Study	Low Priority for Additional Study
1.0 Business Management and Strategy	30%	PHR 1, 2, 3, 4, 5, 6, 7, and 8, and SPHR 61–73	0–10 correct	11–15 correct	16–20 correct
2.0 Workforce Planning and Employment	17%	PHR 8, 9, 10, 11, 12, 13, 14, 15, 16, 17, 18, 19, 20, and 21	0–7 correct	8–10 correct	11–14 correct
3.0 Human Resource Development	19%	PHR 22, 23, 24, 25, 26, 27, 28, 29, 30, 31, and 32, and SPHR 74 and 75	0–6 correct	7–9 correct	10–13 correct
4.0 Compensation and Benefits	13%	PHR 33, 34, 35, 36, 37, 38, 39, 40, 41, 42, and 43	0–5 correct	6–7 correct	8–11 correct
5.0 Employee and Labor Relations	14%	PHR 44, 45, 46, 47, 48, 49, 50, 51, 52, 53, 54, and 55	0–6 correct	7–8 correct	9–12 correct
6.0 Risk Management	7%	PHR 56, 57, 58, 59, and 60	0–2 correct	3 correct	4–5 correct

Business Management and Strategy

This functional area includes coverage of the following responsibilities and knowledge objectives.

Business Management and Strategy—Responsibilities Objectives

- **01** Interpret and apply information related to the organization's operations from internal sources, including finance, accounting, business development, marketing, sales, operations, and information technology, in order to contribute to the development of the organization's strategic plan.

- **02** Interpret information from external sources related to the general business environment, industry practices and developments, technological advances, economic environment, labor force, and the legal and regulatory environment, in order to contribute to the development of the organization's strategic plan.

- **03** Participate as a contributing partner in the organization's strategic planning process (for example: provide and lead workforce planning discussion with management, develop and present long-term forecast of human capital needs at the organizational level) (SPHR only).

- **04** Establish strategic relationships with key individuals in the organization to influence organizational decision-making.

- **05** Establish relationships/alliances with key individuals and outside organizations to assist in achieving the organization's responsibility and community partnership.

- **06** Develop and utilize business metrics to measure the achievement of the organization's strategic goals and objectives (for example: key performance indicators, balanced scorecard) (SPHR only).

- **07** Develop, influence, and execute strategies for managing organizational change that balance the expectations and needs of the organization, its employees, and other stakeholders.

- **08** Develop and align the human resource strategic plan with the organization's strategic plan (SPHR only).

- **09** Facilitate the development and communication of the organization's core values, vision, mission, and ethical behaviors.

- **10** Reinforce the organization's core values and behavioral expectations through modeling, communication, and coaching.

- **11** Provide data such as human capital projections and costs that support the organization's overall budget.

- **12** Develop and execute business plans (i.e., annual goals and objectives) that correlate with the organization's strategic plan's performance expectations to include growth targets, new programs/services, and net income expectations (SPHR only).

- **13** Perform cost/benefit analyses on proposed projects (SPHR only).

- **14** Develop and manage an HR budget that supports the organization's strategic goals, objectives, and values (SPHR only).

- **15** Monitor the legislative and regulatory environment for proposed changes and their potential impact to the organization, taking appropriate proactive steps to support, modify, or oppose the proposed changes.

- **16** Develop policies and procedures to support corporate governance initiatives (for example: whistleblower protection, code of ethics) (SPHR only).

- **17** Participate in enterprise risk management by ensuring that policies contribute to protecting the organization from potential risks.

- **18** Identify and evaluate alternatives and recommend strategies for vendor selection and/or outsourcing (SPHR only).

- **19** Oversee or lead the transition and/or implementation of new systems, service centers, and outsourcing (SPHR only).

- **20** Participate in strategic decision-making and due diligence activities related to organizational structure and design (for example: corporate restructuring, mergers and acquisitions [M&A], divestitures) (SPHR only).

- **21** Determine strategic application of integrated technical tools and systems (for example: new enterprise software, performance management tools, self-service technologies) (SPHR only).

Business Management and Strategy—Knowledge Objectives

- **01** The organization's mission, vision, values, business goals, objectives, plans, and processes

- **02** Legislative and regulatory processes

- **03** Strategic planning process, design, implementation, and evaluation

- **04** Management functions, including planning, organizing, directing, and controlling

- **05** Corporate governance procedures and compliance (for example: Sarbanes-Oxley Act)

- **06** Due diligence processes (for example: M & A, divestitures) (SPHR only)

- **07** Transition techniques for corporate restructuring, M & A, offshoring, and divestitures (SPHR only)

- **08** Elements of a cost-benefit analysis during the life cycle of the business (such as scenarios for growth, including expected, economic stressed, and worst-case conditions) and the impact to net worth/earnings for short-, mid-, and long-term horizons
- **09** Business concepts (for example: competitive advantage, organizational branding, business case development, corporate responsibility)

Human Resources has come a long way from its role as a back office administrative function. It is strong business acumen that pulls HR out of the back and into the front line, driving overall strategy and organizational objectives. Today, the successful human resource professional must have a clear understanding of overall business management and strategy concepts.

Business structures, finance, strategic planning, organizational alignment, branding, culture, and change management are among the many areas in which HR professionals must demonstrate strong knowledge and skill. These concepts and much more are tested in this section.

Business Management and Strategy—Responsibilities Objectives

Objective 01   Interpret and Apply Information Related to the Organization's Operations from Internal Sources, Including Finance, Accounting, Business Development, Marketing, Sales, Operations, and Information Technology, in order to Contribute to the Development of the Organization's Strategic Plan

1. A company has experienced a 15 percent drop in revenue because of the recession. Financial projections indicate that unless there is a major shift in costs or revenue, there will be a negative impact to the bottom line. The decision has been made to move up the roll-out of a new innovative service. If the new service is rolled out effectively, not only will it improve revenue but it will increase market share over competitors. The CEO has asked all senior leaders to present a plan to ensure an effective rollout of the new service. As part of the senior leadership team, you must present ideas for the new service delivery plan from the HR perspective. Which action step would you take to ensure a significant contribution to the company's strategic plan?

   A. Determine when, how, and what kind of training should occur; who should attend; and whether it should be mandatory.

   B. Identify ideal skills for a competitive advantage, determine the skills gap, and develop a plan to resolve any gaps.

   C. Develop a cost-per-hire metric and reporting system to ensure cost-effective recruitment of new employees.

   D. Develop a policy restricting the use of overtime, volunteering for extra shifts, and other premium pay benefits.

2. The process by which key stakeholders of an organization envision its future and develop a mission, objectives, and procedures to achieve that future is called:

   A. Goal planning

   B. Future planning

   C. Succession planning

   D. Strategic planning

3. The CFO of your company has presented year-to-date consolidated financial statements. The statements indicate labor costs equal over 50 percent of operating expenses. Leadership wants to take proactive steps in managing costs. Which of the following would you proactively evaluate as a key cost driver?

   A. Salary and benefits

   B. Voluntary benefits

   C. Paid time off accruals

   D. Tuition reimbursements

4. An organization has completed an analysis of the number of employees that report to each supervisor. As a cost saving measure, the organization increased the number of employees that report to each supervisor, thus eliminating several manager roles. The analysis conducted is referred to as:

   A. Headcount reporting

   B. Budget planning

   C. Span of control

   D. FTE modeling

5. The marketing leader of your company has presented results from a customer market survey. The results indicate that consumers are confused on what services your organization provides. The decision is to implement a consistent communication campaign that defines what kind and the type of service your organization provides. Marketing and recruitment can partner together to develop what kind of strategy?

   A. Marketing strategy

   B. Branding strategy

   C. Succession strategy

   D. Communication strategy

6. It is time for your company to complete its annual budget. This year, the CFO announces that this will be a zero-based budget. In building the HR budget this year, you would account for which of the following rationales?

A. Expenditures are made upward or downward to the existing budget based on return on investment.

B. All expenditures, whether increased or decreased, must be re-justified for each new budget period.

C. Any increased or new expenditures are strictly prohibited yielding no budget change.

D. Adjustments are all carefully evaluated and approved so that there are zero risks.

7. Which of the following are considered part of HR's strategic role?

A. Recruitment, compensation, benefits, and development

B. Cost containment, retention, labor relations, and employee engagement

C. Planning, objective attainment, cross-functional credibility, and partnership

D. HRIS implementation, reducing paper, improving turnover, and establishing metrics

Objective 02   Interpret Information from External Sources Related to the General Business Environment, Industry Practices and Developments, Technological Advances, Economic Environment, Labor Force, and the Legal and Regulatory Environment, in Order to Contribute to the Development of the Organization's Strategic Plan

8. Which of the following refers to the process that systematically surveys and interprets relevant data about the economy, government, laws, and demographic factors to identify external opportunities and threats?

A. Market analysis

B. Supply and demand evaluation

C. Customer survey

D. Environmental scanning

9. A company is considering acquiring another business. This business transition will significantly improve your company's market share. However, a due diligence analysis must be completed. What key components would you include to ensure an effective due diligence analysis?

A. Financial, operational, marketing, legal, and technology.

B. Financial, marketing, legal, technology, and administration.

C. Financial, operational, legal, technology, and customer service.

D. Financial, operational, legal, technology, and people.

10. A company has a new CEO and wants to set a new direction for the future. A new three to five year strategic plan will need to be created. Which of the following would you ensure was part of an effective strategic plan?

   A. Mission statement, SWOT analysis, list of prioritized action items, and review of measurements

   B. Mission statement, customer and employee feedback, SWOT analysis, and a risk assessment

   C. Mission statement, employee satisfaction survey results, risk assessment, and a list of prioritized action items

   D. Mission statement, SWOT analysis, list of prioritized action items, and a communication plan

11. A global company has multiple locations that span across the globe. The decision has been made to transition internal services such as information technology, finance, and HR to a shared service business model. To ensure a smooth transition, what would you include as part of the overall plan?

   A. The creation of a center of excellence and becoming a lead competitor in all functions

   B. The empowerment and distribution of functions to separate local entities or units

   C. The consolidation or centralization of business functions and internal processes

   D. The improvement of performance and measures among internal business functions

12. Employees report on daily performance to the project manager whose authority flows horizontally across departmental boundaries. The employees also report overall performance to the department head whose authority flows vertically within the department. The best description of this organizational structure is which of the following?

   A. Divisional structure

   B. Matrix structure

   C. Project structure

   D. Functional structure

13. A company is completely focused on finding a sustainable product and market niche that produces enough profit for the company to continue as a viable entity. Which organization life cycle stage does this best describe?

   A. Entrepreneur (introduction, embryonic)

   B. Growth (break-even, expansion)

   C. Mature (established, stability)

   D. Decline (waning, reduction)

14. The time allowed for the public to express its opinions and concerns regarding an action of a regulatory agency refer to which of the following?

    A. Lobbying comment period

    B. Grievance comment period

    C. Town hall comment period

    D. Public comment period

▬ SPHR ▬ Objective 03   Participate as a Contributing Partner in the Organization's Strategic Planning Process (SPHR only)

15. An organization is preparing for a strategic planning session. The main goal is to have a comprehensive strategic plan that projects two to three years into the future. The challenge is that with the uncertain economic recovery, there are many unknown forces that can affect the organization making the future unpredictable. You are expected to facilitate a workforce planning discussion with the leadership team to identify economic, social, political, and technology trends and explore the implications of projecting them two to three years in the future. Which strategic planning method would you most likely use to lead this discussion with the leadership team?

    A. SWOT analysis

    B. Needs assessment

    C. Scenario planning

    D. Balanced scorecard

16. A computer products organization wants to create a business strategy that will enable it to be a strong competitor in the industry. In order to achieve this vision, the leaders want to assess existing internal strengths and weaknesses. In addition, they want to take into account external forces that may yield success as well as derail the vision. You will be asked to lead this discussion in the upcoming planning session and provide insights from an HR perspective. Which strategic planning method will you most likely use to assess the current situation the organization faces?

    A. SWOT analysis

    B. Scenario planning

    C. Balanced scorecard

    D. Needs assessment

17. A pharmaceutical organization has experienced disappointing financial performance over the last two years. The organization must seek ways to improve shareholder value in order to realize long-term success. In response, the organization has conducted a SWOT analysis as part of its strategic planning process. The strengths include a strong organizational culture with low turnover. Most leaders have been promoted from within. The weaknesses of the organization include a lack of innovative thinking within employee and management levels. The opportunities include a strong growth potential in emerging markets with continued aging populations. The threats include the ferocity of generic competitors and increasing speed and intensity of product competition. You are asked to lead a discussion with leadership on implementing a workforce plan addressing the SWOT analysis findings. Which strategy would you most likely use as a basis for discussion and resolution?

A. Identify low performers, establish a performance correction or development plan for each of those employees, and seek leadership buy-in.

B. Identify critical leadership competencies (for example: competitive, innovative thinking) for adjusting recruitment, development, and succession plans.

C. Identify cost-savings measures such as overtime abuse, pay wage freezes, and headcount reviews to assess if a reduction in force is necessary.

D. Identify strategic metrics that link to shareholder value (i.e., revenue per FTE), establish a delivery method, and meet to discuss results.

Objective 04   Establish Strategic Relationships with Key Individuals in the Organization to Influence Organizational Decision-Making

18. An electric company wants to expand into the wind energy sector within six months. After a job analysis of the current staff, you determine that a significant number of wind-turbine fabricators, installers, and operators will be needed but the available workforce does not have enough individuals with this training readily available. As the HR Director, how would you advise senior management?

A. Extend the target market segment entry date.

B. Partner with a local college to identify new graduates with skill sets needed.

C. Extend the target market segment entry date and staff new positions with a mix of contractors and internal staff who have been trained.

D. Implement a recruiting strategy with a goal of identifying internal talent and external recruiting.

19. The executive team of a for-profit private school decides to close all Macon, Georgia, locations before the end of the academic year. The Macon locations have not been profitable for two years and because they only go up to kindergarten, the team believes that it will have very little impact on the students. From an HR perspective, which of the following would be a basis for facilitating a discussion about this situation with the executive team?

A. Terminating teachers mid–school year will make it difficult to recruit teachers in the future for the other Georgia locations.

B. A for-profit organization has to make abrupt decisions at times to ensure financial solvency.

C. The kindergarteners can transfer to public schools or another location.

D. The locations were not profitable for two years so the staff should have had a sense that something like this might happen.

20. Over 50 percent of the employees of a fast food chain of restaurants are part-time employees. Historically, the company offered health insurance benefits to anyone who worked 25 or more hours per week. Because of an increase in premiums, the company has decided to no longer offer this benefit. As the HR Director, how would you be of most assistance to the company?

A. Advise the executive team to increase prices to customers or reduce profits to shareholders but maintain this benefit because keeping it would prevent a decline in employee morale.

B. Locate health insurance options and provide this information to affected employees.

C. Identify the employees affected; craft the type, mode, and timing of communications to the employees; prepare a recruiting strategy to fill positions if there is significant attrition.

D. Set up a group session where affected employees can ask questions and gather information on other resources that can help offset the cost of health insurance.

21. Which of the following is an example of an internal HR strategic relationship?

A. HR collaborates with line supervisors to identify employees who may fill future management openings.

B. HR ensures compliance with the Fair Labor Standards Act (FLSA).

C. HR completes a compensation analysis.

D. HR audits education records of all employees.

22. What is the primary reason that HR engages in human resources capital management planning?

    A. To shorten the time to fill in-demand positions

    B. Establish a pipeline for the high turnover positions

    C. Provide a framework to guide management and HR through the task of ensuring that the workforce has the skill needed to execute company strategic plan

    D. Determine what other business ventures the company can pursue

23. The Chief Technology Officer (CTO) has been criticized by the CEO for her department's inability to respond to end-user requests in a timely fashion and with acceptable resolutions. How can HR support the CTO in her effort to improve her department in these areas?

    A. Perform a business process analysis to identify bottlenecks.

    B. Analyze IT jobs and collaborate with CTO to develop performance metrics.

    C. Recruit more talented IT personnel.

    D. Assist the CTO with selecting a better tracking system to determine the outcome of every service call.

24. A company sets a goal to reduce turnover among the outside sales staff. Which of the following is an example of an internal strategic relationship that would be beneficial in achieving this goal?

    A. Weekly planning sessions with the CEO

    B. Bi-weekly informal meetings with the top performing outside sales staff and National Sales Director

    C. Review of the HR budget with the CFO to determine modifications to the sales compensation structure

    D. Periodic review of turnover ratio with sales staff

Objective 05 Establish Relationships/Alliances with Key Individuals and Outside Organizations to Assist in Achieving the Organization's Responsibility and Community Partnership

25. A school district is faced with a growing need for higher credentialed healthcare professionals because of an increase in the complexities of student health needs. Which of the following external partnerships would have the most immediate impact on the school district's staffing needs with respect to recruiting registered nurses?

    A. Partnering with a local university that specializes in training healthcare professionals

    B. Partnering with a healthcare recruiting agency

C. Partnering with a local hospital

D. Partnering with a local senior care facility

26. A food service company provides dining services at a university with a leading agricultural program. Which of the following strategic partnerships would support the sustainability of the company's contract with the school and potentially help in recruiting and retaining future staff?

A. Work through the career services department to recruit on campus.

B. Offer discounted dining services to students in the agricultural program.

C. Purchase food from the school's agricultural program and offer internships to students.

D. Promote a fitness program on campus and allow students to observe operations.

27. A pharmaceutical company states in its mission that it will support and enhance the quality of care in the communities it serves. A not-for-profit hospital is built one mile away from its headquarters. What advice would you provide to the CEO in regards to leveraging this recent development?

A. Establish a partnership with the hospital to offer the patients experimental medications for free.

B. Provide discounted or free products to the hospital.

C. Offer to involve hospital employees in research projects, as appropriate.

D. Open a pharmacy adjacent to the hospital.

28. Senior leadership of a toy manufacturer encourages employees to be active participants in their local communities. With this in mind, which of the following is the type of activity they would support?

A. Establishing a charitable foundation

B. A matching gifts program

C. Staff participation in a walk for cancer research

D. Donating toys to the Grant Wishes foundation

29. You are the HR Director of a car seat manufacturing company. You have set a goal of developing a total rewards package that attracts top talent. Which of the following external relationships would be most beneficial in completing this task?

A. Monthly business professionals networking luncheon

B. Monthly check-in meeting with the coordinator who organizes the company's wellness program

C. Quarterly meeting with the health insurance provider the company currently uses

D. Partnering with a compensation analyst

30. Which of the following would be an appropriate alliance for an automotive safety technology company whose mission is to provide safe transportation services for children?

   A. Hosting community workshops on child restraint devices

   B. An ad campaign against drinking and driving

   C. Employees participating in crash testing

   D. Installing GPS devices in school buses

31. Which of the following is the best description of the reason for fostering strategic external relationships in the field of HR?

   A. To gain an external perspective on policies and procedures

   B. To be responsive to the company's stated mission

   C. To ensure ease of access to information about the best places to source for talent and shop for employee services such as benefits

   D. To ensure that services needed can be acquired at a reasonable cost

SPHR Objective 06 Develop and Utilize Business Metrics to Measure the Achievement of the Organization's Strategic Goals and Objectives (SPHR only)

32. A credit card organization has established a balanced scorecard approach to monitoring its performance. The latest scorecard is distributed among leadership. The results show that financial perspective is not meeting targets, the customer perspective is not meeting targets, the internal processes perspective is meeting targets, and the learning and growth perspective, measuring training participation rates, is meeting target. What action would you take that would contribute significantly to the balanced scorecard and overall organizational effectiveness?

   A. Establish a recruitment plan that screens and hires only those who have financial and customer service knowledge.

   B. Create and implement mandatory customer service training, track attendance, and report training results on the scorecard.

   C. Evaluate cost-cutting options such as overtime abuses, staffing levels, and pay practice usage to help meet financial targets.

   D. Evaluate the effectiveness of the existing measures, align with organizational objectives, and communicate new measures.

33. An organization's vision is to be a leading innovator in the industry. Leaders want to establish a balanced scorecard approach to measuring performance and to ensure alignment of objectives. You have been asked to own the learning and growth perspective of the balanced scorecard. Which key question would

you ask that provides a solid foundation for key performance indicators in the learning and growth perspective of the balanced scorecard?

A. How is our ability to innovate, improve, and execute?

B. How is our ability to find and hire talent quickly?

C. How is our ability to manage performance of low performers?

D. How is our ability to achieve employee satisfaction scores?

34. An organization wants to establish a balanced scorecard in order to monitor its performance. The CEO has asked you to oversee the creation of the balanced scorecard for the organization. Which of the following should be the first action step in the process of setting up a balanced scorecard?

A. Formulate the project plan

B. Gain executive sponsorship

C. Develop the strategic objectives

D. Develop a communication plan

Objective 07 Develop, Influence, and Execute Strategies for Managing Organizational Change That Balance the Expectations and Needs of the Organization, Its Employees, and Other Stakeholders

Use the following scenario to answer questions 35-38. A web development company with approximately 100 employees (30 employees work remotely from home) is considering options to reduce healthcare costs. The company is considering an outsourcing relationship to administer and provide benefits following the recent 25 percent annual increase from its current benefit provider.

35. Based on Donald Kirkpatrick's work as a change management theorist and his change management model, what would be the first step the HR Manager would want to take to reduce benefit costs?

A. Prepare tentative plans.

B. Investigate need or desire for change.

C. Discuss alternatives.

D. Discuss probable reactions of staff.

36. Once the need and desire for changing benefit providers has been established in an outsourcing relationship, what is the best role that the HR Manager can assume during this process?

A. Project manager

B. Employee advocate

C. Management advocate

D. Chief Financial Officer

37. What would be a plausible option the HR Manager could recommend to the CEO in response to the increase in healthcare costs?

  A. Company could freeze raises in order to cover increase in healthcare premiums.

  B. Company could no longer sponsor healthcare benefits.

  C. Company could raise out-of-pocket maximums.

  D. Company could freeze new hires in order to cover increase in healthcare premiums.

38. In the third step of Donald Kirkpatrick's *How to Manage Change Effectively*, what should HR do next to effectively manage the change process?

  A. Conduct focus groups with employees to inform them of the new healthcare provider.

  B. Conduct focus groups to ask employees whether they prefer an increase in health costs or a decrease in wages.

  C. Conduct focus groups to ask employees if they know of any outsourcing/healthcare providers.

  D. Conduct focus groups with employees to discuss concerns about changing healthcare providers.

39. A nonprofit organization that helps homeless animals, located on a large sanctuary in Ohio, is moving from a Microsoft Outlook e-mail system to Google Mail for all of its 45 employees. What would be the best step that HR should take to communicate the change?

  A. Hold webinars to communicate the change.

  B. Hold company-wide meetings and then followup meetings in each department to discuss the change.

  C. Have employees submit questions anonymously to ask questions about the change.

  D. Discuss the change with each employee individually.

40. A publicly held company is going through a merger-acquisition with a new company in the next three months. Employees are unsure of what the future will hold. During this major change for the organization, HR needs to be most aware of which of the following?

  A. Employees will focus on their fears and expected loss.

  B. Employees will focus on the new company and the re-branding.

  C. Employees will focus mainly on their personal commitment to the company.

  D. Employees will focus on watching top management's every move in the workplace.

41. An HR Manager can help employees develop flexibility during organizational change. Which of the following is the best action step the HR Manager can take to help facilitate this?

   A. Look for ways to reduce headcount.

   B. Staying focused on the bottom-line revenue.

   C. Reinforce change with incentives.

   D. Hire additional HR staff to help.

SPHR Objective 08 Develop and Align the Human Resource Strategic Plan with the Organization's Strategic Plan (SPHR only)

42. As an HR leader, you are participating in the organizational strategic planning process. Which of the following is one of the key strategic advantages of ensuring close alignment between HR and the overall business strategy?

   A. Strengthens benefits and compensation strategies and creates an avenue of understanding of direction and adjustments.

   B. Strengthens employee and labor relations ability to understand the organization's direction and to respond swiftly to changes.

   C. Strengthens recruitment ability to know of key position vacancies and respond swiftly to talent acquisition changes and needs.

   D. Strengthens the organization's ability to anticipate and respond to customers, ultimately enabling the organization to maintain a competitive advantage.

43. An organization is focused on developing an effective overall strategic plan. What are four critical questions to ask as part of the strategic planning process?

   A. How many key vacancies? Can we evaluate the job pool? How can we narrow the job pool? What is the timeline?

   B. Where are we now? Where do we want to be? How do we get there? How will we know if we are on track?

   C. What are our strengths? What are our weaknesses? What are our opportunities? What are our threats?

   D. What are the HR barriers? What are the HR opportunities? What resources do we need? What have we accomplished?

44. You have started a new HR leadership position with a complex organization. The organization has been operating for 25 years, has multiple locations, and has several competitors. Upon review, you discover that the organization's

strategic plan previously established is not effective. What action step should you take to evaluate and redirect strategy?

A. Perform a gap analysis (actual versus targeted performance).

B. Analyze employee satisfaction scores (year over year results).

C. Review turnover metrics (benchmark with other competitors).

D. Assess employee exit survey feedback (feedback about HR).

Objective 09 Facilitate the Development and Communication of the Organization's Core Values, Vision, Mission, and Ethical Behaviors

45. Three entrepreneurs decide to start a weight loss company. They determine that a bank loan is needed for start-up costs. As a part of building the business plan, they work to define who the company is and the overall reason for establishing the company. What are they in the process of formulating?

A. Vision statement

B. Mission statement

C. Values statement

D. Corporate goals

46. An appliance sales company is in the process of establishing corporate goals. Which of the following statements would you consider a valid goal?

A. Increase sales on ranges and clothes dryers

B. Increase sales by 7 percent per quarter for the next four quarters

C. Increase refrigerator sales by 150 percent over last year

D. Increase overall sales

47. One of the corporate values of a cable TV company is to provide best-in-class customer service. Which of the following goals would you consider characteristic of this organization?

A. Always refer customers with problems to a supervisor.

B. E-mail a survey to every customer.

C. Award every one hundredth customer with a coupon for free premium channels.

D. Answer customer calls within two rings with a live person and resolve customer issue in one phone call.

48. The executive board of a beauty products supplier wants to diversify the business. During the strategic planning process, the executive board identifies the company's core competencies as logistics and supply chain management.

Which of the following would you consider a good direction to take the business that will allow them to capitalize on these core competencies?

A. Open a beauty school that offers salon services to the public and focus heavily on retailing beauty products through the salon.

B. Open additional stores with diversified product lines and heavily promote the new product offerings.

C. Open a beauty school that offers salon services to the public and focus on offering high quality educational opportunities for students.

D. Expand existing stores by stocking diverse product lines and heavily promote the new product offerings.

49. A national construction company establishes as a part of its corporate values that it empower employees to take initiative and do what is right in their communities. A natural disaster destroys homes in the area of one of the locations. Keeping the corporate values in mind, which of the following statements presents the best response by the local branch?

A. Help the local government craft a better disaster recovery plan.

B. Volunteer to assist in rebuilding homes.

C. Wait for the local government to request corporate financial assistance and donate money.

D. Determine what level of response the corporate office will allow before offering assistance.

50. The statement "We aspire to be a great place to work for all employees" is an example of_____.

A. A values statement

B. A vision statement

C. A mission statement

D. A core competency

51. The words integrity, teamwork, and superior customer service would likely be a part of _____.

A. A values statement

B. A vision statement

C. A mission statement

D. A core competency

Objective 10   Reinforce the Organization's Core Values and Behavioral Expectations Through Modeling, Communication, and Coaching

52. An HR Manager is taking steps to develop an ethical workplace. When drafting corporate values statements in conjunction with senior management, what would be considered the best action step when writing and communicating corporate value statements?

    A. Post corporate value statements in the break room.

    B. State corporate value statements in no more than a couple of sentences and publish it where employees and customers can see.

    C. Post value statements on the home page of the company's intranet.

    D. Value statements should be at least two to three paragraphs long.

53. An employee has brought a possible ethical violation to the HR Director involving a sales colleague selling company data to competitors. What is the best course of action the HR Director should take in this situation?

    A. Put employee on leave of absence until it is safe to return to work.

    B. Speak to the employee's manager to see if they can provide additional information.

    C. Inform the employee's manager of the suspected violation and ensure that an investigation is initiated.

    D. Put the employee in question on a performance improvement plan for selling company data.

54. What is the Chief Executive Officer's main responsibility when it comes to creating a corporate ethics program?

    A. Establish necessary ethical standards and conduct business in a consistent manner with the policies.

    B. Ensure an organization's financial records are accurate.

    C. Provide legal guidance and ensure corporate and governmental compliance.

    D. Ensure accurate reporting and compliance along with the organization's external auditors.

55. A high level manager at a public company releases confidential earnings information to his brother-in-law. The brother in-law acts on this information and buys shares in the company. This is an example of what?

    A. Kickback

    B. Bribe

    C. Payoff

    D. Insider trading

56. What is the best strategy to involve employees in Corporate Citizenship Programs?

    A. Make the cause part of the culture and philosophy of the company.

    B. Focus on a particular cause niche.

    C. Focus on benevolent and business results.

    D. Demonstrate how the program affects the bottom line.

57. What is the most important reason why a CEO of a company would want to hire a Chief Ethics Officer?

    A. To decrease discrimination in the workplace

    B. To allow for consistent policies and standards

    C. To free up time that HR is currently spending on ethical complaints

    D. To reduce time for the dispute resolution process

58. What is the first step an organization would make in developing a Corporate Citizenship program?

    A. Make a wide variety of small charitable donations.

    B. Contributions are made on a strategic level.

    C. The organization has a full long-term engagement with those who have an interest in the company.

    D. Involvement includes in-kind donations such as donation of staff time.

Objective 11   Provide Data Such as Human Capital Projections and Costs That Support the Organization's Overall Budget

59. The nation is at the highest unemployment rate in 10 years. In response, your company has implemented a hiring freeze. Simultaneously, the company decides to enter a new market segment but the existing staff does not have all of the skills required for the company to make significant profits in this new segment. As the HR Director, what kind of data would be most beneficial to senior management to facilitate a discussion regarding an investment in human capital?

    A. The reduced cost of human capital on the open market and the cost of training for existing personnel vs. the ROI

    B. Savings achieved from the hiring freeze

    C. Projected loss of revenue due to lack of talented staff

    D. Cost of entry into the new market segment

60. Which of the following is an example of an objective of a human capital management plan (HCMP)?

    A. Hire an IT Recruiter with expertise in sourcing candidates with telecommunications experience.

    B. HR will improve the retention rate of new hires.

    C. Reduce time to hire.

    D. Hire 40 new programmers by September 1.

61. A company wants to increase the research and development (R & D) staff. To do so, the company must streamline operations in other areas. Which of the following decisions would impact HR but not significantly reduce HR's ability to deliver great internal customer service?

    A. Assign portions of the HR Director responsibilities to direct supervisors and eliminate the HR Director position.

    B. Implement an employee self-serve option as a part of the HRIS to eliminate the need for calls to HR to make demographic changes for employees.

    C. Reduce the availability of company paid professional development for existing staff.

    D. Eliminate the tuition reimbursement program.

62. A manufacturing company sets a goal to reduce the number of workers' compensation claims by 15 percent. Which of the following investments in human capital would have the most direct impact on this goal?

    A. Implement an improved new-hire onboarding process.

    B. Implement a safety training program.

    C. Implement a mentoring initiative to give new hires better support.

    D. Implement HR systems training.

63. A company wants to cut the HR training budget to save money during an economic downturn. Which of the following will help you show the return on investment for the CEO?

    A. Number of additional hammers produced, cost to produce training materials

    B. Cost to produce training materials, overall sales of hammers

    C. Net profits, cost to produce training materials

    D. Cost to produce training materials, training budget

64. The executive board of an airplane parts manufacturing company anticipates a need to increase its technician staff by 30 percent to produce its newest jet.

As you work with the CEO and CFO to develop this year's HR budget, what is a key consideration?

A. Is there a facility large enough to house the additional staff?

B. What are the raw materials costs?

C. Will production of this new jet increase market share?

D. Is there a recruitment plan that will address possible skill deficiencies in the current workforce?

65. Which of the following is the best example of an HR strategic function?

A. HR department maintains accurate personnel records and information for federal reports.

B. HR department measures the quality of talent decisions made by hiring managers.

C. HR department audits workers compensation records.

D. HR department ensures accuracy of health benefits data.

SPHR Objective 12   Develop and Execute Business Plans That Correlate with the Organization's Strategic Plan's Performance Expectations to Include Growth Targets, New Programs/Services, and Net Income Expectations (SPHR only)

66. An organization wants to expand its existing service line to meet increasing customer orders. In order to expand, the organization is dependent on securing a new investor. In developing the business plan, the targeted investor is requesting a five-year forecast of the new expanded service line. The requested forecast will need to provide detail of what financial and workforce resources will be needed in a five-year time frame. Because of the fast-paced nature of the business, it has been difficult to predict what is needed a year from now, let alone five years from now. How would you best go about creating a five-year workforce forecast for the organization's strategic plan?

A. Base the forecast on carefully researched and/or historical evidence in the organization or industry.

B. Base the forecast on newly established workforce metrics such as headcount, turnover, and cost-per-hire.

C. Create the forecast by surveying employees and managers, obtaining opinions on the best staffing plan.

D. Create the forecast by obtaining the status of the existing job pool and anticipated graduate information.

67. Because of market changes, an organization wants to shift its direction and implement a new strategic plan. The new strategic plan will help the organization exceed net revenue goals. However, the plan is complex and hard to understand. There are concerns that the employees will not understand it, let alone see their role in the plan. As the HR leader, you are asked to provide recommendations and ultimately develop and facilitate the organization-wide communication. What is the first key component of the strategic plan that you should evaluate for clarity and effectiveness?

A. The five-year forecast

B. The market analysis

C. The goals and objectives

D. The business description

68. An organization is building an operating plan that will create a new service line. The mission of the new plan is to become a service provider of choice. Each division of the organization is expected to develop objectives that will help the operating plan be successful. As an HR leader, you are asked to develop objectives from the HR perspective. Which of the following would be an example of an effective objective?

A. Our goal is to reduce turnover and improve employee satisfaction scores.

B. We will implement a new training program and software to monitor participation.

C. We will improve the time-to-hire, cost-per-hire, and time-to-productivity metrics.

D. We will enhance the workforce customer service skills by 80 percent in 12 months.

SPHR Objective 13 Perform Cost/Benefit Analyses on Proposed Projects (SPHR only)

69. As an HR leader, you are considering purchasing a software program that will automate the job analysis tasks for your compensation department. The cost of the software program, including service fees, is $300,000. When job classes are misclassified, the cost to the organization is estimated to average $3,000 per year, per employee. An average of 150 employees are misclassified every year. Over two years, the average reduces to 125 employees per year. In order to determine whether the benefit is worth the investment, you decide to do a return on investment (ROI) analysis. Which ROI calculation and result would apply in this case?

A. $750,000 − $300,000 / $300,000 = 150%

B. $450,000 − $300,000 / $450,000 − 33.3%

C. $450,000 – $300,000 / $300,000 = 50\%$

D. $750,000 – $450,000 / $300,000 = 100\%$

70. While conducting a cost/benefit analysis, you've discovered the costs match the benefits of a project. This is an example of what factor in the analysis?

    A. Break even point

    B. Itemized statement

    C. Return on investment

    D. Zero-based budget

71. You are preparing a cost/benefit analysis to assess the purchase of a Human Resource Information System (HRIS). Which of the following is an example of an assumption?

    A. A new system will reduce costs of processing newly hired employees by $200 per employee.

    B. A new system will include an upfront cost of $900,000, plus an annual maintenance fee of $10,000.

    C. The cost reduction of the benefits enrollment process will be reduced by 40 percent.

    D. There will be an estimated cost reduction in processing HR paperwork.

SPHR Objective 14 Develop and Manage an HR Budget That Supports the Organization's Strategic Goals, Objectives, and Values (SPHR only)

72. The finance department has launched a new approval process for anticipated capital expenses for the new budget year. Which of the following will most likely be included in that process?

    A. The payment of a building monthly lease

    B. One time purchase of training materials

    C. Anticipated payroll for the next fiscal year

    D. Purchase of computers and laser printers

73. The CFO has announced that the organization will move to a zero-based budgeting system. Which of the following is one of the key strategic advantages of implementing a zero-based budgeting system?

    A. It minimizes time spent planning for the year.

    B. It minimizes the chance of unaccounted dollars.

    C. It minimizes conflicts with each department.

    D. It minimizes the complexity of the budget.

74. As the HR leader of a manufacturing organization, you are expected to project direct and indirect labor costs for the new fiscal year. Which of the following is one of the key strategic advantages of distinguishing between direct and indirect labor costs?

    A. To determine accurate product costs

    B. To ensure accurate payroll records

    C. To ensure accurate job class records

    D. To keep track of job duties and tracking

Objective 15 Monitor the Legislative and Regulatory Environment for Proposed Changes and Their Potential Impact to the Organization, Taking Appropriate Proactive Steps to Support, Modify, or Oppose the Proposed Changes

75. The CEO has asked that you chair the legislative advocacy committee of the organization. What is a key strategic advantage for an organization involved in legislative advocacy matters?

    A. The organization will be able to keep updated policies and procedures.

    B. Training programs will meet changing legislative compliance requirements.

    C. Proactively identifying threats and opportunities enables a competitive advantage.

    D. The organization will be knowledgeable in what is legal versus illegal activity.

76. You are asked to keep the senior leadership team apprised of Patient Protection and Affordable Care Act's (PPACA) current status and make recommendations on how they may get involved in the legislative process. Which of the following actions would be the best recommendation for getting involved in complex legislation such as the PPACA?

    A. Writing to the media and newspaper outlets

    B. Calling and writing letters to local representatives

    C. Establishing a blog and posting the organization's position

    D. Posting comments on the organization's Facebook page

77. A new safety law will have a significant impact on how the manufacturing lines of an organization operate. Which of the following actions would provide the most significant contribution to the organization's operating plan?

    A. Inform management of the new law and the implementation timeline.

    B. Create a list of business activities that can no longer be performed.

C. Conduct a cost/benefit analysis and provide business recommendations.

D. Create a memo informing the organization of the new regulation.

78. Early in session, Congress passes a workplace-related bill and sends it to the president. The president takes no action on the bill for 10 days. In developing a proactive legislative plan for the workplace, which of the following is the best conclusion?

A. The bill automatically becomes law, assess impact to the workplace.

B. The bill has not been signed by the president, so it will not become law.

C. The bill will be sent back to Congress for a two-thirds majority vote.

D. The timeframe for the president signing the bill will be extended.

79. A regulatory agency has proposed a new rule that will significantly impact your organization. You are developing a proactive advocacy plan to effectively influence the proposed new rule. Which of the following actions will most likely be included in the advocacy plan?

A. Wait before taking action until the regulatory agency has issued a final rule.

B. Begin developing policies and procedures that support the new rule.

C. Develop a "get out the vote" campaign encouraging employees to vote.

D. Actively participate in the public hearings providing clear comments.

80. You are implementing an environmental scanning process as part of the strategic planning process. Which of the following strategies would be most appropriate to implement to ensure effective monitoring of the legislative and regulatory environment?

A. Wait until you hear from law attorneys on new regulations.

B. Partner with legislative advocacy or industry associations.

C. Regularly watch the news and read newspaper headlines.

D. Regularly survey leadership or employees on their opinion.

81. The National Labor Relations Board (NLRB) is required to have a minimum number of members present before official business may be conducted and decisions made. Which of the following defines this concept?

A. Quorum

B. Agenda

C. Minutes

D. Schedule

Objective 16   Develop Policies and Procedures to Support Corporate Governance Initiatives (SPHR only)

82. An organization's leaders want to effectively improve the corporate ethics governance process. Which of the following strategies would be the best strategic action to take?

   A. Conduct an employee satisfaction survey asking about organizational ethics.

   B. Create an ethics code of conduct policy and provide organizational training.

   C. Establish an internal audit process that promotes organizational involvement.

   D. Create an employee and leadership development program emphasizing ethics.

83. You are developing a business case to achieve leadership buy-in on establishing a code of ethics in the organization. What is a key strategic advantage of having a code of ethics?

   A. It will minimize employee complaints, grievances, and turnover.

   B. The organization will be less likely to be sued by customers and employees.

   C. It will minimize ethical issues the human resource department addresses.

   D. It will enable a positive reputation and the ability to expand market share.

84. As an HR leader, you've decided that it's time to implement a whistleblower protection policy. Which of the following is a key factor for a whistleblower protection policy to be effective?

   A. Metrics that measure employee satisfaction

   B. The ability to find and recruit top talent

   C. A competitive compensation program

   D. Leadership buy-in and support

Objective 17   Participate in Enterprise Risk Management by Ensuring That Policies Contribute to Protecting the Organization from Potential Risks

85. An organization will be expanding its service to locations across the globe. You have been asked to develop a plan and supporting policy that address any unexpected crisis that could impact the organization's reputation, brand, and workforce. Which of the following best describes this policy planning effort?

   A. Workforce risk forecasting

   B. Enterprise risk management

   C. Proactive action planning

   D. Legal risk management

86. You have discovered an employee's overtime was not calculated correctly, resulting in minimal back pay of less than $200. There is the potential of minimal payroll issues such as this one that could occur from time to time. Which of the following is the best policy to implement to help manage the risk?

A. A policy that requires payment to the employee of the correct amount out of the company's existing resources

B. A policy that requires purchasing an employment practices liability insurance policy worth several thousands of dollars

C. A policy that requires the creation of metrics that track if employees are leaving the organization due to payroll mistakes

D. A policy that requires the use of an employee survey to measure satisfaction of payroll practices within the organization

87. You have been asked to review and recommend if it is appropriate to purchase an employment practices liability insurance (EPLI). Which of the following is a key advantage of having EPLI coverage?

A. To replace burdensome and complex human resource practices

B. To replace the employee handbook and any related procedures

C. Protection when litigating and settling wrongful discharge lawsuits

D. Protection when employees enforce their rights under Federal law

88. You have decided to conduct an audit to evaluate existing HR policies and practices for risk exposure. Which of the following is one of the key strategic advantages of conducting an HR audit?

A. To understand which policies are outdated and need to be replaced

B. To understand if HR practices help or hinder organizational objectives

C. To understand if there is confusion about policies or practices

D. To understand if leadership development training needs updating

89. It is time for a periodic HR audit to ensure policies are still effective in protecting the organization. Which of the following steps should be first in an HR audit?

A. Develop the audit questionnaire.

B. Provide feedback about the audit.

C. Create a culture of continuous improvement.

D. Determine the scope and type of audit.

90. An organization wants to implement a social media plan to achieve overall branding objectives. You have been asked to provide recommendations in mitigating risk. Which of the following policy recommendations would contribute significantly in protecting the organization?

   A. Monitor online reputation and conduct drills in dealing with a crisis.

   B. Provide information indicating social media is a fad and not worth the time.

   C. Create a human resource social networking policy and procedure.

   D. Develop and establish mandatory training on the use of social media.

Objective 18   Identify and Evaluate Alternatives and Recommend Strategies for Vendor Selection and/or Outsourcing (SPHR only)

91. A technology company is considering the use of HR outsourcing as a way to help with the administrative HR burden of running a business. The CEO/Founder asked the HR department to shop and purchase an outsourced HRIS system for their department. What should be HR's first step in the outsourcing process?

   A. Create a request for a proposal.

   B. Define the budget.

   C. Analyze needs and define goals.

   D. Send RFP to chosen contractors.

92. The VP of HR at a 200-person company is looking for ways to make the HR department more efficient and strategic. A friend in the industry has introduced the idea of outsourcing to the VP of HR. What would be an ideal HR task to outsource?

   A. Employee call centers

   B. HR Strategy

   C. Succession planning

   D. Organization development initiatives

93. Which action step should HR take first to ensure an effective third-party contractor (outsourcing) relationship?

   A. Decide how work disputes will be handled.

   B. Create an in-depth request for proposal that exactly outlines the services that are required.

   C. Develop a strong alliance with the outsourcing partner.

   D. Communicate to the staff about the change.

Objective 19   Oversee or Lead the Transition and/or Implementation of New Systems, Service Centers, and Outsourcing (SPHR only)

94. As an HR leader, you are developing a business case to outsource some of the transactional functions of your department. Which of the following is one of the key strategic advantages in outsourcing certain activities?

    A. It saves the cost of wages, benefits, and headcount.

    B. It frees up people to focus on more strategic initiatives.

    C. It supports smaller companies by giving them business.

    D. It allows a better use of space by freeing up offices.

95. An organization is going to implement a shared service business model. The top objective is to improve efficiency and ensure excellent internal customer service. Which strategy would best ensure clear alignment with the customer satisfaction organizational objective?

    A. Implement a service level agreement.

    B. Implement management training.

    C. Implement a succession plan.

    D. Implement a talent management plan.

96. As an HR leader of an organization, you have chosen to evaluate the effectiveness of an existing recruitment outsourcing arrangement. Which of the following is the best way to measure a return on investment of the recruitment outsourcing arrangement?

    A. Track and analyze metrics that measure the skill of an applicant pool.

    B. Track and analyze metrics that measure the workplace diversity.

    C. Track and analyze metrics that measure cost and quality per hire.

    D. Track and analyze metrics that measure succession planning.

SPHR   Objective 20   Participate in Strategic Decision-Making and Due Diligence Activities Related to Organizational Structure and Design (SPHR only)

97. An organization is planning to merge with another company in order to widen its competitiveness in the market. Which action step would best ensure a significant contribution to the company's strategic plan in a merger or acquisition?

    A. Establish a recruitment plan in anticipation of increased turnover of skilled talent and potential conflicts.

    B. Conduct an employee satisfaction survey to learn how employees feel about the other organization.

C. Wait until you learn more details from your supervisor about the transition such as the timeline and the plan.

D. Assess culture and talent strengths and weaknesses of both organizations to evaluate opportunities and threats.

98. Your organization is going to acquire another company. You have just learned the organization being acquired has pending litigation from the Equal Employment Opportunity Commission (EEOC). Which of the following actions would best protect the acquiring organization's interests?

A. No actions are necessary as the liability strictly stays with the company being acquired.

B. Recommend that an indemnification provision is built into the acquisition agreement.

C. Delay the acquisition decision until the matter with the EEOC is completely resolved.

D. Cancel the acquisition decision as a pending litigation issue is considered too risky.

99. To achieve cost savings and avoid layoffs, an organization implemented a strict hiring freeze. A 5 percent reduction in headcount resulted through attrition. However, this created an imbalance in the organization's structure with some departments lacking in skilled talent while others have an oversupply of skilled talent. Which of the following strategies would best reduce the skilled talent imbalance?

A. Restructure the departments so that skilled talent can be optimally utilized.

B. Implement a plan to rehire all the employees who left and were not replaced.

C. Establish a recruitment plan to hire all new employees with new skills.

D. Develop leaders of understaffed departments to better manage the talent shortfall.

SPHR Objective 21 Determine Strategic Application of Integrated Technical Tools and Systems (SPHR only)

100. You are preparing to attend a leadership meeting that will discuss the house-wide information technology needs. What is a key advantage of purchasing an integrated information (enterprise-wide) solution versus best-of-breed (specialized based on functional area) solutions?

A. It reduces the requirement for time and people needed to implement the system.

B. It offers limitless customization options because of the large-scale implementation.

C. It reduces the need to manage multiple and overlapping technological systems.

D. It is easy to upgrade the system as it will have no impact on functional areas.

101. One of the organization's top objectives is to improve operational efficiency house-wide. The HR department manages open enrollment for annual benefits selection for 10,000 employees annually. Which of the following would be the best way to improve efficiency for the open enrollment process?

A. Assume there will be no changes in benefit selections.

B. Start the open enrollment process earlier in the year.

C. Reduce how many dependents can enroll in benefits.

D. Implement an employee self-service system approach.

102. As an HR leader of a global organization, you are preparing a business case for implementing a manager self-service addition to the HRIS system. What is a key strategic advantage to implementing a management self-service solution?

A. It allows human resources to become a paperless department.

B. It provides executives access to HR forecasting and costing data.

C. It provides recruitment department information to applicants.

D. It provides employees access to their W-2 information.

Business Management and Strategy—Knowledge Objectives

Objective 01   The Organization's Mission, Vision, Values, Business Goals, Objectives, Plans, and Processes

103. In which phase of strategic planning would a company develop its mission and vision statement?

A. Strategy evaluation

B. Strategy development

C. Strategy formulation

D. Strategy implementation

104. Which of the following is an example of a vision statement?

A. Maintain a culture of diversity and inclusion.

B. Develop innovative software.

C. Work with clients in a global marketplace.

D. Be the first choice provider in the marketplace.

105. A tech startup company has just received funding to begin business operations. What is the main risk that a company could face without composing a mission and vision statement?

   A. Employees will leave the company.

   B. Waste time and resources.

   C. Go out of business.

   D. No clear direction for the future.

Objective 02   Legislative and Regulatory Processes

106. A legislative bill is being considered for passage into law that will have a significant negative impact on an organization. You have just learned that the legislative committee reviewed the bill but did not act on it. In reporting back to the senior leadership team on the status of the bill, which of the following is the best conclusion?

   A. The bill will go no further in the process.

   B. The bill is still pending further review.

   C. The bill is being re-routed for editing.

   D. The bill automatically becomes a law.

107. The Department of Labor (DOL) has announced a proposal to expand the Family Medical Leave Act (FMLA) coverage to include military caregivers. Which of the following will most likely be the next step for the Department of Labor in this legislative change process?

   A. A final rule will be issued.

   B. It will be referred to a committee.

   C. Public comment will be invited.

   D. The rule will go to Congress.

108. Which regulatory agency is responsible for enforcing the Americans with Disability Act (ADA) of 1990?

   A. The National Labor Relations Board (NLRB)

   B. The Occupational Safety and Health Administration (OSHA)

   C. Securities and Exchange Commission (SEC)

   D. The Equal Employment Opportunity Commission (EEOC)

109. If the Equal Employment Opportunity Commission (EEOC) creates a new employment requirement, which regulatory process would it follow?

    A. It would introduce legislation by first creating a bill for Congress.

    B. It would follow the rule-making process by first proposing a rule.

    C. It would refer the new proposal to a legislative subcommittee.

    D. It would schedule the new proposal for the Senate or House floor.

Objective 03   Strategic Planning Process, Design, Implementation, and Evaluation

110. An organization has just completed its strategic plan. However, it will be critical to gain support from key stakeholders for the strategic plan to be successful. Which of the following actions would best contribute to the success of the strategic plan?

    A. Involve key stakeholders in the strategic planning process.

    B. Develop a succession plan that will build up leaders to execute on the plan.

    C. Create an employee development program that will teach goal setting skills.

    D. Conduct an applicant satisfaction survey that assesses opinion of the plan.

111. An organization has completed its strategic plan. Some leaders expressed concern about their ability to execute the strategic plan. Which of the following actions significantly contribute to the effective execution of the plan?

    A. Establish metrics that measure recruitment, onboarding, and new employee orientation effectiveness.

    B. Institute a leadership development initiative that instills resource management, communication clarity, and aligning practices.

    C. Create an incentive pay that rewards employees for coming to work on time and providing good customer service.

    D. Implement an employee survey that gathers employees' ideas on how to achieve the strategic plan and its objectives.

112. The first question that is typically asked in a strategic planning process is which of the following?

    A. Where do we want to be?

    B. How do we get there?

    C. What do we have to work with?

    D. Where are we?

Objective 04   Management Functions, Including Planning, Organizing, Directing, and Controlling

113. Implementing a quality management system is an example of which basic management function?

    A. Planning

    B. Organizing

    C. Controlling

    D. Directing

114. The executive board of a home improvement store is considering franchising. What would be the best organizational structure?

    A. Centralized

    B. De-centralized

    C. Matrix

    D. Functional

115. Senior leadership of a retail store chain is considering reducing the number of managers. What should be considered when determining which areas could be effectively managed with fewer supervisors?

    A. Which stores have the lowest financial performance?

    B. Do the employees perform repetitive simple tasks or is the work complex?

    C. Which stores are unionized?

    D. What is the highest level of education completed by the current management staff?

Objective 05   Corporate Governance Procedures and Compliance

116. What is HR's primary responsibility when it comes to the Sarbanes-Oxley Act (SOX) of 2002?

    A. Work with local government officials to advocate for change to the SOX requirements.

    B. Post SOX requirements in all break rooms.

    C. Ensure staff is training on SOX requirements.

    D. Ensure top management and board members are thoroughly trained on their responsibilities under SOX.

117. Which of the following laws covers insider trading and whistleblowing issues?

    A. Employee Retirement Income Security Act

    B. Sarbanes-Oxley Act of 2002

C. WARN Act

D. Family Medical Leave Act

118. What is the best way HR can help fulfill the ethical responsibilities of the board of directors as well as comply with Sarbanes-Oxley requirements?

A. Ensure privacy in the workplace.

B. Provide specialized and continuing education for board members.

C. Develop policies that comply with the Foreign Corrupt Practices Act.

D. Develop policies on potential cultural clashes.

SPHR Objective 06   Due Diligence Processes (SPHR only)

119. The sale, liquidation, or separation of a division, unit, or subsidiary is an example of what kind of business transition?

A. Start-up

B. Acquisition

C. Divestiture

D. Merger

120. Two organizations are considering merging. You are part of a task force that will conduct a due diligence assessment. Which of the following will provide strategic insights and impact for the due diligence assessment from the HR perspective?

A. Culture compatibility information

B. Skilled applicant pool information

C. Recruitment process information

D. Leadership development information

121. An organization is acquiring another company to improve its competitive advantage. You are asked to put together and lead a due diligence task force. Which of the following is a key capability of the task force in ensuring success in the due diligence process?

A. The ability to create metrics and a balanced scorecard

B. The ability to assess your company's marketing strategy

C. The ability to thoroughly evaluate another company

D. The ability to evaluate your company's financial statements

Objective 07   Transition Techniques for Corporate Restructuring, M & A, Offshoring, and Divestitures (SPHR only)

122. An organization is restructuring all of its departments to be better aligned with overall objectives. This will change the way the departments conduct business. What is one of the key strategic roles HR plays in major restructure initiatives?

    A. Leading recruitment initiatives to replace those who choose to leave the company

    B. Leading and facilitating the changes necessary to achieve organizational objectives

    C. Developing metrics and a balanced scorecard that reflects HR activity and initiatives

    D. Developing leadership development and performance improvement courses

123. An organization is restructuring to become more flexible so it can adjust faster to market conditions. Which of the following is a proactive strategy that would assess the ability to succeed through this organizational change?

    A. Preparing leadership development courses

    B. Creating metrics and a balanced scorecard

    C. Preparing a recruitment plan for possible turnover

    D. Assessing organizational readiness for change

124. What kind of strategy can significantly increase employee acceptance of change?

    A. A clear corrective disciplinary program

    B. Increasing the benefits of a retirement plan

    C. Effective employee communication strategies

    D. Robust new employee onboarding strategies

Objective 08   Elements of a Cost-Benefit Analysis During the Life Cycle of the Business and the Impact to Net Worth/Earnings for Short-, Mid-, and Long-Term Horizons

125. Costs that have already been incurred, cannot be recovered, and have become irrelevant from future decision-making are examples of which of the following?

    A. Intangible costs (unquantifiable costs)

    B. Tangible costs (quantifiable costs)

    C. Benefit costs (healthcare costs)

    D. Sunk costs (embedded or stranded costs)

126. An organization in the maturity life cycle stage wants to create a new service line requiring a different skill set than what currently exists. This means hiring 60 new people. Which type of information would be best to use in a cost/benefit analysis of the new service line?

   A. Projected cost of new wages, benefits of revenue earned from new service line compared to existing service line

   B. Projected recruitment costs, benefits of revenue earned from new service line compared to existing recruitment costs

   C. Projected costs of turnover, benefits of revenue earned from new service line compared to existing service line costs

   D. Projected costs of disengagement, benefits of revenue earned from new service line compared to existing service line

127. An organization in the maturity life cycle stage wants to create a new service line requiring a different skill set than what currently exists. To make room for the new opportunity, the organization will be closing an obsolete service line that will impact 60 employees. Which type of information would be best to use in a cost/benefit analysis of a potential layoff?

   A. Costs of turnover and health premiums, benefit of new service line revenue

   B. Costs of severance and any payout requirements, benefits from wages savings

   C. Costs of recruiting new employees, benefits from wages and health benefit savings

   D. Costs of developing new employees, benefits from wages and health benefit savings

Objective 09   Business Concepts

128. What is the main reason why a company should be concerned with corporate social responsibility?

   A. New trend in the market, candidates and employees are seeking companies with this attribute.

   B. All organizations have a vested interest in the condition of the environment and society.

   C. Employees are at an all-time high for fraudulent behavior, which therefore increases the need for such higher corporate social responsibility.

   D. Regulations have increased; therefore, the need for such programs exists.

129. When a company chooses to focus on a cost leadership strategy for a competitive advantage, what should HR focus on?

   A. Providing product knowledge and quality training to employees

   B. Increasing efficiency and productivity

   C. Creating strong research and development

   D. Decentralizing decision making for quicker speed to market

130. When a company chooses to focus on human capital as a competitive advantage, what should HR focus on?

   A. Aligning recruitment with the strategic plan to hire the types of employees that are needed for the future

   B. Providing product knowledge to staff

   C. Promoting technological changes that allows employees to share information about customers

   D. Selecting employees who are skilled at helping customers manage change

1. B	34. C	67. C	100. C
2. D	35. B	68. D	101. D
3. A	36. A	69. C	102. B
4. C	37. C	70. A	103. C
5. B	38. D	71. D	104. D
6. B	39. B	72. D	105. C
7. C	40. A	73. B	106. A
8. D	41. C	74. A	107. C
9. D	42. D	75. C	108. D
10. A	43. B	76. B	109. B
11. C	44. A	77. C	110. A
12. B	45. B	78. A	111. B
13. A	46. B	79. D	112. D
14. D	47. D	80. B	113. C
15. C	48. A	81. A	114. B
16. A	49. B	82. C	115. B
17. B	50. B	83. D	116. D
18. A	51. A	84. D	117. B
19. A	52. B	85. B	118. B
20. C	53. C	86. A	119. C
21. A	54. A	87. C	120. A
22. C	55. D	88. B	121. C
23. B	56. A	89. D	122. B
24. B	57. B	90. A	123. D
25. B	58. A	91. C	124. C
26. C	59. A	92. A	125. D
27. B	60. C	93. B	126. A
28. C	61. B	94. B	127. B
29. A	62. B	95. A	128. B
30. A	63. A	96. C	129. B
31. C	64. D	97. D	130. A
32. D	65. B	98. B	
33. A	66. A	99. A	

1. ☑ **B.** Identifying ideal skills for a competitive advantage, determining the skills gap, and developing a plan to resolve any gaps would contribute significantly to the strategic plan. This focus would leverage the workforce to support the new service rollout and achieve a competitive advantage.

    ☒ **A, C, and D** are incorrect. **A** is incorrect because setting up training, including the determination of the when and how of training, is tactical in nature. **C** is incorrect because the mere setting up of a metric without any linking to overall objectives does not contribute significantly to a strategic plan. **D** is incorrect because policy writing alone does not provide a significant contribution to the strategic plan.

2. ☑ **D.** The definition of strategic planning is indeed the process by which key stakeholders of an organization envision its future and develop a mission, objectives, and procedures to achieve that future.

    ☒ **A, B, and C** are incorrect. **A** is incorrect because establishing goals is part of the larger planning process. We are looking for the best term to describe the overall planning process. **B** is incorrect because although it is true that the larger planning process may require that you look into the future, that is only a part of the process. We are looking for the best term to describe the overall planning process. **C** is incorrect because although succession planning is an action that may result from the larger planning process, "succession planning" is not the term describing the overall planning process.

3. ☑ **A.** Salary and benefits traditionally equal over 50 percent of any organization's operating expenses. In some cases, it is reported that salary and benefits can exceed 70 percent of the operating expenses.

    ☒ **B, C, and D** are incorrect. **B** is incorrect because voluntary benefits generally do not result in additional costs to the employer. There would be no direct impact to financial statements. **C** is incorrect because although paid time off accruals are accounted for in financial statements, they do not generally equate to the largest line item for operating expenses. **D** is incorrect because tuition reimbursements may be an expense but they are generally not the highest expense item on financial statements.

4. ☑ **C.** Span of control is the analysis of how many employees report to each supervisor. This analysis can provide insight to possible cost savings and supervisory effectiveness.

    ☒ **A, B, and D** are incorrect. **A** is not correct because headcount reporting generally counts people per department. This is not the best way to determine how many employees report to each supervisor. **B** is not correct because the analysis described in this question may be an action leading to budgeting, but is not the budget analysis alone. **D** is not correct because FTE modeling refers to an analysis that provides multiple scenarios for staffing purposes. FTE modeling is not the same as span of control analysis.

5. ☑ **B.** Branding refers to establishing and clarifying for customers not only what product and services a company offers, but also how it is different from competitors. In addition, recruitment and marketing can partner on messaging for job advertisements and outreach for job candidates using the same branding strategy.

☒ **A, C,** and **D** are incorrect. **A** is incorrect because a marketing strategy is an overall functional plan. A marketing plan does not necessarily refer to clearly defining and clarifying customer understanding of products or services. **C** is incorrect because succession planning ultimately addresses key position vacancies and development. This strategy is not related to customer branding strategy. **D** is incorrect because the term "communication strategy" is over-broad and does not necessarily refer to product or service clarity and differentiation.

6. ☑ **B.** A zero-based budgeting process refers to all expenditures, which, whether increased or decreased, must be re-justified for each new budget period.

☒ **A, C,** and **D** are incorrect. **A** is incorrect because adjustments that are made upward or downward to the existing budget based on return on investment describe incremental budgeting and not zero-based budgeting. **C** is incorrect because zero-based budgeting does allow increases to the budget. However, it does require that there are reductions to match whatever line item(s) increased. In other words, adjustments within a zero-based budget method must equal zero changes to the bottom line. **D** is incorrect because while each budgeting cycle may require an approval process, this does not adequately meet the definition of zero-based budgeting.

7. ☑ **C.** These are considered part of the big picture of an organization. The strategic role of HR is big picture planning, achieving organization objectives, building credibility, and partnering with cross-functional leaders and departments.

☒ **A, B,** and **D** are incorrect. **A** is incorrect because these are considered functional responsibilities of HR. If these functions are not tied to overall objectives, they may not be considered a "strategic" role of HR. **B** is incorrect because these items are actions driven by the larger picture, or again functional areas, of HR. These are not necessarily considered the strategic role of HR. **D** is incorrect because these are considered functional goals and not necessarily tied to the organization's overall objectives. When you engage in activities that are not tied to overall organization objectives, it is known as operating "in the weeds."

8. ☑ **D.** Environmental scanning meets the definition of the systematic survey and interpretation of relevant data about the economy, government, laws, and demographic factors to identify external opportunities and threats. Environmental scanning is an important step to strategic planning as it enables companies to assess opportunities and threats to their overall objectives.

   ☒ **A, B,** and **C** are incorrect. **A** is incorrect because while market analysis refers to evaluating the market only, it does not necessarily include information about the economy, government, laws, and demographic factors to identify external opportunities and threats. **B** is incorrect because supply and demand evaluation is just another way to state market analysis. A supply and demand evaluation does not review all external environmental factors such the economy, government, laws, and demographic factors. **C** is incorrect because a customer survey is narrowly focused and does not include all external environmental factors such as the economy, government, laws, and demographic factors.

9. ☑ **D.** The ideal due diligence analysis will include financial, operational, legal, technology, and people aspects of the business. When both parties fully discover opportunities and risks considering all of these components, they stand a better chance of making a successful acquisition decision.

   ☒ **A, B,** and **C** are incorrect. **A** is incorrect because it lacks the people aspect of the acquisition. There are many examples of how mergers and acquisitions have failed because people, and ultimately culture alignment, were overlooked. **B** is incorrect because it, too, overlooks the people aspect of the acquisition. A thorough due diligence assessment will include the people aspect of the business. **C** is incorrect because it lacks the people aspect of the due diligence process.

10. ☑ **A.** The consideration of the mission statement, SWOT analysis, list of prioritized action items, and a review or evaluation of measures represent the four phases of strategic planning, which are strategy formulation, development, implementation, and evaluation. If an organization is seasoned and has had multiple strategic planning sessions, it may wish to revisit these key components and adjust them to meet changing times.

    ☒ **B, C,** and **D** are incorrect. **B** is the incorrect answer because while customer feedback is important, it is at the micro level. Strategic planning is generally at a higher level of planning. Customer feedback may be brought up but roll up under the SWOT analysis or action items. **C** is incorrect because it lacks a review of strengths, weakness, opportunities, and threats (SWOT). While employee satisfaction and risk assessment may roll up under the SWOT analysis, it is just as important to discover the company's strengths and opportunities as part of the strategic planning process. **D** is incorrect because it lacks a review or evaluation of measures. The communication plan may be only one part of what needs to be accomplished to drive the strategic plan.

11. ☑   C. The transition to a shared service business model is the consolidation or centralization of business functions and internal processes.

    ☒   A, B, and D are incorrect. A is incorrect because a center of excellence does not adequately describe the business transition of moving to a shared service business model. Often, companies will use this term to name the center where services and processes are located, but it does not refer to the business transition itself. B is incorrect because the empowerment and distribution of functions to separate local entities or units refer to decentralization. D is incorrect because performance improvement is one of the desired outcomes of transitioning to a shared service business model. But this is not the definition of a shared service model.

12. ☑   B. A matrix structure occurs when employees report on daily performance to the project manager whose authority flows horizontally across departmental boundaries. The employees also report overall performance to the department head whose authority flows vertically within the department.

    ☒   A, C, and D are incorrect. A is incorrect because the term "divisional structure" refers to grouping organizational functions into divisions. C is incorrect because the term "project structure" describes how a project is set up. It does not describe the multiple reporting structures that a matrix structure holds. D is incorrect because the term "functional structure" refers to grouping departments together by function. This is the same as a divisional structure.

13. ☑   A. In this phase, it is critical that the company finds a sustainable product and market niche that produces enough profit for the company to continue as a viable entity.

    ☒   B, C, and D are incorrect. B is incorrect because organizations in the growth phase are more focused on running the business in more formal ways. Better accounting and management systems are put into place during this phase. C is incorrect because businesses in the mature or established phase have already identified the successful product and market niche. Organizations in the mature life cycle phase are more focused on productivity and performance improvement. D is incorrect because organizations in the decline phase are not focused on finding a niche. Instead, organizations in this phase are focused on innovation, exit strategies, mergers, or acquisitions.

14. ☑   D. A public comment period is the time allowed for the public to express its opinions and concerns regarding an action of a regulatory agency. This is an important part of the regulatory process as it enables employers to voice their concerns and make recommendations on new agency rules.

    ☒   A, B, and C are incorrect. A is incorrect because it is not the formal process that enables members of the public to express their opinions and concerns regarding an action of a regulatory agency. B is incorrect because it is not the formal process that enables members of the public to express their opinions and concerns regarding an action of a regulatory agency. C is incorrect because although legislators may host town hall meetings, this is not the process that enables members of the public to express their opinions and concerns regarding an action of a regulatory agency.

15. ☑ **C.** Scenario planning is a good method that allows a leadership team to consider multiple probabilities. Once multiple probabilities are identified, the leadership team can establish a plan for each of those possibilities.

☒ **A, B,** and **D** are incorrect. **A** is incorrect because the SWOT analysis is used to identify current strengths, weaknesses, opportunities, and threats. It does not project into the future possible scenarios and implications. **B** is incorrect because a needs assessment addresses current challenges and needs. It does not project into the future. **D** is incorrect because a balanced scorecard is a strategy performance management tool that is used to monitor progress toward organizational objectives.

16. ☑ **A.** The SWOT analysis is an effective strategic planning method that assesses the current strengths, weaknesses, opportunities, and threats an organization faces. Dell computer utilized the SWOT method to assess its strengths, weaknesses, opportunities, and threats. With that method, they were able to determine that they could leverage their capability of customizing computers and selling direct to consumers. They attribute the ability to create this competitive advantage to utilizing the SWOT analysis strategic planning method.

☒ **B, C,** and **D** are incorrect. **B** is incorrect because scenario planning is utilized to project into the future multiple probabilities and assess and plan for implications for each of those scenarios. **C** is incorrect because a balanced scorecard is used to monitor progress toward organizational objectives. **D** is incorrect because a needs assessment is used to determine internal needs of an organization.

17. ☑ **B.** Identify critical leadership competencies (i.e., competitive, innovative thinking) for adjusting recruitment. A development and succession plan is an ideal direction to go in this case. When a workforce becomes stagnant and lacks innovative thinking, it is time to review what competencies are required and then seek out adjustments to how you recruit, develop, and promote people. In addition, this provides a solid foundation for an organization to begin expanding to emerging markets to generate revenue.

☒ **A, C,** and **D** are incorrect. **A** is incorrect because this is reactive in a punitive way and does not address the workplace culture effectively. **C** is incorrect because implementing cost-saving measures is a tactical approach that does not effectively address the organization's need to create an innovative culture. **D** is incorrect because while having metrics that are tied to shareholder value is good, this approach still does not address the need for the organization to transform its culture to one that is innovative.

18. ☑ **A.** In this case, it is already determined that the workforce just isn't available to make entry into this market this quickly. With some creative recruiting solutions, you could potentially enter the market in a year. Perhaps the discussion with senior management is to find international candidates or provide internal

training to staff who may be interested in taking their career in this direction. In either case, the HR Director has to look at this situation strategically and ensure that they are engaging the stakeholders to ensure sound staffing decisions. It would be a financial and brand disaster for the company to enter a new market segment and not have the staff to execute the company's strategic plan.

☒ B, C, and D are incorrect because all of these approaches could only work with more time. The question makes it clear that the workforce simply is not available.

19. ☑ A. As an HR professional, this decision makes your ability to recruit quality teachers difficult. An abrupt layoff of staff damages the employer brand. Strategically, this decision warrants further discussion with the executive team. It is HR's responsibility to raise these concerns and facilitate discussion around this important decision.

☒ B, C, and D are incorrect because they do not take into consideration the impact of this decision from an HR strategic standpoint. They would not aid HR in guiding a discussion on any major HR issue such as staffing, recruiting, and employee relations.

20. ☑ C. The decision has already been made that this benefit will be eliminated. You can assume that the cost versus the potential loss of staff and brand loyalty from the community has already been considered, and it was determined that the elimination of the benefit is still in the company's best interest. At this point, HR's best support to the company is to strategically minimize the impact of any negative backlash by carefully crafting the content of any employee communication, determining how the communication will be delivered (in person, e-mail, intranet, mailers, and so on), and coordinating the timing of the communication. In addition, HR should prepare for the inevitable, which is that some will leave who need the level of insurance coverage offered by the company in favor of companies who still offer a comparable benefit to part-time workers.

☒ A, B, and D are incorrect. A is incorrect because, as stated before, the decision has been made and one can assume from the question that the pros and cons have been weighed. Advising the executive team to consider these options should have already taken place. B and D are incorrect because both options would likely happen after communicating the changes, as stated in choice C.

21. ☑ A. Collaborating with supervisors to identify talent is an internal strategic relationship that would influence recruiting and hiring strategy.

☒ B, C, and D are incorrect. B is incorrect because ensuring FLSA compliance is an HR function but not an example of a strategic internal partnership. C is incorrect because for this to be a strategic internal relationship, the questions of what the compensation analysis is for and what will be done with the information gathered should be answered as well. D is incorrect because it is more of a task-oriented function specific to HR. It would not be considered strategic.

22. ☑ **C.** The overall purpose of human resources capital management planning is to identify what skill sets are needed for the company to successfully execute the its strategy.

☒ **A, B,** and **D** are incorrect. **A** and **B** are incorrect because these are both part of the purpose for a recruiting plan but not the overall purpose of an HCMP. **D** is incorrect because an HCMP supports the company's business plan. Its purpose is not to decide which strategic direction the company should pursue.

23. ☑ **B.** The best choice is for the HR professional and the CTO to form a strategic relationship focused on defining the competencies that exist in the IT department, determine the competencies needed, and develop a way for the CTO to measure performance.

☒ **A, C,** and **D** are incorrect. **A** and **D** are incorrect because these are not appropriate functions for HR. **C** is incorrect because before recruiting more talented personnel, it must first be determined what is causing the slow response time by the IT staff and the problematic resolutions to employee technology issues.

24. ☑ **B.** Whether formal or informal, collaborating with the Sales Director and successful employees will help HR determine the true causes of turnover and how best to approach the company's desire to improve in this area. The Sales Director and salespeople have the most familiarity and direct knowledge of the characteristics and competencies of successful outside sales professionals.

☒ **A, C,** and **D** are incorrect because although these relationships are useful to achieving the goal of reducing turnover, the best choice in this case is to collaborate directly with the people in the sales function or managing the sales function.

25. ☑ **B.** Partnering with a recruiting agency that specializes in healthcare would have the most immediate impact on the school district's recruiting needs. A recruiting agency will likely have a pipeline of candidates that they will be able to place in the open positions. It is important for HR to forge relationships with organizations that may be able to be a source for creative solutions that will support a company's strategic goals.

☒ **A, C,** and **D** are incorrect because a university, hospital, and a senior care facility are not appropriate places to source for candidates to meet long-term needs.

26. ☑ **C.** Purchasing food from the agricultural program is beneficial to all stakeholders—students, the university, and the food service company. The university earns revenue, which it can reinvest in the program to sustain its ability to remain a highly respected program, which, in turn, has the potential to increase enrollment. If the food service company also offers internships to students of the agricultural program, the company can use this opportunity to train future talent in the company's way and it allows the company to have an extended interview of these candidates. If HR decides to bring graduates of the internship program on board, it is likely that they will remain committed employees and have a longer tenure.

☒ **A**, **B**, and **D** are incorrect because although they all present good strategic moves, none are as strong as the strategic partnership formed by utilizing the university as a food supplier and employing the university's students.

27. ☑ **B**. Providing discounted or free medications directly to the hospital would be in line with the company's mission to "…support and enhance the quality of care in the communities it serves…"

☒ **A**, **C**, and **D** are incorrect. **A** is incorrect because it is not congruent with the company's mission. Offering experimental drugs, even if for free, does not support the idea that the company cares about its local community receiving quality healthcare. Experimental medications may have unknown side effects and are not yet be approved by the Food and Drug Administration (FDA). **C** is incorrect because this is also not congruent with the company's mission. **D** is incorrect because opening a pharmacy gives those who utilize the hospital a convenient option to fill prescriptions but given that this is a charity hospital, paying full price for medications does not help the less fortunate in the company. The mission states that the company wants to enhance the quality of care for the community.

28. ☑ **C**. Supporting employees in a walk for cancer research is consistent with the company's position on community involvement.

☒ **A**, **B**, and **D** are incorrect because all three choices are types of ways the company could support charitable organizations but none are originated by employees. The company's position on community involvement is that employees should take the initiative to be a volunteer in their communities.

29. ☑ **A**. A monthly business professional networking event allows the HR Director to form alliances with other professionals who may be of value to the company in the future. One approach for the HR Director is to determine if there is an insurance broker in the network and to solicit his or her assistance to shop for the best insurance package available.

☒ **B**, **C**, and **D** are incorrect. **B** is incorrect because the wellness coordinator can share data on utilization of wellness initiatives that could help when putting together the total rewards package but the contribution is minimal given the scope of the task. **C** is incorrect because it is limited to the data the current insurance company can provide. This is useful but not the only piece of information needed to formulate a new total rewards package. **D** is incorrect because the relationship should be pre-existing. This response assumes that the HR Director will now begin to shop for a compensation analyst.

30. ☑ **A**. A part of the company's mission is to provide safer transportation for children. To that end, partnering with a community organization to host workshops on proper use of child restraints is in line with the mission. The relationship built with the community organization fulfills the company's corporate responsibility and may also support future recruitment efforts as this helps to brand the company as an ethical company that invests in the community's children.

☒ **B**, **C**, and **D** are incorrect because these alliances don't have a direct impact on the mission of promoting safety for children.

31. ☑ C. Building strategic partnerships and alliances prior to there being a need is the best way to secure quick responses and easy access to individuals or companies that can help HR resolve employment-related issues (for example: recruiting, retention).

☒ A, B, and D are incorrect because these are all secondary purposes for forming these alliances. The question asked for the *best* answer.

32. ☑ D. Relevant key performance measures are critical to an effective balance scorecard. In this case, evaluating the effectiveness of the existing measure, aligning with organizational objectives, and communicating new measures are the best actions to take.

☒ A, B, and C are incorrect. A is incorrect because establishing a recruitment plan is an action after the fact. It is not the action that enables an effective balanced scorecard. B is incorrect because mandatory customer service training is an after-the-fact action, but does not contribute to an overall effective balanced scorecard. C is incorrect because implementing cost-cutting measures will not significantly contribute to the balanced scorecard and overall organizational effectiveness.

33. ☑ A. Measuring the ability to innovate, improve, and execute is a key question to ask. This is especially critical if an organization has a vision or mission to be an innovative leader. In answering that question, then, an organization is in a good place to identify key performance indicators that measure progress.

☒ B, C, and D are incorrect. B is incorrect because having the ability to find and hire talent quickly does not adequately address the organization's overall objectives. C is incorrect because managing performance is only one part of the equation and does not adequately address the overall organizational objectives. D is incorrect because employee satisfaction scores, as a stand-alone measure, are not linked to overall organizational effectiveness.

34. ☑ C. Developing the strategic objectives of the scorecard is critical for effectiveness. Otherwise, the effort will be meaningless.

☒ A, B, and D are incorrect. A is incorrect because formulating the project plan is a step that comes well after determining overall objectives. B is incorrect because gaining executive sponsorship comes after determining overall objectives of the balanced scorecard. D is incorrect because developing a communication plan is the last step in the process of developing a balanced scorecard.

35. ☑ B. A thoughtful determination of needs and a desire for change is the first step.

☒ A, C, and D are incorrect because these choices occur later than Kirkpatrick's Model for change.

36. ☑ A. Assuming a project manager role and beginning to put together a team to accomplish the change is the best role an HR Manager can take during the change process.

☒ B, C, and D are incorrect because these choices are not the most important role the HR Manager will take on during this process.

37. ☑ C. This choice will be the least disruptive to the staff.

☒ A, B, and D are incorrect because these choices would negatively impact the staff and could be a possible retention risk.

38. ☑ D. The third step is discussing alternatives and probable reactions. The key here is that HR conducts the focus groups to discuss concerns and questions.

☒ A, B, and C are incorrect. A is incorrect as this step includes discussing alternatives and possible reactions but does not inform staff of the change. B and C are incorrect because these choices would not benefit the employees or the company as the decision would be made by top management; it is not the employee's place to make the decision.

39. ☑ B. A two-way exchange is important for the change to be communicated properly. The first imperative is to create awareness of the need for change followed by a vision of where you want to go.

☒ A, C, and D are incorrect. A and C are incorrect because all the employees are in one location so a webinar would disconnect the group dynamic. Because the staff is relatively small, a group meeting would be ideal. D is incorrect because it would be too time consuming to meet with everyone concerning this particular, less important organizational change. In addition, it would take away from the group learning process as questions and feedback are given during the group meetings.

40. ☑ A is correct because fear of the unknown and what will happen to relationships can impair employee productivity in the workplace. When HR gets involved at the beginning of merger and acquisition planning, loss of employee productivity can be minimized.

☒ B, C, and D are incorrect because these choices are possible options that employees might experience but fear is the most traumatic feeling that employees will face and HR must be aware of this as it is similar to other losses.

41. ☑ C. Reinforcing with incentives to the employee will help facilitate the change and improve employee buy in.

☒ A, B, and D are incorrect because these choices might be part of the process but HR can provide the most benefit by positively reinforcing the change with incentives.

42. ☑ **D.** Human Resources has the ability to contribute to the overall strategic plan by providing human capital information, implications, and workforce environmental scanning information that can enable an organization to become competitive through its workforce. So the key advantage of alignment between HR and the overall business strategy is that it strengthens the organization's ability to anticipate and respond to customers, ultimately enabling the organization to maintain a competitive advantage.

☒ **A, B,** and **C** are incorrect. **A** is incorrect because compensation and benefits planning is a tactical benefit of aligned strategic planning. **B** is incorrect because employee and labor relations are a tactical benefit of planning versus a strategic benefit. Tactical benefits yield a minimal return on investment versus a strategic benefit. **C** is incorrect because, like answer B, recruitment is a tactical benefit versus a strategic benefit. The key question to ask in any HR strategic planning is "How will the organization and its customers benefit?"

43. ☑ **B.** To begin the strategic planning process, the four key questions to ask are: Where are we now? Where do we want to be? How do we get there? How will we know if we are on track? These questions guide the strategic planning process from assessing the existing state of the organization through the point of developing objectives that help with plan execution.

☒ **A, C,** and **D** are incorrect. **A** is incorrect because this addresses only one aspect of HR and does not link to overall business strategy. The most effective HR strategic plans focus on the "big picture" first, and then align the functional areas such as recruitment as steps to achieving the overall plan. **C** is incorrect because these questions represent the SWOT analysis. It is true the SWOT analysis is a good tool to use but it is not the first key questions that are asked in developing a strategic plan. **D** is incorrect because these questions are narrowly focused and past tense. An effective strategic plan is forward-thinking and focuses on the overall organizational strategy.

44. ☑ **A.** The most effective approach to evaluating and redirecting strategy is to perform a gap analysis. Comparing actual to targeted performance will help create understanding of what actions to take to correct any variance to overall organization strategy.

☒ **B, C,** and **D** are incorrect. **B** is incorrect because employee satisfaction scores will not adequately provide insight into misalignment between HR and organizational strategy. **C** is incorrect because turnover metrics will not provide effective insights into a misalignment between HR and organizational strategy. **D** is incorrect because employee exit surveys will most likely provide subjective information and will not be effective in evaluating and redirecting strategy.

45. ☑ **B.** The mission statement communicates the purpose of the company to employees, vendors, investors, and customers. As a part of a business plan, it is used to explain to a lender such as a bank why the company is in existence and the overall purpose of formulating.

☒ **A, C, and D are incorrect. A** is incorrect because a vision statement describes how the company will look in the future. It is an aspirational statement whose purpose is to inspire employees. **C** is incorrect because a values statement is the moral compass of the organization. It is used to describe what the company believes in. **D** is incorrect because corporate goals are established after the vision and mission statements. The purpose is to define how the company will achieve its mission and vision in the mid and long terms.

46. ☑ **B.** Corporate goal setting should follow the SMART model. Goals should be Specific, Measureable, Action-Oriented, Realistic, and Time-Based. "Increasing sales by 7 percent" is measurable. "Over the next four quarters" is time-based. The overall goal is specific and the word "increase" is action-oriented. This answer meets all the SMART criteria.

☒ **A, C, and D are incorrect. A** is incorrect because it is not a measurable or time-based goal. **C** is incorrect because increasing sales by 150 percent is not realistic. A goal like this would actually discourage employees and affect morale. **D** is incorrect because it is not a measureable goal and is not specific.

47. ☑ **D.** Customers appreciate quick, accurate, and thorough resolutions to issues. Answering their phone calls quickly, allowing them to talk to a live person as opposed to an automated system, and resolving any issue in that first call would all be characteristic of a company that wants to be a top-notch customer service organization.

☒ **A, B, and C are incorrect. A** is incorrect because customers expect that a world-class customer service organization would have first line responders who are able to resolve their issues without escalation. **B** is incorrect because e-mailing a survey has very little to do with the overall customer experience. **C** is incorrect because it is gimmicky and because giving away free items after the fact doesn't ensure that the customer's overall experience was positive.

48. ☑ **A.** Opening a beauty school would satisfy the board's desire to diversify. Continuing their mastery of retailing beauty products through the school's salon would allow them to capitalize on their identified core competencies of logistics and supply chain management. A core competency is something the organization does well and that differentiates them or gives them a competitive edge over the competition.

☒ **B, C, and D are incorrect. B** is incorrect because while leadership knows the retail business well, opening another store is not diversifying as much as it is expanding. **C** is incorrect because it is expected that by opening a school, leadership would seek to provide a quality education to students, but this alone does not address the desire to make the most of their core competencies. **D** is incorrect because adding more products to the store is simply that. They would just be offering more beauty products to their consumers. There isn't any diversification or change to their already existing business model.

49. ☑ **B.** Making the decision locally to volunteer to rebuild homes would be in keeping with the corporate values. It shows initiative on the part of the local management, and they are volunteering in an area where they have expertise—construction.

☒ **A, C, and D** are incorrect. **A** is incorrect because it is an incongruous way to offer disaster support. This isn't the company's area of expertise and doesn't offer immediate assistance to the victims of the natural disaster. **C and D** are incorrect because the corporate values encourage taking initiative. Sitting and waiting for the corporate office or the local government to give direction would be the opposite of initiative.

50. ☑ **B.** A vision statement is an aspirational statement that is developed to answer the question of what the company does, who it does it for, and where the company aspires to be in the future.

☒ **A, C, and D** are incorrect. **A** is incorrect because a corporate values statement explains how the company will conduct business and make decisions even if daily business operations change. **C** is incorrect because a mission statement defines how the company will achieve the vision. **D** is incorrect because core competencies are what gives the company its competitive edge.

51. ☑ **A.** A corporate values statement explains how the company will conduct business and make decisions even if daily business operations change.

☒ **B, C, and D** are incorrect. **B** is incorrect because a vision statement is an aspirational statement that is developed to answer the question of what the company does, who it does it for, and where the company aspires to be in the future. **C** is incorrect because a mission statement defines how the company will achieve the vision. **D** is incorrect because core competencies are what gives the company its competitive edge.

52. ☑ **B.** Corporate values should be no more than a few sentences and HR should ensure they are posted/published and understood by customers and employees.

☒ **A, C, and D** are incorrect. **A and C** are incorrect because they are also important to do but **B** encompasses the best action step HR could take. **D** is incorrect because corporate values should be no more than a couple of sentences.

53. ☑ **C.** The employee's manager should be informed and an investigation begun to find out if the alleged activity took place.

☒ **A, B, and D** are incorrect. **A** is incorrect because putting the employee on leave of absence could be seen as retaliation for voicing an ethical concern. **B and D** are incorrect because these choices would not be beneficial to the company or the employees.

54. ☑ A. The basic responsibility of the CEO of an organization is to establish necessary ethical standards and conduct business in a consistent manner with the policies.

☒ B, C, and D are incorrect. B is incorrect because this would be the responsibility of the Chief Financial Officer. C is incorrect because this would be the responsibility of an organization's general counsel. D is incorrect because this would be the responsibility of an organization's internal auditing group.

55. ☑ D. Insider trading is the trading of a public company's stock or other securities by individuals with access to non-public information about the company.

☒ A, B, and C are incorrect. These are other types of ethical issues that may arise from time to time in an organization.

56. ☑ A. Making the cause part of the culture and philosophy of the company is the best way to effectively involve employees in the company's Corporate Citizenship Program.

☒ B, C, and D are incorrect because these choices do not adequately involve employees in the company's Corporate Citizenship Program. Without involving employees in new programs, lack of buy-in and complacency is a certain behavioral outcome.

57. ☑ B. Hiring a Chief Ethics Officer would allow for standard communication/values and standards to be set up for the company.

☒ A, C, and D are incorrect because these choices would be items to consider when hiring a Chief Ethics Officer. While minimizing time spent on ethical issues or the number of discrimination complaints is good goals, they by themselves do not rise to the higher strategic objective of the position.

58. ☑ A. The objective of Corporate Citizenship is to embrace responsibility for the company's actions and encourage a positive impact on communities through the company's activities.

☒ B, C, and D are incorrect because these choices are examples of later phases of developing a corporate citizenship program.

59. ☑ A. The high unemployment rate could potentially be a competitive advantage for this company. They can "shop" for people who have the skill set they need to earn significant profits in the new market segment. The company may also invest in training existing staff with the skills the company needs to obtain the same results. It is unlikely that in a period of high unemployment that the company will lose the employees it chooses to train to the competition. An analysis of the return on investment (ROI) for both of these scenarios will provide valuable information to senior decision makers.

☒ B, C, and D are incorrect because none of these choices provide data that would support the reasons why the company should invest in additional or better trained personnel.

60. ☑ **C.** Reduce time to hire would be an objective of an HCMP. A valuable HCMP has at least six components: a statement of strategic direction, goal, objective, actions needed to reach the goal, method/mode of communicating goal to organization, and a way to measure the success of the plan.

    ☒ **A, B, and D are incorrect. A** is incorrect because this is an example of an action that would be taken to achieve a stated objective of reducing time to hire. **B** is incorrect because this is an example of a goal of an HCMP. **D** is incorrect because this is an example of the measurement component of an HCMP.

61. ☑ **B.** An employee self-service system allows employees to immediately update tax exemption information and certain demographic changes as they happen. This actually increases HR's support to employees but saves the company money because it eliminates the need for an actual person to field the phone calls and make the changes in the system.

    ☒ **A, C, and D are incorrect. A** is incorrect because it is never a good idea to remove the strategic leader of the HR department. Line managers carry out some HR-related duties already but cannot effectively manage retention, turnover, training, employee relations, EEO reporting, and so on without that central support of an HR department lead. **C and D** are incorrect because in both cases the impact to the employee may be negative and reduce morale. If employees feel as though a company is not committed to their growth and development, they are likely to seek employment elsewhere or not do the best job possible while with the current employer.

62. ☑ **B.** Implementing a safety training program will have the most impact on workers' compensation claims. If employees are more aware of safety measures, they will be less likely to incur an injury, thereby reducing the number of claims.

    ☒ **A, C, and D are incorrect. A and C** are incorrect because while it is true that better preparation for the job delivered through the onboarding process and the support of a mentor will assist a new employee in making better safety choices initially, an on-going safety training plan will remind and update workers about current safety measures, which will have the most direct impact on injuries and workers' compensation training. **D** is incorrect because a training on HR systems would not enhance workers' knowledge of safety. Therefore, it has no impact on reducing workers' compensation claims.

63. ☑ **A.** ROI is calculated by dividing the output by the cost of the investment. In this case, the increased number of hammers produced divided by the cost of training employees on making hammers shows that investing in training is in the financial best interest of this company—positive ROI.

    ☒ **B, C, and D are incorrect. B and C** are incorrect because the overall sales of hammers will not show the CEO how the hammer production training directly impacted an increase in sales. It simply shows that sales have increased overall. **D** is incorrect because knowing the training budget does not aid the CEO in determining a training sessions' effect on the bottom line.

64. ☑ **D.** Ensuring that there is a recruitment plan in place to address any possible deficiencies in the current workforce in skills that are needed to support the company's strategic plan is an important part of the budgetary activity of human capital projection. The cost of any human capital that may have to be acquired is calculated and the potential return on investment of that capital evaluated as a part of the overall HR budget.

☒ **A, B,** and **C** are incorrect. **A** and **B** are incorrect because the facility size and raw materials cost are of more concern to the operations leader as opposed to the HR leader. **C** is incorrect because prior to making the decision to pursue the production of this new jet, this is a question most appropriate for the CFO and CEO to ponder. Again, it is not directly related to the HR budget.

65. ☑ **B.** Measuring employment decisions by non-HR managers is a higher level strategic function of HR. These metrics can be used to make data-driven decisions regarding future hires and training/coaching needs of managers whose hiring history shows a lean toward lower-quality human capital acquisitions.

☒ **A, C,** and **D** are incorrect because maintaining and tracking information for reporting or reliable benefits management are more administrative functions of HR.

66. ☑ **A.** It is true many consider forecasting too far out into the future to be subjective. However, when a forecast is based on carefully researched and/or historical evidence in the organization or industry, it's possible to identify a trend in what resources may be required if service lines are doubled or tripled.

☒ **B, C,** and **D** are incorrect. **B** is incorrect because newly established metrics do not provide a much needed historical perspective. **C** is incorrect because while obtaining opinions is good for eventual buy-in, it would not provide an objective historical perspective. **D** is incorrect because an existing job pool may provide an indicator of what skills are available but does not provide a complete picture for a forecast.

67. ☑ **C.** Clearly articulated goals and objectives would overcome any complex business plan. Employees can see their role in new strategies when goals and objectives are clearly communicated.

☒ **A, B,** and **D** are incorrect. **A** is incorrect because a five-year plan would still need goals and objectives for employees to remain engaged. **B** is incorrect because a market analysis, while good information, does not necessarily connect employees to the overall objectives. **D** is incorrect because the business description does not connect employees with the big picture.

68. ☑ **D.** The most effective objectives are those that are specific, measureable, attainable, realistic, and timely. "We will enhance the workforce customer service skills by 80 percent in 12 months" is the most effective objective statement because it provides a specific percentage and a specific time period.

☒ **A, B,** and **C** are incorrect. **A** is incorrect because the statement is not specific. **B** is incorrect because the statement is also not specific or measurable. **C** is incorrect because the statement is not specific.

69. ☑ C. A return on investment (ROI) analysis is calculated by subtracting the cost of the investment from the value of the investment and dividing the result by the cost of the investment times 100. The correct calculation and ratio is $450,000 – $300,000 / $300,000 = 50%. The result of this analysis indicates the investment is worthwhile because the benefit gained from purchasing this software program outweighs the cost of the new system.

☒ A, B, and D are incorrect. A is incorrect because the calculation of the purchase of the system is for only one year. B is incorrect because this calculation accounts for only one year both on the cost and benefit side of the equation. D is incorrect because the equation accounts for only one year of benefits at $450,000.

70. ☑ A. A breakeven point occurs when the costs match the benefits of a project or initiative.

☒ B, C, and D are incorrect. B is incorrect because an itemized statement lists out details of costs or expenses. C is incorrect because a return on investment is a performance measure that evaluates the effectiveness of an investment. D is incorrect because a zero-based budget starts from zero and justifies every line item in the budget.

71. ☑ D. An assumption is an estimated factor that cannot necessarily be narrowed down to a specific number. There is a factor of uncertainty to it but still may be relevant to a cost benefit analysis.

☒ A, B, and C are incorrect because these are specific and measurable factors in a cost benefit analysis.

72. ☑ D. A capital expenditure includes acquiring or upgrading assets such as equipment, property, or buildings. Capital expenses are long-term investments in which money is typically paid up front.

☒ A, B, and C are incorrect. A is incorrect because capital expenditures do not include day-to-day expenses such as lease payments. B is incorrect because training materials are considered day-to-day expenses and do not qualify as a capital expenditure. C is incorrect because payroll is considered a day-to-day expense and does not qualify as a capital expenditure.

73. ☑ B. The key advantage of zero-based budgeting is that is minimizes the chance of budgetary slack. Every department starts from zero and justifies each line item.

☒ A, C, and D are incorrect. A is incorrect because zero-based budgeting is a time-consuming process. C is incorrect because having to justify every budgetary line item creates anxiety and underlying conflict for some department leaders. D is incorrect because zero-based budgeting maintains, if not increases, budgetary complexity.

74. ☑ **A.** To ensure accurate product costs is a key strategic advantage of distinguishing between direct and indirect labor costs. This is a key financial measure that can impact profits.

☒ **B, C,** and **D** are incorrect. **B** is incorrect because maintaining accurate payroll records is tactical in nature. **C** is incorrect because maintaining accurate job class records is tactical in nature. **D** is incorrect because tracking job duties is not an adequate key strategic advantage.

75. ☑ **C.** A key strategic advantage of getting involved in legislative matters is that it provides a proactive approach to identifying threats and opportunities, ultimately leading to a competitive advantage.

☒ **A, B,** and **D** are incorrect. **A** is incorrect because keeping updated policies and procedures is tactical in nature and does not provide a significant strategic advantage. **B** is incorrect because keeping updated training programs is tactical and reactive. **D** is incorrect because becoming knowledgeable in what is legal and illegal, while important, is tactical and is not a key strategic advantage.

76. ☑ **B.** Calling and writing letters to local representatives is a good proactive action plan in expressing concerns, support, or opposition for specific legislative activity.

☒ **A, C,** and **D** are incorrect. **A** is incorrect because writing to media outlets is not effective in expressing support or opposition to legislators and ultimately influencing new laws. **C** is incorrect because posting a blog is not the best action step in influencing the legislative process. **D** is incorrect because posting on social networks is not the best step in influencing new laws.

77. ☑ **C.** Conducting a cost/benefit analysis and providing business recommendations contributes significantly to the organization's strategic plan. Leaders can take information from a cost/benefit analysis and assign priority and take action accordingly.

☒ **A, B,** and **D** are incorrect. **A** is incorrect because simply informing management of the new law does not adequately provide a significant contribution to the strategic plan. **B** is incorrect because providing a list of business activities that can no longer be done (also called a don't do list) stops short of a significant contribution to the organization's strategic plan. **D** is incorrect because creating a memo informing the organization of a new law alone is not a significant contribution to the strategic plan. It is not enough.

78. ☑ **A.** Because Congress is still in session, the bill automatically becomes law. If it is relevant to the workplace, it is wise to go ahead and assess the impact to the organization.

☒ **B, C,** and **D** are incorrect. **B** is incorrect because if Congress is still in session and the president has not signed the bill, it automatically becomes law. **C** is incorrect because in this case the bill automatically becomes law and there is no need for it to be sent back to Congress. **D** is incorrect because there is a formal timeline for every legislative process.

79. ☑ D. Actively participating in the public hearings and providing clear and concise comments form a proactive strategy for an advocacy plan.

☒ A, B, and C are incorrect. A is incorrect because waiting before taking action until the regulatory agency has issued a final rule is not proactive and not effective for an advocacy plan. B is incorrect because developing policies and procedures that support the new rule is not a proactive strategy. C is incorrect because voting is not part of a regulatory rule-making process.

80. ☑ B. Partnering with legislative advocacy or industry associations is a proactive and effective strategy for monitoring the regulatory environment. In addition, this is a good source for cost/benefit analysis information.

☒ A, C, and D are incorrect. A is incorrect because waiting to hear news from any source is not proactive. C is incorrect because watching news may provide some insight on changes but is not an adequate source for cost/benefit information. D is incorrect because surveying internal sources does not provide an adequate picture of the external regulatory influence.

81. ☑ A. The definition of a quorum is a requirement to have a minimum number of members present before official business may be conducted and decisions made.

☒ B, C, and D are incorrect. B is incorrect because an agenda is a document meant to guide the meeting proceedings. C is incorrect because minutes are notes of a meeting. D is incorrect because a schedule does not adequately define a quorum.

82. ☑ C. Establishing an internal audit process that promotes organizational involvement is a good way to improve organizational governance. An internal audit will determine where the risks are and will allow priorities to be established and actions decided on.

☒ A, B, and D are incorrect. A is incorrect because while employee opinion on ethics is important, it is tactical in nature and subjective. B is incorrect because policy and training creation is tactical and something that may come later on after an audit is completed. D is incorrect because providing leadership development training may be a recommendation after an internal audit is completed.

83. ☑ D. An organization that has a code of ethics and is committed to it can build a positive reputation and obtain the ability to expand market share as a result.

☒ A, B, and C are incorrect. A is incorrect because while it is important for employees to know how to handle ethical situations, it does not provide a strategic advantage. B is incorrect because avoiding lawsuits, while desired, is not a strategic advantage. C is incorrect because reducing ethical issues for the Human Resource department does not provide an overall strategic advantage.

84. ☑ D. Leadership can create or impede a culture in which employees feel safe in reporting something wrong. A whistleblower protection policy relies on leadership to be supportive in order for it to be effective.

☒ A, B, and C are incorrect because these factors alone do not influence the effectiveness of whistleblowing protection policies.

85. ☑ B. Enterprise risk management is a practice of forecasting possible risks to the organization and takes steps to mitigate the impact on an organization.
☒ A, C, and D are incorrect. A is incorrect because workforce risk forecasting does not adequately define the practice of forecasting possible risks on an organizational level. C is incorrect because proactive action planning is an overbroad term and not specific to risk management. D is incorrect because legal risk management is not an adequate definition of forecasting possible risks to the organization.

86. ☑ A. Policies that manage risks will take into account the level of risk. If there is a payroll mistake resulting in minimal dollars, most organizations will pay the employee correctly, learn from it, and move on.
☒ B, C, and D are incorrect. B is incorrect in this case because purchasing an Employee Practices Liability Insurance policy is overkill for a minor issue that can be remedied directly from the organization's resources. C and D are incorrect because these actions do not effectively address minor risks.

87. ☑ C. Employment practices liability insurance typically covers litigating and settling wrongful discharge and discrimination lawsuits.
☒ A, B, and D are incorrect. A is incorrect because employment practices liability insurance does not replace human resource policies and procedures. B is incorrect because employment practices liability insurance does not replace a handbook. Typically, the insurance company will want to review the employer's handbook as part of the vetting process. D is incorrect because employment practices liability insurance does not prevent employees from exercising their rights under federal law such as FLSA and ERISA.

88. ☑ B. A key strategic contribution of an HR audit is to understand if HR practices help or hinder organizational objectives.
☒ A, C, and D are incorrect. A is incorrect because understanding which policies need to be replaced may be an outcome of an HR audit but it does not rise to the level of a strategic contribution. C is incorrect because understanding if there is policy confusion is not a key strategic contribution. D is incorrect because updating leadership development is a tactical outcome.

89. ☑ D. Determining the scope and type of audit should be the first step of an HR audit.
☒ A, B, and C are incorrect. A is incorrect because developing the audit questionnaire comes after deciding on the type and scope of HR audit. B is incorrect because providing feedback about the audit results is one of the final steps of an HR audit process. C is incorrect because creating a culture of continuous improvement comes after establishing the type and scope of the audit.

90. ☑ **A.** Monitoring one's online reputation and conducting drills for dealing with a crisis enable an organization to actively leverage social media strategies while mitigating risk.

    ☒ **B, C,** and **D** are incorrect. **B** is incorrect because organizations are finding a return on investment by utilizing a social media strategy. **C** is incorrect because creating a policy and procedure is tactical. **D** is incorrect because developing a training program is tactical and does not necessarily support an overall branding strategy.

91. ☑ **C.** A thoughtful needs analysis is the most critical and first step in the process.

    ☒ **A, B,** and **D** are incorrect. The organization's needs must be determined and specific goals identified before the steps identified in choices **A, B,** and **D** are taken.

92. ☑ **A.** Employee call centers are a great way to streamline the efficiency of an organization while not taking away any strategic tasks.

    ☒ **B, C,** and **D** are incorrect because these choices are typically less frequent tasks that are outsourced due to their complex nature and probably best serviced internally.

93. ☑ **B.** This choice sets the tone for the outsourcing relationship going forward and will clearly specify the intended goals of the outsourcing partnership.

    ☒ **A, C,** and **D** are incorrect because these choices are necessary to develop but they will come later in the outsourcing process.

94. ☑ **B.** Outsourcing transactional components of human resources can free up people to perform more strategic roles. For example, if an organization outsources COBRA benefit administration, it can free up a benefits professional to focus on enhancing the value of other benefit programs.

    ☒ **A, C,** and **D** are incorrect. **A** is incorrect because while saving the cost of wages and benefits may be true, it is tactical in nature. **C** is incorrect because while outsourcing may support smaller businesses, it is not a key strategic advantage. **D** is incorrect because the freeing up of office space is not necessarily a key strategic advantage.

95. ☑ **A.** A service-level agreement is a document that includes details such as what, when, and how a service item will be delivered. Implementing a service-level agreement can go a long way in ensuring internal customer satisfaction and buy-in from key stakeholders.

    ☒ **B, C,** and **D** are incorrect. **B** is incorrect because management training is not necessarily connected to customer service objectives. **C** is incorrect because succession plans are meant to build a leadership pipeline and are not related to a service agreement between the outsourcing firm and customer. **D** is incorrect because a talent management plan is not relevant to an agreement between an internal customer and an outsourcing vendor.

96. ☑ **C.** Assessing the effectiveness of a recruitment outsourcing arrangement can be done by measuring cost-per-hire and quality of hire. Cost-per-hire metrics

can be used to compare and contrast the return on investment for the recruitment source. A quality of hire metric can assess the level of competent and high potential candidates being sourced through this arrangement.

☒ **A**, **B**, and **D** are incorrect. **A** is incorrect because measuring the applicant pool will not necessarily provide effective assessment of the recruitment outsourcing firm. **B** is incorrect because measuring workplace diversity does not adequately reflect the effectiveness of a recruitment firm. **D** is incorrect because a succession plan is not relevant to the effectiveness of a recruitment firm.

97. ☑ **D**. The rate of merger and acquisition failures is often attributed to human resource factors such as conflicting cultures, poor leadership, and organization-wide mistrust. As such, assessing culture and talent strengths and weaknesses of both organizations can contribute significantly to the strategic plan.

☒ **A**, **B**, and **C** are incorrect. **A** is incorrect because implementing a recruitment plan is a premature step. **B** is incorrect because an employee survey may only produce subjective information not adequate for strategic impact. **C** is incorrect because waiting for information is not proactive and will not produce a strategic impact.

98. ☑ **B**. An acquiring organization can inadvertently assume risk from pending litigation from the selling company. The best approach to protecting an acquiring organization's best interests is to include an indemnification in the acquisition agreement. An indemnification provision protects an acquiring company from assuming unreasonable risks particularly from pending litigation matters.

☒ **A**, **C**, and **D** are incorrect. **A** is incorrect because it is not true. The risk from pending litigation from the EEOC or the NLRB does not stay strictly with the selling company and can roll to the acquiring company. **C** is incorrect because delaying an acquisition until pending litigation is resolved is not practical. Sometimes litigation can last for years and the rationale for buying a company can become obsolete in a fast moving business era. **D** is incorrect because it is not practical to resist business decisions if there is any risk involved. The truth is risk is at every business turn. Assessing those risks and considering all alternatives is the best course to take.

99. ☑ **A**. A common method of reducing headcount is through hiring freezes and attrition. A good practice in balancing the skilled talent through an organization after this type of action is to restructure departments so that they are realigned with business objectives.

☒ **B**, **C**, and **D** are incorrect. **B** is incorrect because rehiring employees is contrary to the initial business objective of reducing headcount. **C** is incorrect because, as in answer B, the objective was to reduce headcount, so hiring employees is contrary to the business objective. **D** is incorrect because while developing managers to handle change is good, it is not an adequate solution in this case. A better option is to consider restructuring the organization where skilled talent is aligned with business objectives.

100. ☑ **C.** An integrated information system (enterprise-wide) encompasses multiple departments and reduces the need to manage multiple and overlapping technological systems. The intent of an integrated information system is to enable various departments to communicate and process workflows seamlessly from one to another.

☒ **A, B,** and **D** are incorrect. **A** is incorrect because an integrated system many times will take more time and people to implement. After all, it involves multiple departments versus a single functional best-of-breed system. **B** is incorrect because of an integrated system's size; there is little room for customization, and if there is a custom option, it may be cost prohibitive. **D** is incorrect because of the multiple departments and functions involved; upgrades can be at times just as complex as the implementation itself.

101. ☑ **D.** Technology has come a long way in terms of supporting the open enrollment process. A self-service approach enables employees to log into a computer system from the privacy of their own homes and make whatever benefit selections that appeal to them. This saves the Human Resource department the time-consuming work of manually processing paperwork.

☒ **A, B,** and **C** are incorrect. **A** is incorrect because assuming no changes in benefits from year to year is not practical. This is especially true as organizations shift their benefits offerings to meet organizational objectives. As such, employees most likely have decisions to make in what benefit options work for them. **B** is incorrect because no matter what time open enrollment starts, the paperwork associated with the process is time consuming. **C** is incorrect because reducing dependents from benefits is a decision that may relate to costs but not to efficiency. It is not the most effective way to become efficient in processing open enrollment.

102. ☑ **B.** A key strategic advantage for most organizations is for executives to have access to relevant and timely HR forecasting and costing information at their fingertips. It enables effective decision-making.

☒ **A, C,** and **D** are incorrect. **A** is incorrect because while a self-service solution may reduce some paper-related processes, it is not known to completely eliminate the need for paper. **C** is incorrect because recruitment information about candidates is often housed in an applicant tracking system. **D** is incorrect because employees having access to their W-2 information refers to an employee self-service system.

103. ☑ **C.** Developing the mission and vision is the first step in the process and part of the strategy formulation stage.

☒ **A, B,** and **D** are incorrect because these choices are later in the strategic planning process.

104. ☑ **D.** This statement provides a guiding image of the company's desired future.
☒ **A, B,** and **C** are incorrect. **A** is incorrect as this choice is an example of an organization's values. **B** and **C** are incorrect because these statements are examples of an organization's mission.

105. ☑ **C.** Going out of business can occur when a company has no mission and vision statement. It is also the biggest risk to investors and employees.
☒ **A, B,** and **D** are incorrect because these are possibilities but not the greatest risk to the company.

106. ☑ **A.** If the legislative committee did not act on the bill, the bill will go no further. This is also called "killing the bill." Lawmakers may use a discharge petition to remove the committee from further consideration of the bill. But this could be difficult, as the action would be subject to a majority vote and potential filibustering action. In a lot of cases, the bill is considered killed if not acted on by the committee.
☒ **B, C,** and **D** are incorrect. **B** is incorrect because if there is no action from the committee then the bill is essentially killed and not pending for further review. **C** is incorrect because when the committee doesn't act on the bill, it doesn't go any further for editing or any other actions. **D** is incorrect because when the committee doesn't act on the bill, it does not automatically become law. The bill goes no further and is considered killed.

107. ☑ **C.** There are two avenues to follow: one is legislation (or law making) and the other is regulatory (agency rule-making or law clarity rules). Because the Department of Labor (DOL) is an agency, the regulatory process it would follow is the rule-making procedure. The next step after a proposal is to open the action up for public comment.
☒ **A, B,** and **D** are incorrect. **A** is incorrect because a final rule is last in this regulatory process. **B** is incorrect because referring a bill to a committee is part of the law-making legislative procedure and not the agency rule-making process. **D** is incorrect because this is a rule that would follow the regulatory process and would not go to Congress.

108. ☑ **D.** Regulatory agencies will enforce and provide clarity on particular laws. In this case, the Equal Employment Opportunity Commission (EEOC) enforces the Americans with Disability Act of 1990 among others, such as Title VII of the Civil Rights Act and the Equal Pay Act.
☒ **A, B,** and **C** are incorrect. **A** is incorrect because the National Labor Relations Board (NLRB) oversees and enforces union-related matters such as elections and unfair labor practices (ULPs) in the private sector. **B** is incorrect because the Occupational Safety and Health Administration (OSHA) enforces health and safety requirements in the workplace. **C** is incorrect because the Securities and Exchange Commission (SEC) enforces the federal securities laws and regulates the securities industry and the U.S. stock and options exchanges.

109. ☑ **B.** Under section 717 of Title VII of the Civil Rights Act of 1964, the EEOC is responsible for the administration and enforcement of equal employment opportunity in federal employment. As such, the EEOC is authorized to issue rules, regulations, orders, and instructions as necessary and appropriate to carry out its EEO responsibilities. Because the Equal Employment Opportunity Commission (EEOC) is an agency, it would follow the rule-making process. The first step of the rule-making procedure is to introduce a proposal.

☒ **A, C,** and **D** are incorrect. **A** is incorrect because the rule-making regulatory process would not introduce a bill to Congress. **C** is incorrect because the rule-making regulatory process does not refer bills to the committee or any sub-committee as lawmakers would in the legislative process. **D** is incorrect because a rule proposal would not follow the same path as a bill and head to the House or Senate floor for debate and vote.

110. ☑ **A.** Getting stakeholder buy-in is critical to most strategic plans. It is best to involve key stakeholders and clearly communicate values, goals, and priorities. This saves confusion and helps minimize resistance.

☒ **B, C,** and **D** are incorrect. **B** is incorrect because a succession plan is generally created to proactively ensure that there are no vacancies in key leadership positions. **C** is incorrect because while goal setting is a good skill, it is not directly related to the need to gain stakeholder buy-in. **D** is incorrect because an applicant opinion survey is not directly related to a strategic plan and will not yield the desired results.

111. ☑ **B.** The American Management Association reports results of an executive survey that a mere 3 percent of executives said their organizations are very successful in executing strategy, and 62 percent reported they are moderately successful. Instituting a leadership development initiative that instills resource management, communication clarity, and aligning practices would go a long way in giving leaders plan execution skills and in supporting the strategic plan.

☒ **A, C,** and **D** are incorrect. **A** is incorrect because recruitment metrics are unrelated to the need to support leaders on strategic plan execution. **C** is incorrect because helping employees come to work on time and develop customer services skills is tactical and does not support the larger picture of plan execution. **D** is incorrect because while getting employee involvement is a good practice, it is not related to the need to develop leadership plan execution skills.

112. ☑ **D.** The first step in strategic planning is assessing the organization's current status. So "Where are we?" is usually the first question asked in a strategic planning process. This question kicks off the strategic planning process with techniques such as the SWOT analysis and environmental scanning.

☒ **A, B,** and **C** are incorrect. **A** is incorrect because assessing the desired strategic point by asking "Where do we want to be" is second in the series of typical strategic planning questions. **B** is incorrect because the question "How do we get there?" is usually the last question asked in a strategic planning process.

C is incorrect because assessing what resources are available usually comes after determining where an organization wants to be. This provides an indicator of whether an organization has the resources necessary to get to the desired end point of the strategic plan.

113. ☑ **C.** The control function is used by managers to measure whether the functions they lead are on course to properly execute corporate goals developed during strategic planning. Quality management systems are a way to measure success toward a set of goals. Therefore, they are a part of the control function.

☒ **A, B,** and **D** are incorrect. **A** is incorrect because planning is the act of formulating the strategy. **B** is incorrect because organizing is the management function where structure is provided for employees as a guide for how they will complete their work. **D** is incorrect because directing is the management function where managers develop relationships with employees to support them in completing their work.

114. ☑ **B.** A decentralized structure is best for franchises or any organization with a wide geographic reach. The corporate office provides support in the form of product development and national marketing but the franchise owner has the independence to make decisions based on knowledge of the local market.

☒ **A, C,** and **D** are incorrect. **A** is incorrect because a centralized structure is most appropriate for small business or companies with a small geographic reach. **C** is incorrect because matrix organizations are a combination of centralized and decentralized models where an employee may report to multiple supervisors or report into multiple divisions. This level of complexity is not best for a franchise. **D** is incorrect because a functional structure refers to a structure that is set up along business units or functional areas. This structure works best in companies that are not very agile and focus on a single product or service.

115. ☑ **B.** A wide span of control works best when the employees perform repetitive or simple tasks. For more complex, specialized functions, a narrow span of control is more fitting. The problem the senior leadership is trying to solve, in this case, is whether they can reduce management staff without negatively impacting employee supervision. It would make sense to look at the pros and cons of adjusting spans of control.

☒ **A, C,** and **D** are incorrect because the financial performance, union status, or management education levels have no determination on whether or not employees can be effectively managed if the company had fewer managers.

116. ☑ **D.** Top management and board members are mostly at risk for violating the act as it involves financial data reporting.

☒ **A, B,** and **C** are incorrect. **A** and **B** are incorrect because these choices are not required of HR under SOX. **C** is incorrect because it is more important for top management and board members to be trained than employees, as top management and board members typically handle the financial reporting of the company, and that is where the majority of the burden lies within SOX.

117. ☑ B. The Sarbanes-Oxley Act of 2002 covers insider trading and whistleblowing.

☒ A, C, and D are incorrect as these choices do not cover insider trading and whistleblowing.

118. ☑ B. It is unrealistic to think that all board members have been previously trained in SOX requirements or are up-to-date with their knowledge of the law.

☒ A, C, and D are incorrect because these choices are examples of items for HR to address as far as ethical conduct or requirements, but they would not provide the best benefit to the company as far as compliance.

119. ☑ C. A divestiture occurs when an organization wants to spin-off a division into its own separate entity, or closes down a division and liquidates any remaining assets.

☒ A, B, and D are incorrect. A is incorrect because a start-up is a company that starts from the ground up with no resources from an existing corporate relationship. B is incorrect because an acquisition refers to an organization that purchases another company. D is incorrect because a merger refers to when two companies join together as one company.

120. ☑ A. Statistics indicate that most merger and acquisition deals fail because the cultures of the two companies are incompatible, as in the case of AOL and Time Warner. Uncovering as much information about cultures and determining compatibility information can be invaluable to the success of the arrangement.

☒ B, C, and D are incorrect. B is incorrect because applicant pool information is not a key strategic point that can make or break the success of a merger or acquisition arrangement. If anything, the merger of two companies could widen the pool of potential applicants. C is incorrect because process information will most likely merge over time but is not key information that has significant impact on the arrangement. D is incorrect because leadership development information is a nice-to-know item but does not rise to the level of strategic impact as culture compatibility.

121. ☑ C. The success of a due diligence team rests on its ability to evaluate another company. Factors such as leadership, culture, risk, and resources are critical for the due diligence process. Uncovering those factors about another company is essential for the due diligence success.

☒ A, B, and D are incorrect. A is incorrect because developing a balanced score card is not relevant to the due diligence process. If anything, a balanced scorecard may be developed after the acquisition took place to ensure that organizational performance is on track. B is incorrect because a marketing plan is not relevant to the due diligence process. Marketing may apply strategy during and after an acquisition has taken place to inform and align customers with new changes. D is incorrect because while understanding financial statements is important, it is critical to understand the financial statements of the company being purchased.

122. ☑ **B.** HR's role in restructuring initiatives oftentimes includes the leading or facilitating changes that are aligned with organizational objectives. This includes the implementation of change management, communication, and leadership partnership strategies.

☒ **A, C,** and **D** are incorrect. **A** is incorrect because leading recruitment activities is tactical and not necessarily connected with the organizational objectives. **C** is incorrect because developing metrics and scorecards are only relevant if connected to overall organizational objectives. In this case, it is tactical at best and HR has a higher level of strategic responsibility to an organization going through major changes. **D** is incorrect because leadership and performance improvement initiatives are only relevant if connected to the overall organizational objectives. In this case, you can implement these initiatives after major changes take place. A strategic HR role is activated at the beginning of any major changes.

123. ☑ **D.** Assessing an organization's readiness for change is a proactive approach to major restructures. This enables HR to understand where the potential barriers and opportunities are to success before any major changes commence.

☒ **A, B,** and **C** are incorrect. **A** is incorrect because preparing a recruitment plan alone is not connected to the overall objectives and need to restructure. **B** is incorrect because developing metrics alone is not a proactive approach to supporting the overall organization objectives of restructuring. **C** is incorrect because preparing leadership development courses, as a stand-alone initiative is not proactive or connected to the overall organizational objectives.

124. ☑ **C.** A clear and effective communication plan is known to more than double the employees' rate of acceptance of change. Oftentimes, employees need to know "why" changes are needed and how they can help, and this information moves many to a level of acceptance more quickly.

☒ **A, B,** and **D** are incorrect. **A** is incorrect because simply having a correct disciplinary procedure is not what motivates employees to accept organizational changes. In fact, threatening employees with discipline if they do not accept changes can grow into further resentment and create an environment of actively disengaged employees. Actively disengaged employees can sabotage or poison any positive thinking from other employees, which can lead to an erosion of any success overall. **B** is incorrect because increasing benefits of a retirement plan is not relevant to the need to facilitate a successful change initiative. **D** is incorrect because an onboarding program is used to acclimate new employees to the organization but is not necessarily connected or impactful for an organizational change initiative.

125. ☑ **D.** Costs that have already been incurred, cannot be recovered, and have become irrelevant from future decision-making are an example of sunk costs. This is also called embedded costs. Some organizations sometimes make the mistake of overlooking the point of no return (sunk costs) and throwing money hand over fist trying to get its original investment back out.

  ☒ **A, B, and C are incorrect. A** is incorrect because intangible costs refer to those items that cannot be easily quantified, such as the cost of low morale. **B** is incorrect because tangible costs are referred to as costs that can be quantified, such as the cost to produce a product. **C** is incorrect because benefit costs refer to the cost to provide benefits for employees.

126. ☑ **A.** A cost benefit analysis of a new service line may require that new employees be hired and include elements such as the cost of projected new wages or benefits of revenue earned from the new service line. In addition, the analysis would ideally be compared to the existing service line. Such a comparison would provide information about whether a new service line would produce a significant return on investment in terms of wages invested.

  ☒ **B, C, and D are incorrect. B** is incorrect because comparing recruitment costs between the new and the old service line will not yield adequate information. It would leave open too many variables, such as different recruitment sources, skill levels, and quantity of employees for it to yield a true comparison and produce meaningful information. **C** is incorrect because the cost of turnover is irrelevant to learning the cost and benefit of a new service line. **D** is incorrect because the projected cost of disengagement is irrelevant to learning the cost and benefit of a new service line.

127. ☑ **B.** A cost benefit analysis can be used when identifying if a layoff is going to produce a return. Elements that can go into that analysis would be the cost of severance and any payout requirements such as vacation pay. The benefits would include any savings in wages and benefit costs.

  ☒ **A, C, and D are incorrect. A** is incorrect because a comparison of the costs of turnover to revenue of the new service lines provides confusing and irrelevant information. **C** is incorrect because tracking the cost of recruiting employees is not aligned with the need to lay off employees. The information calculated is a cost benefit analysis and would not be relevant. **D** is incorrect because the cost of developing new employees for a new service line is not aligned with understanding the cost and benefit of a layoff.

128. ☑ **B.** Consumers are increasingly aware of environmental and ethical factors when conducting business.

  ☒ **A, C, and D are incorrect** because while these choices may play a role, they are not the main reason why a company would want to implement a corporate social responsibility program.

129. ☑ **B.** This will allow for a greater cost advantage if efficiency and productivity are high.

☒ **A, C,** and **D** are incorrect because these choices are not strategies that enable a market cost-leader organizational objective.

130. ☑ **A.** This choice will provide the most value to the organization when utilizing a human capital competitive advantage strategy.

☒ **B, C,** and **D** are incorrect because these choices reflect a customer intimacy competitive advantage strategy.

Workforce Planning and Employment

This functional area includes coverage of the following responsibilities and knowledge objectives.

Workforce Planning and Employment—Responsibilities Objectives

- **01** Ensure that workforce planning and employment activities are compliant with applicable federal laws and regulations.

- **02** Identify workforce requirements to achieve the organization's short- and long-term goals and objectives (for example: corporate restructuring, workforce expansion or reduction).

- **03** Conduct job analyses to create and/or update job descriptions and identify job competencies.

- **04** Identify, review, document, and update essential job functions for positions.

- **05** Influence and establish criteria for hiring, retaining, and promoting based on job descriptions and required competencies.

- **06** Analyze labor market for trends that impact the ability to meet workforce requirements (for example: federal/state data reports).

- **07** Assess skill sets of internal workforce and external labor market to determine the availability of qualified candidates, utilizing third-party vendors or agencies as appropriate.

- **08** Identify internal and external recruitment sources (for example: employee referrals, diversity groups, social media) and implement selected recruitment methods.

- **09** Establish metrics for workforce planning (for example: recruitment and turnover statistics, costs).

- **10** Brand and market the organization to potential qualified applicants.

- **11** Develop and implement selection procedures (for example: applicant tracking, interviewing, reference and background checking).

- **12** Develop and extend employment offers and conduct negotiations as necessary.

- **13** Administer post-offer employment activities (for example: execute employment agreements, complete I-9/e-Verify process, coordinate relocations, and immigration).

- **14** Develop, implement, and evaluate orientation and onboarding processes for new hires, rehires, and transfers.

- **15** Develop, implement, and evaluate employee retention strategies and practices.
- **16** Develop, implement, and evaluate the succession planning process (SPHR only).
- **17** Develop and implement the organizational exit/off-boarding process for both voluntary and involuntary terminations, including planning for reductions in force (RIF).
- **18** Develop, implement, and evaluate an Affirmative Action Plan (AAP) as required.
- **19** Develop and implement a record retention process for handling documents and employee files (for example: pre-employment files, medical files, and benefits files).

Workforce Planning and Employment—Knowledge Objectives

- **11** Applicable federal laws and regulations related to workforce planning and employment activities (for example: Title VII, ADA, EEOC Uniform Guidelines on Employee Selection Procedures, Immigration Reform and Control Act)
- **12** Methods to assess past and future staffing effectiveness (for example: costs per hire, selection ratios, adverse impact)
- **13** Recruitment sources (for example: employee referral, social networking/ social media) for targeting passive, semi-active, and active candidates
- **14** Recruitment strategies
- **15** Staffing alternatives (for example: outsourcing, job sharing, phased retirement).
- **16** Planning techniques (for example: succession planning, forecasting)
- **17** Reliability and validity of selection tests/tools/methods
- **18** Use and interpretation of selection tests (for example: psychological/ personality, cognitive, motor/physical assessments, performance, assessment center)
- **19** Interviewing techniques (for example: behavioral, situational, panel)
- **20** Impact of compensation and benefits on recruitment and retention
- **21** International HR and implications of global workforce for workforce planning and employment (SPHR only)
- **22** Voluntary and involuntary terminations, downsizing, restructuring, and outplacement strategies and practices
- **23** Internal workforce assessment techniques (for example: skills testing, skills inventory, workforce demographic analysis)
- **24** Employment policies, practices, and procedures (for example: orientation, on-boarding, and retention)
- **25** Employer marketing and branding techniques
- **26** Negotiation skills and techniques

Workforce Planning and Employment is the functional area of the Human Resources Body of Knowledge that addresses how workforce strategies such as recruiting, retaining, developing, and managing employees are linked to desired business outcomes. It is the most quantifiable and measureable of all HR functions and when done well can really show the value of HR as a strategic partner in an organization.

Workforce Planning and Employment begins by identifying candidates that have the knowledge, skills, and abilities to perform a job effectively combined with the personal drive and ambition that complement the organization. The employee is then onboarded into the organization, is managed, and at some point exits the organization. Fair and equitable processes for off-boarding both voluntary and involuntary exits are critical to ensuring that employees who stay with the organization remain committed to the company's goals. This section tests your knowledge in all responsibilities and core knowledge areas of the exam covering items from applicable federal laws and regulations, strategic workforce planning, staffing programs, organization exit processes, and reporting.

Workforce Planning and Employment— Responsibilities Objectives

Objective 01   Ensure That Workforce Planning and Employment Activities are Compliant with Applicable Federal Laws and Regulations

1. An African-American female candidate was interviewed for an IT Manager position at a company. After the first interview, the recruiter told her that she was the top candidate but there was concern about her professional appearance. The recruiter advised her to cut her hair, which was styled in "locs," before meeting with the CTO. She refused to cut her hair citing religious reasons and was told the day after the second interview that she would not be hired because they were looking for someone with more current IT knowledge. The company hired a white male for the position two months later. The candidate filed a complaint with the EEOC. What steps should the HR Director take to eliminate future potential discriminatory hiring practices?

   A. The HR Director should train staff on Title VII of the Civil Rights Act of 1964 and as amended in 1972, 1978, and 1991.

   B. The HR Director should terminate the recruiter who made such an obvious error.

   C. The HR Director should just respond to any requests by the EEOC having confidence that this case has no merit given that the reason for the decision not to hire had nothing to do with race.

   D. The HR Director should contact the candidate and apologize for any misunderstanding on behalf of the recruiter.

2. A local government is recruiting police officers. The advertisement states that all applicants must be 21–50 years old and a high school graduate. Norman applies. He is 51 and a college graduate and was not called for an interview. Does Norman have a viable discrimination complaint?

   A. Yes, because according to the Age Discrimination in Employment Act, a company or municipality can't set an age requirement for candidates.

   B. No, because the 21–50-year-old requirement may be a bona fide occupational qualification (BFOQ) given the nature of the work.

   C. No, because the hiring of police officers is a specific exception of the Age Discrimination in Employment Act.

   D. Yes, because all employers must adhere to Title VII.

3. A company is recruiting for a coastal scientist. The position requires a Ph.D. in physics. There are no Hispanic candidates. As the HR Director, what would concern you the most about this scenario?

   A. Potential disparate treatment of Hispanic candidates.

   B. Discriminatory access to training for Hispanic candidates.

   C. Ineffective recruiting strategies as it relates to Hispanic candidates.

   D. Potential disparate impact on Hispanic candidates.

4. A manufacturing plant is hiring forklift drivers. Female employees are absent more due to injuries sustained while operating the forklift. As a result, the shift supervisors decide that all female applicants must score 4 out of 5 on the forklift driving test, and all male applicants can be considered for employment with a score of 3 out of 5. As the HR Director, what would be the *best* response to the shift supervisors once you are made aware of this intended change?

   A. This practice is allowable because it is a bona fide occupational qualification (BFOQ), which is supported by the absenteeism rate of female forklift drivers.

   B. This new practice results in disparate treatment of female workers and is prohibited by Title VII.

   C. This new practice will have disparate impact on female applicants and is prohibited by Title VII.

   D. This practice is allowable because women are not a protected class defined by Title VII of the Civil Rights Act of 1974.

Objective 02 Identify Workforce Requirements to Achieve the Organization's Short- and Long-Term Goals and Objectives

5. Over the past 10 years, a school district has experienced an increase in students requiring bilingual services, which translates into a need for additional bilingual staff and a reduction in general education staff. A significant number of teachers are assigned to general education classes who are bilingual and may be interested in completing the additional coursework needed to become certified in bilingual education. Which of the following workforce strategies would be most appropriate to implement?

   A. Workforce expansion

   B. Workforce reduction

   C. Reengineering

   D. Restructuring

6. A plastics manufacturer determines that if the business was relocated to Lagos, Nigeria, it would be able to develop its products for less than half its current manufacturing cost because the cost of labor is significantly less expensive in Lagos. Which of the following workforce planning strategies would most likely be implemented?

   A. Outsourcing and workforce reduction

   B. Corporate restructuring and workforce reduction

   C. Merger and acquisition

   D. Reengineering and workforce reduction

7. An owner of a small sports marketing firm has decided that the goal for the next fiscal year is to increase profits by 25 percent. This is an aggressive goal. As the HR Director, what workforce planning strategy do you think would best support this goal?

   A. Reduce the number of administrative staff resulting in a savings in labor costs.

   B. Expand the workforce by five sales people.

   C. Purchase a competing firm.

   D. Reduce general administrative costs by eliminating wasteful spending in the company.

8. A financial services company has multiple divisions. The insurance sales division continually shows 10 percent gains year after year. The securities division has not been faring as well. Often, the success of the insurance sales division is what keeps the rest of the company profitable. As the HR Director, what workforce planning strategy should you most likely be prepared to support?

   A. Workforce reduction

   B. Merger

   C. Corporate restructuring

   D. Divesture

Objective 03   Conduct Job Analyses to Create and/or Update Job Descriptions and Identify Job Competencies

9. Wendy was the Finance Director at a company. She was promoted to VP of Finance and her former position needs to be filled quickly. The responsibilities of the Finance Director have expanded some over the years due to the growth of the business. As the HR Manager, what would be your best next step?

   A. Include Wendy in interviews so she can explain the magnitude of the position to candidates.

   B. Promote from within so the position can be filled quickly.

   C. Begin recruiting for the position.

   D. Conduct a job analysis.

10. The Sales Manager is preparing to interview candidates for Account Representative positions at a pharmaceutical sales company. He wants to ask a mixture of situational and behavioral questions. What would be the best source from which to develop these types of questions?

    A. List of job competencies

    B. List of essential functions

    C. List of job specifications

    D. List of job duties

11. Job descriptions at a company have been out of date for almost a decade. Recent hires have complained that the job they currently have is not what they thought they were applying for initially. As the HR Director, you want to keep employees

informed of expectations but not disrupt daily operations. What strategic workforce planning process would you implement to achieve both goals?

A. Conduct meetings with employees and direct supervisors to inform them of the expectations

B. A company-wide project to bring all job descriptions up-to-date starting immediately

C. A job analysis conducted annually and job descriptions revised accordingly

D. Conduct training with staff weekly to bring them up-to-date about job expectations

12. A Recruitment Process Outsourcing (RPO) company decides to launch a new division. This division would help colleges and universities recruit and retain students. The new division needs to be fully staffed within six months. Which of the following would be the best first step in a comprehensive strategic selection process?

A. Determine who can staff the new division from internal applicants.

B. Determine hiring criteria.

C. Develop pre-employment skills testing for appropriate positions.

D. Identify the qualifications necessary to do the jobs in the new division.

Objective 04   Identify, Review, Document, and Update Essential Job Functions for Positions

13. What would be the first step for an HR Director when an employee requests an accommodation under the Americans with Disabilities Act?

A. Assess reasonableness of accommodations.

B. Choose job accommodations.

C. Identify job accommodations.

D. Identify the essential job functions and barriers to performance.

14. At a 50-person company, a 40-year-old employee sends her manager a text message stating she needs to undergo rehabilitation treatment for drug use. The manager passed along the information to the HR Department. How should the HR department proceed?

A. No action taken, as the ADA does not cover drug rehabilitation.

B. Let the employee go as drug dependency conflicts with their drug-free workplace policy.

C. Begin the interactive ADA process with the employee.

D. Communicate to the employee that the manager will reply with a response.

15. An employee is requesting an additional elevator to be installed at his place of work due to his use of a wheelchair for cerebral palsy. The employer is a small nonprofit that helps homeless families and has 23 employees. What would be an appropriate response from his employer regarding this reasonable accommodations request?

    A. Let the employee know that this additional elevator would cause an undue hardship due to limited resources and it could not be accommodated at this time.

    B. Say yes to the accommodation even though funds are not available to do so.

    C. Try to raise additional funds from other employees to accommodate the request.

    D. Try to raise funds from donors to accommodate the request.

16. Which of the following is the best action item for HR to take in determining if job functions are essential job functions under the Americans with Disabilities Act?

    A. Conduct a job analysis.

    B. Review job competencies.

    C. Review job specifications.

    D. Review job description.

Objective 05   Influence and Establish Criteria for Hiring, Retaining, and Promoting Based on Job Descriptions and Required Competencies

17. An employee is questioning why additional work is being requested of him and demands his job description be updated to accommodate the extra duties that are now being required. The employee has filed a complaint with HR and is considering leaving the company. What could HR have done differently to prevent this problem?

    A. Added FLSA status to the job description

    B. Added an appropriate disclaimer such as "other work as assigned" in job description

    C. Changed employee's title to accommodate the extra duties

    D. Offered the employee a promotion because the extra duties were not in the job description

18. A large engineering firm is looking for strategies to obtain workers with the knowledge, skills, and abilities needed for its 10-year plan. The firm realizes that there is a skill gap between the knowledge, skills, and abilities it is looking for

and actual knowledge, skills, and abilities of college graduates. What would be the most strategic approach to ensure that future applicants have the knowledge, skills, and abilities (KSA's) needed to meet the needs of the firm's 10-year plan?

A. Outsource products to different countries where math and science skills are higher.

B. Train workers once they enter the company.

C. Invest in extra-curricular high school activities in math and science to spark interest and enhance KSA's.

D. Invest additional training efforts to increase math and science KSA's once new hires are with the company for one year.

19. Which of the following is the best example of a managerial competency for a patient care clinic that the HR Department should use when completing a competency model?

A. Provide excellent customer care, 100 percent patient satisfaction.

B. Manage a staff of 10 employees.

C. Enhance profits.

D. Collect and summarize data.

20. Which of the following is the best example of a core competency related to quality for a business analyst that HR should use to complete a competency model?

A. Identifies gaps in processes that effect the project to excel

B. Conducts cost/benefit analyses

C. Takes notes at meetings and produces monthly outlines

D. Manages the staff

Objective 06   Analyze Labor Market for Trends That Impact the Ability to Meet Workforce Requirements

21. An HR manager must forecast HR needs for the upcoming five years as part of her strategic plan. What would be the best action to start to project future HR needs?

A. Survey managers to see if employees are likely to stay with the company.

B. Decide if equipment in the future will help current employees.

C. Survey employees to see if they plan on staying with the company.

D. Complete a trend analysis.

22. As the CEO of ServiceMaid, you read an article that the Department of Labor has forecasted a major shortage of low-skill workers in the labor market. As a service company that mainly employs low-skill workers, this is of concern to you. Which of the following would be your first course of action?

A. Begin recruiting for new staff members.

B. Conduct market analysis to forecast your future employee needs.

C. Provide additional training to current staff.

D. Provide current workers with additional money to stay longer.

Objective 07   Assess Skill Sets of the Internal Workforce and External Labor Market to Determine the Availability of Qualified Candidates, Utilizing Third-Party Vendors or Agencies as Appropriate

23. A business has been operating for 20 years. Filling key vacancies has been a relatively easy process throughout the history of the company, until recently. Over the last two years, time-to-fill hiring metrics have been getting longer in duration. Efforts made to expand recruitment outreach have not changed the time-to-fill metric, which is getting worse as the weeks go by. Diagnose the most likely underlying issue.

A. Low labor demand, high labor supply

B. High labor demand, low labor supply

C. Low labor demand, low labor supply

D. High labor demand, high labor supply

24. A company is finding it harder to compete in the market for skilled technology professionals. Upon review of its staffing condition, it was identified that the company needed to find a better way to define job roles, provide compensation, and match skills to company needs in ways that enable it to compete for talent. What strategy would you employ to help solve this issue?

A. Implement a market survey of compensation.

B. Implement an employee satisfaction survey.

C. Implement a skills inventory measurement.

D. Implement an employee development initiative.

25. A company is expanding and adding a critical service line. This new service line will enable the company to improve its market share. The service line will be in need of a specific skill set in order to operate properly. You have identified the

need to assess the internal skill set of the organization. What steps would you take to complete an internal skills assessment?

A. Define critical skills needed, determine existing skill assets, address the skills gap, monitor skill levels.

B. Define open positions, create or update job descriptions, recruit top talent, evaluate ongoing performance.

C. Define key positions, create or update job descriptions, recruit top talent, evaluate ongoing performance.

D. Define critical skills needed, develop internal staff, evaluate performance, monitor performance.

26. A high-technology company relies on science, technology, engineering, and mathematic (STEM) skills in order to operate effectively and competitively. You've noted in workforce analysis reports that retirements are on the rise. Existing staff that are not close to retirement seem to lack these skills. What is the best way to assess the external job pool for STEM skills?

A. Conduct a survey of existing staff meeting the requirements of targeted classification to gather opinions.

B. Conduct a survey of management and collect their opinion on the status of the external job market.

C. Analyze all turnover data of former staff meeting the requirements of the targeted classification.

D. Analyze current and projected number of graduates from schools meeting the requirements of the targeted classification.

Objective 08   Identify Internal and External Recruitment Sources and Implement Selected Recruitment Methods

27. A company is a federal contractor. It maintains and monitors an Affirmative Action Plan (AAP). Upon analysis of the affirmative action plan, it is discovered that minorities are underrepresented in technical job classifications. What key step would you take to influence this issue?

A. Implement a diversity outreach plan.

B. Implement a succession plan.

C. Implement a management buy-in plan.

D. Implement a development plan.

28. A key business objective is to improve the organization's competitiveness by expanding service lines. The timeline to expanding these new service lines is six months. To get ahead of the curve, the tactical goals are to reduce turnover of existing staff and time to hire for newly created positions. What is the best action to take to achieve these objectives?

A. Hire outside contractors to fill positions.

B. Implement an employee referral program.

C. Launch an external recruitment campaign.

D. Improve efficiency of on-boarding processes.

29. A company has found it increasingly difficult to find skilled individuals in a particular job classification. It appears the only way to find people interested in working for the company is to develop relationships with them beforehand. The budget is tightening up this fiscal year. What is one of the most effective strategies to implement to recruit talent?

A. Network with prospective candidates at popular career fairs.

B. Network with prospective candidates at industry conferences.

C. Network with prospective candidates through social media.

D. Network with prospective candidates in open house job fairs.

30. A warehousing and distribution company is adding six warehouses for an increase in product storage needs. It is uncertain that this increase in product will stay in place for any duration of time. The company needs to increase forklift drivers to meet the immediate increase in storage needs. However, if the storage need reduces over time then these forklift drivers will not be needed. What would be the best recruitment strategy?

A. Wait until the organization obtains more details.

B. Don't hire new forklift drivers and use overtime.

C. Inform forklift drivers of layoff possibilities.

D. Recruit temporary agency forklift drivers.

Objective 09   Establish Metrics for Workforce Planning

31. A call center depends on the level of sales completed per phone call for its success. An employee's ability to establish credibility and achieve customer satisfaction is critical for optimal performance. The company wants to establish

a development program for those who may not be performing to expectations. What metric would you use to measure workforce effectiveness under these circumstances?

A. Customers per employee

B. Expenses per employee

C. Revenue per employee

D. Labor cost per employee

32. A company operates in a very competitive market. In order to be successful, they need to be able to attract top talent. Part of the objective is to determine if they are competitive with benefits, compensation, and a reputation as a great place to work. What metric would you use to measure how effective the company is in hiring talent?

A. Ratios of offers made to acceptances

B. Involuntary resignation turnover

C. Hires as a percentage of total employees

D. Voluntary employee turnover within 90 days

33. A recruitment department wants to assess all of its hiring sources. The objective is to find out which hiring sources are more cost effective in finding talent they need. Which metric would you use to measure hiring sources?

A. Cost per hire

B. Time to fill jobs

C. Time to start jobs

D. Quality per hire

34. A public sector agency is struggling to meet fiscal responsibilities. The concern is that public retirement funds are outpacing revenues being generated. You are being asked to analyze and present your findings to the leadership team. Which metric would be one of the best to measure?

A. Benefit costs as a percentage of revenue

B. Benefit costs as a percentage of expense

C. Retiree benefit cost as a percentage of expense

D. Compensation as a percentage of expense

Objective 10 Brand and Market the Organization to Potential Qualified Applicants

35. A national youth agency went through a 10-year period of litigation 20 years ago. Several employees during that time raised allegations of sexual harassment and racial discrimination. Since that time, the environment has dramatically improved, salaries increased, promotional opportunities expanded, and the individuals who perpetuated the negative culture have been removed. However, the agency continues to struggle with attracting top female and minority talent. As an HR Director, what would be one of your considerations in determining an effective rebranding strategy?

    A. Where is the agency recruiting?

    B. How do current employees view the promotional opportunities for women and minorities?

    C. Is the agency advertising job openings on the websites of Historically Black Colleges and Universities (HBCUs)?

    D. Are the pre-employment tests used causing a disparate impact on women and minorities?

36. What is the most important reason to manage the employer brand?

    A. Attract and retain quality employees even during times of economic downturn.

    B. To support the existence of robust compensation packages for key positions.

    C. Set the stage for promotional opportunities for internal candidates.

    D. Improve company image on social networking sites.

Objective 11 Develop and Implement Selection Procedures

37. A new career college campus will be in need of admissions representatives. The campus President knows a few talented salespeople from a past employer and wants to interview them ASAP. HR will post the position in one week and standard procedure for interested candidates is to complete an online application. As the HR Director, what would you suggest the Campus President do next?

    A. Set up interviews with the salespeople ASAP so she doesn't lose good candidates.

    B. Contact the salespeople and tell them to submit resumes directly.

C. Contact the salespeople and tell them to complete online applications when the position posts.

D. Set up phone screens with the salespeople ASAP so she doesn't lose good candidates.

38. A high volume customer service call center is recruiting for customer service representatives. The turnover rate is 65 percent. Ninety percent of the former employees who returned exit interviews stated that the reason for leaving was that the actual job was not like what they prepared for in training, especially the volume of calls and noise level of the customer service floor. What would you suggest be incorporated into the interviewing process going forward?

A. Aptitude test

B. Assessment center

C. Realistic job preview

D. Cognitive ability test

39. At the conclusion of interviews for a new financial analyst, a member of the interview team rates one of the candidates poorly but could not articulate why. The other three members of the interview team have a very different view of the same candidate. Which of the following best describes the kind of interviewer bias displayed in this case?

A. Horn effect

B. Negative emphasis

C. First impression

D. Stereotyping

40. A financial services firm hires a trader who spent the last four years in state prison for committing a battery against a coworker. The financial services firm is in Wyoming, but the trader did his jail time in state prison in Arizona. In an effort to reduce costs, HR did a background check but only for the state of Wyoming. How would you safeguard the company from any legal exposure in the future?

A. This is an example of negligent hiring. The company should conduct complete background and reference checks including a check of both state and FBI records going forward.

B. The company is in violation of the Fair Credit Reporting Act and should get consent before performing a background check.

C. The company is guilty of negligent hiring and may be in violation of the Privacy Act of 1974.

D. This is an example of negligent hiring, so HR should place the employee on leave for not disclosing this during the interview process.

41. A company hires a youth counselor. During the course of his employment, several teenage girls have reported that he looks at them in a way that makes them uncomfortable. Following these complaints, the company conducts an investigation, which uncovers that he had been suspended without pay by two prior employers because of similar allegations. Which of the following best practices performed during the selection process may have brought to light this youth counselor's prior history?

    A. Conduct in-depth reference checks.

    B. Conduct a criminal history check.

    C. Conduct a personality test.

    D. Conduct an integrity test.

42. The pre-employment tests for Administrative Assistants measure typing speed and accuracy. The current company need for administrative support is in the area of competency with computer software programs such as Microsoft Office and payroll/finance software. The new Supervisor decides to develop a test and administer it after each interview. As the HR Director, what would concern you the most about this scenario?

    A. The tests should only be given after an offer of employment is made.

    B. The tests have not been proven to be reliable and valid predictors of job success.

    C. The tests were administered without prior approval from HR.

    D. The physical space that the test was administered in wasn't adequate.

Objective 12 Develop and Extend Employment Offers and Conduct Negotiations as Necessary

43. When should an HR professional offer employment to a candidate during the hiring process?

    A. After HR has run the background check

    B. One week following the decision to hire the candidate

    C. As soon as possible following the decision to hire a candidate

    D. After HR has run the drug test

44. What should an HR Manager do in regards to offer-letter timing?

    A. Set a reasonable timeline for acceptance.

    B. Allow the employee as much time as he/she needs to make a decision.

    C. Set a 24-hour deadline for the candidate to accept.

    D. For positions that require relocation, they must accept within 48 hours.

45. Nick, the HR Manager at a large Atlanta law firm, is looking to hire 15 attorneys in the next year. What should Nick include in the offer letter for contract terms?

    A. Tenure guidelines

    B. Requirements for community service

    C. Rights to patents and copyright during employment

    D. Restrictions to perform services exclusively for the employer

46. What would HR want to include in an offer letter when specifically referring to telecommuters?

    A. Publishing requirements

    B. A limit on post-employment competition by the greatest extent of the law

    C. Maintaining confidential company information

    D. Limits on conflicts of interest

Objective 13 Administer Post-Offer Employment Activities

47. A mechanical engineering company with federal contracts at approximately $150,000 is required to complete which process on all newly hired employees?

    A. The PERM (Program Electronic Review Management) process

    B. The E-Verify process

    C. The WARN (Worker Adjustment and Retrain Notification) requirements

    D. The Congressional Accountability Act requirements

48. How long is the HR department required to keep the I-9 (Employee Eligibility Verification) forms for all employees?

    A. Three years after date of hire or one year after termination, whichever is later

    B. One year after hire or three years after termination

    C. Employee's tenure only

    D. Two years

49. When should the HR Department complete the Form I-9, section 1 with the employee during the hiring process?

    A. As part of the resume submission process

    B. Within the first three days of employment

    C. In conjunction with the application process

    D. Due on first day of employment

50. A tech company is moving an employee and spouse from Tampa to Denver because of new market opportunities on the West Coast. What would be HR's primary goal when relocating an employee from Tampa to Denver?

A. Provide cost of living analysis to employee.

B. Give employee resources for their spouse to find a job in Denver.

C. Provide the best service to the employee at the most reasonable cost to the company.

D. Find the employee an apartment.

Objective 14 Develop, Implement, and Evaluate Orientation and Onboarding Processes for New Hires, Rehires, and Transfers

51. Steve has expanded the Funnel Cakes & More Company to 45 locations nationwide. He wants new employees to embody the humble beginnings of the company as opposed to viewing them as just another big corporation. To achieve this goal, which of the following would most likely be included during a new hire orientation session?

A. Review of the mission and vision statements

B. Review of policies and procedures

C. Review of job descriptions

D. Review of the employee handbook

52. After completion of the new hire orientation, there have been anecdotal reports of employees unable to punch in and not having access to the e-mail system. HR would like to get continual comprehensive reports of any issues a new hire experiences in an effort to help identify process improvements. Which of the following strategies would be most appropriate to implement to assist HR with determining the effectiveness of onboarding activities?

A. E-mail an evaluation of the IT department to new hires within 30 days of employment.

B. Set up a time to meet with each new employee within 30 days of employment.

C. E-mail a survey to new hires within 30 days of employment.

D. E-mail an evaluation of the HR department to new hires within 30 days of employment.

53. Teachers are routinely transferred to new buildings at a public school district. Some teachers have reported not feeling completely a part of the new building's culture.

Which strategy would be the most effective in helping to bridge the gap for transferring teachers?

A. Assign a peer mentor to transferring teachers, establish goals for the mentor and employee, and monitor progress.

B. Ensure that the principal of the new building introduces staff and asks coworkers to be welcoming of transferring teachers.

C. Assign a department head to answer any questions the transferring teacher may have throughout the year.

D. E-mail all building staff when a transferring teacher is coming onboard and ask for their support in helping that person feel welcome.

54. New hire orientation surveys reveal that customer service representatives at a wireless communications company leave training excited about their new jobs and the company as a whole. After three months of employment, confidential surveys reveal that the same representatives feel unequipped to do their jobs effectively and begin to search for new employment. As the HR Director, what strategy would you implement to reduce the significant change in employee engagement?

A. Establish follow-up training sessions to refresh skills learned during new hire orientation.

B. Form a task force of new and seasoned employees with the goal of implementing periodic team-building activities to keep new hires engaged.

C. Establish a career-path program with the goal of providing new hires with opportunities for advancement to keep them engaged.

D. Collaborate with department supervisors to develop, implement, and enforce a post new-hire orientation on-boarding plan.

Objective 15 Develop, Implement, and Evaluate Employee Retention Strategies and Practices

55. A review of the last four quarters shows higher than normal turnover at a grocery store. Exit interviews reveal that most people who decide to leave the organization cite dissatisfaction with management. Which of the following strategies would be most appropriate to implement?

A. Invest in training for store management focused on selecting more committed employees.

B. Implement longevity bonuses for store employees.

C. Invest in training for store management focused on improving leadership and motivational skills.

D. Only hire people who express a willingness to have a long-term career with the company.

56. A company has experienced a reduction in employee morale and an increase in turnover. Over the course of the year, employees have been reassigned to new business units or locations as a result of a merger with a smaller company. Which of the following retention strategies would best support the company's goal of bringing turnover back to pre-merger levels?

A. Provide additional training opportunities for the employees who have been reassigned.

B. Provide formal and informal socialization activities for employees who are in new business units or new locations.

C. Link rewards to longevity (for example, additional vacation days).

D. Provide advancement opportunities for the employees who have been reassigned.

57. A school district recruits new teachers exclusively from six local universities. A recent review of the teacher preparation programs at the universities shows that a high number of graduates of the programs at two of the universities leave the teaching profession only two years after graduation while the other four show an average of 20 years in the profession. What retention strategy would best address the high teacher turnover for the school district?

A. The school district should provide a better mentoring program for new teachers so they feel supported in their first two years.

B. The school district should offer a career path to teachers that gives them opportunities to advance to management positions.

C. The school district should provide formal and informal socialization activities to help new teachers integrate into the culture.

D. The school district should focus recruitment and selection activities at universities where the teacher preparation program better prepares teachers for the early challenges of the profession.

58. HR is asked to review overall turnover throughout a company. The current retention strategy was implemented four years ago and turnover is still high. As the HR Director, what would you recommend going forward to ensure the company reaches its retention goals?

A. Periodic review and adjustments to the retention strategy

B. More team-building activities to keep employees engaged

C. An overhaul of the total rewards program to remain competitive

D. A review of the recruitment and selection process

59. A recent report identified that the number of college graduates is expected to continue to decrease over the next five years while the number of retirees will increase during the same timeframe. For a local manufacturing company this means that over the next five years they will have four openings for chemists due to retirements. As the HR Manager, how would you increase the company's ability to fill these key positions?

    A. Identify the KSAs necessary to be successful as a chemist and identify current employees who could be groomed for the positions.

    B. Develop a recruiting strategy focused on local colleges with strong science programs.

    C. Identify skill gaps and training needs among current employees.

    D. Boost employee morale in an effort to retain the other chemists.

60. Senior management implemented a succession plan five years ago. It was a lengthy and cumbersome process that the new CEO isn't convinced was worth the effort. As the HR Director, how would you convince the CEO that a formal succession planning process is necessary to ensure smooth transitions for key positions?

    A. Provide the CEO with a report on the reasons for a reduction in turnover.

    B. Provide the CEO with a summary of employee retention results.

    C. Provide the CEO with the ROI in the areas of cost per hire and quality of hire of the participants in the program.

    D. Provide the CEO with a comparison of the number of open positions currently to the number of openings five years ago.

61. Far too often, applicants for technology positions do not have the right combination of skills for the complex mid-career level positions at a company. Senior management has decided that they would like HR to coordinate the development of a succession plan. Which of the following would be your next step in implementing a strategic succession plan process?

    A. Assess the current situation.

    B. Articulate a desired outcome.

    C. Formulate the strategy.

    D. Implement the strategy.

Objective 17   Develop and Implement the Organizational Exit/Off-Boarding Process for Both Voluntary and Involuntary Terminations, Including Planning for Reductions in Force (RIF)

62. A company decides to close four of its North American locations in three months. The layoff affects 2,500 full-time employees, 200 of which are on leaves of absence. Is the organization subject to the provisions of the Worker Adjustment and Retraining Notification (WARN) Act?

    A. Yes, because the WARN Act requires that organizations provide 60 days notice to employees or their union representatives if the organization has 100 or more employees.

    B. Yes, because the WARN Act requires that organizations provide 30 days notice to employees or their union representatives if the organization has 100 or more full-time employees.

    C. No, because the WARN Act is only applicable to companies that operate large manufacturing plants.

    D. No, because the WARN Act only applies in this case if the employer counts the 200 employees who are on leave in its total employee count.

63. A corporation determines that 10 percent of its workforce in specific business units has to be laid off in order for the company to remain profitable. As the HR Director, you are asked to craft the criteria by which employees will be selected for layoff. What criterion would most likely be included?

    A. Performance as determined by performance appraisals of employees in the targeted business units

    B. The cost of a reasonable severance package

    C. The cost of outplacement services and unemployment compensation

    D. The company cost of COBRA in order to continue to provide health benefits for affected employees

64. When an employee resigns from a company, which of the following essential part of the exit process will help the organization reduce future turnover?

    A. Distribution of HIPAA and COBRA notices

    B. Final payment of wages

    C. Exit interview

    D. Promotion of qualified employees to the vacated position

65. Half of a manager's department is slated to be laid off. As the HR Manager, how would you advise the manager to handle the layoff meeting?

A. Because so many people are affected, a group meeting with time for questions would be most efficient.

B. Hold a group meeting with the affected employees. Be sure to be completely clear regarding the conditions of the layoff. Show compassion.

C. Hold individual meetings. Provide the employee with a clear message regarding the conditions of the layoff. Show compassion. Meet with the remaining employees to offer support.

D. Hold individual meetings with affected employees. Give them a few weeks to properly say good-bye to their coworkers.

Objective 18 Develop, Implement, and Evaluate an Affirmative Action Plan (AAP) as Required

66. A private company wants to secure a $200,000 federal contract and needs to establish an Affirmative Action Plan (AAP). Which of the following will most likely be included as essential parts of that plan?

A. Action-oriented goals and a process for evaluating the plan's effectiveness

B. Goals for increasing the number of women hired

C. Placement goals for African-American men

D. The name and title of the HR Director and CEO

67. Anderson Construction, a government contractor with 100 employees, has a written Affirmative Action Plan (AAP) in place. However, a recent review of workforce demographics shows an underutilization of women. What should be included in the AAP that would address this discovery?

A. The AAP should include the number of women the contractor commits to hiring by a specified date.

B. The AAP should specify procedures the contractor will follow to improve its utilization rates among women.

C. The AAP should include the number of minorities the contractor commits to hiring by a specified date.

D. The AAP should specify procedures the contractor will follow to reach a set number of women hired.

68. During a compliance review, the officer from the Office of Federal Contract Compliance (OFCCP) determines that a federal subcontractor is in serious non-compliance with Executive Order 11246. What action would the OFCCP most likely take to remedy this situation?

A. Issue a conciliation agreement with the subcontractor.

B. Recommend a formal hearing with a judge.

C. Impose sanctions such as declaring contractor ineligible for future government contracts.

D. Recommend administrative enforcement through the Office of the Solicitor General.

69. Five years ago, a company was awarded a government contract that requires an Affirmative Action Plan (AAP). Since that time, they have exceeded their plan's established goals for women professionals. What is a key strategic advantage of continuing their outreach efforts even though their established goals have been met and exceeded?

A. Their outreach efforts should be discontinued because with a more diverse workforce, it is inevitable that minority managers will gravitate toward minority candidates, thus keeping an acceptable balance of minorities at the company

B. AAP programs are costly to establish and maintain. The best decision would be to discontinue the program because the program goals have been exceeded.

C. If allegations of discriminatory hiring practices are made in the future, then the fact that there is an AAP in place will help the company prove that the allegations have no merit.

D. A diverse workforce fosters creativity and innovation, which gives the company a competitive edge.

Objective 19 Develop and Implement a Record Retention Process for Handling Documents and Employee Files

70. Employment offers at a private social services organization are made contingent upon employment/education verification and the results of fingerprint-based criminal background checks after obtaining written permission from the applicant. HR Specialists have historically placed the results of these background checks in the main personnel files viewable by any supervisor who makes a request to review the file. As the new HR Director, how would you redesign the records management policy?

A. No change because the employment offer was already made so the background check didn't affect the selection process.

B. No change because this is perfectly legal and compliant with personnel records retention laws.

C. Remove the background check results each time a supervisor requests a file review.

D. Store criminal background check results in a separate file.

71. An employee alleges that he was passed over for a promotion because he was convicted of assaulting a police officer during a civil rights protest 40 years ago. Which of the following types of information would best assist the Equal Employment Opportunity Commission (EEOC) in determining the reason why the employee was not awarded the position?

A. Performance evaluations of the selected employee and the accuser

B. Employment tests and job applications for all candidates

C. Criminal background check results of the selected employee and the accuser

D. Training attended by all employees

72. Which of the following require a five-year record retention period?

A. OSHA forms 300, 301, and 300A

B. Performance evaluations

C. I-9 Forms

D. Job descriptions

73. Consolidated Omnibus Budget Reconciliation Act (COBRA), which provides the continuation of health coverage for a limited time after the loss of a job, is an amendment to which of the following?

A. Health Insurance Portability and Accountability Act

B. Uniformed Services Employment and Reemployment Rights Act (USERRA)

C. Patient Protection and Affordable Care Act (PPACA)

D. Employee Retirement Income Security Act (ERISA)

Workforce Planning and Employment— Knowledge Objectives

Objective 11   Applicable Federal Laws and Regulations Related to Workforce Planning and Employment Activities

74. Which of the following addresses religion, sex, or national origin as a bona fide occupational qualification (BFOQ) exception in making employment decisions?

A. Age Discrimination in Employment Act of 1967 (ADEA)

B. Executive Order 11246

C. Americans with Disabilities Act of 1990

D. Rehabilitation Act of 1973

Objective 12   Methods to Assess Past and Future Staffing Effectiveness

75. Which group is experiencing adverse impact?

Group	Applicants	Hired
Native American	22	2
Asian	30	8
Caucasian	120	35
African-American	48	5

   A. Native Americans and Asians

   B. Caucasians and Native Americans

   C. African-Americans and Asians

   D. Native Americans and African-Americans

76. The recruiting manager at a hospital is doing an analysis on "in demand" positions. The goal is to review historical data in an effort to determine the cost per hire for registered nurses, occupational therapists, and physical therapists, and then shift the advertising dollars away from the easier to fill positions to support the recruiting efforts for these select positions. Which of the following will have the *most* impact on the recruiting manager's decision?

   A. Turnover rate

   B. Replacement cost

   C. Hiring manager's salary

   D. Accession rate

Objective 13   Recruitment Sources for Targeting Passive, Semi-Active, and Active Candidates

77. Which of the following is the best online recruiting source for finding passive candidates?

   A. Company website

   B. Personal networks used to mine for candidates (i.e., LinkedIn)

   C. Job fairs

   D. Employment agencies

78. The three top performing veterinarians hired at an American medical research company are from the same Ugandan university. However, HR has not recruited from that university in over a decade. There are currently two veterinarian openings.

What should be the *first* consideration of the HR Director when determining when, how, and where to recruit for these two positions?

A. Promoting the employee referral program

B. Arranging an on-campus job fair at the university

C. Sourcing methods used in the past to attract the top three performers

D. Determine if anyone from the university has applied for the openings

Objective 14   Recruitment Strategies

79. Which of the following is an exclusive internal recruiting method?

A. Job board

B. Job bidding

C. Job fair

D. Posting on company website

80. For the past 10 years, a school district has seen a growing number of students in need of state-mandated bilingual education because English is not the first language spoken in the child's home. This has placed increased attention on the talent acquisition process. It is October and all bilingual teacher positions for the current school year are filled. It is anticipated that next year there will be 30 percent more openings due to retirements, certification issues, and dismissals for performance. In developing a recruitment strategy, which of the following will have the *most* impact on whether or not the best candidates are aware of the teaching opportunities?

A. When the recruiting cycle begins

B. The total rewards package

C. The employer brand

D. Existing pipeline

Objective 15   Staffing Alternatives

81. The staffing manager is looking to hire an experienced CFO. He is deciding whether he should use the company's internal hiring process or outsource the hire to an executive search firm. What is the biggest drawback to using an executive search firm?

A. Search firms charge high fees to find qualified candidates.

B. Search firms are not able to find good matches with the managers.

C. Search firms add additional time to the hiring process.

D. Search firms typically find too many candidates making it harder to pick from.

82. What is contingency fee–based recruiting?

    A. A recruitment service funded by the federal government

    B. A temporary staff agency

    C. A type of executive search firm that charges a fee but only after the candidate is found

    D. A type of executive search firm where a fee is charged whether or not the candidate is found

Objective 16   Planning Techniques

83. What would be the best planning technique HR should use to forecast what skills are available within the internal labor pool?

    A. Performance reviews

    B. Interviews

    C. Assessment centers

    D. Job Descriptions

Objective 17   Reliability and Validity of Selection Tests/ Tools/Methods

84. An HR professional is tasked with designing valid employee selection procedures for her organization. She is hiring a secretary for the Executive Director. What would be an example of a content-valid testing item for this secretarial position?

    A. IQ of 180

    B. A typing test

    C. Mechanical comprehension

    D. Personality tests

85. What is the best definition of reliability as it relates to selection testing and tools?

    A. The ability of an instrument to measure the same results consistently

    B. The ability of an instrument to measure validity

    C. The ability of an instrument to measure time

    D. The ability of an instrument to measure the accuracy of a test

Objective 18   Use and Interpretation of Selection Tests

86. A company has decided to implement integrity tests for all new hires. What should HR be aware of as the main criticism from applicants on integrity tests?

A. Personal time activities are not related to job performance.

B. Not relevant to hiring.

C. Not directly related to the position in which they are applying.

D. Invasion of privacy.

87. Why would the HR department want to conduct a psychomotor test on a group of applicants applying for firefighter positions?

A. To test the physical dexterity to operate the equipment

B. To test personality to see if temperament is a match

C. To test mathematical skills needed for the position

D. To test general ability to learn

88. When conducting psychomotor testing for pre-employment, what is the main concern that HR should focus on when preparing and implementing these tests?

A. Ensure the test is validated on the essential job functions.

B. Ensure the test reveals possible substance abuse.

C. Ensure that the test reveals abnormal behavior.

D. Ensure the test measures mental processes.

89. Which of the following would be the most expensive form of employment testing?

A. Integrity tests

B. Assessment centers

C. Cognitive ability tests

D. Aptitude tests

Objective 19 Interviewing Techniques

90. What is the disadvantage of conducting a panel interview?

A. Scheduling the interview.

B. The interview will take too long.

C. Too many opinions on who to hire.

D. Can be threatening to the candidate.

91. What steps should HR take to ensure the candidate's level of comfort with a panel interview?

A. Have hiring manager sit at the head of the table.

B. Have CEO sit at the head of the table.

C. Arrange chairs in a circle or a curved pattern.

D. Arrange chairs to face all candidates.

Objective 20 Impact of Compensation and Benefits on Recruitment and Retention

92. What is the main risk that a company runs if an employee feels their contributions and talent are not being rewarded fairly?

    A. Employees will not share their ideas openly and honestly.

    B. Employees will start showing up late for work.

    C. Employees will require additional training therefore adding time and money to the organization.

    D. Employees will suffer from morale and motivation problems.

93. Besides the monetary investment made in an employee, what is the greatest drawback of employee turnover?

    A. Loss of knowledge, skills, and abilities.

    B. New employees will need to be hired, causing a burden to the HR department.

    C. Loss of that employee will impact the morale of the whole team.

    D. New employees will need more intense supervision, therefore causing additional time and resources for the organization.

SPHR Objective 21 International HR and Implications of Global Workforce for Workforce Planning and Employment (SPHR only)

94. What is the impact of an ethnocentric approach on staffing to an international business?

    A. Talent acquisition policies are unique to each country.

    B. Talent and skills transfer essentially one way.

    C. Limited cross-border movement of talent and skills.

    D. Headquarters-country personnel have little impact.

Objective 22 Voluntary and Involuntary Terminations, Downsizing, Restructuring, and Outplacement Strategies and Practices

95. A contracted service supplied by companies that specialize in helping employees prepare for job searching after a layoff or job loss is defined as which of the following?

    A. Search firm

    B. Outplacement firm

    C. Brokerage firm

    D. Outsourcing firm

96. In response to the recession, a company needs to eliminate 100 jobs over the course of six months in order to remain financially viable. The company values employee morale and engagement. While the leaders recognize an involuntary downsizing may be necessary, they would like to avoid that action if possible. What is the best action to support the company's objective of reducing jobs but maintaining morale?

   A. Offer resume building and interviewing skills training to those that may be affected by a downsizing (reduction in force).

   B. Develop leadership training sessions that teach how to support a surviving workforce after a downsizing.

   C. Offer support through an Employee Assistance Program for those remaining in the workplace after a downsizing.

   D. Offer a voluntary early retirement option and evaluate open positions and close non-critical open positions (attrition).

Objective 23 Internal Workforce Assessment Techniques

97. A new competitor has moved into your company's market. The competitor has an advertising campaign that reaches through all media (television, radio, and social media). There are already signs of diminishing sales for your company. All senior leaders are asked to provide information on addressing this new competition. What information will you present in the upcoming meeting that will contribute the most to the company's strategic objectives?

   A. A headcount report and staffing plan that supports optimal customer service operating hours

   B. A human capital assessment of workforce qualities that provide a competitive advantage

   C. A turnover report indicating how many employees have left the company to go work for the competitor

   D. A report that provides information of how competitive wages and benefits compare to market

98. A skills inventory that includes information such as qualifications, abilities, capacities, and career goals of employees would provide what kind of advantage for a company?

   A. It provides internal candidates eligible for promotions.

   B. It provides an opportunity to set a new leadership direction.

   C. It requires little time to collect, measure, and report.

   D. It doesn't require much update or maintenance of skills.

Objective 24 Employment Policies, Practices, and Procedures

99. A business has had vacancies for hard-to-fill positions for quite a while. As a result, once a skilled candidate is found and hired, a key objective is to shorten their learning curve and move them to a productive state quickly. What key activity would you invest time in to achieve this objective?

    A. Application process

    B. Skills inventory

    C. Employee orientation

    D. Employee development

100. A tuition reimbursement program that requires an employee to agree to stay with the company for two years is an example of what type of employment practice objective?

    A. Retention

    B. Onboarding

    C. Orientation

    D. Recruitment

Objective 25 Employer Marketing and Branding Techniques

101. A company recognizes that each employee has the potential to be an ambassador of company products and services. Each employee connects with numerous people daily in the community as they run errands, connect with neighbors, and communicate with family members. What would be effective in conveying the company's message on its products and services to the surrounding community?

    A. Send periodic and timely e-mails to employees about new product developments.

    B. Provide employees an elevator speech in answering the question "What do you do?"

    C. Develop and conduct mandatory customer service and sales training for all employees.

    D. Invite guest speakers from marketing to attend all monthly staff department meetings.

102. A statement that provides the overall value of working for a company in exchange for the employee's skills, qualifications, and time is an example of what type of branding strategy?

    A. Product statement proposition

    B. Marketing value proposition

    C. Customer value proposition

    D. Employer value proposition

Objective 26   Negotiation Skills and Techniques

103. What best describes the negotiation/ad hoc approach to international compensation?

    A. The employer pays a lump sum amount instead of allowances.

    B. The employer and each assignee negotiate a mutually agreeable package.

    C. Potential assignees are offered several options.

    D. Pay exactly what local nationals in equivalent positions are paid.

104. Valerie, the HR Director for a U.S.-based international company, is hiring for positions in London. She has decided to use the negotiation/ad hoc process to negotiate an international compensation package. What is the biggest advantage to using the negotiation/ad hoc process?

    A. Simple and convenient but tends to be relatively costly

    B. Easy to administer and communicate

    C. Promotes perception of equity among assignees

    D. Offers tax advantages to assignees

1. A	27. A	53. A	79. B
2. C	28. B	54. D	80. A
3. D	29. C	55. C	81. A
4. B	30. D	56. B	82. C
5. C	31. C	57. D	83. C
6. A	32. A	58. A	84. B
7. B	33. A	59. A	85. A
8. D	34. C	60. C	86. D
9. D	35. B	61. B	87. A
10. A	36. A	62. A	88. A
11. C	37. C	63. A	89. B
12. D	38. C	64. C	90. D
13. D	39. D	65. C	91. C
14. C	40. A	66. A	92. D
15. A	41. A	67. B	93. A
16. A	42. B	68. A	94. A
17. B	43. C	69. D	95. B
18. C	44. A	70. D	96. D
19. A	45. D	71. B	97. B
20. B	46. C	72. A	98. A
21. D	47. B	73. D	99. C
22. B	48. A	74. A	100. A
23. B	49. D	75. D	101. B
24. C	50. C	76. C	102. D
25. A	51. A	77. B	103. B
26. D	52. C	78. C	104. A

1. ☑ **A.** It is clear that, at a minimum, training and clarification is needed by all of the individuals involved in the hiring process. Title VII of the Civil Rights Act of 1964, and as amended in 1972, 1978, and 1991, prohibits discriminatory recruiting, selection, and hiring on the basis of race whereby race is a protected class. "Locs" are a culturally specific hairstyle most naturally worn by people of African descent. To require that "locs" be cut as a prerequisite to obtaining employment may be deemed discriminatory.

☒ **B, C,** and **D** are incorrect. **B** is incorrect because terminating the recruiter doesn't solve a possible systemic problem. The hiring manager (CTO) may also have a similar misunderstanding as to what is an appropriate action during the selection process. Further, there is no evidence to support that the recruiter really did say these things. **C** is incorrect because it would be irresponsible on the HR Director's part not to take the allegation seriously. He or she is not in a position to draw conclusions on the merits of the case. That is the responsibility of the EEOC. A forward thinking HR Director should recognize this unfortunate incident as an opportunity to further educate staff and streamline processes. **D** is incorrect because neither the HR Director nor anyone involved in preparing responses to the complaint should have direct contact with the candidate. All contact should be directly to the EEOC or through the company's attorneys to the EEOC. Direct contact with the candidate presents litigation risks for the company.

2. ☑ **C.** The Age Discrimination in Employment Act specifies certain exceptions. The hiring of firefighters and police officers is an exception.

☒ **A, B,** and **D** are incorrect because a municipality can set an age requirement when hiring firefighters and police officers; the age requirement is not a BFOQ but it is a separate exception and all employers do not have to adhere to Title VII if their situation is covered by one of the exceptions.

3. ☑ **D.** The HR Director should be most concerned with disparate impact. Disparate impact is an unlawful practice where a practice seems fair on its face but has an adverse impact on a protected group. Adverse impact is illegal unless justified by job-related business necessity. In this case, there may be a very valid reason why the position requires a Ph.D. in physics, but the fact that there is not a single Hispanic applicant is something the HR Director should take a closer look at, modifying recruiting practices if necessary.

☒ **A, B,** and **C** are incorrect because disparate treatment is when an employer intentionally treats one group of candidates differently than another. **B** is incorrect because this example does not offer up enough information to indicate that Hispanics have less access to training, and access to training is usually an issue after a candidate becomes an employee. **C** is incorrect because while it is possible that a recruiting strategy that focuses on increasing Hispanic candidates for these positions is necessary, the HR Director in this case should focus immediately on the potential ramifications of engaging in an unlawful hiring practice.

Chapter 3: Workforce Planning and Employment

4. ☑ **B.** This is a clear case of disparate treatment. The test for a forklift driver has to be the same regardless of the link of absenteeism to job injury. It is more likely that there is an issue related to the training of female forklift drivers than there is to the ability of female forklift drivers.

   ☒ **A, C,** and **D** are incorrect. **A** is incorrect because this is not a BFOQ. **C** is incorrect because this is a case of disparate treatment not disparate impact. Disparate impact is unintentional. **D** is incorrect because women are a protected class. Title VII prohibits discrimination on the basis of sex.

5. ☑ **C.** Reengineering would be the best strategy in this case. This would realign the general education teachers who could meet the bilingual education requirements into bilingual classes. By definition, reengineering is realigning operations in a way that adds more value to customers.

   ☒ **A, B,** and **D** are incorrect. **A** is incorrect because expanding the workforce would mean there were staff members who were being paid to essentially do nothing. There is a need for more bilingual education teachers but not a need for a total overall increase in staff. **B** is incorrect because while there is a need to reduce the number of general education staff, there is no need for a reduction in the overall workforce. Because there are potential ways to realign existing staff, that option should be exhausted first. **D** is incorrect because restructuring involves looking for redundancies and process inefficiencies across the corporation and finding ways to eliminate or reduce them. Restructuring does not apply to this scenario.

6. ☑ **A.** Outsourcing/offshoring and workforce reduction are the two most likely strategies that would be applied in this case. To cut labor costs, the plastics company may relocate their plant to Lagos, Nigeria, and downsize the American plant workers.

   ☒ **B, C,** and **D** are incorrect. **B** is incorrect because corporate restructuring involves looking for redundancies and process inefficiencies across the corporation and finding ways to eliminate or reduce them. **C** is incorrect because a merger/acquisition is the decision to acquire or market share by purchasing other companies. **D** is incorrect because reengineering is to realign operations in a way that creates value for clients.

7. ☑ **B.** Workforce expansion would work best in this case because the goal is aggressive so the focus should be on increasing revenue. An expanded sales force will have the most direct impact on increasing revenue and, in turn, profit, all other things being equal.

   ☒ **A, C,** and **D** are incorrect. **A** is incorrect because reducing the administrative personnel will likely result in a reduction in the company's ability to manage day-to-day operations effectively. Even with an increase in sales, this lack of daily operational management could cost more than it saves. **C** is incorrect because it would be a riskier move to attain this aggressive 25 percent goal to purchase a competitor who may or may not achieve enough financial success for the purchasing company to break even in the first year. **D** is incorrect because the scenario is about increasing profits. It is true that reducing wasteful spending will contribute to a better bottom line, but the aggressive 25 percent increase in profits is best addressed by making more sales.

8. ☑ **D.** A divesture is the likely outcome in this scenario. A divesture involves the sale of a portion of a business or company's financial or physical assets that could result in the reduction or transfer of staff. It is likely that the decision would be made to divest the securities division.

    ☒ **A, B, and C** are incorrect. **A** is incorrect because the question asks for the most likely outcome and while a divesture could also result in workforce reduction, it is most likely that a successful company would attempt to sell its less successful holdings rather than close the division without some financial gain. If a sale is made, then HR should be prepared to support what happens with the employees of the affected division. **B** is incorrect because purchasing another company does not address the issue presented. **C** is incorrect because corporate restructuring is focused on eliminating and reducing inefficient and bureaucratic processes in an organization.

9. ☑ **D.** Conducting a job analysis is needed because the position has changed. The goal of a job analysis is to identify the knowledge, skills, and abilities (KSAs) that candidates will need to be successful in the job to support organizational goals.

    ☒ **A, B, and C** are incorrect. **A** is incorrect because it could be helpful to have the outgoing Director in interviews, especially since this position still reports into his division. However, a candidate should know as much as possible about the job responsibilities before investing time in applying or interviewing. In fact, it may turn off a candidate if she goes in for an interview and feels blindsided by differing job expectations than what was described. **B** is incorrect because promoting from within is great and would help fill the position quickly, but the question asked for the best next step. It is best to identify the core competencies required to do the job successfully to ensure that the person selected for the position is the best available fit. **C** is incorrect because recruiting should not begin before conducting a job analysis.

10. ☑ **A.** Job competencies guide interviewers in that they help them formulate questions that seek feedback from the candidate that is more expansive. Responses to questions developed from job competencies help to determine how well a candidate fits the overall culture and not just whether or not they are able to perform the tasks associated with a job. An example would be hiring a Campus Director for a small school that is experiencing rapid growth. This person would have to display a job competency of adaptability and flexibility.

    ☒ **B, C, and D** are incorrect. **B** is incorrect because lists of essential functions aren't the best source for developing behavioral and situational questions. Essential functions are the barest minimum tasks required to perform a job.

The Sales Manager, in this example, is seeking to identify behaviors both past and present that will help her determine a candidate's overall fit for an Account Representative job. **C** and **D** are incorrect because job specifications are simply a detailed listing of work to be done or job duties coupled with minimum qualifications such as education, certifications, and so on.

11. ☑ **C.** A job analysis done on a regular cycle such as once per year will cause little interruption to daily operations while keeping descriptions current.

   ☒ **A, B,** and **D** are incorrect. **A** is incorrect because reducing the administrative personnel will likely result in a reduction in the company's ability to manage day-to-day operations effectively. Even with an increase in sales, this lack of daily operational management could cost more than it saves. **B** is incorrect because an immediate company-wide project to update job descriptions through the job analysis process will be disruptive for business. An effective job analysis includes interviewing supervisors, coworkers, and incumbents; creating a task list; and so on. **D** is incorrect because providing weekly staff meeting updates is not an effective way to maintain a current catalogue of job descriptions.

12. ☑ **D.** Identifying the qualifications to do the jobs in the new division is the best first step because this is equivalent to conducting a job analysis. There has to be a job analysis from which to build a job description, which, in turn, helps HR to make the best job-to-person fit.

   ☒ **A, B,** and **C** are incorrect. **A** is incorrect because selecting from a pool of internal applicants proceeds completing the job analysis. **B** and **C** are incorrect because both developing pre-employment tests and hiring criteria take place after the job analysis. The components of both are built from the information compiled through the job analysis.

13. ☑ **D.** Identifying essential job functions and then identifying barriers to performance is the first step to determine if a company can accommodate the disability

   ☒ **A, B,** and **C** are incorrect. These are all later steps in the interactive process under the ADA.

14. ☑ **C.** The first step would be to start the interactive process with the employee, as drug use is covered under the ADA if they are undergoing treatment or are rehabilitated.

   ☒ **A, B,** and **D** are incorrect. **A** is incorrect because drug use is covered under the ADA if they are undergoing treatment or are rehabilitated. **B** is incorrect because a drug-free workplace would not apply in this particular situation, as the drug user is rehabilitated or seeking treatment. **D** is incorrect because it is best for HR to handle the communication regarding ADA.

15. ☑ **A.** This employer is small and likely the cost of an additional elevator would cause an undue hardship to the employer. A less expensive option may be a better choice in this situation. The ADA does not require an employer to accommodate the request if it would cause an undue hardship.

☒ **B, C,** and **D** are incorrect. They are not required under the ADA and would cause an undue financial hardship on the organization.

16. ☑ **A.** A comprehensive job analysis will show what job functions are essential and nonessential.

☒ **B, C,** and **D** are incorrect. B is incorrect because is not relevant to this example. C and D are incorrect because they are part of the job analysis process. The job analysis as a whole is the best action item to take in this situation.

17. ☑ **B.** Adding the verbiage "other duties as assigned" in the first job description would have communicated to the employee that there are extra tasks that could be assigned at any time and therefore prevented employee discontent.

☒ **A, C,** and **D** are incorrect. A is incorrect because the FLSA status is a component of a job description and should be listed, but it wouldn't have prevented the problem. C and D are incorrect because they would not be required to accommodate the employee's discontent, nor would it address the root cause of the disconnect.

18. ☑ **C** is correct because investing in early education will likely help companies in the future to develop the knowledge, skills, and abilities needed for the future workforce. This would be the most strategic option.

☒ **A, B,** and **D** are incorrect. They are not strategic in nature as they do not plan for the future; they only react to the current problem (lack of knowledge, skills, and abilities in graduating college students).

19. ☑ **A.** This addresses a skill that is tied to the organizational vision (100 percent patient satisfaction).

☒ **B, C,** and **D** are incorrect. They are generic examples of managerial competencies but not the best choice.

20. ☑ **B.** Conducting a cost/benefits analyses would be an example of a core competency for a business analyst.

☒ **A, C,** and **D** are incorrect. A and D are incorrect because they are examples of core competencies for a manager. C is incorrect because that would be an example of core competencies of an administrative assistant.

21. ☑ **D.** Completing a trend analysis is the most systemic way to see the relationship between two variables and begin to project what future HR needs will be.

☒ **A, B,** and **C** are incorrect. These choices would not provide much useful information for the HR forecast.

22. ☑   B. A market analysis will provide you with the most accurate information to predict future staffing needs.

☒   A, C, and D are incorrect. They are preemptive and will likely not provide any value at this beginning point until a proper analysis is complete.

23. ☑   B. It will take a longer time to find and recruit talent when there is a high labor demand and low labor supply scenario. For example, highly skilled talent in the areas of science, technology, engineering, or mathematics (STEM) may fall into this category. The demand is high for these skills. However, the supply doesn't match the demand.

☒   A, C, and D are incorrect. A is incorrect because a low labor demand and high labor supply would indicate that there is plenty of talent but little need for it. A time-to-fill metric would be relatively low in this scenario. C is incorrect because a low labor demand and low labor supply would indicate there is no talent in a particular area and no need to search for it. D is incorrect because high labor demand and a high labor supply would indicate that hiring talent in this scenario would not be difficult to find, therefore not causing any delay in time-to-fill metrics.

24. ☑   C. Implementing a skills inventory measurement or management system will enable the company to understand the level of skill needed to achieve its objectives. Recruitment, compensation, and development strategies can be focused on what the skills inventory reveals.

☒   A, B, and D are incorrect. A is incorrect because a market survey of compensation reveals how the employer ranks in compensating its existing workforce. It does not address skill level in order to compete. B is incorrect because an employee satisfaction survey measures engagement levels and does not address skill level needs of the business. D is incorrect because employee development would not be the first step in analyzing workforce skill levels. Employee development would come later on in the process of upgrading the skill level of a business.

25. ☑   A. An internal skills assessment requires defining critical skills needed, determining existing skill assets (also called "as is"), addressing the skills gap, and monitoring ongoing skill levels.

☒   B, C, and D are incorrect. B is incorrect because defining open positions, creating job descriptions, recruiting top talent, and evaluating ongoing performance come after a skills analysis has been conducted. C is incorrect because defining key positions, creating or updating job descriptions, recruiting top talent, and evaluating ongoing performance are either not related or come after an internal skills analysis. D is incorrect because while these activities may relate to skill gaps within an organization, they are not part of the actual internal skills analysis.

26. ☑   D. A good way to assess the external job pool for targeted skills is by analyzing the current and projected number of graduates from schools meeting

the requirements of targeted classifications. Not only does that provide an anticipated number of potential graduates, but those numbers can also be compared with anticipated future need of those skills. This enables HR to build a proactive strategy in filling any critical skill gaps.

☒ A, B, and C are incorrect. A is incorrect because existing staff opinion does not provide an objective measure of the external job pool. B is incorrect because management opinion does not provide an objective measure of the external job pool. C is incorrect because turnover data of former staff does not provide an adequate picture of the external job pool skills.

27. ☑ A. Once a business realizes minorities are under-represented in specific job classifications, the best strategy is to implement a diversity outreach recruitment plan. This entails attending specific career fairs, advertising in diversity-related publications, or recruiting from schools that rank high in diversity populations.

☒ B, C, and D are incorrect. B is incorrect because a succession plan relates to filling key management positions. C is incorrect because getting management buy-in, while important, does not contribute to correcting minority under-representation in specific job classifications. D is incorrect because a development plan relates to existing staff, not to recruitment of external candidates.

28. ☑ B. Implementing an employee referral program can improve morale, reduce turnover, and speed up hiring timelines.

☒ A, C, and D are incorrect. A is incorrect because hiring outside contractors does not address the turnover issue. C is incorrect because launching a recruitment campaign is overbroad and does not address turnover. D is incorrect because improving the efficiency of on-boarding processes does not address turnover issues.

29. ☑ C. Social media is proving to be an effective and cost-efficient recruitment force. It enables companies to showcase their culture and develop relationships with prospective candidates prior to hiring them.

☒ A, B, and D are incorrect. A is incorrect because career fairs entail travel and lodging expenses. B is incorrect because much like career fairs, industry conferences are an expense for a company. D is incorrect because while it brings candidates in-house, there is still an expense associated with the event.

30. ☑ D. Hiring temporary forklift drivers will enable a company to fill a temporary need without having to lay off workers later on. If the temporary need becomes permanent, the employer has the option of hiring the temporary workforce onto its own payroll.

☒ A, B, and C are incorrect. A is incorrect because waiting for additional details is not the best action toward filling open positions. B is incorrect because increasing overtime expenses is not the best action. C is incorrect because while being upfront with employees is a good practice this is not the best action to take to fill open positions.

31. ☑ **C.** Revenue per employee would be a good place to capture how effective each employee is in completing sales.

☒ **A, B, and D** are incorrect. **A** is incorrect because customers-per-employee measures the quantity of customers each employee manages. It does not measure how effective an employee is in closing sales. **B** is incorrect because expenses-per-employee measures how much is spent per employee. It does not measure how effective an employee is in closing sales. **D** is incorrect because labor cost per employee measures how much a company spends on wages and benefits per employee. It does not measure employee effectiveness.

32. ☑ **A.** A ratio of offers to acceptances measures the company's ability to hire. If a large number of top talent declines a company's offer to work for competitors, that is a sign that the compensation, benefits, or overall company reputation is not competitive.

☒ **B, C, and D** are incorrect. **B** is incorrect because regrettable voluntary turnover measures retention. It does not necessarily measure how competitive a company is at attracting top talent. **C** is incorrect because hires is a percentage of employees measured on recruitment activity. It does not necessarily reflect on the ability to attract top talent. **D** is incorrect because voluntary turnover within 90 days still reflects retention. It does not reflect the company's ability to attract top talent.

33. ☑ **A.** Cost per hire metrics can be grouped by hiring source. This will enable recruitment departments to assess the cost effectiveness per hiring source.

☒ **B, C, and D** are incorrect. **B** is incorrect because time to fill measures how fast open positions are filled. It does not necessarily reflect on the cost effectiveness of a hiring source. **C** is incorrect because the time to start jobs metric measures on-boarding process efficiency. **D** is incorrect because quality per hire measures if new hires are high performers.

34. ☑ **C.** Retiree benefit cost as a percentage of expense will provide insight into the cost of retirement benefits in relation to overall expenses.

☒ **A, B, and D** are incorrect. **A** is incorrect because benefit costs as a percentage of revenue measures health, dental, and vision and does not necessarily narrow in on retirement costs. **B** is incorrect because benefit costs as a percentage of expense, as in answer A, includes all things related to benefits. It does not narrow in on retirement costs. **D** is incorrect because compensation as a percentage of expense does not measure retirement costs.

35. ☑ **B.** Determining and communicating to the potential workforce that women and minorities view promotional opportunities in a positive light would be a part of an effective branding strategy. Because the agency was plagued with allegations of racial discrimination and sexual harassment, it is likely that the agency's inability to recruit top talent among these groups results from the fact that it has a reputation in the marketplace as being unsupportive of women and minorities.

☒ A, C, and D are incorrect. They are not elements of a branding strategy. They are questions a recruiter would ask to determine if the agency is utilizing the appropriate resources to attract targeted candidates.

36. ☑ A. Attracting and retaining quality employees are the most important reasons for managing the employer brand. Even during times where there is slow growth, no growth, or a decline in business, employers with a strong brand are able to maintain commitment by employees. To be effective, the official brand must actually match the reality of the environment, of course.

☒ B, C, and D are incorrect. None of these responses really support why the employer brand is most important.

37. ☑ C. The Campus President should contact these salespeople and make them aware of the upcoming opening. It is a smart move to get them engaged. Posting a position and then interviewing applicants is an orderly and systematic way to consider applicants and it is in accordance with the principles of the Uniform Guidelines on Employee Selection Procedures (UGESP). The UGESP was developed by the Equal Employment Opportunity Commission (EEOC), the Civil Service Commission (CSC), the Office of Federal Contract Compliance Programs (OFCCP), and the Department of Justice (DOJ). The purpose of the UGESP is to give employers a guide to ensure compliance with Title VII, Executive Order 11246, and related employment legislation.

☒ A, B, and D are incorrect. A is incorrect because interviews should never be set before a position is posted. A component of the applicant tracking process for Internet applicants is for the employer to "act" to fill a position. The normal procedure for this school is to post positions online, and then interested candidates apply and set interviews accordingly. Posting of the position online, in this case, is the employer "acting" to fill the position. B is incorrect because direct resume submission is not the school's normal process. Another component of the applicant tracking process related to Internet applicants is that the individual follow the employer's normal process for applying. D is incorrect because setting up phone screens is the same as setting up in-person interviews, which should not happen prior to posting the position.

38. ☑ C. A realistic job preview would be best because it has a direct impact on turnover. A realistic job preview is an opportunity for a candidate to explore what happens on a day-to-day basis in a given job. In a call center environment, candidates could shadow another representative for an extended period of time (1–2 hours) to get a sense of the kinds of calls the typical representative could handle and to get a sense of the overall work environment (for example, noise level with lots of reps talking, desk drawers opening and closing, the sound of typing; proximity of one reps desk to another; and so on). If, during the RJP, a candidate decides that this may not be the kind of environment he could work in, then he will self-select out of the process, thereby reducing potential future turnover.

☒ A, B, and D are incorrect. These are all variations of tests that could be used during the selection process but would not have as much impact on reducing turnover as the realistic job preview.

39. ☑ **D.** This is stereotyping. This interviewer is drawing a conclusion based on intuition without any facts to support his opinion of the candidate. Stereotyping is forming a generalized opinion about how people of a particular gender, religion, or race appear, think, act, feel, or respond.

☒ **A, B,** and **C** are incorrect. **A** is incorrect because the horn effect occurs when the interviewer draws a conclusion based on one negative trait of the candidate. **B** is incorrect because negative emphasis happens when the interviewer uses a small amount of negative information to draw an unfavorable opinion of the candidate. **C** is incorrect because the first impression bias occurs when the interviewer determines his opinion of the candidate, whether negative or positive, from the first impression.

40. ☑ **A.** The company is guilty of negligent hiring and should conduct complete background and reference checks, including a check of both state and FBI records going forward. Negligent hiring occurs when a company knew, or should have known, that a candidate is prone to be a danger to employees, customers, vendors, and anyone else he comes in contact with. If a thorough background check was done, including a search of the FBI database, it could have easily been uncovered that this employee was convicted and found guilty of battery.

☒ **B, C,** and **D** are incorrect. **B** is incorrect because, as it relates to HR, the FCRA requires that employers not use information obtained about an applicant's background in an adverse manner until certain criteria are met and that employers obtain consent prior to conducting any background check. **C** and **D** are incorrect because while it is negligent hiring, the Privacy Act of 1974 regulates how information collected is stored, requires that the candidate know what is being collected, and prevents information collected from being used for any purpose other than that which was intended. This does not apply in this case.

41. ☑ **A.** In-depth reference checks, including speaking with prior supervisors and/or determining if the employee was eligible for rehire, may have revealed this pattern prior to extending an offer.

☒ **B, C,** and **D** are incorrect. **B** is incorrect because based on the information provided, the employee was never convicted of a related crime so a criminal history check would have revealed nothing. **C** is incorrect because a personality test simply measures how well a person will fit a particular job. For example, an applicant for a sales job may need to have a personality that can handle consistent rejection because in sales people often refuse to buy what you are selling. **D** is incorrect because integrity tests measure ethics, such as whether or not a person would steal from an employer.

42. ☑ **B.** It is a requirement of the UGESP that any pre-employment test be both valid and reliable. *Reliability* refers to whether or not the test produces similar results over time. *Validity* refers to whether the test is measuring what it is intended to measure. In this case, what should be measured is computer software proficiency.

☒ **A, C,** and **D** are incorrect. **A** is incorrect because a pre-employment test can be given before an offer of employment is made. **C** and **D** are incorrect because neither of these are most concerning about the scenario presented. It is true that no pre-employment test should be administered without being thoroughly vetted by HR, and the physical space within which any test is administered matters to the reliability of the test. However, these tests have already been administered, which may have affected the hiring decision made in regards to some of the candidates. At this point, as the HR Director, it would be best to remove the tests from use immediately, review the scores of the candidates who may have been affected, and take corrective action as necessary to protect the company from liability.

43. ☑ **C.** Employment offers should be made as soon as possible after the decision is made to hire; delays increase the risk that the candidate will not accept.

    ☒ **A, B,** and **D** are incorrect. **A** and **D** are incorrect because these tasks happen after the employment offer is made. **B** is incorrect because in delaying the offer, the company increases the risk that the candidate will not accept.

44. ☑ **A.** HR should set a timeline for acceptance, but it should be a reasonable amount of time (not too long, wherein the candidate can become disinterested, nor too short, wherein the candidate feels pressured).

    ☒ **B, C,** and **D** are incorrect. These would not be HR best practices in regards to hiring. Setting deadlines that are too short could result in candidates feeling pressured. Giving a candidate too much time can lead to the candidate becoming disinterested or finding another opportunity.

45. ☑ **D.** A staff attorney would be expected to perform services exclusively for the employer.

    ☒ **A, B,** and **C** are incorrect. **A** is incorrect because tenure requirements would be for professors. **B** is incorrect because involvement in community service would be a requirement of an executive. **C** is incorrect because rights to patents and copyright during employment would be applicable primarily in high tech or research fields.

46. ☑ **C.** Maintaining company confidential information is an important term of a contract for telecommuters; parameters must be set around this to secure confidential information.

    ☒ **A, B,** and **D** are incorrect. **A** is incorrect because publishing requirements would be more applicable for professors. **B** is incorrect because this would apply to workers in the high tech or research fields. **D** is incorrect because this would primarily be for executives.

47. ☑ **B.** Companies with federal contracts and subcontracts are required to perform the E-Verify process for all newly hired employees.

    ☒ **A, C,** and **D** are incorrect. These choices are programs that do not specifically apply to federal contractors or newly hired employees.

48. ☑ **A.** Companies are required to retain the completed I-9 for three years after the hire date or one year after termination, whichever is later.

☒ **B, C,** and **D** are incorrect. They are not the proper requirement for form I-9.

49. ☑ **D.** Employers are required to complete section 1 (employee section) of the I-9 form no later than the first day of employment.

☒ **A, B,** and **C** are incorrect. Although the review and verification requirements associated with the I-9 form do not have to be completed before three business days, section 1 of the form must be completed by the end of the day of the first day of employment.

50. ☑ **C.** The primary goal of a corporate relocation process is to provide the best service to the employee at the most reasonable cost to the company.

☒ **A, B,** and **D** are incorrect. These choices are a part of a relocation process but are too specific and are not a primary goal of corporate relocation.

51. ☑ **A.** Reviewing the mission statements will help to clarify for a new employee the company's overall belief and values.

☒ **B, C,** and **D** are incorrect. A review of policies and procedures, job descriptions, and the employee handbook will assist the employee in understanding what is expected of her as a new team member. However, none of these focus in on what makes the company unique.

52. ☑ **C.** It would be most useful to e-mail new hires a survey that includes questions about their overall onboarding experience. Included could be questions related to how many days they were working before being able to punch in, when they were made aware that their e-mail was set up and were able to log in. Included could also be questions regarding their current overall impression of the company as it compares to their initial experiences.

☒ **A, B,** and **D** are incorrect. **A** and **D** are incorrect because the issues related to e-mail and punching in may not be exclusive to HR or IT. Those functions are interrelated so the bottleneck could be in multiple departments at multiple places throughout the process. **B** is incorrect because this would be cumbersome depending on how many new hires a company has in a month and because the questions would not be uniform. Standardized questions in a survey format will help the HR professional identify trends and make process improvement recommendations.

53. ☑ **A.** Assigning a mentor, establishing goals, and monitoring progress toward those goals will be most effective in engaging a transferring teacher. Peer support/mentor/buddy programs are used as a way to informally provide additional support to new team members.

☒ **B, C,** and **D** are incorrect. Although all of these activities are positive and will help support the effective onboarding of a new or transferring staff member, the most effective strategy would be to provide individual one-on-one support. The staff member will feel as though they have a secure place to ask questions and gain advice and support.

54. ☑ **D.** The best solution to this issue is to collaborate with supervisors so you gain their commitment in establishing a full onboarding program. The onboarding program should include department supports, possibly mentors for each new hire, periodic reviews of how to handle customer calls, coaching, and so on. All the activities of the onboarding program should be focused on providing effective supports to each new hire.

☒ **A, B,** and **C** are incorrect. All of these activities are good elements of building a positive company culture and encouraging employee engagement; however, the new customer service representatives in the scenario specifically report that they did not feel like they had the tools necessary to do their jobs effectively. A successful onboarding program would best address these concerns.

55. ☑ **C.** Because the consistent complaint is that employees are leaving due to dissatisfaction with store management, focus should be placed on ensuring that front line managers are creating a positive environment for employees. It is often said that people don't leave jobs. They leave managers.

☒ **A, B,** and **D** are incorrect. **A** is incorrect because the exit interviews show dissatisfaction with store management as the most commonly noted reason for leaving. Some work could also be done to improve the selection process but that doesn't address the main issue stated. **B** is incorrect because a longevity bonus, if used properly, may help to reduce turnover but if management is mistreating employees they will still leave at some point even possibly right after the bonus is received. **D** is incorrect because even if a person states during the interview process that she is interested in a long-term career, again, if management mistreats her, she will likely become disengaged and seek a long-term career with another grocery store.

56. ☑ **B.** Turnover is highest among new hires. Even though these employees are not new hires, they are new to their business units or locations. In addition to the uneasiness that mergers bring, these employees may also feel like they don't fit into their new environments, begin feeling dissatisfaction with their jobs, and seek employment elsewhere. Establishing both formal and informal activities designed to help employees get to know each other will help to integrate the transferred employees in the culture of their new location or new business unit.

☒ **A, C,** and **D** are incorrect. The question, as stated, does not indicate that lack of training, lack of rewards, or lack of advancement opportunities are what is causing these employees to disengage. The only change that has taken place is their reassignment or transfer.

57. ☑ **D.** The best fix here is to adjust the recruitment and selection process. The high turnover at the two universities warrants a review and perhaps severing ties with the universities until their teacher preparation programs provide enrollees with a realistic job preview and produces high quality graduates.

☒ **A, B,** and **C** are incorrect. The other four university graduates are not leaving the teaching profession in large numbers. Their average teaching career is 20 years. Therefore, one cannot point to lack of mentoring, socialization, or advancement opportunities as the reason for the high turnover.

58. ☑ A. Scheduled audits of the retention program are important in helping management determine what drivers of turnover are. Is it that turnover is highest among middle management employees who are being recruited by competitors? Is it mostly lower skilled workers?

☒ B, C, and D are incorrect. These are all solutions to aspects of turnover. In this example, HR has not yet determined the exact causes for turnover so it does not make sense to apply any of these solutions.

59. ☑ A. Succession planning is beneficial to all companies. In this case, there is predictive data early enough for the company to implement a succession plan that should minimize the possibility of these key positions going unfilled.

☒ B, C, and D are incorrect. B and C are incorrect because these are all great strategies that would be useful if the company needed to fill the positions relatively quickly. However, the company is five years out from expecting an issue so a well thought-out and implemented succession plan would best serve their needs. Generally speaking, if you have at least one and a half to three years to fill a position, then implementing a succession plan is the most appropriate way to address a future staffing need. D is incorrect because positive employee engagement strategies help the organization overall. However, this is not a targeted strategy that would address the need of specifically attracting or retaining more chemists.

60. ☑ C. The best way to communicate the value of a succession plan to senior management is to translate the success of the program into return on investment (ROI). In this case, the cost per hire for a program participant versus the cost per hire for an external candidate would be a valuable way to quantify the program's success. Another measure is the quality of hire, as shown through employee evaluations and the achievement of specific company goals by the program participants. If the succession planning program is a success, the candidates promoted internally should have a shorter learning curve and a more significant and relatively quick impact on the organization's goals.

☒ A, B, and D are incorrect. Turnover rates, employee retention rates, and a reduction in open positions are likely influenced by several factors that may or may not include the implementation of a succession plan.

61. ☑ B. Senior management has already assessed the situation, which is that there are not enough qualified candidates in the marketplace to fill the mid-career technology positions. Therefore, the next logical step in a strategic plan would be to articulate the objectives of the plan.

☒ A, C, and D are incorrect. A is incorrect because the situation has already been assessed. C and D are incorrect because formulating and implementing a strategy would have to follow the establishment of the objectives that the strategy is intended to address.

62. ☑ A. The WARN Act provisions apply if an organization has 100 or more full-time employees or 100 or more full- and part-time employees who work

an average of 4,000 or more hours per week. This would be considered a mass layoff by the definition provided in the WARN Act because the act defines mass layoff as 500 or more affected employees.

☒ **B, C,** and **D** are incorrect. **B** is incorrect because full- and part-time employees are considered in the 100-employee minimum count. **C** and **D** are incorrect because the WARN Act provisions are not exclusive to plants, and employees on leave are always considered a part of the total employee count.

63. ☑ **A.** The use of performance appraisals to determine who remains employed and who is released is the most equitable way to document a layoff decision. If an affected employee were to subsequently raise an EEO concern, the use of performance appraisals to determine which employees are laid off would be legally defensible.

☒ **B, C,** and **D** are incorrect. **B** and **C** are incorrect because the cost of a severance package or outplacement services are of lesser concern at this point. Once you determine who will be laid off using a relatively objective tool such as a performance review, then you can review what it might cost if the company chooses to offer a severance package or outplacement services. **D** is incorrect because the cost of COBRA coverage for continued health benefits is almost exclusively that of the employee's.

64. ☑ **C.** The exit interview is an extremely useful tool for a company. The information gathered should include reason for leaving, suggestions for process and culture improvements, and issues that need to be addressed immediately. This information will help a company make decisions that will impact future turnover.

☒ **A, B,** and **D** are incorrect. While these are significant parts of a smooth exit process, they have very little impact on turnover. The promotion of an employee into the vacated position may have the positive effect of retaining that employee but that has little to no impact on the company's overall turnover ratio.

65. ☑ **C.** To allow for the smoothest possible exit, managers should address affected employees individually with compassion. There should be complete clarity regarding the conditions of the layoff (indefinite, may be recalled, unemployment compensation eligibility). Following the completion of the individual meetings, managers should meet with the employees who survived the layoff collectively and answer questions candidly and clearly. This is an important emotional transition for those employees as well.

☒ **A, B,** and **D** are incorrect. **A** and **B** are incorrect because layoffs should rarely be done in a group setting. The effect on the employee is complicated and potentially devastating. It should not be about maintaining efficiency. The layoff meeting should be focused on ensuring a proper exit for affected employees. Some considerations for management are the occurrence of workplace violence and the retention of the employees left behind. **D** is incorrect because those who have been laid off should not be allowed to linger. Their understandable angst toward the company will have a negative impact on the remaining employees.

66. ☑ **A.** Essential components of an AAP would be action-oriented goals with specific steps that have to be taken to correct the problem areas.

☒ **B, C,** and **D** are incorrect. **B** and **C** are incorrect because specific goals should be established for the affected groups. **D** is incorrect because the AAP should include the titles of employees responsible for the effective implementation of the plan. Those employees may not specifically be the HR Director or CEO.

67. ☑ **B.** A contractor need only show that it is making a good faith effort to ensure equal opportunity. In this case, women are being underutilized so the plan should specify the procedures in place to improve these rates.

☒ **A, C,** and **D** are incorrect. A federal contractor need only show a good faith effort; thus, any answer that requires that a target number of women be hired is incorrect.

68. ☑ **A.** If the Office of Federal Contract Compliance Programs (OFCCP) finds a contractor to be in serious non-compliance with Executive Order 11246, it will issue a conciliation agreement with the violating employer. A conciliation agreement is a contract that requires corrective steps to the serious out-of-compliance matters. Serious violations can include blatant discrimination issues, lack of required documentation, and failure to comply with past commitments.

☒ **B, C,** and **D** are incorrect. Failure to reach a conciliation agreement will result in additional enforcement actions such as fines and debarring from government contracts for up to five years.

69. ☑ **D.** One of the benefits of diversifying your workforce is that it brings fresh, new perspectives to the work. This fosters creativity and innovation, which leads to an increase in profitability.

☒ **A, B,** and **C** are incorrect. **A** is incorrect because this assumes a bias. **B** is incorrect because this sets the company up for losing the diverse workforce balance it has worked hard to establish. Creating a diverse workforce is best achieved when deliberate planned actions govern hiring and promotional decisions. **C** is incorrect because just the mere existence of an AAP does not ensure that a company is making a good faith effort to maintain equity in its hiring practices.

70. ☑ **D.** Utilizing a separate and secure location to store background checks is the best decision. Hiring managers should never be able to review this kind of information. In accordance with the Fair Credit Reporting Act (FCRA), the employer obtained permission from the candidate to obtain the background check for limited use, which was to fulfill the contingencies of the employment offer. Further, questionable background information could lead a supervisor to pass someone over for a promotion in favor of another employee, which may result in multiple civil rights violations.

☒   A, B, and C are incorrect. A is incorrect because the offer was contingent, in part, on the results of the criminal background check. It can be rescinded. B is incorrect because it is not a best practice due to equal employment opportunity considerations. As the new HR Director, your goal should be to improve processes in support of the organization's overall goals, not simply encourage meeting minimum requirements. C is incorrect because it increases the probability that removal of the background check may not happen consistently due to human error. Finding a new location for the record is the best of the choices given.

71.   ☑   B. The results of any employment test given and job applications of all applicants are relevant to this investigation. Prior to administering the employment test, it is in the company's best interest to ensure that the test is valid and reliable, and that it does not result in disparate impact.

☒   A, C, and D are incorrect. A is incorrect because prior performance evaluations may not have been the only reason for denying or granting the promotion. Also, just providing performance evaluations for the selected employee and the accuser does not provide the EEOC with a full picture of the candidates considered for the promotion. In addition, the selected candidate may be an external hire; thus, prior performance evaluations would not be available. C is incorrect because unless there is also a similar conviction in the selected candidate's background, the criminal background records are irrelevant. D is incorrect because training attendance is only relevant to the extent that the company is trying to demonstrate that it provides training opportunities to all employees equally. An employee may or may not have actually attended an offered training session. A better data point would be what total training is offered and to which employee groups.

72.   ☑   A. OSHA requires that forms 300, 301, and 300A be retained five years after the relevant year.

☒   B, C, and D are incorrect. B is incorrect because performance evaluations are considered documents controlled by the FLSA, which requires three years' retention after termination. C is incorrect because I-9s are controlled by IRCA, which requires retention three years after hire or one year after termination. D is incorrect because job descriptions are considered employee recruitment and hiring records controlled by the FLSA and EPA.

73.   ☑   D. COBRA is an amendment to ERISA. ERISA was passed in 1974 and set minimum standards for pension and health plans of private employers.

☒   A, B, and C are incorrect. A is incorrect because HIPAA is another amendment to ERISA. B is incorrect because USERRA is a law that protects the reemployment rights of armed service personnel when they return from a period of service. It has nothing to do with health insurance. C is incorrect because it is a separate law passed during the most recent administration. It works in conjunction with other healthcare-related statutes but is not an amendment to any prior statute such as ERISA.

74. ☑ A. The Age Discrimination in Employment Act of 1967 and Title VII of the Civil Rights Act of 1964 both have exclusions for bona fide occupational qualifications (BFOQ). When religion, sex, or national origin are "reasonably necessary to the normal operation" of the business, a BFOQ occurs. An example of this would be hiring models for a male clothing line. In this case, it would be a BFOQ to only advertise for male models.

☒ B, C, and D are incorrect. B is incorrect because Executive Order 11246 was a broad order that expanded the definition of protected class as defined by the Civil Rights Act to include the prohibition of employment discrimination on the basis of race, creed, color, or national origin and requires that certain parameters be met in advertising jobs, recruiting, promotions, access to training, employee compensation, and termination. C and D are incorrect because the Americans with Disabilities Act of 1990 was an expansion of the Rehabilitation Act of 1973. It extended protected class status to qualified persons with disabilities. The Rehabilitation Act of 1973 established an equal playing field for individuals with disabilities.

75. ☑ D. Native Americans and African-Americans would experience adverse impact in this case. To calculate adverse impact, first divide the number of new hires by the number of applicants in that particular group to determine the selection rate. Then, multiply the highest selection rate by the 80 percent (4/5ths rule). The selection rate for African-Americans is 10 percent and for Native Americans it is 9 percent. The highest selection rate is for Caucasians at 29 percent. Four-fifths of 29 percent is 23 percent. The selection rate for Asians is 27 percent, which is above the 23 percent benchmark.

☒ A, B, and C are incorrect. When applying the 4/5ths rule, neither Asians nor Caucasians are adversely impacted. All three of these answers include either Asians or Caucasians as a choice.

76. ☑ C. The hiring manager's salary is a part of an effective cost per hire calculation. A meaningful cost per hire calculation should include advertising costs, recruiter costs, HR team salaries for people directly involved in activities such as developing an advertisement or scheduling interviews, the hiring manager's salary and anyone else on the interview team, and the cost of administering any pre-employment tests.

☒ A, B, and D are incorrect. A is incorrect because turnover rate is most beneficial for a manager when determining why people leave an organization and what organizational change should happen to retain quality employees. B is incorrect because the Recruiting Manager is specifically trying to determine the cost per hire. Replacement cost expands cost per hire by including training costs, lost productivity, and a number of other factors. D is incorrect because the accession rate measures the number of new employees versus the overall number of employees at the end of a period.

77. ☑ **B.** Personal networks such as LinkedIn, Twitter, and Facebook are excellent sources for finding passive candidates. A passive candidate is a person who is not seeking employment but may have the experience that matches the needs of the organization. In that case, a recruiter would contact them, gauge their interest, and encourage them to apply for an opening.

    ☒ **A, C,** and **D** are incorrect. It is most likely that candidates who are seeking employment (active candidates) would be the ones visiting a company's career page on the company's website. Job fairs are designed to invite active candidates to meet employers, and the candidates who are registered with an employment agency are usually actively seeking employment.

78. ☑ **C.** The HR Director should consider the sourcing method(s) used in the past that recruited the top three performers to the organization. It would be a good starting point that will help determine the best sourcing method going forward.

    ☒ **A, B,** and **D** are incorrect. **A** is incorrect because the employee referral program would only help if the top three performers knew the new graduates of the university and could refer them to the company. **B** is incorrect because it assumes that a job fair would be a good way to recruit similar talent and doesn't take into account the exorbitant costs associated with having an in-person job fair in another country. **D** is incorrect because it suggests a passive strategy. Simply hoping that a talented person from the university will apply is not assertive enough to achieve the recruiting goal.

79. ☑ **B.** Job bidding is an internal recruitment method whereby a current employee expresses an interest in a position before it becomes available.

    ☒ **A, C,** and **D** are incorrect. A job board is simply a posting location: It could be online or a physical posting but it is not exclusively an internal recruiting method. A job fair is not internal and a posting on the company website can be viewed by both internal and external candidates.

80. ☑ **A.** From a purely recruiting standpoint, one of the main issues the Recruiting Manager must resolve is when to start recruiting. Now may seem like the most obvious answer, but it is October so there may not be many new teaching graduates or qualified teachers still left in the market.

    ☒ **B, C,** and **D** are incorrect. While the total rewards package, employer brand and an existing candidate pipeline are all important to the recruiting process, none of these choices will attract the right candidate if the right candidates are not available and aware of the opportunities. When to recruit is the most important issue to resolve.

81. ☑ **A.** Executive search firms typically charge anywhere from 20 to 30 percent of an employee's first-year salary.

    ☒ **B, C,** and **D** are incorrect. They are untrue statements about hiring an executive search firm.

82. ☑ C is correct because that is what a contingency fee–based search firm charges.
☒ A, B, and D are incorrect. A and B are incorrect because they do not accurately reflect a contingency fee–based search firm. D is incorrect because the statement is describing a type of search firm with a retained fee.

83. ☑ C is correct because assessment centers can fully evaluate an internal candidate's knowledge, skills, and abilities through a battery of testing options.
☒ A, B, and D are incorrect. These choices would not be the best option for retrieving all the information needed.

84. ☑ B. Content validity is the degree to which a test—for example, a typing test—measures the actual job KSAs.
☒ A, C, and D are incorrect. None of these choices measures the KSAs associated with a secretarial position.

85. ☑ A. Reliability is the ability to measure results consistently.
☒ B, C, and D are incorrect. None of these choices address consistency, a required characteristic of reliability.

86. ☑ D. The main concern from applicants is invasion of privacy.
☒ A, B, and C are incorrect. Although these choices may be criticisms of integrity testing, they are not the main concern for the employer and HR.

87. ☑ A. A firefighter is required to have high physical dexterity skills in order to operate the equipment and that would be determined by a psychomotor test.
☒ B, C, and D are incorrect. B is incorrect because this choice would be used in conjunction with a personality test. C is incorrect because this choice would be determined by completing a cognitive ability test. D incorrect because this choice would be determined by completing an aptitude test.

88. ☑ A. Determining if the test is valid based on essential job functions will decrease chances of discriminating against disabled job applicants.
☒ B, C, and D are incorrect. B is incorrect because substance abuse would be revealed using an honesty/integrity test. C is incorrect because abnormal behavior could be revealed through a personality test. D is incorrect because mental processing would be the result of a cognitive ability test.

89. ☑ B. This choice is the most expensive because of the high costs associated with the trained assessors using a battery of tests.
☒ A, C, and D are incorrect. These choices are significantly less expensive than assessment centers.

90. ☑ D. Facing a group of interviewers at the same time can be threatening.
☒ A, B, and C are incorrect. Although these are factors to consider, they do not threaten the integrity of the interview.

91. ☑ C. Shaping chairs in a circle or a curved patterns allows for a conversational or free flowing interview.
☒ A, B, and D are incorrect. These options would be uncomfortable and threatening to the employee.

92. ☑ **D.** The main risk is that morale and motivation will become a problem for the employee and employer.

☒ **A, B,** and **C** are incorrect. It is possible for these to happen as a result but it is the not main concern.

93. ☑ **A.** Knowledge, skills, and abilities are very difficult to replace.

☒ **B, C,** and **D** are incorrect. These are possible considerations, but it is not the biggest drawback.

94. ☑ **A.** In an ethnocentric approach to staffing, key positions at home and abroad are staffed by people at the headquarters.

☒ **B, C,** and **D** are incorrect because these describe a polycentric approach to staffing.

95. ☑ **B.** An outplacement firm is a contracted service supplied by companies that specialize in helping employees prepare for job searching after a layoff or job loss.

☒ **A, C,** and **D** are incorrect. **A** is incorrect because a search firm focuses on filling open positions for clients. **C** is incorrect because a brokerage firm is a liaison between a company and service providers. **D** is incorrect because an outsourcing firm is an outside organization that manages functional services for companies.

96. ☑ **D.** A voluntary early retirement program as well as reducing jobs through attrition is less disruptive to the workforce than an involuntary downsizing (reduction in force). When handled well, morale is maintained and the dignity of those who sign up for early retirement is protected.

☒ **A, B,** and **C** are incorrect. **A** is incorrect because offering resume building and interview skills training is a nice thing to do but it does not avoid a downsizing. **B** is incorrect because training managers in supporting those employees who remain in the workplace after a downsizing may not necessarily maintain morale. **C** is incorrect because offering an employee assistance program for those who survive a downsizing may repair poor morale and aid those who are anxious in the workplace, but it does not maintain good morale.

97. ☑ **B.** A human capital assessment of workforce qualities that provide a competitive advantage contributes significantly to a company's objective of competing in the marketplace. Once an assessment of this type is created, a company can plan on developing and deploying staff based on these critical findings.

☒ **A, C,** and **D** are incorrect. **A** is incorrect because a headcount report and staffing plan for customer service operating hours will contribute significantly to the company's objective to raise the competitive advantage bar. **C** is incorrect because while it would be helpful to know why employees are leaving to work for a competitor, it will not contribute significantly because it is reactive in nature. It is true that for retention purposes, it would be helpful to know why employees leave to work for a competitor, but it would not be the type of information to raise the bar in the consumer's eyes. **D** is incorrect because, much like answer C, a comparative compensation and benefits report would aid in retention but not be a significant driver in raising the competitive advantage bar in the consumer's eyes.

98. ☑ **A.** A skills inventory can provide information on prospective internal candidates for promotion opportunities.

☒ **B, C,** and **D** are incorrect. **B** is incorrect because most companies will hire external candidates when they want to set a new leadership direction. **C** is incorrect because creating and maintaining a skills inventory is time-consuming. **D** is incorrect because a skills inventory does require maintenance as employees continue to develop and add new skills.

99. ☑ **C.** The employee orientation is an opportunity to acclimate the new employee to a company's culture, key expectations, and other items that might impede their productivity.

☒ **A, B,** and **D** are incorrect. **A** is incorrect because an application collects contact information and past employment history of a candidate, but it is not an effective tool for reducing a learning curve for a new employee. **B** is incorrect because a skills inventory collects existing skills and does not reduce an employee's time to productivity. **D** is incorrect because while an employee development plan may eventually improve an employee's performance, it would not necessarily reduce the learning curve a new employee faces.

100. ☑ **A.** A tuition reimbursement program that offers to reimburse a portion of an employee's tuition in exchange for an agreement that they will stay with the employer for two years is an example of a retention strategy.

☒ **B, C,** and **D** are incorrect. **B** is incorrect because onboarding is the process that collects information from new employees and prepares them to begin work in the company. **C** is incorrect because orientation introduces an employee to the company culture, key policies, and other important information. **D** is incorrect because recruitment is the location and acquisition of key talent.

101. ☑ **B.** We are all asked the question "What do you do" whether it be at the store or at a family gathering. Providing employees an easy-to-remember elevator speech is an example of an effective employer branding strategy.

☒ **A, C,** and **D** are incorrect. **A** is incorrect because sending out periodic e-mails is not necessarily effective. Not everyone opens their e-mails or does so in a timely fashion. **C** is incorrect because mandatory training is not necessarily effective in empowering employees to speak confidently while off duty about the products or services their company provides. **D** is incorrect because employees may not retain information in department meetings to adequately relay key messages while off duty.

102. ☑ **D.** An employer value proposition is a statement that provides the overall value of working for a company in exchange for the employee's skills, qualifications, and time.

☒ **A, B,** and **C** are incorrect. **A** is incorrect because a product statement proposition relates only to a company's product. **B** is incorrect because it does not apply to the employment proposition. **C** is incorrect because it relates to customers and not the employment proposition.

103. ☑ **B.** In the negotiation/ad hoc negotiation process, the employer and each individual assignee negotiate a mutually acceptable compensation package.

☒ **A, C,** and **D** are incorrect choices.

104. ☑ **A.** The negotiation/ad hoc approach is simple but tends to be relatively costly.

☒ **B, C,** and **D** are incorrect choices.

Human Resource Development

This functional area includes coverage of the following responsibilities and knowledge objectives:

Human Resource Development—Responsibilities Objectives

- **01** Ensure that human resources development activities are compliant with all applicable federal laws and regulations.

- **02** Conduct a needs assessment to identify and establish priorities regarding human resource development activities.

- **03** Develop/select and implement employee training programs (for example: leadership skills, harassment prevention, computer skills) to increase individual and organizational effectiveness.

- **04** Evaluate effectiveness of employee training programs through the use of metrics (for example: participant surveys, pre- and post-testing) (SPHR only).

- **05** Develop, implement, and evaluate talent management programs that include assessing talent, developing career paths, and managing the placement of high-potential employees.

- **06** Develop, select, and evaluate performance appraisal processes (for example: instruments, ranking and rating scales) to increase individual and organizational effectiveness.

- **07** Develop, implement, and evaluate performance management programs and procedures (includes training for evaluators).

- **08** Develop/select, implement, and evaluate programs (for example: telecommuting, diversity initiatives, repatriation) to meet the changing needs of employees and the organization (SPHR only).

- **09** Provide coaching to managers and executives regarding effectively managing organizational talent.

Human Resource Development—Knowledge Objectives

- **27** Applicable federal laws and regulations related to human resources development activities (for example: Title VII, ADA, Title 17 [Copyright law])

- **28** Career development and leadership development theories and applications (for example: succession planning, dual career ladders)

- **29** Organizational development (OD) theories and applications
- **30** Training program development techniques to create general and specialized training programs
- **31** Facilitation techniques, instructional methods, and program delivery mechanisms
- **32** Task/process analysis
- **33** Performance appraisal methods (for example: instruments, ranking and rating scales)
- **34** Performance management methods (for example: goal setting, relationship to compensation, job placements/promotions)
- **35** Applicable global issues (for example: international law, culture, local management approaches/practices, societal norms) (SPHR only)
- **36** Techniques to assess training program effectiveness, including use of applicable metrics (for example: participant surveys, pre- and post-testing)
- **37** Mentoring and executive coaching

Human Resource Development (HRD) is a functional area of Human Resource (HR) that focuses on investing in the human capital strength within an organization. An organization's human capital strength is considered by many to be a competitive advantage in the marketplace.

Human Resource Development (HRD) aligns the right knowledge, skills and abilities, and employee performance to achieve this competitive advantage and to meet the complex demands of the organization's strategic short- and long-term goals. This is done through the use of training and development, performance management, organizational development, and the change management process.

Human Resource Development—Responsibilities Objectives

Objective 01 Ensure That Human Resources Development Activities Are Compliant with All Applicable Federal Laws and Regulations

1. Which of the following is a form of legal protection granted to the ornamental design of a functional item?

   A. Plant patent

   B. Task patent

   C. Design patent

   D. Utility patent

2. Max is looking for training materials for use in his training courses and wants to ensure he is not violating The Copyright Act of 1976. Which of the following training materials would fall under this exception?

   A. Works in the public domain

   B. Works protected under the Fair Use Provision

   C. Work-for-Hire Domain

   D. Works protected under the U.S. Patent Act

3. An IT Developer at Bay Testing, Inc. who has been with the company for five years, has developed code to be utilized for the company's clients. He believes that because he is the creator of the code, he should receive the credit as the author. He has brought his concerns to the HR department. What exception to The Copyright Act should the HR department explain to him regarding The Copyright Act?

   A. Employees who design work in their free time

   B. Works that are covered by the Trademark Act

C. Employer who hires the employee to create the work as part of regular job duties

D. Works that enter the public domain

4. Grace Banks, the HR Manager at Mentor County Schools, needs to ensure that training is provided to all employees in a fair and consistent manner. What is the *primary* reason why Grace has an obligation to ensure training programs are administered fairly and consistently?

   A. Employee engagement could decrease as a result of training.

   B. If they select individuals for training, employers are required to show that they are not discriminating or creating an adverse impact on a particular group of employees.

   C. Employers are required to track all training for participants.

   D. Managers need to have access to all training records.

5. According to The Copyright Act of 1976, copyrights protect original works for the life of the author plus ___ years?

   A. 120

   B. 70

   C. 95

   D. 90

6. Family Resources is a nonprofit that provides back-to-work training resources, specifically CompTIA courses to individuals below the poverty line taught by employees of Family Resources. The organization wants to ensure that they are complying with the Fair Use provision of the U.S. Copyright Act. What is the *best* course of action?

   A. Develop a copyright compliance policy and educate employees on the organization's intent to comply with the law.

   B. Tell trainers they may use copyrighted material without asking for permission because they are a not-for profit organization.

   C. Allow pages of magazines to be copied and used in training but not pages from a book.

   D. Allow trainers to use copyrighted material only for those courses they do not charge for.

Objective 02   Conduct a Needs Assessment to Identify and Establish Priorities Regarding Human Resource Development Activities

7. As Human Capital Director, you realize from employee surveys that there is a major lack of knowledge regarding benefit management. What should be your *first* step in conducting a Needs Assessment for training?

A. Identify goal.

B. Gather data.

C. Analyze data.

D. Propose solutions.

8. The Kids R Fun Learning Center corporate office has tasked the Training Director to gather and analyze organization-specific data for a needs assessment for training. What is the *best* place to gather this information?

A. Online resources

B. Textbooks

C. Customer complaints

D. Turnover rates

9. Stephanie, the CEO and founder of FastJet, an online booking service, is conducting a needs analysis for a training program. She is considering her employees and their learning styles. Stephanie prefers a fast-paced "learn by doing" style and she feels her employees will too. Which of the following styles should she implement?

A. Visual learning style

B. Kinesthetic learning style

C. Auditory learning style

D. Virtual learning style

10. A gap analysis is being conducted by the HR Director in conjunction with a needs analysis at Nationwide Galleries. Which of the following is the most important consideration as it relates to this gap analysis?

A. Identifying constraints that may impede the efforts to close them

B. Lack of support from senior leaders

C. Time and cost involved to fully complete the analysis

D. Lack of long-term focus among senior leaders

11. TriBex is developing a new benefits training program for its staff. The company has decided to start the process by conducting a needs analysis to obtain the necessary information to move forward with the project. What is the *first* question they will want to ask themselves when beginning a needs analysis?

A. What gaps currently need to be fixed?

B. Where do we want to be in one, five, and ten years?

C. Do we have the right people on the team?

D. How will we fill this gap in knowledge?

12. Oats and Such, an organic food distributor is considering implementing a new Point of Sale system. While conducting the needs analysis for developing a new training plan to train all employees on the new POS system, they have discovered that training has already taken place (On the Job Training, OJT) in some areas of the company. After finding out this information, what should the company do next in terms of a needs analysis?

    A. Train additional staff on new POS system.

    B. Design course content, goals, and objectives and determine if the OJT should be used.

    C. Recommend solutions to fill this gap.

    D. Hire a third party to facilitate the training

Objective 03   Develop/Select and Implement Employee Training Programs to Increase Individual and Organizational Effectiveness

13. The payroll department of a company has experienced six months of repeated payroll errors. Two payroll clerks complain that the new payroll software that was implemented nine months ago is the source of the problem. However, the first three months of processing payroll through the new system was not riddled with as many errors as has been consistently observed over the last six months, and the two payroll clerks were recently hired. You suspect that the issue may be a lack of training. Which of the following describes the *best* first step?

    A. Gather/analyze data.

    B. Identify the target audience.

    C. Develop a training objective.

    D. Design training materials.

14. A customer service call center has established a goal of answering customer calls within four rings and 1 percent dropped calls. The Call Center Manager reviewed the statistics of the last three months and determined that, on average, calls are being answered after 20 rings and the drop rate is 7 percent. In discussion with the Call Center Manager, you both conclude that the data is skewed negatively by the response time of second shift employees. If senior management agrees to fund training for this group, this level of training is called:

    A. Task-level training

    B. Organizational-level training

    C. Department-level training

    D. Individual-level training

15. A school district is required by the state to perform fingerprint-based criminal background checks on all incoming employees. They have chosen to purchase a fingerprinting machine and handle the process in-house. Which of the following learning curve *best* describes what the HR employees will experience who are being trained on this repetitive task?

    A. Increasing returns

    B. Plateau

    C. Decreasing returns

    D. S-shaped

16. The corporate office of a national retail store has received several harassment and discrimination complaints in the past three months from the female employees at one location. In addition to investigating, HR has been asked to facilitate company-wide training on all forms of harassment (sexual, bullying, and so on). Which of these choices would be the *best* training delivery mechanism to use for the out-of-state employees?

    A. Classroom training

    B. Blended learning

    C. E-learning

    D. Socratic seminar

17. Teachers are invited to a workshop on the new math curriculum. The training session will require the participants to work in several small groups, simulating lessons using blocks, markers, and an abacus. Which seating arrangement would work *best* in this situation?

    A. Chevron-style

    B. Banquet-style

    C. Conference-style

    D. U-shaped

18. At Trimix Engineering, new maintenance mechanics complete a five-day training session where they dismantle devices using cranes, power tools, and hoists. What training method does this describe?

    A. Vestibule training

    B. Facilitation

    C. Demonstration

    D. Socratic seminar

19. According to HofStede's Value Dimensions, when discussing the masculinity/ femininity dimensions, what important motivational concepts should HR include in its list of needs to be aware of to design a culturally appropriate training programs for feminine cultures?

    A. Feminine cultures value relationships and assertiveness.

    B. Feminine cultures value relationships, quality of life, and clear gender roles.

    C. Feminine cultures value flexible gender roles and ambition.

    D. Feminine cultures value competiveness and flexible gender roles.

20. The training manager seeks to develop new training applications for his workforce. Based on the principle that states that "Adults best benefit from learning experience when they have a need for knowledge," what could the training manager do to apply this principle in his training programs?

    A. Apply training to both current and future needs.

    B. Promote a collaborative learning environment between instructor and participant.

    C. Allow students to participate in planning the training programs.

    D. Incorporate a "what's in it for me concept" in the training programs.

21. Which of the following is the term that describes how adults learn?

    A. Pedagogy

    B. Andragogy

    C. Trainability

    D. Kinesthetic

22. If an HR Manager wanted to positively reinforce employees in a call center for attaining sales goals at a variable ratio, what action would the HR Manager take?

    A. Weekly or monthly paychecks for meetings the sales goals

    B. Piece rate or sales commissions for meeting the sales goals

    C. Give random checks with praise for meeting the sales goals

    D. Give unscheduled positive comments for meeting the sales goals

23. The average experience level of employees at a fast food restaurant chain is 0–1 years. Applying the Hersey-Blanchard Theory, which of the following leadership style would be most successful at motivating this team?

    A. Delegating

    B. Participating

    C. Telling

    D. Selling

24. Which leadership concept uses concern for people and concern for production as measurements to determine quality leadership?

    A. Theory X and Theory Y

    B. Blake-Mouton Managerial Grids

    C. Path-Goal Theory

    D. Fielder's Contingency Theory

25. The research and development team at a car seat manufacturing company is searching for a new leader because of a recent early retirement. The team is highly skilled and generally motivated to produce cutting edge products built on the company's mission to provide the safest child restraint systems in the market place. What type of leader would you advise the CEO recruit for this position?

    A. Authoritarian and transactional

    B. Transformational and directive

    C. *Laissez-faire* and transformational

    D. Transformational and democratic

SPHR Objective 04 Evaluate Effectiveness of Employee Training Programs Through the Use of Metrics (SPHR only)

26. A trainer just completed safety training for 150 employees at a manufacturing plant. At the end of the development session, the trainer hands out a questionnaire. The questionnaire asks the participants what they thought about the training. This describes which training evaluation type?

    A. Learning

    B. Reaction

    C. Results

    D. Behavior

27. A trainer has developed a new customer service development program to achieve organizational customer satisfaction goals. The trainer wishes to measure results of the training. Which of the following measures *best* describes the results evaluation method?

    A. A 360-degree feedback process is implemented after the training program.

    B. An online evaluation was distributed to participants to complete and return.

    C. The number of customer complaints is measured before and after the training.

    D. A test is distributed to participants before and after the training session.

28. An organization has implemented a mandatory service excellence training house-wide. The desire of leadership is to see a change in customer service behavior after the training session. Essentially, they want to see employees smiling more in front of customers. Which question below would *best* measure the success of training?

   A. Is there a change in performance observed in the participant after the training session?

   B. Is there a reduction in customer service complaints after the training session?

   C. Did the participants learn what the intended objectives were in the training session?

   D. Did the participants consider the training relevant and a good use of their time?

Objective 05   Develop, Implement, and Evaluate Talent Management Programs That Include Assessing Talent, Developing Career Paths, and Managing the Placement of High-Potential Employees

29. Prior to rolling out training on the use of the new Point of Sale (POS) system to all 50 stores, a beauty supply store decides to train just those employees at its Pennsylvania location. Attendees are asked to evaluate the effectiveness of the training session and HR uses their feedback to make modifications to future training sessions. Which of the following *best* describes this type of evaluation?

   A. Summative evaluation

   B. Trainer evaluation

   C. Formative evaluation

   D. Results evaluation

30. After the completion of a six-module computer-based test, participants are asked to complete a 30-minute online test. What aspect of summative evaluation is this?

   A. Learning

   B. Behavior

   C. Results

   D. Reaction

31. The HR Department at Concorde International Airlines has developed a series of training workshops for new flight attendants. Training will be delivered by local HR representatives across 4 continents and 38 countries. To ensure that training delivery is consistent across the company, senior management has decided to

gather all trainers at the Dallas, Texas training facility and conduct train-the-trainer sessions. Which stage of the ADDIE model is HR currently in?

A. Design

B. Delivery

C. Implementation

D. Development

32. In an effort to improve turnover, senior management has tasked HR with shifting its recruitment strategy to include more internal candidates promoted into mid to senior level positions even if there are no present openings. HR has decided to survey entry-level employees to determine if there is an interest in moving into leadership positions and develop a mentorship program for these individuals. HR also reviewed the most recent employee engagement surveys and found that entry-level employees wanted a more positive environment and better benefits package. HR then took steps to address those concerns. Which answer *best* describes the kind of program HR developed?

A. Knowledge management program

B. Succession planning program

C. Career pathing program

D. Talent management program

33. The board of Genoa Corporation determined that they are in need of a formal succession plan. Twenty percent of the senior management team will be retiring within the next 10 years. Which of the following is the *best* first step in the succession planning process?

A. Identify competencies in key leaders.

B. Select the high-potential members who will participate in succession planning.

C. Interview and select a member for the new leadership position.

D. Determine the key leaders for whom successors will be needed.

34. During the development phase of the purchase order module training of a financial software implementation, it was determined that participants would be secretly observed while doing their jobs at set intervals of 6 and 12 weeks. Trainers would use this information to determine if training was effective and what supplemental training would need to be developed. What level of summative evaluation is described here?

A. Learning

B. Results

C. Behavior

D. Reaction

35. HR is in the process of revamping the management trainee program for a rental car company. HR decides that a case study should be required and that trainees would work on it as a group. Which stage of the ADDIE model is HR currently in?

A. Design

B. Development

C. Analysis

D. Implementation

Objective 06   Develop, Select, and Evaluate Performance Appraisal Processes to Increase Individual and Organizational Effectiveness

36. An evaluation rater maintains a log of behavioral incidents that represent both effective and ineffective performance for each employee. This is an example of what type of performance appraisal method?

A. Critical incident

B. Behavior observation

C. Paired comparison

D. Forced distribution

37. An employee exhibits outstanding performance in customer friendliness. However, this employee does not perform well in any other category such as timely reports, attendance, or teamwork. The performance evaluator assigns a high overall rating on this employee's appraisal. This describes what type of appraisal error?

A. Leniency error

B. Halo effect

C. Regency of events

D. Central tendency

38. An evaluator is given a set of traits and asked to rate the employee on each of them. The available ratings range from 1 to 5. For example, a rating of 1 represents unsatisfactory performance. A rating of 5 represents outstanding performance. Which of the following does this appraisal method best describe?

A. Paired comparison

B. Behavior observation

C. Forced distribution

D. Graphic rating scale

39. An organization values feedback as part of the overall performance appraisal process. However, the leaders do not want to rely only on the supervisor to provide feedback on performance. Which appraisal process would *best* meet the performance appraisal objectives of this business?

   A. Behavior observation

   B. Paired comparison

   C. 360-degree feedback

   D. Critical incident

40. An organization has several objectives that must be met in the following year. As part of the appraisal process, goals have been developed for each employee of the company. Employees will participate in establishing these goals. Each of the employee's goals will be based on the organization's overall objectives. Which of the following *best* describes this appraisal method?

   A. Behavior observation

   B. Forced ranking

   C. Management by objectives

   D. Paired comparison

41. An evaluator writes explanations of an employee's weaknesses and strengths and provides recommendations for improvement. The written explanations include examples of behavior and performance. Which of the following appraisal methods most typically characterize this approach?

   A. Narrative essays

   B. Management by objectives

   C. Critical incident

   D. Ranking method

Objective 07   Develop, Implement, and Evaluate Performance Management Programs and Procedures

42. At Laureate Linguistics, LLC mid-level managers are evaluated annually. This year HR and senior management decide that in order to get an objective view of each mid-level manager's performance, the tool used should include feedback from all stakeholders (vendors, direct reports, coworkers, and so on). Which of these evaluation formats would *best* support this goal?

   A. Management by Objectives (MBO) review

   B. Ratings scale

   C. 360-Degree review

   D. Peer review

43. At Global Integration Systems, the Chief Technology Officer notices that the IT department supervisors are consistently retaining Level 1 Technicians whose performance is perceived as below average by the end users they support. HR is asked to review the Level 1 Technician job description and the prior two years of performance reviews. The evaluations reveal that the items the technicians are appraised on are generally not related to their job descriptions or the expectations of the end users. HR is tasked with developing a new evaluation tool that appropriately rates and ranks the competencies Level 1 Technicians are expected to master. Which of the following appraisal tools would be the *best* choice to achieve this goal?

    A. Rating scale

    B. Behaviorally anchored rating scale (BARS)

    C. Ranking method

    D. Narrative method

44. After only two months as a Sales Representative at Transamerica Flotation, Gina exceeded her sales goals by 200 percent. Since that time, she has vacillated between 60 to 70 percent of her overall sales goals. However, the Sales Manager consistently rates Gina as significantly exceeding expectations on performance evaluations. Which *best* describes this type of rater bias?

    A. Halo effect

    B. Positive leniency

    C. Recency effect

    D. Horn effect

45. Sandoval Automotive employs 15,000 employees across 17 states. HR is asked to come up with a performance appraisal format that will help senior management quickly identify top performers and lowest performers. The goal of this assessment tool is to identify those employees who are potential prospects for future management and those employees who are detrimental to Sandoval's financial success. The lowest performers would be terminated in an effort to manage involuntary turnover. Which comparison method would *best* address this need?

    A. Forced ranking

    B. Ranking

    C. Paired comparison

    D. Narrative method

46. Leslie is the Marketing Director of a mid-sized sports marketing firm. She supervises a copy editor and two marketing specialists. Leslie meets with her employees at the beginning of their performance periods to establish mutually

agreeable annual performance standards in line with her company's goals. In the past 12 months, one of Leslie's marketing specialists conducted herself in an unprofessional manner at least twice at a client worksite. As a result, Leslie issued a verbal warning and two written warnings to this specialist. Leslie received positive feedback several times regarding the work performed by her other specialist and the copy editor during the same period. Leslie is now drafting the annual performance appraisals for her three employees using the feedback she received over the past year. Leslie's actions reflect her performance _____ role, a key element in her company's talent management program.

    A. Review

    B. Management

    C. Evaluation

    D. Appraisal

47. R2 Linguistic Masters has experienced significant growth without a formalized performance appraisal process, which has resulted in employee performance issues. HR has been directed to implement a formalized appraisal program and conduct supervisory training prior to its implementation. What are the key elements that should be addressed in this training?

    A. Overall company strategic goals

    B. Supplemental training courses for employees who rank low on certain performance criteria in the appraisal

    C. Types of performance appraisal tools, whether used by the company or not

    D. Purpose of performance reviews, review of common rater errors and acceptable methods, or providing feedback

SPHR Objective 08   Develop/Select, Implement, and Evaluate Programs to Meet the Changing Needs of Employees and the Organization (SPHR only)

48. An organization wants to explore implementing a telecommuting program. You have been asked to evaluate and provide recommendations on which job position would be ideal for a telecommuting program. What type of job would fit the ideal criteria for a telecommuting program?

    A. Receptionist

    B. Transcriptionist

    C. Manufacturer

    D. Retail clerk

49. You are preparing a business case for the senior leadership team on implementing a diversity program. Which of the following is one of the key strategic advantages of implementing an effective diversity program?

A. It will enhance compliance with EEOC workplace requirements.

B. Employees are less likely to file complaints based on discrimination.

C. It will satisfy corporate social responsibility requirements.

D. It will increase market share and a satisfied diverse customer base.

50. A global business found that turnover rates are high for repatriates. Many of the reasons cited for leaving the company include high stress, lack of support upon return to their home country, and reverse culture shock. Which strategy would *best* reduce reverse culture shock for repatriates?

A. Provide top-down news updates for the repatriate employees.

B. Provide training for both the repatriate and family members.

C. Provide a promotion for the returning employee.

D. Provide housing options for the returning employee.

Objective 09   Provide Coaching to Managers and Executives Regarding Effectively Managing Organizational Talent

51. A department head chooses to motivate employees by promising rewards or the threat of discipline. This leadership style is known as which of the following?

A. Micromanaging

B. *Laissez-faire*

C. Transactional

D. Talent management

52. A leadership development initiative of a company is to improve leaders' emotional intelligence (EI). Part of the development program includes an assignment that will help improve emotional intelligence for each of the leaders. Which of the following will most likely be included in that development assignment?

A. Practice putting yourself in others' shoes and listening

B. Attendance at all holiday parties and company picnics

C. Speaking up more at meetings to show you're engaged

D. Showing emotion when an issue or conflict arises

53. An organization focuses its development activities based on what good leaders do. This includes the study of autocratic, democratic, or *laissez-faire* leadership styles. What type of leadership theory is most likely adopted?

A. Contingency

B. Behavioral

C. Trait

D. Power and influence

54. An organization has decided that transformational leadership will be a key development focus enterprise-wide. Which of the following is a key component of transformational leadership?

A. Control

B. Discipline

C. Influence

D. Position

55. An organization has adopted a mentorship program as part of an ongoing commitment to leadership development. Of the following choices, which would be considered essential to an effective mentorship program?

A. The mentee picks the mentor from a list of choices.

B. The mentor has time to spend with a mentee.

C. The company allocates budget dollars to the program.

D. The company has a long-term commitment to the program.

56. A manager is in need of an interactive process aimed to resolve performance issues and further develop capabilities. Which of the following strategies would be most appropriate to implement?

A. Mentoring

B. Coaching

C. Performance management

D. Development

Human Resource Development—Knowledge Objectives

Objective 27 Applicable Federal Laws and Regulations Related to Human Resources Development Activities

57. The recently revised job description of an Administrative Assistant III at the Unified School District of Montage, which has 6500 employees, lists as one of the essential functions that applicants must be able to lift up to 50 pounds. Jonathon is a 56-year-old Administrative Assistant II who was denied a promotion to Administrative Assistant III because of his medically supported inability to lift over

10 pounds. His performance evaluations over the past 15 years have been average to above average and there are other Administrative Assistant IIIs with various documented limitations that the school district has made accommodations for. Which of the following laws would be *most* applicable in this case?

A. Title VII of the Civil Rights Act of 1964

B. Americans with Disabilities Act

C. Age Discrimination in Employment Act of 1967

D. Fair Labor Standards Act of 1938

58. Made law in 2009, this Act resets the 180-day statute of limitations regarding pay discrimination lawsuits to commence with the issuance of each paycheck deemed discriminatory.

A. Equal Pay Act

B. Fair Labor Standards Act

C. Lily Ledbetter Fair Pay Act

D. Equal Pay for Equal Work Act

59. Sarah works for International Visions Publishing as a travel writer. She recently authored a book for ex-pats on relocating and opening a restaurant in Paraguay. Who is the owner of the copyright?

A. Sarah, because she is the original author of the work

B. International Visions Publishing who paid Sarah for this work as a part of her normal job duties

C. The Paraguay government due to an agreement with International Visions Publishing

D. Sarah, because no one can replicate the original works of an author without their permission

Objective 28   Career Development and Leadership Development Theories and Applications

60. The CEO of a company decided to commit time and resources to a succession plan. There had not been a succession plan in previous years. Which of the following steps should be first in a systematic succession plan process?

A. Identify the long-term vision and direction.

B. Identify core and technical competencies.

C. Identify talent with critical competencies.

D. Identify recruitment and retention strategies.

61. A technology organization wants to develop and motivate its staff. However, upward mobility into managerial or supervisory roles is limited. Instead, it has created an alternate career path that includes the ability to achieve levels of mastery within each employee's technical field. Employees can achieve higher levels by learning specific new skills. This is an example of what type of career development plan?

    A. Education career ladder

    B. Leadership career path

    C. Dual career ladder

    D. Development career path

62. A company has every management position filled with qualified individuals. The opportunity for promotion is limited. In order to engage and develop employees, leadership decided to create a career development opportunity that would enable employees to move from one field to another within the same company. Which of the following defines this career development technique?

    A. Purpose-centered career path (project based)

    B. Cross-functional career path (multi-functional)

    C. Job-centered career path (job rotation)

    D. Single functional career path (subject matter expert)

Objective 29   Organizational Development (OD) Theories and Applications

63. A CEO has uncovered an internal process that is leading to employee and customer dissatisfaction. He has communicated the reasons why change needs to take place to his senior staff. Which of the following describes what stage of Change Process Theory the company is currently in?

    A. Moving

    B. Unfreezing

    C. Refreezing

    D. Communication

64. As an HR Professional at StarSpen Publishing, Inc., your company is acquiring many smaller companies to merge with your larger company. Employees are hesitant and resistant to change for a variety of reasons. Productivity and morale are suffering because of this. As an HR professional, what is the *first* step in helping the change process?

    A. Talk to employees about their concerns after the change has taken place.

    B. Work with senior leaders to develop new policies.

C. Develop focus groups with employees and provide abundant communication prior to any changes taking place.

D. Understand hesitation in the change process.

65. What is the most important task an HR Manager can do during a change initiative?

A. Listen to employee concerns.

B. Act as a change agent to balance needs of employees and senior leadership.

C. Work with supervisory staff to communicate change to employees.

D. Discuss changes with senior leadership.

Objective 30 Training Program Development Techniques to Create General and Specialized Training Programs

66. A growing IT company is interested in expanding the skill set of entry-level employees. What is the *first* call to action before beginning a training program?

A. Find out the root cause of the organizational problem and analyze if training is an appropriate solution.

B. Balance HR budget to ensure proper funds are available.

C. Ask employees which training is needed.

D. Access organization for system defects.

67. Mary Ann, a sales representative with an outstanding track record of exceeding sales goals, is suddenly seeing a decrease in sales with new products. As the HR Manager, you are tasked with finding out the root cause of the decrease in sales. When analyzing the situation, you begin looking at all factors that may have contributed to the decrease in sales. What is the most likely explanation of this occurrence?

A. The sales quota has been increased by 40 percent.

B. A new product has been introduced to market and product training has not occurred for sales staff.

C. Mary Ann's employee engagement has decreased.

D. The company has hired a new CEO.

68. The ADDIE Model is an acronym that describes the five elements of ____ design?

A. Training

B. Interactive

C. Development

D. Instructional

69. As an organization's HR leader, you decided it is time to create an effective leadership development program. To ensure adult learning effectiveness, you want the development program to leverage top adult learning characteristics. Which of the following represent top adult learning characteristics?

   A. Self-directedness, experience, readiness to learn, orientation to learning, and motivation to learn

   B. Self-actualization, self-esteem and achievement, sense of love and belonging, sense of safety and security, physiological needs met

   C. Openness to experience, conscientiousness, extrovert/introvert, agreeableness, sensitivity

   D. Flexibility, communication style, courage, leadership presence, accountability, and responsibility

70. A corporate training professional is designing a new leadership development program. The trainer wishes to implement elements of the andragogical (adult) learning theory into the program. Which of the following would most likely be a part of the new development program?

   A. Meet with supervisors and ensure buy-in for the leadership development program.

   B. Create an evaluation that asks supervisors how they feel about quality of the training.

   C. Involve participants in diagnosing their own need for learning and setting objectives.

   D. Develop metrics and a balanced scorecard that measures the effectiveness of training.

71. An organization wants to motivate employees in all levels of the Maslow Hierarchy of needs. Which of the following actions would appeal to employees in a self-actualized level of motivation?

   A. Provide opportunities to join small groups and teams.

   B. Provide challenging projects and responsibilities.

   C. Provide competitive salary and opportunities to save money.

   D. Provide employee feedback opportunities on workplace hazards.

Objective 31   Facilitation Techniques, Instructional Methods, and Program Delivery Mechanisms

72. A small, remote nonprofit college is offering career training courses to the general public. Because of its remote location, sometimes Internet connectivity can be a problem. The school anticipates 10–15 students per training course. Based on this information, what would be the *best* Program Delivery Mechanism?

A. Self study

B. Classroom training

C. Blended learning

D. Computer-based training

73. Christian, a Senior Marketing Analyst, is leading a workshop entitled "Cutting Edge Practices in Digital Marketing" at which he will need to train a large audience of approximately 150 participants. Which of the following would be the *best* instructional method to use?

A. Demonstration

B. Group discussion

C. Case study

D. Presentation

74. Under which circumstances would banquet-style seating be best used?

A. Participants will be taking part in small group discussions.

B. Participants are listening to presentations and taking notes.

C. Lectures, videos, or films are being used.

D. When food is served to a large group of people.

Objective 32   Task/Process Analysis

75. The VP of HR is trying to show the Board of Director the impact that absenteeism has on company performance. Which of the following would be the *best* illustration of these two variables?

A. Histogram

B. Process-flow analysis

C. Control chart

D. Scatter diagram

76. A Pareto principle states that:

A. 70 percent of effects come from 30 percent of causes.

B. 90 percent of effects come from 10 percent of causes.

C. 80 percent of effects come from 20 percent of causes.

D. 60 percent of effects come from 40 percent of causes.

77. A task inventory includes which of 9 the following items?

A. Tasks needed for the position

B. Education needed for the position

C. Skills needed for the position

D. Knowledge needed for the position

Objective 33   Performance Appraisal Methods

78. Which of the following is a comparative method of performance appraisal?

A. Rating scale

B. Critical incident

C. Ranking

D. BARS

79. An evaluation method that uses 1) Unsatisfactory 2) Fair 3) Satisfactory 4) Good 5) Excellent to evaluate an employee is an example of what kind of performance appraisal method?

A. Ranking

B. Checklist

C. Comparison

D. Graphic rating scale

80. The Superintendent of the Division of Planning & Natural Resources has decided that the traditional performance evaluation tool for his Cabinet members does not effectively capture their overall value to the department's strategic goals. He has asked you as the HR Manager to develop a tool that allows him more of an opportunity to expound on these key employees' strengths and weaknesses. The tool will be implemented during the next performance evaluation cycle. Which of the following performance appraisal methods would *best* meet the Superintendent's needs?

A. Essay

B. BARS

C. Forced comparison

D. Checklist

Objective 34   Performance Management Methods

81. When setting a SMART performance goal for performance reviews, what does the acronym SMART stand for?

A. Specific, Measurable, Attainable, Realistic, and Timely

B. Smart, Measurable, Attainable, Relevant, and Timely

C. Specific, Measurable, Accurate, Relevant, and Timely

D. Specific, Measurable, Attainable, Relevant, and Timely

82. On a recent employee survey, it was revealed that employees wanted a more effective and fair performance management process when it came to job promotions. As the HR Manager, you have been tasked to improve the current performance management system. What would be the most effective way to accomplish this goal?

   A. Give employees 360 reviews to assess peer performance.

   B. Implement twice-yearly performance feedback.

   C. Organize a focus group to address the issue and provide feedback to management.

   D. Offer ongoing performance management throughout the year.

83. At XYZ Aero , Inc., the company is growing at a steady pace and hiring on average 10 new employees each year. Understanding that growth means new employees will be hired, the company places greater importance on setting goals in relation to performance management. What is the *best* approach for setting goals in Performance Management to obtain the company's overall goals?

   A. The employee's personal goals are discussed in conjunction with department goals.

   B. The manager tells the employee which goals should be focused on for the year.

   C. The manager and employee agree on development goals and jointly create a goal to achieve those plans.

   D. Goals are decided upon by peers during a 360-degree review.

▄▄ SPHR ▄▄ Objective 35   Applicable Global Issues (SPHR only)

84. An organization headquartered in the United States has just set up locations in countries outside of the U.S. However, employees in various countries are not responding to its communications. In some cases international employees have found some of the communications coming from headquarters offensive. You have been asked to audit the communication strategy and provide recommendations to improve effectiveness. Which of the following actions would contribute the *most* in an effective international communication plan?

   A. Provide a list of all U.S. analogies, terminology, and their meanings to employees and managers.

   B. Implement an across the board translation of every written and oral communication for employees and managers.

   C. Remove U.S.-based analogies (i.e., football) and localize the communication style to each country.

   D. Provide mandatory training for all employees to learn about United States culture and analogies.

85. A perfume company expanded its operations to Brazil. The expatriate managers decided to market Camellia flower–scented perfume. However, the managers didn't realize the Camellia flower is used for funerals. The product launch failed. What type of strategy could help prevent this outcome?

A. Product training

B. Cultural training

C. Diversity training

D. Management training

86. What are Geert Hofstede's five cultural dimensions?

A. Power distance, individualism, masculinity, uncertainty avoidance, and long-term organization.

B. Power distance, individualism, discrimination prevention, uncertainty avoidance, and long-term organization.

C. Power distance, team building, discrimination prevention, uncertainty avoidance, and long term organization.

D. Power distance, individualism, masculinity, long-term job security, and long-term organization.

87. A company that is headquartered in the United States but also outsources products and employees to India is investigating ways to provide motivational training for its international staff. What issue should HR address first when designing a training program for its international staff?

A. Motivation models of western cultures cannot be assumed in other cultures.

B. Language translations need to be considered when developing its course materials.

C. Work ethic and lifestyles may be different among eastern cultures.

D. Training materials will need to be multilingual in order to accommodate language barriers.

Objective 36 Techniques to Assess Training Program Effectiveness, Including Use of Applicable Metrics

88. Which of the following would be *most* effective in evaluating training effectiveness?

A. Small group discussion

B. Large group discussion

C. Measurement of enhanced job performance

D. Grade in training program

89. Your company has tasked the training department to determine if and what learning has occurred after the in-depth four-week series on "Achieving Customer Satisfaction." Which of the following would the *best* method in measuring if and what learning has actually taken place?

   A. Pre/post test

   B. Group discussion

   C. Lower turnover rates

   D. Increased employee morale

90. The HR Manager at a mid-size software company is conducting a training evaluation after new product training that recently took place. She is analyzing data from observations, interviews, tests, and surveys to see if new skills were successfully transferred to the job. The analysis she is completing is an example of_____ evaluation?

   A. Behavior

   B. Results

   C. Learning

   D. Reaction

Objective 37   Mentoring and Executive Coaching

91. A company has adopted a development program where mentors and mentees self-select on the basis of personal chemistry. Goals are not set and outcomes are not measured. Access is limited. The focus is exclusively on the mentee. The mentoring relationship typically lasts for many years. Which of the following defines this type of mentorship program?

   A. Informal

   B. Formal

   C. Social

   D. Developmental

92. Paul, a leader within an organization is friendly and motivated. He enjoys his work and his performance exceeds most expectations. However, feedback from staff indicates that when Paul is under pressure his communication style becomes direct and inpatient. As a result, his relationship with team members has deteriorated. You are asked to provide a recommendation to resolve this issue. What action would contribute significantly in resolving the issue?

A. Terminate Paul's employment because the team is dissatisfied with his communication style when under pressure.

B. Assign Paul to an executive coach that will help him identify better communication choices while under pressure.

C. Provide Paul with a disciplinary or corrective action plan calling his attention to a poor communication style.

D. Meet with Paul privately and praise his overall performance and ask him to improve his communication style.

1. C	24. B	47. D	70. D
2. A	25. D	48. B	71. A
3. C	26. B	49. D	72. D
4. B	27. C	50. B	73. C
5. B	28. A	51. C	74. A
6. A	29. C	52. A	75. C
7. A	30. A	53. B	76. A
8. C	31. C	54. C	77. C
9. B	32. D	55. D	78. B
10. A	33. D	56. B	79. D
11. A	34. B	57. B	80. A
12. B	35. A	58. C	81. A
13. A	36. A	59. B	82. C
14. A	37. B	60. A	83. C
15. C	38. D	61. C	84. C
16. C	39. C	62. B	85. B
17. D	40. C	63. B	86. A
18. A	41. A	64. C	87. A
19. B	42. C	65. B	88. C
20. D	43. B	66. A	89. A
21. B	44. A	67. B	90. A
22. C	45. A	68. D	91. A
23. C	46. B	69. B	92. B

1. ☑ **C.** A design patent is a legal protection granted for the ornamental design of a functional item

   ☒ **A, B,** and **D** are incorrect. **A** is incorrect because a plant patent protects asexually reproduced variety of plants. **B** is incorrect because a task patent is not a viable option in this question. **D** is incorrect because a utility patent protects new processes, machines, manufacture, or composition of matter.

2. ☑ **A.** Works that are in the public domain do not require permission to be used.

   ☒ **B, C,** and **D** are incorrect. These choices do not accurately reflect the circumstances that do not require permission to be used.

3. ☑ **C.** The Copyright Act of 1976 allows for an exception for employers who hire employees to create the original works as part of their normal job duties.

   ☒ **A, B,** and **D** are incorrect because they are not exceptions as part of The Copyright Act of 1976.

4. ☑ **B.** According to the Title VII of the Civil Rights Act of 1964, employers are required to prohibit discrimination based on color, race, religion, national origin, and gender in all aspects of employment, including selection for training.

   ☒ **A, C,** and **D** are incorrect. These choices are incorrect because while they may be applicable to the organization, they are not the most important reason to ensure that training programs are administered fairly.

5. ☑ **B.** Copyrights protect original works for the life of the author plus 70 years.

   ☒ **A, C,** and **D** are incorrect. **A** is incorrect because 120 years reflects the protection given to work-for-hire creations. **C** is incorrect because works for hire are protected for 95 years from the first year of publication. **D** is incorrect because 90 years is not a correct option for this question.

6. ☑ **A.** To stay compliant, an organization must develop a copyright policy and train employees on the intent and expectation that the organization will comply with the law.

   ☒ **B, C,** and **D** are incorrect. **B** is incorrect because nonprofit organizations are not exempt from copyright laws. **C** is incorrect because the fair use provision will only cover an excerpt that is extremely short and a magazine article would not always qualify under that doctrine. Also, pages from a book cannot be copied and used without permission. **D** is incorrect because it is untrue that just because you are not charging for a training course that you can use copyrighted material at your discretion.

7. ☑ **A.** Identifying a goal is the first step in beginning the needs assessment process.

   ☒ **B, C,** and **D** are incorrect. **B** is incorrect because gathering data is the second step in the needs analysis process. **C** is incorrect because analyzing data is part of the second step in conducting a needs analysis. **D** is incorrect because proposing solutions is the third step in the needs analysis process.

Chapter 4: Human Resource Development

8. ☑ **C.** Customer complaints can be a great source of organization specific defect information

☒ **A, B, and D are incorrect.** A and B are incorrect because these choices would not provide specific organization data. D is incorrect because turnover rates would be specific to the organization but would not point to specific training opportunities.

9. ☑ **B.** Kinesthetic learners learn by trying and completing tasks hands on.

☒ **A, C, and D are incorrect.** A is incorrect because visual learners learn by seeing or reading the information. C is incorrect because auditory learners learn by hearing the information. D is incorrect because virtual learning does not apply to this example.

10. ☑ **A.** It is extremely important to identify constraints early on that impede the process as it will help you to understand what roadblocks lie ahead.

☒ **B, C, and D are incorrect** because all are considerations in the gap analysis but A is the most important consideration.

11. ☑ **A.** Asking "What gaps need to be fixed?" is the first step in a needs analysis.

☒ **B, C, and D are incorrect** because asking "Where do we want to be in the future?" is the second step. The questions "Do we have the right people on the team" and "How do we fill this knowledge gap?" are all subsequent steps when conducting a needs analysis.

12. ☑ **B.** The next step would be to determine course content, goals, and objectives, and to determine if they should include the OJT training after the goals and objectives have been decided upon.

☒ **A, C, and D are incorrect.** A is incorrect because training staff on the POS system would be the last step. C is incorrect because recommending solutions cannot take place until you fully understand where the gaps lie. D is incorrect because hiring a third party would be premature at this stage given that you are unsure of where the gaps lie.

13. ☑ **A.** Gathering/analyzing data is contained within the first phase of the ADDIE model. In this phase, data is collected to identify gaps between actual and desired organizational performance.

☒ **B, C, and D are incorrect.** B and D are incorrect because identifying the target audience takes place during the design phase of ADDIE and designing training materials happens after assessment. C is incorrect because training objectives are statements with measureable outcomes that are established during the design stage of instructional design.

14. ☑ **A.** Task-level training is designed to address a single process in a single job category. The call center is experiencing a significantly higher than normal rate of dropped calls during the second shift. These employees need to be retrained on answering calls within the company-set goal of four rings.

☒ **B, C, and D are incorrect.** B and C are incorrect because organizational-level training would be delivered to the entire company or the entire department.

In this case, training is targeted to second-shift employees only. **D** is incorrect because individual-level training would focus on one employee's performance and need for assistance in a particular area.

15. ☑ **C.** Decreasing returns are representative of repetitive tasks. Once HR employees learn how to properly fingerprint a candidate, they will repeat the same steps. There is a rapid increase in learning in the beginning, and then learning slows down over time.

☒ **A, B,** and **D** are incorrect. **A** is incorrect because increasing returns occur when the comprehension of the learner starts off slowly, but as the learner gains more familiarity, she is able to complete more complex tasks. An example would be an entry-level computer technician learning how to write software programs. **B** is incorrect because a plateau learning curve occurs when there is a rapid increase in learning that eventually levels off. In the scenario, if there is an HR employee who fingerprints a new candidate only five times a year, the HR employee may know the steps but never become proficient. **D** is incorrect because an S-shaped learning curve is a combination of the positive and negative learning curve. This occurs when an employee learns quickly in the beginning and then learning tapers and then picks up again.

16. ☑ **C.** E-learning is best for companies where employees are located at multiple sites or work remotely. Computer-based training is a blend of presentations, simulations, and one-on-ones.

☒ **A, B,** and **D** are incorrect. **A** is incorrect because classroom training requires that all trainees gather in the same location. Either the company would have to send trainers to various locations or transport trainees to a central training site. **B** is incorrect because blended learning utilizes several methods of delivery. The instructor-led portions of blended learning training would be challenging to deliver to remote employees. **D** is incorrect because a Socratic seminar is a method of instruction rather than a delivery mechanism. It requires that trainees all be in the same location to benefit from training.

17. ☑ **D.** Small U-shaped groups would be a better method because all participants have a clear view of the facilitator throughout the training. A U-shaped setting maintains a better connection throughout the training between participants and the facilitator and vice versa while still providing excellent contact between participants in each U-shaped setting.

☒ **A, B,** and **C** are incorrect. **A** is incorrect because a chevron style works best when the participants have some interaction with the trainer and some interaction with each other in several activities, including lecture, audiovisual presentations, and some small group activities. **B** is incorrect because a banquet-style setup allows for interaction of the participants in small groups but will leave some participants with their backs to the facilitator. **C** is incorrect because a conference style is best when the training session is run by a facilitator, and visual aids are not primarily used.

18. ☑ **A.** Vestibule training is simulated training used primarily when participants will be handling dangerous or hazardous materials.

☒ **B, C, and D are incorrect. B** is incorrect because facilitation is used for small groups where there is a moderator who guides the group discussion while participants solve problems. **C** is incorrect because demonstration is a form of on-the-job training where the trainer demonstrates the activity, and then the trainee performs the same task with the guidance of the trainer. **D** is incorrect because a Socratic seminar is an active training method that involves the trainer posing a question to a group at the beginning of the session. Participants then discuss amongst themselves to gain an understanding of the topic. It is modeled after the Greek philosopher Socrates.

19. ☑ **B.** Feminine cultures place more value on relationships, quality of life, and clear gender roles than male cultures.

☒ **A, C, and D are incorrect.** Assertiveness, ambition, and competitiveness are male values.

20. ☑ **D.** The need of adults to seek out a learning experience when they have a need to be taught, including "What's in it for me" techniques, will improve training results.

☒ **A, B, and C are incorrect** because none of them address the principle that adults best benefit from the learning experience when they have a need for knowledge.

21. ☑ **B.** Andragogy is the discipline that studies adult learning.

☒ **A, C, and D are incorrect. A** is incorrect because pedagogy is the study of education of children. **C** is incorrect because trainability is the interaction between forces within the individual and the environment. **D** is incorrect because that choice is not applicable in this question.

22. ☑ **C.** Variable ratio would be giving reinforcement after a random number of responses, for example, random checks with praise.

☒ **A, B, and D are incorrect. A** is incorrect because this would be an example of a fixed interval reinforcement schedule. **B** is incorrect because this would be an example of a fixed ratio reinforcement schedule. **D** is incorrect because this would be an example of variable interval.

23. ☑ **C.** The Hershey-Blanchard Theory purports that leadership should be guided by the maturity level of those being led. Telling works best when the followers lack experience. The leader provides direct guidance to the team.

☒ **A, B, and D are incorrect. A** is incorrect because delegating works best when the team is experienced and self-motivated. The leader's role here is to articulate the goal and ensure accountability. **B** is incorrect because participating works best when the team is experienced but may not be self-motivated. A leader in this instance must provide support to the team to keep them motivated and focused on the goal. **D** is incorrect because selling works best when the team is motivated but may not be as experienced. The leader in this situation spends a great deal of time being motivational and supportive to help the team maintain the confidence needed to achieve the goal.

24. ☑ **B**. The Blake-Mouton Managerial Grid is a situational theory that uses nine levels, with (1,1) representing the leader who does not care about people or production. This extreme represents the worst kind of manager. At the other end of the spectrum, (9,9) represents a leader who shows equal concern for people and production. According to Blake and Mouton, this is the best kind of leader.

    ☒ **A, C,** and **D** are incorrect. **A** is incorrect because Douglas McGregor's Theory X and Theory Y is a behavioral theory that measures two traits: the behavior of focusing only on the rules and regulations of a job (X) versus the people's needs of the job (Y). **C** is incorrect because the Path-Goal Theory is a situational theory that suggests that leaders can affect the behavior of the team by focusing on goal setting and supporting the team to reach those goals. Depending on the situation, a leader could adapt one of four styles: directive, supportive, participative, or achievement. **D** is incorrect because Fielder's Contingency Theory approaches leadership development from the position that leaders have particular styles already so it is imperative that a company identify the situations where a leader would be most effective and place the leader into those team situations. The situations are grouped into three areas: leader-member relations, task structure, and position power.

25. ☑ **D**. Transformational and democratic leadership styles are inspiring to followers. These styles support the innovative and idealistic thought needed to foster a research and development team's goal of producing the safest child restraint systems on the market. Transformational and democratic leaders care about the interpersonal work relationships and leverage them to achieve desired results.

    ☒ **A, B,** and **C** are incorrect. **A** and **B** are incorrect because an authoritative/directive style is best in situations where a quick decisive response is needed. This would work best in a military setting or for first responders like 911 operations or firefighters. This style does not encourage innovative or independent thought. Further, transactional leaders focus rules and seek out opportunities to discipline those not following the rules. This strict adherence to rules and lack of support for independent thought would not work well in this situation. **C** is incorrect because a *laissez-faire* style normally results in low production levels. This style doesn't support the focus needed to achieve the best in market results this company seeks.

26. ☑ **B**. Reaction is the correct answer. Measuring training effectiveness by asking participants how they felt about the training is called a reaction type of evaluation. This method is also called "happy sheets" or "feedback forms."

☒ A, C, and D are incorrect. A is incorrect because the learning evaluation type tests to find out to what extent participants gained knowledge or skills. C is incorrect because the results training evaluation looks at the tangible outcomes of training such as reduced costs, reduced customer complaints, increased sales, or increased quality. D is incorrect because the behavior training evaluation seeks to answer what changes in performance have occurred after training.

27. ☑ C. Capturing a before and after picture of the number of customer complaints is a results training evaluation type. Using key performance indicators such as customer complaints is a popular method of measuring training effectiveness.

☒ A, B, and D are incorrect. A is incorrect because the 360-degree feedback is typically used to measure behavior after the training session. B is incorrect because it measures a participant's impression of the training, which is associated with the reaction evaluation type. D is incorrect because pre- and post-tests are typically used for the learning evaluation method.

28. ☑ A. This method measures behavior changes after the training is complete, which is consistent with the behavior evaluation method.

☒ B, C, and D are incorrect. B is incorrect because this question is answered by using the results evaluation method. C is incorrect because this question is answered by using the learning evaluation method. D is incorrect because this question is answered by using the reaction evaluation method.

29. ☑ C. Formative evaluation is done during the design phase of instructional design. It involves participants taking part in a training session and providing feedback. The evaluations are then reviewed and the feedback used to modify future training sessions.

☒ A, B, and D are incorrect. A is incorrect because summative evaluations happen at the conclusion of training. They may be at the reaction, learning, behavior, or results level. B is incorrect because trainer evaluation refers to the assessment of the trainer's delivery. D is incorrect because results evaluation is a method that compares an objective statement to an end result.

30. ☑ A. The learning evaluation method involves administering a test to participants to determine if participants learned the material presented. It does not measure improvements in job performance due to training.

☒ B, C, and D are incorrect. B is incorrect because the behavior evaluation method measures training effectiveness at predetermined intervals. This does tell the trainer if training transferred to effectiveness on the job. C is incorrect because the results evaluation method measures training effectiveness at predetermined intervals and what effect the training had on actual business performance. This also tells the trainer if training transferred to effectiveness on the job. D is incorrect because the reaction evaluation method involves providing participants with a survey immediately after the completion of training. It does not measure improvements in job performance due to training.

31. ☑ C. The implementation phase is where all of the preceding work of identifying training needs, and designing and developing training comes together. If the trainer sessions are determined to be necessary, they would take place in this phase.

    ☒ A, B, and D are incorrect. A is incorrect because during the design phase the trainer is engaged in activities such as determining who the target audience is and developing the training objectives. B and D are incorrect because during the development phase the method(s) of delivery are determined and the presentation is developed. The instructional designer is involved in activities such as compiling manuals, setting up the content of case studies, and preparing handouts.

32. ☑ D. A talent management program is the strategic and integrated approach an organization takes to ensure that the company has a continuous supply of quality individuals to fill the right jobs at the right time. An effective plan considers an employee's professional goals, company culture, and overall compensation plans.

    ☒ A, B, and C are incorrect. A is incorrect because knowledge management is focused on creating systems that allow the organization to create and easily access knowledge needed to run the organization. B is incorrect because succession planning is an aspect of a talent management program. It is heavily focused on training and developing internal talent. C is incorrect because career-pathing is sometimes employee driven. Employees determine their desired career path within an organization. Then management collaboratively with HR determines what knowledge, skills, and abilities are necessary for the employee to achieve the desired progress in her/his career.

33. ☑ D. The steps in the succession planning process are 1) Determine the key leaders for whom successors will be needed, 2) Identify competencies in key leaders, 3) Select the high-potential members who will participate in succession planning, 4) Interview and select a member for the new leadership position, and 5) Evaluate succession planning efforts and make changes.

    ☒ A, B, and C are incorrect. All of the choices listed are steps in the succession planning process. The question asks you to identify the first step, which is to determine which key leaders will need successors.

34. ☑ B. The results evaluation method measures training effectiveness at predetermined intervals and what effect the training had on actual business performance. This also tells the trainer if training transferred to effectiveness on the job.

    ☒ A, C, and D are incorrect. A is incorrect because the learning evaluation method involves administering a test to participants to determine if participants learned the material presented. It does not measure improvements in job performance due to training. C is incorrect because the behavior evaluation method measures training effectiveness at predetermined intervals. This does not tell the trainer if training transferred to effectiveness on the job.

D is incorrect because the reaction evaluation method involves providing participants with a survey immediately after the completion of training. It does not measure improvements in job performance due to training.

35. ☑ **A.** During the design phase, the instructional designer is involved in activities related to determining which tasks participants need training on, determining activities for the three learning styles—auditory, kinesthetic, visual—and developing materials and content. In this case, HR has decided that one of the delivery methods for this training program will be a case study.

☒ **B, C,** and **D** are incorrect. **B** is incorrect because during the development phase materials are either developed or purchased. **C** is incorrect because the analysis phase is the needs assessment phase. The end result is a proposal that includes a current status, goals, and desired outcome of training. **D** is incorrect because the implementation phase is when all the prior activities in instructional design meet and training is actually delivered to participants. It is characterized by selecting the training facility, selecting and training the trainers, and establishing the training schedule.

36. ☑ **A.** This example best describes the critical incident appraisal method. The critical incident method refers to when a rater uses a log to record both effective and ineffective behavioral incidents.

☒ **B, C,** and **D** are incorrect. **B** is incorrect because behavior observation refers to when an evaluator observes performance during a specific time and does not necessarily use a log (critical incident) method throughout the year. **C** is incorrect because a paired comparison rates each employee with another employee in the form of pairs. **D** is incorrect because force distribution assumes performance conforms to a normal distribution. The rater is compelled to distribute employees throughout a scale.

37. ☑ **B.** Halo effect is the correct answer. The halo effect is a bias that is most likely to occur when a rater assigns high overall ratings based on one area the employee may excel in, ignoring other performance flaws.

☒ **A, C,** and **D** are incorrect. **A** is incorrect because leniency describes when a rater always gives a favorable rating no matter the reality of performance. Be careful because leniency can be easily confused with the halo effect. Halo effect is based on assumptions of character while leniency is always rated favorably no matter the belief of character. **C** is incorrect because regency of events refers to when a rater forgets past performance or incidents and may be only focused on current events. **D** is incorrect because central tendency refers to leaning toward just selecting average ratings regardless of performance.

38. ☑ **D.** A graphic rating scale is used when an evaluator is given a set of traits and asked to rate the employee on each of them. Typically, the ratings are on a scale of 1 to 3 or 5. In some cases, the ratings may be on a "meets" or "does not meet expectations" scale.

☒ **A, B,** and **C** are incorrect. **A** is incorrect because a paired comparison rating compares one employee with another as a pair. **B** is incorrect because behavior observation refers to when an evaluator rates behavior during a period of time. **C** is incorrect because a forced distribution assumes performance falls within a normal distribution and compels the evaluator to assign ratings within a scale.

39. ☑ **C.** The 360-degree feedback is the ideal method. This method collects feedback from not only the employee's supervisor but also from peers and internal customers of the employee.

☒ **A, B,** and **D** are incorrect. **A** is incorrect because behavior observation does rely on the observations of one evaluator. **B** is incorrect because a paired comparison relies on the observation of one evaluator. **D** is incorrect because a critical incident evaluation method relies on the observation of one evaluator.

40. ☑ **C.** Management by objectives, also known as MBO, correctly describes this appraisal method. Managing by objectives typically focuses on *what* and *how many* goals were achieved versus a focus on *how* they were achieved.

☒ **A, B,** and **D** are incorrect. **A** is incorrect because a behavior observation method of evaluation does not necessarily involve the employees in setting goals as the management by objective (MBO) method does. **B** is incorrect because forced ranking involves a predetermined scale of performance expectations and does involve goal setting. **D** is incorrect because paired comparison does not involve the employees in goal setting.

41. ☑ **A.** Narrative essays are a characteristic of the narrative essay appraisal method. This method allows a short essay describing the performance of the employee. Ordinarily, the appraiser is given several topic areas for comment. A limitation of this method is that appraisers have varying writing skills, which can affect the quality of the appraisal.

☒ **B, C,** and **D** are incorrect. **B** is incorrect because management by objectives does not provide the same opportunity for narrative comment on an employee's performance. **C** is incorrect because a critical incident method reports on observed behavior and not on a set of topic ideas for comment. **D** is incorrect because a ranking method does not include narrative essays on set topic ideas.

42. ☑ **C.** The 360-degree review uses feedback from others to assess the employee. The process is intended to solicit input from vendors, internal and external customers, subordinates, and coworkers.

☒ **A, B,** and **D** are incorrect. **A** is incorrect because the Management by Objectives (MBO) review, made popular by Peter Drucker, requires that managers and employees agree on a specific set of goals and set a deadline to reach those goals. Then the employee has the responsibility of working toward achieving those goals. **B** is incorrect because the ratings scale format requires the employer to set up an intricate grading system for employee performance and the ratings are used to determine employee success or failure in a variety of areas. **D** is incorrect because peer reviews are the type of review where employees review each other.

43. ☑ **B.** A behaviorally anchored rating scale (BARS) utilizes the job description to establish the most important behaviors for doing a job properly. For example, a BARS review method for a receptionist position would include an anchor statement similar to "Answers phone within four rings" rather than "Answers phone promptly." Once the behaviors are established, a numerical scale is established to measure how well or how poorly the employee exhibits those essential behaviors.

☒ **A, C, and D** are incorrect. A is incorrect because rating scales set a value that is used to differentiate levels of performance. The value may be narrative or numeric. An example of a narrative value would be statements similar to "…significantly exceeds expectations, meets expectations, and does not meet expectations." C is incorrect because the ranking method lists employees in order from highest to lowest performers. D is incorrect because narrative methods summarize employee performance through short essays or a summary of critical incidents that have taken place over the review period.

44. ☑ **A.** The halo effect is a bias that happens when an employee extremely competent in one area is therefore rated high in all areas.

☒ **B, C, and D** are incorrect. B is incorrect because positive leniency occurs when the evaluator wants to rate everyone on the team highly. C is incorrect because the recency effect happens when the evaluator rates an employee highly based on a recent success as opposed to the totality of the employee's performance throughout the evaluation period. D is incorrect because the horn effect is a bias that occurs when the evaluator views the employee as a poor performer based on a limited event rather than the totality of the employee's performance throughout the evaluation period.

45. ☑ **A.** Forced ranking requires managers to rank employees along a bell curve. As an example, a small number are always to be ranked highly (20 percent), a small number ranked poorly (10 percent), and most employees ranked as average. This helps management quickly identify which employees perform in accordance with the company's strategic goals and which employees are a strategic liability while recognizing that most employees are adequate.

☒ **B, C, and D** are incorrect. B is incorrect because ranking means that employees are listed in order from worst to best performer. This comparison method does not work well for large groups. C is incorrect because paired comparison is a performance appraisal method that compares each employee in a group to the other employees of that group one at a time. D is incorrect because the narrative method requires that managers describe an employee's performance in written form.

46. ☑ **B.** Performance management is the continuous process of providing employees with both positive and negative feedback regarding their performance as it relates to the organization's strategic goals.

☒ **A**, **C**, and **D** are incorrect because performance review, performance evaluation, and performance appraisal are all used interchangeably to describe the annual review document where a manager summarizes the employee's performance over the course of the evaluation period.

47. ☑ **D**. The purpose of the performance review, a review of common biases (rater errors), and acceptable ways to provide feedback to employees are all important elements of a good evaluator training program. Often, employees dread performance reviews but properly trained, the evaluators may at least allow for an effective evaluation process.

☒ **A**, **B**, and **C** are incorrect. **A** is incorrect because the question asks for the most key element of an effective evaluator training session on performance evaluations. It is always good to review the company's overall strategic goals and how they align with the stated objectives in the performance evaluation but choice **D** states the key elements most thoroughly. **B** is incorrect because again it is encouraged that the evaluator be aware of solutions to potential performance issues such as recommending Microsoft Word training to an administrative assistant who is not maximizing use of the software program. However, the question as stated is asking for the most key elements of an evaluator training, which suggests a high-level analysis of the purpose of this type of training session. **C** is incorrect because the training sessions should focus, in part, on the evaluation tools being utilized by the company as opposed to an exhaustive list of appraisal tools and methods on the market.

48. ☑ **B**. Transcription is an ideal job for telecommuting because it is a role that can be done alone and independent of a physical location.

☒ **A**, **C**, and **D** are incorrect. **A** is incorrect because a receptionist is required to perform job duties at a specific physical location. **C** is incorrect because a manufacturer also has job duties that are required to be performed at a specific physical location. **D** is incorrect because, like in A and C, the duties of a retail clerk are tied to a specific physical location.

49. ☑ **D**. A key strategic advantage of implementing an effective diversity program is that it can increase market share and a satisfied customer base.

☒ **A**, **B**, and **C** are incorrect. **A** is incorrect because enhanced compliance with EEOC is not a key strategic advantage of implementing a diversity program. **B** is incorrect because not only is it not necessarily true that employees will be less likely to file discrimination complaints, but it does not add a significant strategic advantage. **C** is incorrect because while compliance and social responsibility measures benefit the organization, they do not provide a strategic advantage.

50. ☑ **B**. To provide training for both the repatriate and family members is the best strategy to ease reverse culture shock. The open forum enables employees and family members to express concerns and discuss how they are feeling about the return. In addition, the most effective training enables a process for the employee to transfer newly learned knowledge while on assignment.

☒ A, C, and D are incorrect. A is incorrect because providing top-down communication is not adequate in addressing reverse culture shock. C is incorrect because providing a promotion is not practical and it is not adequate in addressing reverse culture shock. D is incorrect because providing housing options does not address reverse culture shock that repatriation might cause.

51. ☑ C. The leadership style that motivates employees by promise of reward or threat of discipline is also called transactional.

☒ A, B, and D are incorrect. A is incorrect because micromanaging is an excessive control of details. This answer does not relate to the transaction leadership style. B is incorrect because *laissez-faire* refers to easing back on control and letting things take their own course. This leadership style relies heavily on delegation. D is incorrect because talent management refers to planning and addressing human capital needs within an organization. This does not adequately define the leadership style of using promises and threats to motivate employees.

52. ☑ A. A key component of emotional intelligence is to have the ability to show empathy and listen to others. Practicing placing yourself in another's shoes or listening goes a long way toward improving emotional intelligence.

☒ B, C, and D are incorrect. B is incorrect because attending parties does not rise to the definition of social intelligence. C is incorrect because being vocal at a meeting does not necessarily mean that a manager possesses social intelligence. Knowing when silence or speech is necessary in a given situation is a mark of emotional intelligence. D is incorrect because simply being emotional does not necessarily reflect emotional intelligence.

53. ☑ B. Behavioral leadership theories focus on what good leaders do. Studies on autocratic, democratic, or *laissez-faire* leaders fit into the behavioral theory of leadership development.

☒ A, C, and D are incorrect. A is incorrect because the contingency leadership style focuses on different environmental variables that influence leadership style. This focuses on environmental influences and not on what good leaders do. C is incorrect because the trait theory assumes individuals inherit qualities that make them a better leader. This theory focuses on inherited traits and not on what good leaders do. D is incorrect because the power and influence theory focuses on the source of the leader's influence.

54. ☑ C. A transformational leader motivates through influence. This style of leader uses inspiration, character, and commitment to motivate others. It is thought that this style of leadership is the most effective in today's business era.

☒ A, B, and D are incorrect. A is incorrect because control represents a transactional leader. B is incorrect because discipline represents a transactional leader. D is incorrect because position represents a transactional leader.

55. ☑ D. A mentorship program is a deliberate process that takes time. A long-term commitment to any mentorship program is critical for its success.

☒ A, B, and C are incorrect. A is incorrect because the option of having a mentee pick a mentor is not a critical contributor to long-term success of a mentorship program. B is incorrect because a mentor can make time if there is buy-in on the program. C is incorrect because having a budget is not the most critical factor of a long-term mentorship program.

56. ☑ B. Coaching is the interactive process by which performance issues are resolved or capabilities are further developed. Coaching is focused on correcting inappropriate behavior and is a short-term approach.

☒ A, C, and D are incorrect. A is incorrect because mentorship is someone helping another individual learn skills or concepts that they otherwise would not have been able to learn on their own. Coaching is a subset of mentorship. Mentorship is a long-term approach to someone's development and addresses overall career development. C is incorrect because performance management is a description that fits under the coaching definition. D is incorrect because development is a description that fits under the coaching definition.

57. ☑ B. Title I of the American with Disabilities Act requires employers with 15 or more employees to provide qualified individuals with disabilities an equal opportunity to benefit from the full range of employment-related opportunities available to others. It requires that employers make reasonable accommodation to the known physical or mental limitations of otherwise qualified individuals with disabilities, unless it results in undue hardship.

☒ A, C, and D are incorrect. A is incorrect because Title VII of the Civil Rights Act of 1964 does not mention disabled Americans. It prohibits unlawful employment practices with respect to race, color, religion, sex, or national origin. C is incorrect because if Jonathon were being denied this promotion due to age then the Age Discrimination in Employment Act of 1967 may be applicable. The Act prohibits denial of promotions and other unlawful employment practices on the basis of a person's age. D is incorrect because the Fair Labor Standards Act of 1938 establishes minimum wage, overtime pay, recordkeeping, and youth employment standards affecting all full-time and part-time workers in the private sector and in Federal, State, and local governments. The Act makes no mention of employees with disabilities specifically.

58. ☑ C. The Lily Ledbetter Fair Pay Act was the first bill that President Barack Obama signed into law. Prior to this, the statute of limitations for bringing a lawsuit regarding equal pay was 180 days from the date of the original discriminatory incident.

☒ A, B, and D are incorrect. A is incorrect because the Equal Pay Act of 1963 prohibits discrimination on account of sex in the payment of wages by employers engaged in commerce or in the production of goods and services. B is incorrect because the Fair Labor Standards Act of 1938 establishes minimum wage, overtime pay, recordkeeping, and youth employment standards affecting all full-time and part-time workers in the private sector and in Federal, State, and local governments. D is incorrect because there is not a statute named the Equal Pay for Equal Work Act.

59. ☑ **B.** International Visions Publishing paid Sarah for this work as a part of her normal job duties. An exception to The Copyright Act of 1976 is that when an employee creates original work in the normal course of their duties, the employer is the owner of the copyright.

☒ A, C, and D are incorrect because of the reasons stated above.

60. ☑ **A.** Identifying the long-term vision and direction is an important first step to any succession planning process. Succession planning must be steered in the direction that is aligned with the long-term vision and values of a company.

☒ B, C, and D are incorrect. B is incorrect because identifying core and technical competencies is not the first step in a systematic succession planning process. C is incorrect because identifying talent with critical competencies is not the first step in developing a systematic succession plan. D is incorrect because identifying recruitment and retention strategies is not the first step in developing a systematic succession plan.

61. ☑ **C.** A dual career ladder is an alternate career path that enables upward mobility or mastery within the employee's technical field.

☒ A, B, and D are incorrect. A is incorrect because this is not an adequate definition of dual career path. B is incorrect because the essence of a dual career path is that it provides an alternate development path to leadership or supervisory roles. D is incorrect because a development career path is not an adequate definition of a dual career path.

62. ☑ **B.** A cross-function career path moves individuals from function or field to another function or field. This technique enables employees to gain a broader scope of the business and keep them engaged despite limitations in promotion opportunities.

☒ A, C, and D are incorrect. A is incorrect because a purpose center career path refers to those who remain in their primary position, but will work on various projects that appeal to their interests. An example of this method is at Lockheed Martin, which provides a list of current projects to attract key talent. C is incorrect because it is job- or task-focused. D is incorrect because this refers to when individuals remain in their area of expertise such as information technology or engineering.

63. ☑ **B.** The unfreezing stage creates the motivation for change by identifying and communicating the need for change.

☒ A, C, and D are incorrect. A is incorrect because the moving stage refers to when resistance is examined and managed. C is incorrect because the refreezing stage refers to adjusting to the new norm, and the outcome is evaluated. D is incorrect because the communication stage is not part of the Change Process Theory.

64. ☑ C. Communication through focus groups with staff will help prepare and enable employees to get used to the change gradually and build commitment to the process.

☒ A, B, and D are incorrect because although they are plausible options and helpful during the change management process, communication prior to change will help the change process most effectively and should be the first step.

65. ☑ B. Acting as a change agent to move the process forward and balance the needs of the organization and the staff will ultimately be the greatest asset to the change management process.

☒ A, C, and D are incorrect. A is incorrect because while listening to employee concerns is important, it is not the most important task in this process. C is incorrect because working with supervisory staff is an important aspect of the process, but it is not the most important task. D is incorrect because discussing the changes with senior leadership is important but is not the most important task in the process.

66. ☑ A. Deciding if training is indeed the proper solution to the problem is the first step.

☒ B, C, and D are incorrect because all of the steps are crucial before beginning a training program, but A is the number one consideration before beginning a training program.

67. ☑ B. Most likely Mary Ann has not received the proper product training to be able to position her product to market appropriately.

☒ A, C, and D are incorrect because all are possible choices but not the most likely explanation of this occurrence.

68. ☑ D. The ADDIE model is an acronym that describes five elements of Instructional Design.

☒ A, B, and C are incorrect because they do not accurately define what an ADDIE model is.

69. ☑ A. Malcolm Knowles is known for the adoption of andragogy—the study of adult learning theory. Knowles identified five characteristics of adult learning: self-directed, experience, readiness to learn, orientation to learning, and motivation to learn.

☒ B, C, and D are incorrect. B is incorrect because self-actualization, self-esteem and achievement, love and belonging, safety and security, and physiology are the motivation levels of Maslow's hierarchy of needs. C is incorrect because openness to experience, conscientiousness, extrovertedness and introvertedness, agreeableness, and sensitivity are communication styles. D is incorrect because flexibility, communication style, courage, leadership presence, accountability and responsibility are leadership styles.

70. ☑ **C.** Involving participants in diagnosing their own need for learning and setting learning objectives is one of the key elements of andragogical (adult) learning theory. This is a key differentiator from the pedagogical model, which is the art and science of teaching children. In the pedagogical model, the teacher assumes all responsibility for learning, such as determining what, how, and when it will be learned.

☒ **A, B, and D are incorrect. A** is incorrect because while achieving leadership buy-in on learning initiatives is important, this is not a key element of andragogical learning. **B** is incorrect because initiating an evaluation process is how learning can be measured but not one of the key elements of andragogical learning. **D** is incorrect because developing metrics and a balanced scorecard is a way to monitor learning effectiveness but is not one of the key elements of andragogical learning.

71. ☑ **B.** A self-actualized individual has all other needs met, such as safety and belongingness, and seeks to be challenged. Providing challenging projects and responsibilities is a key motivator for those in the self-actualized level of Maslow's hierarchy of needs.

☒ **A, C, and D are incorrect. A** is incorrect because providing the opportunity to join small groups or teams appeals to those in the love and belonging level of motivation. **C** is incorrect because providing a competitive salary and teaching skills for saving money appeal to those in the physiological level of motivation. **D** is incorrect because providing employee feedback opportunities on workplace hazards would appeal to those in the safety and security level of motivation.

72. ☑ **B.** Because the group is relatively small and some participants do not have access to the Internet, classroom training would be the best because it does not rely on technology and because classroom training works best with a smaller group.

☒ **A, C, and D are incorrect. A** is incorrect because in self study the learning is directed entirely by the learner. **C** is incorrect because blended learning encompasses multiple ways to enhance learning, one of which is web-based learning. Because some participants may not have access to the Internet, this choice would not be possible. **D** is incorrect because of the potential problems with Internet access; computer-based training would not be possible.

73. ☑ **D.** Presentation style will allow Christian to disseminate the same information to a large group of people at a time.

☒ **A, B, and C are incorrect. A** is incorrect because a demonstration method would require the learner to perform it under the guidance of the trainer and that would not be possible in a large group setting. **B** is incorrect because a group discussion would not be as effective as a presentation as the audience is too large to accommodate that. **C** is incorrect because a case study lets participants investigate, study, and analyze the data with a group of participants.

In the case of a large number of participants, it would not be possible to do such an analysis.

74. ☑ **A.** Banquet-style seating is best used when participants are invited in small group discussion and activities.

☒ **B, C,** and **D** are incorrect. **B** is incorrect because training where participants are taking notes and listening to presentations lends itself better to classroom-style seating. **C** is incorrect because training where lecture and videos are used works best with theater-style seating. **D** is incorrect because this choice is not relative to any of the seating style choices.

75. ☑ **D.** The best way to illustrate a possible relationships between two variables is a scatter diagram.

☒ **A, B,** and **C** are incorrect. **A** is correct because a histogram is the graphic representation of a single type of measurement. **B** is incorrect because a process-flow analysis is a diagram of all the steps involved. **C** is incorrect because a control chart is an illustration of variations from normal in a situation over time.

76. ☑ **C.** The Pareto principle states that 80 percent of effects come from 20 percent of causes.

☒ **A, B,** and **D** are incorrect because they are not the correct percentages in terms of the Pareto principle.

77. ☑ **A.** Tasks are included as part of the task inventory.

☒ **B, C,** and **D** are incorrect because these options are not part of a task inventory.

78. ☑ **C.** Ranking, paired comparison, and forced ranking are all comparative methods of performance appraisals.

☒ **A, B,** and **D** are incorrect. **A** is incorrect because rating scales are a rating method. **B** is incorrect because critical incident is a narrative method. **D** is incorrect because behaviorally anchored rating scales (BARS) are a behavioral review method.

79. ☑ **D.** Graphic rating scales are the oldest, and probably most popular, performance appraisal method. They assign a simple rating (for example, 1–5, or significantly exceeds through does not meet expectations) to employee performance.

☒ **A, B,** and **C** are incorrect. **A** is incorrect because the ranking method lists employees from lowest to best performer. **B** is incorrect because a checklist is a list of phrases on the performance appraisal tool. The evaluator simply checks off those phrases that best describe the employee. **C** is incorrect because the comparison is used to describe several performance appraisal methods that are based on comparing employees to one another in some way.

80. ☑ **A.** An essay format would give the Superintendent the most flexibility of the choices listed. It is also subjective but if managed well can be a useful tool in communicating the areas that the Superintendent views as most important to the success of the person in the role.

☒ **B, C,** and **D** are incorrect. **B** is incorrect because behaviorally anchored rating scales (BARS) offers rating scales for actual behaviors that exemplify various levels of performance. **C** is incorrect because forced comparison places employees on a bell curve with a small number noted as top performers, a small number noted as poor performers, and most employees noted as average performers. **D** is incorrect because a checklist is a list of phrases on the performance appraisal tool. The evaluator simply checks off those phrases that best describe the employee.

81. ☑ **A.** The correct definition of a SMART goal is Specific, Measurable, Attainable, Realistic, and Timely.
    ☒ **B, C,** and **D** are incorrect. While these choices could be part of a well-defined goal, Relevant, Smart, and Accurate are not part of the SMART goal parameters.

82. ☑ **C.** Designing an employee focus group to address problems to report back to management is the most effective way to improve the current performance management process.
    ☒ **A, B,** and **D** are incorrect. **A** is incorrect because 360-degree feedback is important to the performance management process but because of appraisal bias it is not the most effective way to improve a performance management process. **B** and **D** are incorrect because even though increasing the frequency of feedback is important to performance management, neither of them is the most effective way to improve a performance management process.

83. ☑ **C.** Aligning the organizational, department, and personal goals will help to ensure that organization-wide goals are understood by each employee, therefore resulting in a higher functioning organization.
    ☒ **A, B,** and **D** are incorrect. **A** is incorrect because although important to include an employee's personal goals and department goals, goals also need to be aligned with organization-wide goals. **B** is incorrect because it is critical that the employees participate in the setting of goals so they maintain a commitment to achieve them. **D** is incorrect because 360-degree reviews are a part of the performance goals process but not the best overall approach to helping the company with overall organization goals.

84. ☑ **C.** Removing headquarters analogies and localizing the communication style for each country will contribute significantly to effective international communication strategies. This action addresses local cultural norms and ensures effective communication in each foreign country.
    ☒ **A, B,** and **D** are incorrect. **A** is incorrect because while providing a list of home country analogies and culture references may help a little, it does not take into account local cultural norms and will not significantly contribute to an effective communication plan. **B** is incorrect because an across-the-board translation does not account for local cultural norms and may still contribute to a confusing message. **D** is incorrect because it does not take into account local cultural norms.

85. ☑ **B.** Cultural training is the best answer. If the expatriate managers were trained on Brazil's culture, they could have avoided this product launch mistake.

☒ **A, C, and D are incorrect.** A is incorrect because this situation is not so much about a product as it is about cultural awareness. C is incorrect because diversity training relates to expanding your understanding of employee differences. This does not relate to the situation in Brazil. D is incorrect because "management training" is an overly broad term and does not adequately describe the need for cultural training.

86. ☑ **A.** Geert Hofstede's five cultural dimensions are power distance, individualism, masculinity, uncertainty avoidance, and long-term organization. This is a cultural awareness framework that many companies base their training on for expatriates who are preparing to enter foreign countries.

☒ **B, C, and D are incorrect.** B is incorrect because discrimination prevention is not part of the Geert Hofstede's five cultural dimensions. C is incorrect because team building is not part of the Geert Hofstede's five cultural dimensions. D is incorrect because long-term job security is not part of the Geert Hofstede's five cultural dimensions.

87. ☑ **A.** Western approaches to adult motivation such as Maslow's Hierarchy of Needs theory cannot be assumed among different cultures. Values and motivation factors need to be studied and understood for each region.

☒ **B, C, and D are incorrect.** They do not address adult learning theory and motivation factors. Although these are factors to consider, they are not the first concern for HR.

88. ☑ **C.** Measurement of enhanced job performance is the best way to measure training effectiveness as it can quantifiably measure the desired outcome of the training.

☒ **A, B, and D are incorrect.** A and B are incorrect because large and small group discussion cannot be quantifiably measured as a desired outcome of training. D is incorrect because one's grade in a training program is not necessarily a valid indicator of training success; it is merely an indicator of how well a participant can study rather than what they learned.

89. ☑ **A.** Pre/post test is the most effective way to evaluate as it measures knowledge before the training took place and then measures knowledge after training has taken place.

☒ **B, C, and D are incorrect.** B is incorrect because a group discussion is not an effective way to evaluate effectiveness; it is subjective and not quantifiable. C is incorrect because lower turnover rates could mean that learning has taken place but it is likely a small percentage of the reason why lower turnover is occurring. D is incorrect because employee morale could be due to a multitude of things, not an effect of learning conducted by the training program.

90. ☑ **A.** Conducting observations, interviews, tests, and surveys describes the Behavior evaluation method.

☒ **B, C,** and **D** are incorrect. **B** is incorrect because an example of the Results evaluation method is "a 20 percent decrease in customer complaints over a 12-month period," which answers the question of whether training had an impact on business results. **C** is incorrect because an example of Learning evaluation is a pre/post test that answers the question of whether learning took place. **D** is incorrect because an example of Reaction evaluation is measuring the initial reaction of the training participants. It doesn't measure organization impact but provides feedback for the trainer as far as presentation of the material.

91. ☑ **A.** An informal mentorship program typically doesn't have outlined goals and measures. In addition, mentors and mentees will engage in a self-selecting process based on personal chemistry.

☒ **B, C,** and **D** are incorrect. **B** is incorrect because this does not define an informal program. It requires a formal matching of mentor to mentee and measures that indicate success or failure of the program. **C** is incorrect because the term "social" is not the same thing as an informal mentorship program. **D** is incorrect because the term "developmental" does not adequately define an informal mentorship program.

92. ☑ **B.** Assigning Paul to an executive coach who will help him identify better communication choices while under pressure is a more effective option in achieving long-term results. In addition, this will help an otherwise high-performing employee to build a strong team.

☒ **A, C,** and **D** are incorrect. **A** is incorrect because terminating this employee will result in a loss of an otherwise high-performing employee. **C** is incorrect because a disciplinary track can create more pressure while not providing tools and resources to succeed. **D** is incorrect because this option does not provide tools or resources to succeed. The issue with communication is coachable.

CHAPTER 5

Compensation and Benefits

This functional area includes coverage of the following responsibilities and knowledge objectives.

Compensation and Benefits—Responsibilities Objectives

- **01** Ensure that compensation and benefits programs are compliant with applicable federal laws and regulations.
- **02** Develop, implement, and evaluate compensation policies/programs (for example: pay structures, performance-based pay, internal and external equity).
- **03** Manage payroll-related information (for example: new hires, adjustments, terminations).
- **04** Manage outsourced compensation and benefits components (for example: payroll vendors, COBRA administration, employee recognition vendors). (PHR only.)
- **05** Conduct compensation and benefits programs needs assessments (for example: benchmarking, employee surveys, trend analysis).
- **06** Develop/select, implement/administer, update, and evaluate benefit programs (for example: health and welfare, wellness, retirement, stock purchase).
- **07** Communicate and train the workforce in the compensation and benefits programs, policies, and processes (for example: self-service technologies).
- **08** Develop/select, implement/administer, update, and evaluate an ethically sound executive compensation program (for example: stock options, bonuses, supplemental retirement plans) (SPHR only).
- **09** Develop, implement/administer, and evaluate expatriate and foreign national compensation and benefits program. (SPHR only).

Compensation and Benefits—Knowledge Objectives

- **38** Applicable federal laws and regulations related to compensation, benefits, and tax (for example: FLSA, ERISA, FMLA, USERRA)
- **39** Compensation and benefits strategies
- **40** Budgeting and accounting practices related to compensation and benefits
- **41** Job evaluation methods
- **42** Job pricing and pay structures
- **43** External labor markets and/or economic factors

- **44** Pay programs (for example: variable, merit)
- **45** Executive compensation methods (SPHR only)
- **46** Noncash compensation methods (for example: equity programs, noncash rewards)
- **47** Benefits programs (for example: health and welfare, retirement, Employee Assistance Programs [EAPs])
- **48** International compensation laws and practices (for example: expatriate compensation, entitlements, choice of law codes) (SPHR only)
- **49** Fiduciary responsibilities related to compensation and benefits

Objective

Compensation and benefits play a critical role within the human resource function in an organization. They are also closely related to the accounting and payroll function within an organization. Therefore, understanding accounting practices related to payroll, compensation strategies, and benefit administration is also required to master this skill set. Human resources professionals must understand how to design, develop, and implement sound compensation and benefits practices. Human Resources professionals must also be cognizant of federal and state requirements while ensuring best practices of compensation and benefit administration programs.

It is vital that human resources professionals understand that in today's global economy, compensation and benefits are critical to ensuring that an organization is able to attract and retain the best candidates possible for their organization. Compensation and benefits can be of high cost to an organization; therefore, this human resources function is of overall importance to the bottom line of an organization.

Compensation and Benefits—Responsibilities Objectives

Objective 01   Ensure That Compensation and Benefits Programs Are Compliant with Applicable Federal Laws and Regulations

1. The payroll manager is auditing the Fair Labor Standards Act policies and procedures. According to the Fair Labor Standards Act, in order for an employee to be exempt, what does the payroll manager need to ensure?

   A. Make sure they are not being paid overtime

   B. Be paid a minimum salary of no less than $455 per week

   C. Be paid a minimum salary of no less than $650 per week

   D. That the employee has been with the company for at least one year

2. To qualify for the administrative exemption under the Fair Labor Standards Act, what must an HR department ensure for those employees?

   A. Have a primary duty involving performance or office work directly related to the management or general business operations of the employer or the employers customers

   B. Have a primary duty involving management of an enterprise

   C. Direct the work of at least two more full-time employees

   D. Have the authority to hire and fire other employees

3. The HR Director at a growing energy company in Colorado is designing a new pay-for-performance plan. The federal law requires a minimum wage of $7.25 and the state of Colorado requires a minimum wage of $7.78. How should the HR Director establish base pay rates for these employees?

   A. HR should establish the base pay rate at $7.51 to split the difference between the state and federal rates.

   B. HR should establish base pay rate at $7.78 because the state the employee works in will always prevail.

   C. HR should establish base pay rates at $7.25 because the federal rate always supersedes the state rate.

   D. HR should establish base pay rates at $7.78 because this most benefits the employee.

4. Which of the following laws states that the statute of limitations on pay discrimination lawsuits resets as each alleged discriminatory paycheck is issued?

   A. Lily Ledbetter Fair Pay Act

   B. Equal Pay Act

   C. Davis-Bacon Act

   D. Copeland "Anti- Kickback" Act

5. In calculating regular wages, in what situations must the accounting manager pay all non-exempt employees?

   A. The employee arrives to work an hour early in an effort to beat the traffic.

   B. An employee has an hour commute to and from the office and wants to be compensated for that time.

   C. An employee's shift begins at 10 a.m., but on the day of a snow storm, he spends 8–9 a.m. waiting to hear if the company will be open.

   D. An employee's shift begins at 8 a.m., but she must wait until 9 a.m. to begin work because she must wait for the product to arrive to be able to inspect it.

6. What is the main tenet an HR Manager should focus on when deciding if an individual is an employee or an independent contractor?

   A. The nature and degree of control retained by the employer

   B. How much per hour the individual is making

   C. The performance of the individual

   D. How many years of experience the individual has

Objective 02 Develop, Implement, and Evaluate Compensation Policies/Programs

7. A charter school has had challenges retaining exemplary employees. The charter school's current compensation program provides a 1.5 percent pay increase each year up to five years and then a 4 percent increase per year for all employees who remain with the school for more than five years. Which compensation strategy would you recommend to help the school improve the retention rate among high caliber employees?

    A. Internal equity

    B. Performance

    C. Entitlement

    D. Line of sight

8. What type of pay structure would most likely be associated with a union shop?

    A. Merit

    B. Shift

    C. Performance

    D. Seniority

9. A startup company does not have enough capital to hire employees at competitive market base pay rates. As the HR Director, what compensation strategy would you recommend they implement?

    A. Meet the market in base pay and hire fewer people because that is the only way to attract the talent needed to grow.

    B. Lag the market in base pay and offer incentives such as stock options and medical insurance that meet the average total rewards in the external market for similar positions.

    C. Lag the market.

    D. Lead the market because investing in the right talent now will pay off as the company grows.

10. A company has multiple HR Generalists paid within a range of $40,000 to $90,000. The HR Generalists who have been with the company the longest have expressed that they do not believe that their base pay is reflective of their knowledge, skills, and abilities. As the HR Director, what internal condition would you be concerned about in this scenario?

    A. How each employee's pay relates to their performance

    B. The perception that the processes and procedures used to determine pay scales may not be equitable

    C. Whether the employees' pay is competitive with the external market

    D. Whether employees are discussing each other's pay amongst themselves

11. The company sets a goal to increase sales by 5 percent each quarter for the next two years. Recognizing that this is an aggressive goal, the CEO wants to craft a compensation plan that will motivate the sales team to attain this goal. Which of the following would you recommend as the best approach?

    A. Direct compensation in the form of bonuses for each benchmark attained

    B. Indirect compensation in the form of additional vacation days and stock options

    C. Direct compensation in the form of a salary increase of 10 percent for all sales people who meet the establish benchmarks

    D. Direct compensation in the form of an additional pension contribution

12. A Massachusetts-based company is opening a new location in Alabama where cost of living is significantly lower. As the Vice President of Human Resources, you must develop appropriate salary ranges for all positions in Alabama. What would be your best next step?

    A. Review available salary surveys.

    B. Establish salary ranges.

    C. Review compensation components such as base pay, insurance, variable pay, and so on.

    D. Review job descriptions.

Objective 03 Manage Payroll-Related Information

13. Which of the following is an example of an involuntary deduction?

    A. Wage garnishment

    B. State income tax

    C. 401(k)

    D. Social Security

14. What is the record keeping requirement for payroll records?

    A. 7 years

    B. 2 years

    C. 3 years

    D. 3 pay periods

15. Which of the following is a primary function of a payroll system?

    A. Print and distribute paychecks.

    B. Troubleshoot employee pay related questions.

    C. Accurate reporting of payroll information to management.

    D. Input statutory deductions.

16. The payroll department receives a court order for wage garnishment for child support for an employee. The employee's supervisor is also not pleased with the employee's work and wants to terminate employment. As the HR Manager, how would you advise the supervisor?

   A. Move forward with the termination because the company may end a person's employment as it deems necessary.

   B. Move forward with the termination if processing the wage garnishment has become burdensome for the payroll department.

   C. Do not terminate employment because Title III of the Consumer Credit Protection Act (CCPA) protects an employee from being fired if pay is garnished for only one debt.

   D. Do not terminate employee without proper written documentation of his overall performance.

17. An employer receives four wage garnishments requests for an employee totaling over 90 percent of the employee's gross earnings. What guidance would you provide to the payroll department?

   A. Process the garnishments received not to exceed 25 percent of the employee's disposable earnings.

   B. Process all garnishments in their entirety because they are court ordered.

   C. Process all four garnishments, sending a reduced amount to debtors not to exceed 50 percent of the employee's disposable income.

   D. Process the first garnishments received not to exceed 50 percent of the employee's disposable income.

18. A company receives a child support wage garnishment order for an employee. The employer immediately terminates the employee. Which of the following will most likely happen to this employer?

   A. The employer may be forced to reinstate the employee and pay back wages because the Department of Labor tries to resolve violations of Title III of the Consumer Credit Protection Act through informal means.

   B. Nothing because the termination of the employee was not related to the receipt of the child support wage garnishment order.

   C. The employer may be forced to pay garnishments out of its own funds relieving the employee of any liability.

   D. For a willful termination such as this, the employer may be prosecuted criminally, fined up to $1000, and imprisoned for up to one year.

Objective 04 Manage Outsourced Compensation and Benefits Components (PHR only)

19. A small company currently has 13 employees in multiple states and is looking at payroll outsourcing options. What would be the main advantage of this HR department using an outsourced computerized payroll system?

    A. Comply with all federal and state tax rules and withholding in a time-efficient manner.

    B. Comply with internal security controls.

    C. Provide management with accurate reports.

    D. Provide employees with accurate paychecks.

20. What is the main advantage of a small company (25 employees) having a third-party vendor manage its COBRA administration needs?

    A. Less likelihood of error

    B. Having third-party COBRA expert keep up with all applicable laws and regulations

    C. Lower HR staffing costs to administer

    D. Less time of HR staff spent away from strategic functions

21. When HR is considering which outsourced payroll system to utilize to give their employees the best service, what should be their first consideration?

    A. The payroll outsourcing company's current clients

    B. The payroll outsourcing company's corporation status

    C. The payroll outsourcing company's ability to provide the technical capability to support the company's payroll needs

    D. The payroll outsourcing company's financial stability

22. What is the main advantage for using a payroll outsourcing provider for payroll services?

    A. File storage is only accessible to selected persons at the company

    B. More access to data

    C. Company controls the system

    D. Low fixed costs, no initial investment, no maintenance

23. What is the main advantage why an HR manager would possibly decide to not enter payroll and also control the employee database?

    A. To maintain the security of the data

    B. To foster checks and balances within the organization

    C. To lower workload for HR staff

    D. To lower workload for the payroll staff

Objective 05 Conduct Compensation and Benefits Programs Needs Assessments

24. What is HR's final step in conducting a benefits needs assessment?

    A. Analyze the design and utilization date on all benefit plans.

    B. Analyze the demographics of the employers workforce.

    C. Review the organization's strategy.

    D. Compare organizational needs, employee needs, and the existing set of benefits.

25. What action should the HR Manager take if the findings from the benefits needs assessment showed "benefits that are too costly but are heavily used by employees"?

    A. Institute cost-containment strategies.

    B. Revise benefits that are not meetings needs.

    C. Research new benefits.

    D. Drop underutilized benefits.

Objective 06 Develop/Select, Implement/Administer, Update and Evaluate Benefit Programs

26. An employee has come to the HR Generalist at a manufacturing company to let the HR Generalist know of her pregnancy. What would be the first step the HR Generalist would advise the employee to take in regards to partial pay replacement?

    A. Advise her to take social security disability.

    B. Advise her to take long-term disability.

    C. Advise her to take sick time.

    D. Advise her to take short-term disability.

27. An employee comes to the HR department with questions about her paycheck for this week. The employee is questioning why she is being taxed on her life insurance premiums. What would be the HR department's best explanation to her question?

    A. HR should advise the employee she is being taxed because the amount of the life insurance policy is over $25,000 (excess group-term life insurance) so it is taxed as imputed income.

    B. HR should advise the employee she is being taxed because the amount of the life insurance policy is over $50,000 (excess group-term life insurance) so it is taxed as imputed income.

C. HR should advise the employee she is being taxed because the amount of the life insurance policy is over $40,000 (excess group-term life insurance) so it is taxed as imputed income.

D. HR should advise the employee she is being taxed because the amount of the life insurance policy is over $35,000 (excess group-term life insurance) so it is taxed as imputed income.

28. A company that allows for the use of Paid Time Off (PTO) typically sees the following results?

A. Greater company loyalty and stronger productivity

B. Fewer accidents in the work place

C. Fewer benefit claims

D. Higher scores on employee surveys

29. Due to changing demographics in the workplace, an HR department is facing a challenge dealing with the "Sandwich" generation, which takes care of their children and their elders at the same time. What is the best thing HR can do to help employees with this challenge?

A. Offer flex-time, job-sharing, and part-time work.

B. Create a less demanding job for these employees.

C. Offer higher wages to account for the increasing costs of child/elder care.

D. Create a focus group to discuss child/elder care issues.

30. Which of the following is considered non-taxable indirect compensation?

A. Gifts and prizes if over a certain dollar limit

B. Paid time off

C. Business expenses

D. Sick pay

31. An employee at Garden, Inc. has been diagnosed with terminal cancer. The employee has already exhausted the benefits under the short-term disability plan and also was enrolled in the long-term disability plan at the time of diagnosis. What is the next step the HR Manager should take to help this employee with benefits coverage?

A. Advise the employee to apply for life insurance.

B. Advise the employee to apply for long-term disability and to coordinate with social security to avoid duplication of coverage.

C. Advise the employee to draft a will.

D. Advise the employee to pick a richer medical plan to cover the high costs associated with cancer.

Objective 07   Communicate and Train the Workforce in the Compensation and Benefits Programs, Policies, and Processes

32. Which of the following is required communication that HR must provide to employees to comply with federal laws?

    A. Summary Plan Description

    B. Plan brochures

    C. Employee handbook

    D. Reminder on policies

33. When is it required for HR to send out the Summary Annual Review (SAR), which contains financial information about the plan?

    A. Within two months of the end of the plan year

    B. Within one year of the end of the plan year

    C. Immediately after the end of the plan year

    D. Seven months after the end of the plan year

34. The Humane Society has experienced higher than average attrition rates in the past year. They have also received a new executive director in the past month who has brought forth many procedural and organizational changes. Given the amount of change in employees, leadership, and procedures, what would be the *best* course of action for HR in terms of communication?

    A. Verbally discuss old/new policies.

    B. Put in writing new employee handbook and reminder of policies.

    C. Form employee focus groups to discuss changes.

    D. Post federal and state law posters.

35. The HR Department of a growing manufacturing company that currently has 100 employees is realizing the need to shift employees to more self-service paperless options. What is the main potential benefit of Employee Self Service technology?

    A. Enhanced reputation of "green" environmentally friendly company

    B. Checks deposited into employee accounts quicker

    C. Enhanced federal and state compliance

    D. More time spent on employees' job functions

36. What would an HR Generalist want to perform as an HR best practice for a voluntary direct communication in regards to job grade changes?

    A. Meet individually with each employee to discuss job grade changes.

    B. Meet as a group to discuss job grade changes.

C. Send an e-mail to all employees letting them know if they have questions they can contact HR about the job grade changes.

D. Discuss in a group setting and then let employees know that they can contact their manager if they have any questions.

37. What is an example of required communication that HR must provide to employees?

A. Personalized benefit statements

B. COBRA rates when the employee first starts with an organization

C. Notification of Continuation of Benefits under COBRA

D. Benefit manuals

■SPHR■ Objective 08   Develop/Select, Implement/Administer, Update, and Evaluate an Ethically Sound Executive Compensation Program (SPHR only)

38. A private organization has established its strategic plan with agreed upon objectives that have been determined for the year. The CEO has asked you for compensation plan recommendations that will keep the executive team motivated to achieve those objectives throughout the entire year. Which of the following is the best compensation plan strategy?

A. Upfront merit-based pay increase

B. Performance-based cash bonus

C. Defined contribution retirement plan

D. The offering of stock options

39. As an HR leader of an organization, you wish to expand the assessment process of executive pay to ensure effectiveness of the executive incentive pay under every possible scenario. Which of the following is an example of a quantitative risk assessment?

A. Risk evaluation

B. SWOT analysis

C. Scenario planning

D. Stress testing

40. As an HR leader of an organization, you will be responsible for designing the executive compensation strategy. Which of the following is the best strategic focus of executive compensation design?

A. Establish shareholder goal alignment, profitability, and long-term orientation.

B. Structure executive compensation in a way that it avoids media attention.

C. Build a communication plan that helps employees accept pay disparity concerns.

D. Create a plan that can be reviewed and approved by the CEO annually.

SPHR Objective 09   Develop, Implement/Administer, and Evaluate Expatriate and Foreign National Compensation and Benefits Programs (SPHR only)

41. What is the main difference between an expatriate and an inpatriate?

A. An expatriate is an employee hired locally while an inpatriate is an employee on a cross-border assignment.

B. An expatriate is an employee who is sent to another country to work but hired as a local employee, whereas an inpatriate is an employee brought in from another country to work in the headquarters country for a specified period of time.

C. "Inpatriate" describes employees brought in from another country to work in the headquarters country for a specified period of time, whereas "expatriate" describes employees who move to one country and are employed by an organization based in another country.

D. "Inpatriate" describes employees who move to one country and are employed by an organization based in another country, whereas "expatriate" describes employees brought in from another country to work in the headquarters country for a specified period of time.

42. What is the best hiring practice for an HR Manager to implement when addressing competitive labor market practices in a global HR market?

A. Employ people with different skills to get new ideas when competition is high.

B. Employ people with similar skills when industry-specific expertise is in short supply or competition is high.

C. Employ many people with cross-functional skill sets.

D. Employ sparingly with budgetary goals in mind.

43. What should the HR department avoid when considering cultural pay issues in a global market?

A. Avoid replication of headquarters country policies and procedures in risk adverse countries.

B. Avoid lagging the market in compensation.

C. Avoid leading the market in compensation.

D. Avoid conducting market or salary surveys in different regions.

Compensation Benefits—Knowledge Objectives

Objective 38   Applicable Federal Laws and Regulations Related to Compensation, Benefits, and Tax

44. What federal law sets uniform minimum standards to ensure that employee benefit plans are established and maintained in a fair and financially sound manner?

    A. Fair Labor Standards Act (FLSA)

    B. Securities Exchange Act (SEC)

    C. Employee Retirement Income Security Act (ERISA)

    D. Patient Protection and Affordable Care Act (PPACA)

45. An organization wants to track its overtime usage and associated costs more closely. You are asked to track and report on overtime usage. Which of the following is most likely to be included in tracking overtime?

    A. The Chief Executive Officer worked 55 hours last week.

    B. A non-exempt employee worked 43 hours last week.

    C. An exempt employee worked 47 hours last week.

    D. A receptionist worked 32 hours and took 8 hours for vacation.

46. You have decided to conduct an exempt versus non-exempt audit based on the Federal Labor Standards Act (FLSA). Which of the following is most likely to be considered non-exempt?

    A. An employee who regularly performs routine or clerical duties

    B. An employee who is paid $25,000 per year ($481 per week)

    C. A manager who supervises two or more employees

    D. An employee who functions as the employer's attorney

Objective 39   Compensation and Benefits Strategies

47. A startup IT company is looking to hire software engineers with the latest technological skill set, which is vital to getting investors. What compensation strategy should HR implement to attract the candidates with these skill sets?

    A. Lead the market in compensation strategy.

    B. Match the market rate in compensation strategy.

    C. Lag the market in compensation strategy.

    D. Either lag or lead the market in compensation contingent upon candidate preferences.

48. A small after-school tutoring company, Kinder Minds, is hiring three new college graduates as tutors for special needs children. Kinder Minds is finding a huge number of new college graduates with a bachelor's degree in education, all of whom are highly qualified. What compensation strategy should the HR department of Kinder Minds implement when hiring in this situation?

    A. Lead the market to ensure the best possible candidates.

    B. Lag the market because supply of talent is greater than the demand.

    C. Match what the market is paying.

    D. Lead the market as demand is higher than supply.

49. Which of the following is considered a form of indirect compensation?

    A. Differential pay

    B. Short-term incentive pay

    C. Deferred Pay

    D. Long-term incentive pay

Objective 40   Budgeting and Accounting Practices Related to Compensation and Benefits

50. According to the Fair Labor Standards Act and the Age Discrimination in Employment Act, how long must an employer retain payroll records?

    A. 3 to 4 years, depending on the record

    B. 2 to 3 years, depending on the record

    C. 2 years

    D. 3 years

51. The payroll department of a large company is to keep a master file of all employment records. What should the payroll department include in the master file for employees?

    A. Personal data including name, veteran status, date of birth, and social security number

    B. Personal data including name, national origin, date of birth, and social security number

    C. Personal data including name, Form I-9, date of birth, and social security number

    D. Personal data including name, gender, date of birth, and social security number

52. The Department of Labor is investigating a potential Fair Labor Standards Act violation because an employee has complained about not being paid for overtime. The Department of Labor has requested all wage records for this employee. The HR department has only kept electronic copies of these records. What should be HR's next step?

    A. Retrieve electronic copies for the last three years and submit to the Department of Labor.

    B. Reproduce all wage records in a paper format and submit to the Department of Labor.

    C. Print all electronic copies and submit to the Department of Labor.

    D. Retrieve wage data from the employee's manager for the last five years and type on paper.

Objective 41   Job Evaluation Methods

53. The job evaluation process determines which of the following?

    A. The level of performance of every employee in an organization

    B. The job offer that is given to a prospective job applicant

    C. The duties that every employee in the organization must perform

    D. The relative worth of each job by establishing a hierarchy of jobs

54. A large organization wants to shift to a more systematic approach to the job evaluation process. The key objective is that the job evaluation method is understandable and well accepted by employees. It is also important that the system accounts for changes in duties and responsibilities. Which of the following job evaluation methods would best suit this organization's objectives?

    A. Factor comparison method

    B. Job ranking method

    C. Point factor method

    D. Job classification method

Objective 42   Job Pricing and Pay Structures

55. The process for establishing wage rates for jobs using the job evaluation method is known as _____.

    A. Job classification

    B. Factor comparison

C. Point factor

D. Job ranking

56. A company hires a compensation analyst to review all support services positions. Once salary structures are developed, it reveals some positions are paid significantly higher than the average market rate and some significantly lower. The decision is made to achieve internal equity by raising the salaries of those employees on the lower end and freezing the pay of those employees on the higher end. As the HR Director, how would you prepare management to administer the new compensation program?

A. Inform line supervisors that HR will handle the employee relations issues that will result from those employees whose pay was frozen.

B. Develop talking points for managers and refer employees who have questions to them.

C. Develop a compensation handbook accessible to all managers, which includes information on the company's compensation philosophy and how pay increases, new hire salaries, and promotional salaries are determined.

D. Review a compensation handbook with senior management and rely on them to relay the message to immediate supervisors and their employees.

57. Because of the changing needs of a company, administrative assistants once classified as Admin Level III have been performing Admin Level II positions. However, the pay rates of those administrative assistants who were repositioned was not reduced to the corresponding salary range. As a result, the pay for these admin assistants now falls outside the range maximum for an Admin II. This is referred to as _____.

A. Red circle

B. Green circle

C. Wage compression

D. Compa-ratio

Objective 43   External Labor Markets and/or Economic Factors

58. What is the *biggest* advantage to HR using an external published salary survey to inquire how the external labor market pays their employees in a given market?

A. No participation is required and data is widely available.

B. Providing some input into survey design.

C. No input is needed in survey design.

D. Full control of survey design and administration.

59. A company is transferring an employee and her family from the company headquarters in New York City to a satellite location in San Francisco. When deciding on compensation for this employee utilizing salary surveys, what should HR factor in?

   A. Funds for helping her spouse find a position in a new city

   B. Local pay rates as they relate to the national salary survey

   C. Cost of schooling for her children in a new city

   D. Regional benefit plan differences from the national salary survey

Objective 44   Pay Programs

60. As an HR leader of an organization, you are expected to create a strategy that will reward employees' contributions toward an organization's new profitability and productivity objectives. Which of the following pay practices would contribute significantly to the organization's objectives?

   A. Implement a variable pay program based on the attainment of specific objectives.

   B. Maintain the existing compensation program that pays a standard increase annually.

   C. Provide an across-the-board pay increase if supervisors rate high performance.

   D. Implement voluntary benefits allowing employees to choose from a menu of options.

61. Regular increases that are given to employees that meet or exceed established performance expectations reflect what type of pay program?

   A. Regular-based pay

   B. Merit-based pay

   C. Flexible-based pay

   D. Market-based pay

SPHR Objective 45   Executive Compensation Methods (SPHR only)

62. The CEO of Wonderworks Brands is being let go due to an acquisition. As part of her severance final pay agreement (Golden Parachute Clause), she will be receiving a payment of four times her annual salary. What can she expect in terms of taxation?

   A. Her final pay will not be taxed as part of the golden parachute clause.

   B. Her final pay will be subject to an excise tax in addition to income taxes.

C. Her final pay will be taxed at a 25 percent tax rate.

D. Her final pay will not be taxed as the employer will pick up the burden of the taxation.

63. Which of the following is stock ownership without the without participants having to invest any of their own funds?

A. Incentive stock options

B. Phantom stock

C. Restricted stock grants

D. Restricted stock units

64. What is the main reason why a CEO would request that a golden parachute clause be included in his/her executive contract?

A. To provide the executive with job security.

B. To help the executive find another position faster.

C. After years of service and commitment to a company, an executive has the right to request this clause.

D. If a merger or acquisition occurs, both companies will have C-suite executives but they will need only one incumbent for each role after the merger or acquisition.

Objective 46   Noncash Compensation Methods

65. An owner of a mid-sized organization wants to retire. The owner would like to fund his retirement without having to sell the company to outsiders. What would be a viable alternative to selling the organization to outside investors?

A. Establish a 401(k) retirement plan for all employees.

B. Convince relatives of the owner to take over the organization.

C. Establish an Employee Stock Option Plan (ESOP).

D. There are no other alternatives to selling the organization.

66. A defined contribution plan that enables employees to contribute a percentage of their wages on a tax-deferred basis and can also be matched by the employer up to a certain amount is which type of noncash compensation program?

A. A 401(k) plan

B. A pay-for-performance plan

C. A merit increase plan

D. A market increase plan

67. An organization has become limited in its ability to reward employees through cash-related incentives. However, the organization has the ability to reward employees through gifts, awards, and prizes. Which of the following describes this incentive program?

A. Performance share plan

B. Group incentive plan

C. Profit sharing plan

D. Noncash incentive plan

Objective 47 Benefits Programs

68. What is the *main* disadvantage to an employee when using a flexible spending account (FSA)?

A. Employees risk losing their money at the end of year if funds are not used by the year-end deadline.

B. Too many restrictions on what is a qualified health expense.

C. Difficult to keep receipts for qualified health expenses.

D. Difficult to predict future health expenses.

69. Leo, a new hire at Soul Café, is being offered a health reimbursement account by his employer. During a new hire orientation, HR describes for him how this works and what the advantages are. How does HR explain the *biggest* advantage of utilizing a health reimbursement account (HRA)?

A. If a claim occurs, the employee can pay the claim up front.

B. There are no restrictions on types of medical claims that can be reimbursed.

C. He may roll over the remaining funds into the next year.

D. Leo can use this as a savings account for retirement.

70. To be eligible to enroll in a health savings account (HSA), what must the employee be enrolled in?

A. Employee must be enrolled in a health maintenance organization plan.

B. Employee must be enrolled in a high deductible health plan.

C. Employee must be enrolled in a flexible savings account.

D. Employee must be enrolled in a fee for service plan.

71. James is voluntarily leaving his employment at The G & G Institute to pursue personal interests. James is currently enrolled in a health reimbursement account. Knowing that he has stage 1 cancer, his employer can elect the following option under the HRA provisions:

A. To allow James to use the funds in the HRA toward COBRA payments

B. To allow James to close his account and spend the money on whatever he needs

C. To allow James to move the money into a 401(k)

D. To allow James to not be taxed on his last check in order to bring home more money

72. Why do dental plans have a high adverse selection rate?

A. Employees go out of network for their services.

B. Only a small percentage of employees actually enroll in the dental plans.

C. Many dental procedures can be postponed.

D. Only a small percentage of employees utilize the dental benefits once they are enrolled.

73. What is the *main* difference between an Administrative-Services-Only (ASO) plan and a Third-Party Administrator (TPA) plan?

A. TPAs utilize an independent claims department and ASOs utilize the claims department of the insurance plan.

B. ASOs are self-funded and TPAs are fully insured.

C. TPAs are self-funded and ASO's are fully insured.

D. ASOs utilize an independent claims department and TPAs utilize the claims department of the insurance plan.

74. What is the *best* way an HR department can help control healthcare costs while increasing morale at the same time?

A. Require co-insurance on all plans.

B. Let employees pick the programs that best serve their overall need.

C. Redesign policies to increase deductibles and out-of-pocket maximums.

D. Require generic or mail order prescription drugs.

SPHR Objective 48   International Compensation Laws and Practices (SPHR only)

75. How does HR best approach compliance with international compensation laws and regulations?

A. Pay overtime in times of uncertainty.

B. Pay minimum wage of the company headquarters.

C. Engage local international compensation and benefits experts.

D. Involve employees in focus groups to help design fair pay practices.

76. What is the *main* purpose of international social security agreements?

   A. To eliminate government interference into expatriate compensation agreements

   B. To eliminate an employer from having to pay social security on the employees behalf

   C. To eliminate any additional work for the employer and the employee

   D. To eliminate dual social security taxation, which occurs when a worker from one country works in another country where workers are required to pay social security taxes on the same wages

77. What is the *biggest* advantage of a lump-sum approach to international compensation?

   A. A lump sum payment at the start of the assignment is a strong incentive for an assignee to accept the assignment.

   B. It protects the assignee from fluctuating payments during the assignment.

   C. It provides a tax advantage when the assignee is from a high-tax country.

   D. The assignee is able to shelter a larger portion of taxes during the assignment.

Objective 49   Fiduciary Responsibilities Related to Compensation and Benefits

78. An individual, or individuals, who have discretionary decision-making over a group's health plan carry what specific role and responsibility according the Department of Labor, specifically the Employee Retirement Income Security Act (ERISA)?

   A. A profitability responsibility

   B. A fiduciary responsibility

   C. A recruitment responsibility

   D. A talent satisfaction responsibility

79. An organization is beginning the process of hiring a group health plan service provider. As part of the fiduciary responsibility, what is a key action that should be taken when considering a prospective service provider?

   A. Provide specific information to one service provider that is the CEO's relative.

   B. Seek out one provider and ask them to bid on the organization's service need.

   C. Compare all firms based on same information such as services offered and costs.

   D. Minimize documentation because the service provider is an independent contractor.

1. B	21. C	41. C	61. A
2. A	22. D	42. B	62. B
3. D	23. B	43. A	63. A
4. A	24. D	44. C	64. D
5. D	25. A	45. B	65. C
6. A	26. C	46. A	66. A
7. B	27. B	47. A	67. D
8. D	28. A	48. B	68. A
9. B	29. A	49. C	69. C
10. B	30. C	50. D	70. B
11. A	31. B	51. D	71. A
12. D	32. A	52. A	72. C
13. A	33. D	53. D	73. A
14. C	34. B	54. D	74. B
15. C	35. A	55. B	75. C
16. C	36. A	56. C	76. D
17. A	37. C	57. A	77. A
18. A	38. B	58. A	78. B
19. A	39. D	59. B	79. C
20. B	40. A	60. C	

1. ☑ **B.** According to the FLSA standards, exempt employee must be paid a minimum salary of $455 per week.

 ☒ **A, C,** and **D** are incorrect because they are not requirements to be an exempt employee

2. ☑ **A.** To qualify for the administrative exemption, an employee must have a primary duty involving performance of office work directly related to the management or general business operations.

 ☒ **B, C,** and **D** are incorrect because these choices are examples of requirements under the executive exemption.

3. ☑ **D.** Under the FLSA, the general rule when state and federal laws differ is that you should follow the regulation that most benefits the employee.

 ☒ **A, B,** and **C** are incorrect because these are all incorrect statements under the FLSA.

4. ☑ **A.** This is the main tenet of the Lily Ledbetter Fair Pay Act.

 ☒ **B, C,** and **D** are incorrect. **B** is incorrect because the Equal Pay Act prohibits wage discrimination by requiring equal pay for equal work. **C** is incorrect because this refers to establishing prevailing wage and benefit requirements for contractors on federally funded projects. **D** is incorrect because this refers to precluding a federal contractor or subcontractor from inducing an employee to give up any part of the compensation to which he or she is entitled.

5. ☑ **D.** Because the employee's shift started at 8 and she could not complete the work because the order was late, this would be compensable time.

 ☒ **A, B,** and **C** are incorrect because these choices are not considered compensable time under the FLSA.

6. ☑ **A.** The Wage and Hour Division has said that nature and degree of control must be considered to decide if the individual is an independent contractor or an employee.

 ☒ **B, C,** and **D** are incorrect because these choices are not relevant items to look at to decide whether or not someone is an employee.

7. ☑ **B.** A performance-based philosophy is one where an employee's performance is directly tied to his compensation. When looking at compensation strategy, this type of culture will motivate a company's top performers.

 ☒ **A, C,** and **D** are incorrect. **A** is incorrect because internal equity is a pay philosophy that uses a salary range to ensure that each job is compensated according to the jobs above and below it in a hierarchy. **C** is incorrect because an entitlement-based philosophy associates rewards such as pay with longevity or seniority. Typically, this creates commitment and loyalty among employees.

However, in this case, this is already the philosophy that drives the school's compensation strategy and yet the school is losing its top performers. With this in mind, it is time for a change. **D** is incorrect because line of sight is the descriptor used to explain how a performance-based compensation strategy works. Employees have a "line of sight" from their performance to their compensation and rewards (both intrinsic and extrinsic).

8. ☑ **D.** Pay rates in a company where employees are represented by a union are set based on negotiations between the union and management. Therefore, the company's compensation structure may not be considered relevant. In these environments, employees are usually compensated based on seniority or longevity.

  ☒ **A, B, and C** are incorrect. **A** is incorrect because a merit increase is a possible part of a performance-based pay program. **B** is incorrect because "shift pay" refers to the compensation associated with different shifts in a company (swing shifts, night shift, and so on). Shift pay may be a component of a company's pay structure. **C** is incorrect because performance-based pay isn't typical in a union shop. Pay is negotiated by the union and may not match the company's compensation philosophy.

9. ☑ **B.** The company should consider lagging the market in base pay but put together a total rewards package that meets the market. As a startup, the company needs to attract top talent to ensure the best possibility for steady growth. While the base pay may not be competitive with the market, the overall compensation and rewards program should attempt to meet the market average.

  ☒ **A, C, and D** are incorrect. **A** is incorrect because it is clear that the company simply cannot meet the average market base pay. To hedge against this, the company should explore creative ways to make the total compensation package attractive to talented individuals. **C** is incorrect because lagging the market will not attract the kind of talent the company needs to be successful. **D** is incorrect because it is clear that the company is not financially able to lead the market. It is true that the better the compensation package is the more likely a company is to attract quality people. However, for a startup like this, spending large amounts on labor could potentially put the company in such a financial bind that it cannot make a timely profit.

10. ☑ **B.** Of the choices provided, the HR Director should be concerned about the perception that the processes and procedures used to determine pay scales may not be equitable. This can lead to a number of undesired employee behaviors, such as a lack of employee engagement, and it may cause potential labor relations issues.

  ☒ **A, C, and D** are incorrect because the issue here is not how each employee's pay relates to her performance, whether or not her pay is externally competitive or whether or not it is appropriate for pay to be discussed openly. The issue is that there is a belief that employees with the most experience are not compensated appropriately when compared to their peers in similar positions.

11. ☑ **A.** Direct compensation in the form of a bonus that is directly tied to meeting a sales target would work best to motivate this team. This is the clearest line of sight for the employee.

    ☒ **B, C,** and **D** are incorrect. **B** is incorrect because any indirect form of compensation would not be the strongest motivator for a sales professional and is unlikely to push a sales person to achieve an aggressive immediate short-term goal. **C** is incorrect because even though it is direct compensation, which typically is a motivator for a sales professional, it still equates the performance of all sales people the same. For example, if a sales person meets the goal and another exceeds the goal, they both get a 10 percent salary increase. **D** is incorrect because even though an increased pension contribution is a direct form of compensation, it isn't immediately tangible enough to motivate the sales team effectively to meet this aggressive short-term goal.

12. ☑ **D.** The first step when engaging in job pricing is to review job descriptions so that you gain an understanding of the knowledge, skills, and abilities needed to be successful in the positions.

    ☒ **A, B,** and **C** are incorrect because the job pricing process starts with a review of job descriptions, and then a review of available salary surveys, which ensures that the surveys reflect the local market, and finally a review of compensation components. With this information compiled, salary ranges can then be established.

13. ☑ **A.** A wage garnishment is involuntary. An employer receives a court order requiring them to take the deductions and forward them to the appropriate agency.

    ☒ **B, C,** and **D** are incorrect because income taxes and social security are statutory deductions. A 401(k) contribution is a voluntary deduction.

14. ☑ **C.** The record keeping requirement is three years for payroll records, collective bargaining agreements, sales, and purchase records.

    ☒ **A, B,** and **D** are incorrect because the record keeping requirement is three years.

15. ☑ **C.** Among other functions, such as accurately calculating payments and deductions, a payroll system should provide accurate reports on pay-related information to assist management in decision making.

    ☒ **A, B,** and **D** are incorrect because printing and distributing paychecks, troubleshooting pay related questions, and ensuring accurate data entry of statutory deductions are all functions of those responsible for administering payroll.

16. ☑ **C.** Title III of the Consumer Credit Protection Act limits the amount of an employee's earnings that may be garnished and protects an employee from being fired if pay is garnished for only one debt.

    ☒ **A, B,** and **D** are incorrect because once a wage garnishment is in place, Title III of the CCPA provides employment protection if pay is only being garnished for one debt. None of the other considerations matter in this case. If there is more than one garnishment then no protection is offered.

17. ☑ **A.** Title III of the Consumer Credit Protection Act states that for ordinary garnishments (i.e., those not for support, bankruptcy, or any state or federal tax), the weekly amount may not exceed the lesser of two figures: 25 percent of the employee's disposable earnings or the amount by which an employee's disposable earnings are greater than 30 times the federal minimum wage (currently $7.25 an hour).

    ☒ **B, C,** and **D** are incorrect because for child-support garnishments, the percentage can be as much as 50 percent if the employee currently supports a spouse or another child or 60 percent if not.

18. ☑ **A.** It is most likely that the Department of Labor (DOL) would try to resolve this issue without taking legal action. Common remedies are reinstatement of employment and/or paying back wages.

    ☒ **B, C,** and **D** are incorrect. **B** is incorrect because the DOL would take some action. It is unlawful to terminate someone with one debt garnishment and it is especially suspicious for it to happen immediately following the receipt of the court order. **C** is incorrect because this is not an available remedy. It is possible that the employer may be forced to refund an improper garnishment but not pay the employee's debt. **D** is incorrect because while this is a viable penalty, the scenario presented does not indicate that this employer has shown a pattern of similar actions or that this termination was willful in nature. The DOL is only likely to pursue such severe legal action for willful acts on the part of the employer.

19. ☑ **A.** The main advantage would be complying with federal and state laws in an easy-to-use format, thus saving time and money. In-house manual payroll systems for multi-state payrolls can be time-consuming and complicated for a small company to administer.

    ☒ **B, C,** and **D** are incorrect. These choices are also advantages but not the main advantage.

20. ☑ **B.** Because COBRA is ever changing, it is difficult for a small company with limited resources to keep up with the changing regulations.

    ☒ **A, C,** and **D** are incorrect because these choices are not the main advantage of administering COBRA with a third-party vendor.

21. ☑ **C.** In order to provide employees with the best service, the payroll company's ability to provide the technical capabilities to support the company's payroll needs would be the best option.

    ☒ **A, B,** and **D** are incorrect because these choices are not as relevant and important in this situation.

22. ☑ **D.** Advantages are typically lower fixed costs, no initial investment, and no maintenance involved with a payroll service outsourcing provider.

    ☒ **A, B,** and **C** are incorrect because these choices do not reflect the advantages of an in-house server payroll system.

23. ☑ **B.** Having two employees enter the payroll data and maintain the employee database ensures checks and balances within an organization.
☒ **A, C,** and **D** are incorrect because although these choices may also be a factor, they are not the main reason.

24. ☑ **D.** The final step in a needs analysis is to compare the organization's needs with employee needs and then also the existing set of benefits.
☒ **A, B,** and **C** are incorrect. **A** is incorrect because analyzing the design and utilization data would be the fourth step in a benefits needs assessment. **B** is incorrect because reviewing demographics of the workforce would be the third step in a benefits–needs assessment. **C** is incorrect because reviewing an organization's strategy would be the first step in the benefits needs assessment process.

25. ☑ **A.** The best action to take with this statement is to institute cost-containment strategies.
☒ **B, C,** and **D** are incorrect because cost containment is the best action to take.

26. ☑ **C.** The first step of partial income replacement protection would be sick time if the employee has this benefit.
☒ **A, B,** and **D** are incorrect because they are later steps of partial income replacement protection. First is sick time; next is short-term disability; next is long-term disability and possibly even social security disability benefits, if applicable.

27. ☑ **B.** $50,000 is the key as anything over that amount is referred to as excess group-term life insurance and is taxed as imputed income.
☒ **A, C,** and **D** are incorrect because anything over $50,000 is taxed as imputed income.

28. ☑ **A.** The trust factor in treating employees as adults and no longer requiring an accounting of the reason for absences has been shown to improve productivity and increase loyalty.
☒ **B, C,** and **D** are incorrect because these factors are not seen with offering PTO.

29. ☑ **A** is correct because creating flex time, job share, or part-time work will allow employees to take care of personal obligations as well as to be productive employees.
☒ **B, C,** and **D** are incorrect because these choices are not required and would not be the best option to help the employees.

30. ☑ **C.** This is a non-taxable form of indirect compensation if accounted for in a timely manner.
☒ **A, B,** and **D** are incorrect because these choices are all considered taxable income.

31. ☑ **B.** Once short-term disability expires (if applicable in the state in which the employee resides), long-term disability will apply (if enrolled at time of diagnosis). It is important to coordinate with social security disability benefits to avoid duplication of coverage.

    ☒ **A, C,** and **D** are incorrect because these choices may help the employee but they are not the next step in the benefit coverage process.

32. ☑ **A.** Summary Plan Descriptions (SPDs), which include information on what the plan provides and how it operates, are required for employers to give to employees under ERISA requirements.

    ☒ **B, C,** and **D** are incorrect because these choices are all voluntary communication to employees.

33. ☑ **D.** An employer is required to send out the SAR no later than seven months after the end of the plan year.

    ☒ **A, B,** and **C** are incorrect because an employer is required to send out the SAR no later than seven months, and these choices do not reflect SAR requirements.

34. ☑ **B.** Given all the changes that this organization has experienced, it would be a best HR practice to put the employee handbook and reminder of policies in all writing so employees have a guide and can refer back to it.

    ☒ **A, C,** and **D** are incorrect. **A** and **C** are incorrect because although these choices would be helpful, they are not the best course of action. **D** is incorrect as federal and state posters are required and would have no impact on helping with organizational changes.

35. ☑ **A.** The employer could gain the reputation for becoming a "green" environmentally friendly company.

    ☒ **B, C,** and **D** are incorrect. Although these choices may provide a benefit, these choices would not be the main benefit.

36. ☑ **A.** An HR best practice would be to meet with each employee individually to discuss the job grade changes as it will affect each employee differently.

    ☒ **B, C,** and **D** are incorrect because these choices would not be an HR best practice for communicating the job grade changes.

37. ☑ **C.** An organization is required by federal law to provide employees with a notification of continuation of benefits under COBRA.

    ☒ **A, B,** and **D** are incorrect. **A** and **B** are incorrect because these choices are not necessary to achieve organizational goals; this is not the most strategic focus of designing an executive compensation plan. **D** is incorrect because while it is certainly important that the CEO approves all compensation plans, this is not the strategic focus of a well-designed executive compensation plan.

38. ☑ **B.** A performance-based cash incentive plan is a common strategy to keep executives motivated on achieving organizational objectives over a period of time. This is also called a pay-for-performance plan.

   ☒ **A, C,** and **D** are incorrect. **A** is incorrect because an upfront merit-based pay is not an incentive plan that pays out over time or is not necessarily linked to specific objectives. **C** is incorrect because a defined contribution retirement plan is not necessarily linked to performance and not considered an incentive pay plan. **D** is incorrect because stock options are a compensation strategy for publically traded organizations. This question is specific to a private organization.

39. ☑ **D.** Stress testing is a quantitative assessment that evaluates incentive plans under various scenarios. The possible scenarios range from poor performance to exceeding performance expectations. This assessment method enables an organization to determine what risk there may be to sustainability and viability objectives.

   ☒ **A, B,** and **C** are incorrect. **A** is incorrect because a risk evaluation is an overbroad term and not the best definition of stress testing. **B** is incorrect because a SWOT analysis refers to the assessment of internal and external environmental influences of an organization. **C** is incorrect because scenario planning is an overall strategic planning method to determine future possible outcomes for an organization's future.

40. ☑ **A.** The strategic focus of an executive compensation plan should center around shareholder goal alignment, as well as focusing on profits and long-term orientation. Investors are becoming increasingly focused on executive pay and how closely aligned it is to performance. These are key strategic ingredients to an effective executive compensation plan.

   ☒ **B, C,** and **D** are incorrect. **B** is incorrect because structuring an executive pay plan simply to avoid media attention would on its own make it ineffective. It is not aligned with organizational goals such as profitability. **C** is incorrect because establishing a communication plan is in this case tactical in nature. While it is important to clearly communicate compensation strategies so that employees are motivated to achieve organizational goals, this is not the most strategic focus of designing an executive compensation plan. **D** is incorrect because while it is certainly important that the CEO approves all compensation plans, this is not the strategic focus of a well-designed executive compensation plan.

41. ☑ **C.** "Inpatriate" describes employees brought in from another country to work in the headquarters country for a specified period of time, whereas "expatriate" describes employees who move to one country and are employed by an organization based in another country.

   ☒ **A, B,** and **D** are incorrect. **D** is incorrect in this example. **B** is incorrect because the first part of the statement reflects a localization assignment. **A** is incorrect because the first part of the statement reflects a local national or local hire and the second part of the statement reflects an employee on a cross-border assignment.

42. ☑ **B.** Employ people with similar skills when industry-specific expertise is in short supply or competition is high.

☒ **A, C, and D** are incorrect because these choices are not best practices in relation to the competitive labor market in global HR.

43. ☑ **A.** Avoid the country headquarters exact duplication of policies and procedures. It is important to look at the cultural value on team or individual contributions before developing pay practices. Companies need to involve local contacts to understand usual and customary pay practices

☒ **B, C, and D** are incorrect because these choices are not relevant in the discussion of cultural pay practices in global HR.

44. ☑ **C.** The Employee Retirement Income Security Act (ERISA) sets uniform minimum standards to ensure retirement plans are established and maintained in a fair and financially sound manner.

☒ **A, B, and D** are incorrect. A is incorrect because the Fair Labor Standards Act (FLSA) establishes standards for wages and hours. B is incorrect because the Securities Exchange Act (SEC) is responsible for enforcement of United States federal securities law. It protects investors by requiring accurate disclosure of financial statements. D is incorrect because the Patient Protection and Affordable Care Act (PPACA) is a law that relates to widening the health insurance market.

45. ☑ **B.** According to the Fair Labor Standards Act (FLSA), "unless specifically exempted, employees covered by the Act must receive overtime pay for hours worked in excess of 40 in a workweek at a rate not less than time and one-half their regular rates of pay."

☒ **A, C, and D** are incorrect because overtime at the federal level is required for non-exempt employees who must receive overtime pay for hours worked in excess of 40 in a workweek. A CEO who is exempt or an employee who works less than 40 hours in a week is not eligible for overtime pay.

46. ☑ **A.** There are various exceptions to overtime eligibility. However, an employee who regularly performs routine or clerical duties generally would be considered non-exempt and eligible for overtime pay.

☒ **B, C, and D** are incorrect because an employee who is paid $25,000 per year ($481 per week), a manager who supervises two or more employees, and an employee who functions as the employer's attorney are considered exempt and not eligible for overtime pay.

47. ☑ **A.** A company would want to lead the markets and pay in approximately the 75th percentile of what the market is paying to attract the right candidates for these critical positions.

☒ **B, C, and D** are incorrect because these choices would not reach the desired outcome of getting these critical positions filled with the right candidate with the right skill sets.

48. ☑ **B.** The company can choose to lag the market to control labor costs because the supply (of qualified candidates) is high and the demand is low (only three positions to be filled).

☒ **A, C, and D** are incorrect because these choices are not necessary to achieve the desired outcome.

49. ☑ **C.** Deferred pay is a form of indirect compensation.

☒ **A, B, and D** are incorrect because these are examples of direct compensation.

50. ☑ **D.** According to the Fair Labor Standards Act and the Age Discrimination Act in Employment Act, an employer must keep payroll records for three years.

☒ **A, B, and C** are incorrect in this example of payroll record retention as a company is required to keep payroll records for three years.

51. ☑ **D.** The master file should include personal data including name, gender, date of birth, and social security number.

☒ **A, B, and C** are incorrect because although name, date of birth, and social security number should be included in the master file, veteran status, national origin, and Form I-9 should be kept in a separate file to ensure confidentiality.

52. ☑ **A.** There is no federal requirement to maintain paper copies; therefore, retrieving electronic records and submitting is sufficient.

☒ **B, C, and D** are incorrect because there is no federal requirement to maintain paper copies; there is no need to print or reproduce or re-type data.

53. ☑ **D.** The job evaluation process provides a rational foundation to the organization's concern for a total compensation system. The job evaluation process accomplishes this objective by determining the relative worth of each job by establishing a hierarchy of jobs.

☒ **A, B, and C** are incorrect. A is incorrect because the job evaluation process does not measure the performance level of employees. B is incorrect because while the job evaluation process may determine wage information that goes into a job offer, it does not itself initiate a job offer process. C is incorrect because a job evaluation process may look at duties in order to determine job classifications but it does not drive the creation or assignment of job duties.

54. ☑ **D.** The job classification method is a popular job evaluation approach because it is understandable and well accepted by employees. In addition, classifications can change as responsibilities change. The job classification method is a typical approach for large organizations with limited resources.

☒ **A, B, and C** are incorrect. A is incorrect because the factor comparison method requires time and resources. The factor comparison method compares job to job through the use of job descriptions and a thorough job analysis process. B is incorrect because the job ranking method puts jobs into a sequence based on relative value. It is best used in small organizations where there are few jobs to be evaluated. C is incorrect because this process is difficult to explain to employees and would not fit the objectives outlined in this question.

The point factor method is a systematic process that establishes categories based on skill, responsibilities, effort, and working conditions. Each of those factors is divided into levels, which are assigned points.

55. ☑ **B.** The factor comparison method, which ranks each job by each selected compensable factor, then identifies dollar values for each level of each factor to ultimately establish a pay rate for each job.

    ☒ **A, C, and D are incorrect. A** is incorrect because "job classification" refers to a method where jobs are classified into an existing grade/category structure or hierarchy. Each level in the grade/category structure has a description and associated job titles. Each job is assigned to the grade/category providing the closest match to the job. The classification of a position is decided by comparing the whole job with the appropriate job grading standard. **C** is incorrect because the "point factor method" refers to valuing jobs based on elements deemed critical to a company's sustainability. **D** is incorrect because "job ranking" refers to the process of establishing a hierarchy of jobs from lowest to highest based on each job's overall value to the organization. It evaluates the whole job rather than parts of it, and compares one job to another. It is a subjective process.

56. ☑ **C.** HR's role in this scenario is to ensure that immediate supervisors have the tools they need to roll out the new compensation plan. The message needs to be consistent throughout the organization. A compensation handbook will provide that information in a succinct and uniform manner.

    ☒ **A, B, and D are incorrect** because all managers, especially the line supervisors who immediately manage the workforce, should have the tools they need to discuss the new compensation structure readily available. Extending the time an employee has to share his feelings, both positive or negative, about this change will only heighten the employee's concern and create more angst than necessary.

57. ☑ **A.** "Red circle" refers to pay that falls above the maximum of a salary range.

    ☒ **B, C, and D are incorrect. B** is incorrect because "green circle" refers to pay that falls below the minimum of a salary range. **C** is incorrect because wage compression occurs when new hires are paid at a higher rate than existing employees who have similar skills, education, and experience. **D** is incorrect because compa-ratios are a calculation that compares an employee's salary to the midpoint of a range.

58. ☑ **A.** In an external published survey such as the Department of Labor and Bureau of Labor Statistics survey, the data is widely available and no participation is needed, therefore saving time.

    ☒ **B, C, and D are incorrect. B** is incorrect because providing input into survey design would occur with an external survey outsourced to a consulting firm. **C** is incorrect because using an external survey conducted by a consulting firm such as Mercer or Towers Watson would allow for no input in survey design. **D** is incorrect because full control of survey design would occur with an internal custom survey outsourced to a consulting firm.

59. ☑ **B.** Factoring differences in local pay rates in both cities on the national salary survey will help devise an appropriate compensation plan.

☒ **A, C,** and **D** are incorrect because these choices are not necessary or recommended as a way to factor regional pay differences on salary surveys.

60. ☑ **C.** Establishing an Employee Stock Option Plan (ESOP) is a viable option for an organization's owner who wishes to fund employees' retirement without having to sell the company to outside investors. An Employee Stock Option Plan is a defined contribution plan in which a firm sets up a trust and makes tax-deductible contributions to it. An ESOP enables employees to purchase shares in an organization from the selling owners.

☒ **A, B,** and **D** are incorrect. **A** is incorrect because a 401(k) does not offer stock ownership of an organization. **B** is incorrect because there is a noncash compensation option that is more effective than simply trying to convince relatives of the owner to take over a company. **D** is incorrect because an ESOP is a viable alternative to selling the company to outside investors.

61. ☑ **A.** A 401(k) plan enables employees to contribute a percentage of their wages on a tax-deferred basis. The employer also matches contributions up to a certain amount. Employers like this option because it gets employees involved in their own retirement planning process.

☒ **B, C,** and **D** are incorrect. **B** is incorrect because a pay for performance plan is an incentive program. **C** is incorrect because in a merit pay plan, employees are rewarded for performance. **D** is incorrect because in a market pay plan, an employee's pay is adjusted as a result of market changes.

62. ☑ **B.** As a general rule, if a severance payment written in a golden parachute clause is equal to or exceeds three times the executive's total compensation, then the executive will be subject to an excise tax in addition to income taxes on the payment.

☒ **A, C,** and **D** are incorrect because these choices are all incorrect statements when referring to golden parachute clauses written into executives contracts.

63. ☑ **A.** Incentive stock options are a way for employees to achieve stock ownership without the participants having to invest any of their own money.

☒ **B, C,** and **D** are incorrect because these are not ways to provide stock options without employees investing their own money.

64. ☑ **D.** This change of control provision is necessary during a merger or acquisition as only one incumbent will remain as a result and accelerated payments may be necessary.

☒ **A, B,** and **C** are incorrect. **A** and **B** are incorrect because these choices would not be a reason for a golden parachute clause to apply to executive compensation. **C** is incorrect because although an executive may feel/think this way, it is not the most important reason to include a golden parachute clause in the executive's contract.

65. ☑ **C.** Establishing an Employee Stock Option Plan (ESOP) is a viable option for an organization's owner who wishes to fund employees' retirement without having to sell the company to outside investors. An Employee Stock Option Plan is a defined contribution plan in which a firm sets up a trust and makes tax-deductible contributions to it. An ESOP enables employees to purchase shares in an organization from the selling owners.

☒ **A, B,** and **D** are incorrect. **A** is incorrect because a 401(k) does not offer stock ownership of an organization. **B** is incorrect because there is a noncash compensation option that is more effective than simply trying to convince relatives of the owner to take over a company. **D** is incorrect because an ESOP is a viable alternative to selling the company to outside investors.

66. ☑ **A.** A 401(k) plan enables employees to contribute a percentage of their wages on a tax-deferred basis. The employer also matches contributions up to a certain amount. Employers like this option because it gets employees involved in their own retirement planning process.

☒ **B, C,** and **D** are incorrect. **B** is incorrect because a pay for performance plan refers to an incentive program. **C** is incorrect because a merit pay plan refers to how employees are rewarded for performance. **D** is incorrect because a market pay plan refers to the adjustment of employees' pay due to market changes.

67. ☑ **D.** A noncash incentive plan includes rewarding employees through the use of gifts, rewards, or prizes. The key to success in using noncash is to understand what employees value the most and linking it to organizational objectives.

☒ **A, B,** and **C** are incorrect. **A** is incorrect because a performance share plan allows employees to earn stock in their organization. **B** is incorrect because a group incentive plan rewards groups or teams for meeting or exceeding performance expectations. **C** is incorrect because a profit sharing plan rewards employees based on organizational profitability targets.

68. ☑ **A.** If money is left over in an employee's account at the deadline for FSA, all remaining funds will be forfeited.

☒ **B, C,** and **D** are incorrect because these choices, while disadvantages, are mere inconveniences compared to losing money if not used during the plan year.

69. ☑ **C.** Leo and all employees may roll over the remaining funds into the next year.

☒ **A, B,** and **D** are incorrect because these choices are not advantages to an HRA, nor are they accurate reflections on how an HRA works.

70. ☑ **B.** An employee must be enrolled in a qualified High Deductible Health Plan to be eligible to also be enrolled in a health savings account.

☒ **A, C,** and **D** are incorrect as these choices are not mandatory to be enrolled in a Health Savings Account.

71. ☑ **A.** At the employer's discretion, the funds can be used toward COBRA payments if the employee leaves his or her position.

☒ **B, C,** and **D** are incorrect because these are not options at the employer's discretion on a health reimbursement account.

72. ☑ **C.** Unlike medical services, which typically need to be done quickly, employees can postpone dental services so there is typically a high adverse selection rate on dental plans. A dental plan will typically require 100 percent participation to combat this.

☒ **A, B,** and **D** are incorrect because these choices are neither accurate nor relevant to this example.

73. ☑ **A.** In ASO plans, the employer utilizes only the claims department of the insurance company, whereas TPAs utilize an independent claims department that is not usually insurer-related.

☒ **B, C,** and **D** are incorrect. **B** and **C** are incorrect because both ASOs and TPAs are self-funded. **D** is incorrect because in ASO plans, the employer utilizes only the claims department of the insurance company, whereas TPAs utilize an independent claims department not usually insurer-related.

74. ☑ **B.** In letting employees choose which plans best serve their overall needs, the employer is not left overpaying for unwanted health care services. This will help reduce costs and improve employee morale as employees feel they have a choice.

☒ **A, C,** and **D** are incorrect because these choices will reduce costs but most likely will not lead to higher employee morale as the out-of-pocket costs on these will be higher and employees will experience the inconvenience of these plan designs.

75. ☑ **C.** Involve local experts in compensation and benefits laws and regulation to be able to fully comply with each region's laws and regulations.

☒ **A, B,** and **D** are incorrect because these choices are not necessary or recommended as a way to ensure compliance with laws and regulations.

76. ☑ **D.** The main purpose of an international social security agreement is to eliminate dual social security taxation, which occurs when a worker from one country works in another country where workers are required to pay social security taxes on the same wages.

☒ **A, B,** and **C** are incorrect because these choices don't reflect the purpose behind an international social security agreement.

77. ☑ **A.** Providing a lump sum is a strong incentive for the assignee to accept the assignment.

☒ **B, C,** and **D** are incorrect because they would not be the biggest advantages to providing a lump-sum approach.

78. ☑ **B.** A fiduciary is one who exercises discretionary decision-making over a group health plan. The Department of Labor (DOL), specifically the Employee Retirement Income Security Act (ERISA), outlines who is a fiduciary and the responsibilities of fiduciaries.

☒ **A, C, and D are incorrect. A** is incorrect because profitability responsibility is not an ERISA compliance responsibility. **C** is incorrect because recruitment is not tied to health benefit fiduciary responsibilities. **D** is incorrect because talent satisfaction is not an ERISA compliance responsibility.

79. ☑ **C.** The Department of Labor considers the very act of hiring a service provider to be a fiduciary function. As such, the process of hiring a service provider should not be done haphazardly. A key action would be to equally compare all firms based on the same information such as services offered and costs.

☒ **A, B, and D are incorrect. A** is incorrect because the guidance we receive from the DOL is that we should provide equal information to more than one prospective firm. Simply utilizing services from a relative of a CEO, Board Director, or anyone else is not stepping up to the fiduciary responsibility expectations, and potentially you could face personal liability for such an action. **B** is incorrect because, again, the most prudent action is to seek information from more than one provider. **D** is incorrect because the fact that the service provider is an independent contractor is irrelevant in this case. The best action to take is to document the selection and monitoring of the service provider.

CHAPTER 6

Employee and Labor Relations

This functional area includes coverage of the following responsibilities and knowledge objectives.

Employee and Labor Relations—Responsibilities Objectives

- **01** Ensure that employee and labor relations activities are compliant with applicable federal laws and regulations.

- **02** Assess organizational climate by obtaining employee input (for example: focus groups, employee surveys, staff meetings).

- **03** Develop and implement employee relations programs (for example: recognition, special events, diversity programs) that promote a positive organizational culture.

- **04** Evaluate effectiveness of employee relations programs through the use of metrics (for example: exit interviews, employee surveys, turnover rates).

- **05** Establish, update, and communicate workplace policies and procedures (for example: employee handbook, reference guides, or standard operating procedures) and monitor their application and enforcement to ensure consistency.

- **06** Develop and implement a discipline policy based on organizational code of conduct/ethics, ensuring that no disparate impact or other legal issues arise.

- **07** Create and administer a termination process (for example: reductions in force [RIF], policy violations, poor performance) ensuring that no disparate impact or other legal issues arise.

- **08** Develop, administer, and evaluate grievance/dispute resolution and performance improvement policies and procedures.

- **09** Investigate and resolve employee complaints filed with federal agencies involving employment practices or working conditions, utilizing professional resources as necessary (for example: legal counsel, mediation/arbitration specialists, investigators).

- **10** Develop and direct proactive employee relations strategies for remaining union-free in non-organized locations (SPHR only).

- **11** Direct and/or participate in collective bargaining activities, including contract negotiation, costing, and administration.

Employee and Labor Relations—Knowledge Objectives

- **50** Applicable federal laws affecting employment in union and nonunion environments, such as laws regarding antidiscrimination policies, sexual harassment, labor relations, and privacy (for example: WARN Act, Title VII, NLRA)

- **51** Techniques and tools for facilitating positive employee relations (for example: employee surveys, dispute/conflict resolution, labor/management cooperative strategies)

- **52** Employee involvement strategies (for example: employee management committees, self-directed work teams, staff meetings)

- **53** Individual employment rights issues and practices (for example: employment at will, negligent hiring, defamation)

- **54** Workplace behavior issues/practices (for example: absenteeism and performance improvement)

- **55** Unfair labor practices

- **56** The collective bargaining process, strategies, and concepts (for example: contract negotiation, costing, and administration)

- **57** Legal disciplinary procedures

- **58** Positive employee relations strategies and non-monetary rewards

- **59** Techniques for conducting unbiased investigations

- **60** Legal termination procedures

Employee and Labor Relations is the functional area of the human resources body of knowledge that addresses how employers sustain effective working relationships with staff in union and non-union environments. It involves sustaining systems that support positive employee relations programs, effective workplace policies and procedures, and employee performance. Employee and Labor Relations are governed by several common law doctrines and legal statutes that provide both employers and employees with certain rights and responsibilities. Some of the significant legislation in this area includes the National Labor Relations Act and the establishment of the National Labor Relations Board.

Employee and Labor Relations—Responsibilities Objectives

Objective 01 Ensure That Employee and Labor Relations Activities Are Compliant with Applicable Federal Laws and Regulations

1. A company reaches an agreement with a labor union that states that only union members will be employed with the company. Which of the following laws makes it illegal to establish a closed shop except in the construction industry?

   A. National Labor Relations Act

   B. The Wagner Act

   C. Taft-Hartley Act

   D. Labor-Management Reporting and Disclosure Act

2. A non-union company implemented a freeze on raises for the next three years. The tool and dye makers at this plant are unhappy with this decision and begin meeting in small groups to discuss confronting management and possibly forming a union. Which of the following would you most likely use to lead a discussion with management?

   A. Labor-Management Reporting and Disclosure Act

   B. Labor Management Relations Act and Wagner Act

   C. National Labor Relations Act

   D. Wagner Act and the Norris-LaGuardia Act

3. The union representative for the plumbers union at a company leaves a stack of recruiting flyers in the break room. Her supervisor wants to issue a written warning to her stating that she is engaging in union activity on company time. As the HR Director, how would you advise her supervisor?

A. He can proceed with the write-up because, per the National Labor Relations Act (NLRA), an employer can vocalize their opposition to unions as long as it is not done in a threatening manner.

B. He can't proceed with the write-up because, per the Labor-Management Relations Act (LMRA), an employer can question an employee's interest in union representation during work hours.

C. He can proceed with the write-up because, per the NLRA, an employer can prohibit union solicitation during work hours. The break room is used during work hours only and on the employer's property.

D. He can't proceed with the write-up because, per the NLRA, an employer cannot prohibit the union from soliciting members in non-work areas, such as the break room, unless the employer has a published and enforced policy that prohibits all types of solicitation material in the break room.

4. John was offered a job at Rubber Makers International on the condition that he not join the union. His supervisor suggested that there might be a financial incentive after 90 days for adhering to this verbal contract. As the HR Director, what concerns you most about this interaction?

A. This is a potential violation of the Wagner Act.

B. This is a potential violation of the Taft-Hartley Act.

C. This is a potential violation of the Norris-LaGuardia Act.

D. This is a potential violation of the WARN Act.

5. A mine workers' union provides free printing services to a candidate running for union president. Which entity would be most likely to investigate these activities?

A. Office of Labor-Management Standards (OLMS)

B. National Labor Relations Board (NLRB)

C. Department of Labor (DOL)

D. Department of Justice (DOJ)

Objective 02   Assess Organizational Climate by Obtaining Employee Input

6. An automotive manufacturing plant management wants to determine which technology upgrade would increase production efficiency. It is preferred that the employees doing the work provide feedback. Which of the following employee-involvement strategies would work best?

A. Employee-management committees

B. Self-directed work teams

C. Task force

D. Committees

7. A CEO receives conflicting reports from HR regarding the reason for high turnover in the finance department. He wants to take a more hands-on approach to gathering feedback. Which employee engagement measurement tool would you recommend?

A. Skip-level interviews

B. Employee focus groups

C. Employee surveys

D. Exit Interviews

8. A recent regulatory change requires that a multinational organization change its business processes within the next three months. Which of the following would be the best way for the company to get new process flow diagrams out to all staff?

A. Newsletter

B. All-hands Staff meeting

C. Brown-bag lunch

D. Intranet

9. A company has an open-door policy with management. The organizational structure is flat and employees are rewarded when they revamp a process and bring new ideas to the table. Yet the exit interviews from recently departed employees of the payroll department show that they felt as if there was little room for growth and that management ignored their suggestions for improving processing times and system upgrades. As the HR Director, what would you determine is the area you need to focus on in this department?

A. Improving organizational culture

B. Advancing organizational development

C. Improving organizational climate

D. Advancing organizational efficiency

10. Which of the following is the best description of the overall purpose of an effective employee relations program?

A. Establish employee dispute resolution techniques

B. Maximize employee performance

C. Increase employee feedback to management

D. Improve employee communication to management

Objective 03   Develop and Implement Employee Relations Programs That Promote a Positive Organizational Culture

11. A valued employee of 25 years recently had changes in her personal life that require that she start work no earlier than 9 a.m. several days per month. Which of the following modified work schedules would best assist this employee?

    A. Part-time work

    B. Flextime

    C. Job-sharing

    D. Compressed workweeks

12. HR wants to encourage the number of innovative ideas submitted by employees throughout the year. Which of the following employee relations strategies work best to achieve increased employee participation?

    A. List the names of people with the most innovative ideas on the company intranet.

    B. Recognize employees, with an incentive, who submitted innovative ideas that the company has decided to implement at the annual all-hands meeting.

    C. List the names of employees with the most innovative ideas in the company newsletter.

    D. Recognize employees with the most innovative ideas at their department's staff meeting.

13. Which of the following helps to promote inclusion and diversity in the workplace?

    A. Recognition events

    B. Work/life balance programs

    C. Employee committees

    D. Job share

14. At the cornerstone of a positive employee relations strategy is

    _____.

    A. Mutual trust between employees and management

    B. Adherence to all common law statutes

    C. Exclusively communicating positive outcomes to employees

    D. Consistent vocalization of the company's non-union message

15. Which of the following has the most impact on increasing employee productivity?

    A. Increase pay raises.

    B. Review the total rewards package including health benefits.

C. Increase the number of ways that an employee can be recognized.

D. Treat employees with dignity and respect.

Objective 04 Evaluate Effectiveness of Employee Relations Programs Through the Use of Metrics

16. An organization has been steadily losing skilled employees due to turnover. Managers have been complacent and not taking retention initiatives seriously. What would be a most effective metric that would contribute to achieving buy-in on retention initiatives?

A. Time-to-fill

B. Turnover cost

C. Vacancy rate

D. Accession rate

17. An organization has been collecting exit interview data for several years. The data is in a raw form (numbers in a spreadsheet). Which of the following would be the most effective way to apply the data learned from these exit interviews?

A. Because the data reflects the past, ignore it and collect all new information.

B. Distribute the spreadsheets to all supervisors, managers, and leadership.

C. Create a turnover report and a balanced scorecard, and post it on bulletin boards.

D. Organize the data into meaningful categories and report strengths and weaknesses to management.

18. A survey that assesses why good employees remain with the organization and what might make them leave is which type of retention method?

A. Stay interviews

B. Turnover cost tracking

C. Exit interviews

D. Employee safety survey

19. An HR leader starts a new job with an organization and finds that the employees are apathetic to completing the employee engagement survey. The employee sentiments heard are that management does nothing with the information so why bother filling out the survey. Which of the following actions contribute significantly to an effective employee engagement survey?

A. Create turnover metrics and a balanced scorecard to track if the survey has had a positive impact.

B. Have managers create action plans and communicate survey results to their own employees.

C. Launch a communication campaign with the goal of convincing employees that the survey matters.

D. Cancel future employee engagement surveys since employees are not inclined to participate.

20. An organization wants to measure the effectiveness of its cross-cultural mentoring program. Which of the following actions would contribute the most to learning about the effectiveness of the program?

A. Survey prospective applicants to see if they applied because of the program.

B. Survey all employees to see if they would like to join the mentoring program.

C. Survey program participants with questions that measure engagement and retention.

D. Survey leadership to determine their thoughts on the mentoring program.

Objective 05   Establish, Update, and Communicate Workplace Policies and Procedures and Monitor Their Application and Enforcement to Ensure Consistency

21. An organization entering the growth life cycle phase wants to begin developing house-wide policies. In the process of establishing policies, which of the following should be the first step?

A. Identify the need for a policy.

B. Communicate with employees.

C. Determine policy content.

D. Update or revise policies.

22. An HR leader has identified the need to create a new organizational policy. The intention of the policy is to clarify behavioral expectations while maintaining flexibility based on the circumstances involved. Which of the following is the best statement to use that will help achieve the objective of the policy?

A. This policy applies to all permanent employees.

B. Employees who follow this policy will enjoy long-term employment.

C. Employees will be terminated only "for cause."

D. Typical behaviors in violation of this policy include but are not limited to...

23. It is time to implement a new organization-wide policy. The policy will address how employees will respond to potential violent situations in the workplace. Which of the following is the best step to ensure effective employee buy-in and understanding of the new policy?

A. Post the new policy on all bulletin boards located on the organization's premises.

B. Managers give the employees the ability to ask questions in department meetings.

C. E-mail the new policy to all leaders and employees, with an effective date included.

D. No additional steps are necessary because policies are a requirement regardless of buy-in.

24. A job posting policy requires every new job must be posted internally for five full days before outside recruiting activities begin. A supervisor expresses concern that a vacant position requires critical skills that existing employees mostly do not possess. This is a fast-paced work environment and the organization's objective would be limited if this position remains vacant for long. Which of the following actions would contribute significantly to the organization's objectives?

A. Create a time-to-fill metric, monitor the situation, and report to leadership the results of the study.

B. Advise the supervisor that the policy has been in place for years and to be patient.

C. Revise the policy to allow job posting to occur internally and externally concurrently.

D. Immediately post the job internally so that the five-day requirement expires quickly.

Objective 06   Develop and Implement a Discipline Policy Based on Organizational Code of Conduct/Ethics, Ensuring That No Disparate Impact or Other Legal Issues Arise

25. An organization is being threatened with a lawsuit from an employee who was recently terminated. The claim is that the employer terminated him because of his race. However, the employer states that the termination was "for cause." Which of the following would be the best proactive approach to preventing a possible lawsuit?

A. Have a written disciplinary policy and follow it uniformly.

B. Survey terminated employees if they feel discriminated against.

C. Train all employees on cultural awareness and diversity.

D. Create a leadership development program on diversity awareness.

26. An organization wants to establish a formal progressive disciplinary policy. Which of the following will most likely be included as disciplinary steps in the policy?

A. Management discretion in issuing a verbal, written, and final warnings

B. A meeting with the employee, supervisor, and senior leader

C. First, second, and third offense before taking action

D. Minor, intermediate, and severe policy violations

27. A supervisor is being accused of discrimination. The supervisor states that he is trying to correct the performance of this employee and is following the disciplinary policy. Which of the following would be the best action to take to minimize risk?

A. Survey other employees about the supervisor's history and make a decision based on findings.

B. Conduct an investigative meeting with both the supervisor and employee to determine facts.

C. Check the supervisor's personnel record to see if there is a history of complaints filed.

D. The issue is escalated so there is nothing to do but to call an attorney and prepare for a lawsuit.

Objective 07   Create and Administer a Termination Process Ensuring That No Disparate Impact or Other Legal Issues Arise

28. An organization's leaders have decided that it must conduct a reduction in force (RIF) in order to remain financially viable. As the HR leader, you must decide how to select employees to lay off that would minimize any adverse impact. Which of the following are the best criteria to use for a reduction in force selection?

A. Complaint or grievance history, troublemaker reputation, team-player status

B. Popularity, coworker friendliness, and team playing activity

C. Attendance, meeting participation, and project completion timeliness

D. Job categories, prior disciplinary actions, seniority, and skill set

29. A supervisor has approached the HR leader expressing interest in terminating an employee due to ongoing performance issues. Which of the following is the best first step to take?

A. Include the employee in a future reduction in force to minimize risk.

B. In the termination meeting, tell the employee she is being laid off.

C. Check the personnel record for documentation of previous and current performance issues.

D. There are no actions to take as the performance issue will correct itself.

30. A multi-national organization based in the United States has an employee based in Indonesia. The organization's leadership wants to terminate this employee's employment. Which of the following is the best step to take?

   A. Check local requirements and seek the local Industrial Relations Court approval, if applicable.

   B. The company is headquartered in the United States, so you can move forward with the termination process.

   C. All employees have been notified they are "at will," so move forward with the termination process.

   D. Do not move forward with the termination process and give the employee a second chance.

Objective 08   Develop, Administer, and Evaluate Grievance/Dispute Resolution and Performance Improvement Policies and Procedures

31. Liz, an HR Manager, is researching how frequent absenteeism is affecting her department's bottom line. What is the *main* effect of absenteeism on productivity?

   A. Current employees must train new or replacement workers.

   B. High cost of replacement staff.

   C. Overtime payments may need to be paid out for current staff working extra hours.

   D. Insurance premiums may go up.

32. A nursing home employee who has been with the company for five years has been out of work for four consecutive days without notice of her status. The manager is writing up a disciplinary action for the time missed from work. The manager brings it to HR for review. What step should HR take at this point?

   A. Call the employee and let him know he has been terminated for no call/no show.

   B. Find out if the employee has been out of work for FMLA, USERRA, or another state law protected leave of absence.

   C. Have the manager deliver the disciplinary action with HR present.

   D. Find out if the employee is missing work because of dissatisfaction with his position.

33. What is the best preventive measure that a manager can take to avoid disciplinary action?

   A. Talk to each employee on a monthly basis.

   B. Provide positive results on yearly performance reviews.

C. Lead the market with salary rates.

D. Set clear expectations.

34. A restaurant employee in a non-union environment has had repeated tardiness and customer complaints. What should the manager's *first* step be in the disciplinary process?

   A. Oral warning

   B. Termination

   C. Open dialogue and problem solving

   D. Written warning

35. An employee has been caught using the company credit card for fraudulent purchases and profiting from the purchases. What step should HR take in this case?

   A. Oral warning

   B. Termination

   C. Problem solving

   D. Written warning

Objective 09   Investigate and Resolve Employee Complaints Filed with Federal Agencies Involving Employment Practices or Working Conditions, Utilizing Professional Resources as Necessary

36. Union employees of a government agency are prohibited from striking and have agreed to engage in alternative dispute resolution in lieu of legal action for any labor dispute. There is a labor dispute regarding pay raises. Which of the following is likely the next step for the union and management?

   A. Compulsory arbitration

   B. Facilitative mediation

   C. Voluntary arbitration

   D. Constructive confrontation

37. At which stage of the mediation process might the facilitator meet with parties separately?

   A. Fact-finding

   B. Negotiating

   C. Options

   D. Structure

38. A construction worker union refuses to do business with any company that buys supplies from a particular concrete company. This decision was made to support the workers at the concrete company who have reported multiple violations of the Fair Labor Standards Act (FLSA) with regards to overtime pay. As the HR Director at Next Generation Home Builders, what advice would you provide to senior management?

A. This hot cargo contract clause is an unfair labor practice as defined by the National Labor Relations Act (NLRA).

B. This featherbedding contract clause is an unfair labor practice as defined by the Labor Management Relations Act (LMRA).

C. This yellow-dog contract clause is an unfair labor practice as defined by the Norris-LaGuardia Act.

D. This iron-clad contract clause is an unfair labor practice as defined by the Labor Management Relations Act (LMRA).

39. A school district decides to purchase absence management software, which eliminates the need to have an administrative assistant contact and assign substitute teachers on a daily basis. The administrative assistant who currently performs this job was notified that her position will be eliminated at the close of the school year. She files a grievance with the secretarial union, which has an active contract with the district for the next four years. What is the likely outcome of an arbitration proceeding on this matter?

A. The school district must retain the administrative assistant's current position until the end of the contract term.

B. The school district would be engaging in an unfair labor practice by accepting this iron-clad contract.

C. The union would be engaging in an unfair labor practice (ULP) if it does not guarantee the administrative assistant retain employment because she is a dues-paying member.

D. The union would be engaging in an unfair labor practice if it tried to force the school district to keep this position.

40. The cashiers union at Nationwide Appliances is on strike accusing the company of unsafe working conditions. The drivers from One Stop Delivery Services attempt to deliver a shipment of refrigerators and are blocked from doing so by the strikers. As the HR Director, how would you advise the senior management team of One Stop Delivery Services?

A. This is organizational picketing. The company should file an unfair labor practice (ULP) charge with the National Labor Relations Board (NLRB).

B. The cashiers union is within its rights to engage in this economic strike.

C. This is a secondary boycott. The company should file a ULP charge with the NLRB.

D. This is recognition picketing in which the cashiers union is demanding that Nationwide Appliances recognize their group as a lawful union and agree to bargain with them in good faith.

SPHR Objective 10 Develop and Direct Proactive Employee Relations Strategies for Remaining Union-Free in Non-Organized Locations (SPHR only)

41. An organization wishes to remain union-free. The newly hired HR leader is expected to be proactive in union avoidance strategies. Which of the following actions would contribute significantly to the organization's objectives?

A. Implement a generous retirement plan.

B. Give every employee a pay raise.

C. Hire employees with a positive attitude.

D. Conduct a vulnerability assessment.

42. A supervisor in a union-free organization casually tells an HR leader that he heard rumors of employees meeting offsite to discuss union organizing possibilities. He heard the rumor about three months prior to this conversation. Which of the following is the best action the HR leaders should consider taking?

A. Conduct leadership training on proactive union-avoidance strategies.

B. Track down the employee who started the rumor and terminate employment.

C. Send out a memo that all offsite meetings need to be approved by HR.

D. No actions are necessary as it is a three-month-old rumor and no petitions were filed.

43. An organization's leaders want to have a culture that stresses on open, transparent communication and professional integrity philosophy to maintain a union-free status. When it comes to onboarding new employees, which of the following actions contribute significantly to the organization's objectives?

A. Recruit and hire employees who have excellent communication and team-work skills.

B. Utilize the new employee orientation to communicate the organization's philosophy.

C. Create metrics that measure the culture's communication methods and effectiveness.

D. Conduct an employee-engagement survey to measure employee attitudes and opinions.

Objective 11 Direct and/or Participate in Collective Bargaining Activities, Including Contract Negotiation, Costing, and Administration

44. The metal workers union and Trivago Metalworks engage in the collective bargaining process. The relationship between management and the union is characterized by a desire to be amicable and to make the business successful so that employees are able to continue to improve their personal economic situations. Which of the following best describes this type of bargaining?

    A. Positional bargaining

    B. Conjunctive bargaining

    C. Distributive bargaining

    D. Interest-based bargaining

45. South Cob Airlines has three active unions representing flight attendants, pilots, and mechanics. Both management and labor want to standardize certain terms of each contract such as holiday pay and scheduled raises. Which of the following bargaining techniques would you recommend to management and labor?

    A. Single-employer bargaining

    B. Coordinated bargaining

    C. Parallel bargaining

    D. Multi-employer bargaining

46. A secretarial union and management are in negotiations. Traditionally, all administrative assistant positions work from a physical location and the union would like it to stay this way. However, the business needs have changed and because of technological advances, the employer wants to redesign certain administrative assistant positions to include the ability to work remotely. Which position would you advise management to take on this subject?

    A. Scheduling and job design typically is a management right.

    B. Job design is an illegal subject and cannot be negotiated.

    C. This is a term of employment that is a mandatory subject and must be negotiated.

    D. This is a permissible subject and must be negotiated.

47. The collective bargaining agreement for the bakers' union requires that all bakers pay their fair share in union dues even if they decide not to become voting members of the union. This is an example of a(n) _____.

    A. Open shop

    B. Union shop

    C. Agency shop

    D. Closed shop

48. A major restaurant chain acquires a group of restaurants represented by a chefs' union with a contract set to expire in four years. The management wants to make changes to pay rates and hours. As the HR Director, how would you advise management?

  A. The new restaurant group must assimilate into the company culture. It begins with adhering to the conditions of employment, wages, and hours of their new owner.

  B. The National Labor Relations Board (NLRB) may consider them a successor employer. As a successor employer, they can make changes but they must be negotiated through the collective bargaining process.

  C. The NLRB would not consider them a successor employer because they added a small number of new employees with the acquisition. The union contract does not have to be honored.

  D. The union contract must be honored. The new employer will have a chance to negotiate new wages and work hours in four years when the contract expires.

Employee and Labor Relations—Knowledge Objectives

Objective 50 Applicable Federal Laws Affecting Employment in Union and Non-Union Environments, Such as Laws Regarding Antidiscrimination Policies, Sexual Harassment, Labor Relations, and Privacy

49. Which of the following established that employers can be held vicariously liable for the actions of their employees in sexual harassment cases?

  A. *Burlington Industries v. Ellerth*

  B. *Meritor Savings Bank v. Vinson*

  C. *Harris v. Forklift Systems*

  D. *Oncale v. Sundowner Offshore Services, Inc.*

50. Jasmine, an African-American woman, resigns her position as Account Manager citing that she was harassed by the team leader who supervises her on a daily basis. The team leader has no authority to take tangible employment actions in regards to Jasmine. The Sales Director claims no knowledge of the events leading up to Jasmine's resignation. As the HR Director, how would you advise senior management regarding the company's liability in this case?

  A. There is no liability because Jasmine did not report the incidents that led up to her decision to resign.

  B. The company is vicariously liable because the team leader meets the definition of a supervisor as established by the Ellerth and Faragher cases on sexual harassment.

C. The company is not liable for the team leader's actions because the Supreme Court in *Vance v. Ball State University* narrowly defined supervisor as the person who may take tangible employment actions such as demotion or termination of employment.

D. The company is liable because the team leader meets the definition of supervisor as established by the Equal Employment Opportunity Commission (EEOC).

51. A reservist was called to active duty for five years. Upon return to the United States mainland, he was informed that the position he left had been upgraded and filled by a permanent employee. Does the employer have any responsibilities to the reservist related to reinstatement of employment?

A. The reservist has been gone more than 180 days; therefore, the employer has no duty to reinstate her in the same position.

B. The reservist has 90 days following the completion of service to apply to the employer for reinstatement.

C. The employer must reinstate the reservist promptly but may terminate her employment for cause within 60 days.

D. The employer must reinstate the reservist promptly but may terminate her employment for cause after 180 days.

Objective 51   Techniques and Tools for Facilitating Positive Employee Relations

52. A procedure that provides clear guidance for supervisors and employees to systematically and fairly resolve complaints is known as which of the following?

A. An open door policy

B. An HR resolution policy

C. A grievance process

D. A team building process

53. A unionized organization faces negative implications if certain legislation passes into law. The organization will be forced to lay off its workforce as a result. However, the organization has limited resources to spend on opposing the legislation. Which of the following strategies would significantly contribute to the overall organizational objectives?

A. Analyze the potentially new law and inform leadership of the implications.

B. Notify the workforce and union representatives that layoffs are a possibility.

C. No actions are necessary as the new legislation is not yet passed into law.

D. Form a labor-management committee to oppose the new proposed legislation.

54. An organization implemented an employee engagement survey and the results show that there are strengths to be celebrated and weaknesses to be corrected. Which of the following is the best action to hold managers accountable for communicating results and implementing improvements?

    A. Utilize action plan indicators (API) to measure and report on progress.

    B. No action as managers' performance will be reported on the next survey.

    C. Monitor turnover metrics to see if there is an improvement in numbers.

    D. Create a leadership development course on how to read survey results.

Objective 52   Employee Involvement Strategies

55. An organization is in a highly competitive industry. To be successful it is critical for the organization to have an innovative culture. The organization must have highly skilled and critical thinkers to work on many interdependent projects. Which of the following strategies would contribute significantly to the organization's objectives?

    A. Implement a survey to measure employee engagement and skill levels.

    B. Create self-directed teams that are empowered to make project decisions.

    C. Recruit and hire only employees who have innovative thinking skills.

    D. Create metrics and a balanced scorecard to measure employee performance.

56. A manufacturing organization is concerned about an increase in safety incidences. While improvements in safety protocols need to be created, a key concern is ensuring employees have understood and embrace any new changes. Which of the following strategies would contribute significantly to organizational objectives?

    A. Send out a memo asking employees to work more safely.

    B. Establish an employee-management safety committee.

    C. Create metrics that measure and report on safety issues.

    D. Safety protocols are mandatory; no additional actions are necessary.

57. A global organization's workforce operates on a virtual level. Which of the following methods effectively involves a virtual workforce?

    A. Utilize video conferencing and ensure they are invited to all major meetings.

    B. Send update memos, reports, and information to all employees across the globe.

    C. Have supervisors e-mail and call employees with all news, events, and updates.

    D. No actions are required because virtual employees are not concerned about onsite decisions.

Objective 53 Individual Employment Rights Issues and Practices

58. All Meat Fast Food Company is in the process of setting in place guidelines for responding to reference checks of former employees. Which of the following strategies would you recommend?

    A. Provide dates of employment and title only.

    B. Provide only job-related information that is truthful, clear, and supported by the former employees evaluations.

    C. Provide dates of employment and the reason for discharge only.

    D. Provide job-related information that prevents the new employer from making a negligent hire.

59. Gina's supervisor included the following on her last evaluation: "Keep up the good work and you'll have this job for life." How could this statement have affected the concept of employment-at-will?

    A. Contract exception

    B. Statutory exception

    C. Public-policy exception

    D. Fraudulent misrepresentation

60. A company facilitates a program that assists ex-violent offenders with transitioning back into the society. As the HR Director, you want to ensure that the company does not hire anyone who may have had a violent past. What strategy would you put in place in order to prevent negligent hiring?

    A. Ensure that all employees submit to a review of motor vehicle records.

    B. Ensure that all employee submit to a fingerprint-based criminal background check.

    C. Ensure that all employees submit to a drug screen.

    D. Ensure that employees are discharged immediately if violent behavior is exhibited.

Objective 54 Workplace Behavior Issues/Practices

61. Javetz Corporation's latest reports show an increase in absenteeism by 13 percent over last year. As the HR Director, what would you do next?

    A. Determine the change in costs associated with the increase and explore options to revise the absenteeism policy.

    B. Add new punitive measures to the absenteeism policy to discourage employees from taking mental health days or other unintended forms of paid time off (PTO).

C. Change the absenteeism policy by reducing the number of sick days available to employees.

D. Dock employee pay when absenteeism appears to be excessive.

62. Sarah rolls her eyes every time her supervisor asks her to complete a work-related task. The supervisor reports this insubordinate behavior to HR. How would you advise the supervisor to address this?

A. It is clear that the behavior is insubordinate. Write the employee up for insubordination.

B. Write the employee up because this behavior is consistent and there have been repeated offenses.

C. Discuss the behavior with the employee focusing only on the actual rolling of her eyes. Clarify acceptable responses for future reference.

D. Inform the employee that the bad attitude will result in termination if it happens again.

63. An employee is consistently absent, insubordinate, and an all-around poor performer. The employee has been warned both verbally and in writing. You have decided to move to establishing a performance improvement plan (PIP) for this employee. Which of the following is an element of a quality PIP that has the most impact on deterring the employee from repeating the undesirable behaviors?

A. Number of times the behavior was observed

B. Listing of the undesirable behaviors and the time frame within which improvement is expected

C. Information about how the employee is expected to correct the behaviors

D. Corrective action to be taken if PIP is not fulfilled successfully

Objective 55   Unfair Labor Practices

64. Which of the following is an example of a Union Unfair Labor Practice?

A. Picketing in high numbers where nonstriking employees cannot physically enter the building

B. Filing charges with the NLRB

C. Training being denied by employer during union organization

D. Employees suffering from stress of labor contract negotiations

65. When must an affected employee file an unfair labor practice charge with the NLRB?

A. File claim within 9 months after the alleged ULP.

B. File claim within 12 months after the alleged ULP.

C. File claim immediately after alleged ULP.

D. File claim within six months after the alleged ULP.

66. Employees at a 400-person manufacturing plant are beginning to organize to start a union. During that campaign, an employer would most likely take which following action first?

A. Tell the employees that the plant will move to Mexico if a union is established.

B. Try to negotiate a mutually agreeable benefit package with employees.

C. Try to persuade employees not to form a union but be careful not to threaten or intimidate.

D. Tell employees that they will all get raises if the union is not formed.

Objective 56   The Collective Bargaining Process, Strategies, and Concepts

67. During the collective bargaining process in the public sector, which of the following is considered to be generally illegal in regards to bargaining subjects?

A. Methods of performing work

B. Negotiation of wage rates

C. Types of employees or positions assigned to any organizational work project

D. Arrangements for employees in carrying out job tasks that cannot be negotiated

68. What is the primary goal of contract negotiation between union and management?

A. To establish a contract that will contribute to a constructive relationship with effective resolution of issues that may arise.

B. Both parties agree on all the items of the contract on the first draft.

C. To satisfy both parties interests through a verbal agreement.

D. To clarify ambiguous issues with the contract.

69. Felicia, a team member at Fry Foods, Inc., a union organization, feels that she has been unfairly treated at work and wrongly subjected to disciplinary action after reporting a potential safety violation. During the grievance process, she filed a grievance with her immediate supervisor and higher-level management with no resolution. What is Felicia's next step in the grievance process?

A. To work with HR directly to air the grievance

B. To use the determination of a third party who is a neutral outside arbitrator

C. To have internal legal counsel brought in to discuss the grievance

D. To have the manager and the highest ranking HR official sit down to air the grievance

Objective 57 Legal Disciplinary Procedures

70. An employee brings a licensed firearm to work in a concealed carry state. The same employee had a verbal altercation with a vendor two weeks before and made statements regarding the company not doing business with this particular vendor because he might just have to hurt him. What is the best course of action for this company?

    A. Write the employee up because an immediate termination may result in an accusation of wrongful termination.

    B. Terminate his employment immediately because he poses a threat to the workplace.

    C. Suspend the employee pending investigation.

    D. Write the employee up because these incidents have to be documented before termination can be considered.

71. An employee filed a workers' compensation claim that cost the company almost two million dollars. He is subsequently terminated. The employee believes the termination is related to the filing of the workers' compensation claim. What is this an example of?

    A. Wrongful termination

    B. Constructive discharge

    C. Hostile work environment

    D. Constructive dismissal

72. What is HR's strategic role in employee terminations?

    A. Conduct the termination meeting.

    B. Counsel and coach before the meeting to ensure proper documentation and proper ways to conduct the actual meeting.

    C. Ensure company property is returned.

    D. Ensure that the employee's access to company technology is terminated.

Objective 58 Positive Employee Relations Strategies and Non-Monetary Rewards

73. The HR Manager at a call center is looking at ways that he can add job enrichment to the customer service rep's current position. What would be the *best* example of how he could enrich a customer service rep's job?

    A. Giving reps opportunity to train the shipping department

    B. Giving reps authority to issue credits to customers when they are dissatisfied

    C. Giving reps opportunities to train the accounting department

    D. Giving reps the authority to manage their own schedules

74. What is the *main* advantage of a company allowing its employees to use flextime?

   A. Reduction in absenteeism

   B. Allows employees time to pursue outside activities

   C. Helps morale of employees

   D. More time spent on work activities rather than driving at rush hours

75. What is the main benefit for a company that chooses to utilize employee involvement strategies (participative management) to achieve a mutually beneficial relationship for the company and its employees?

   A. Employees' morale improves.

   B. Provide positive results on yearly performance reviews.

   C. Active participation fosters employee commitment.

   D. Sets clear expectations for company.

Objective 59   Techniques for Conducting Unbiased Investigations

76. A transportation company receives complaints from the community that one of its drivers has been observed driving erratically and is possibly a habitual user of cocaine. HR decides to investigate. What is the likely next step?

   A. Prepare a list of questions to ask each witness.

   B. Interview witnesses.

   C. Determine who should conduct the investigation.

   D. Ensure confidentiality for each possible witness.

77. An employee reports to HR that she believes a coworker is being sexually harassed by their supervisor. What is HR's best next step?

   A. Confirm the harassment with the employee and take measures to ensure the harassment does not continue.

   B. Tell the reporting employee to encourage her coworker to come forward or there is nothing HR can do.

   C. Conduct an investigation.

   D. Suspend the supervisor without pay pending investigation.

78. An HR Director at a school district conducts an investigation after a report of racial discrimination in the food service department. Forty-seven people were interviewed during the investigation. The investigation revealed that the claims were unfounded. What advice would you provide to the department's supervisors at the completion of the investigation to help protect the school district from future litigation?

A. Remind them that the fact that the investigation had to take place is an indication that there is something amiss in the department.

B. Remind them that any adverse employment action against the 47 people interviewed may be seen as retaliatory.

C. Remind them to track the 47 people who participated in the investigation closely because they want to seek retribution against the company.

D. Remind the supervisors of the importance of diversity training.

Objective 60 Legal Interviewing Techniques

79. An employer has discovered alleged misconduct by an employee, which may lead to termination. What is the first step HR should take once discovering the alleged misconduct?

A. Investigate promptly and thoroughly.

B. Move to termination.

C. Suspend employee with pay pending investigation.

D. Suspend employee without pay pending investigation.

80. What is the main advantage to an organization using the Alternative Dispute Resolution process?

A. Decreases HR/management time spent on disputes

B. Decreases costs related to conducting investigations

C. Decreases conflict within the organization

D. Decreases the number of disputes that might end up in court

1. C	21. A	41. D	61. A
2. B	22. D	42. A	62. C
3. D	23. B	43. B	63. D
4. C	24. C	44. D	64. A
5. A	25. A	45. B	65. B
6. C	26. A	46. A	66. C
7. A	27. B	47. C	67. B
8. D	28. D	48. B	68. A
9. C	29. C	49. A	69. B
10. B	30. A	50. C	70. C
11. B	31. A	51. B	71. A
12. B	32. B	52. C	72. B
13. C	33. D	53. D	73. B
14. A	34. C	54. A	74. A
15. D	35. B	55. B	75. C
16. B	36. A	56. B	76. C
17. D	37. A	57. A	77. A
18. A	38. A	58. B	78. B
19. B	39. D	59. A	79. A
20. C	40. C	60. B	80. D

1. ☑ **C.** The Taft-Hartley Act amended the National Labor Relations Act and outlawed closed shops. A *closed shop* is a company where employees are required to join a union as a condition of employment.

   ☒ **A, B,** and **D** are incorrect. **A** and **B** are incorrect because the National Labor Relations Act, also known as the Wagner Act, established the basic rights of employees to form unions. **D** is incorrect because the Labor-Management Reporting and Disclosure Act established reporting requirements for unions, union officers, employees, and employers; set standards for electing union officers; and established safeguards for protecting the assets of labor organizations.

2. ☑ **B.** The Labor Management Relations Act (LMRA), also known as the Taft-Hartley Act, provides the employer with the right of employers to promote an anti-union message in the workplace so long as the employer is not threatening employees or bribing employees to discourage them from forming a union. The Wagner Act, also known as National Labor Relations Act (NLRA), protects the rights of employees to form a union and collectively bargain for wages, benefits, hours, and other working conditions. As the HR leader, it would be your responsibility in this case to arm management with this knowledge and recommend a dual approach to resolution. Management should carefully craft with their legal representatives a message that expresses the company's position on unions but be mindful that they should not infiltrate any attempt for the tool and dye makers to organize and bargain collectively.

   ☒ **A, C,** and **D** are incorrect. **A** is incorrect because the Labor-Management Reporting and Disclosure Act established reporting requirements for unions, union officers, employees, and employers; set standards for electing union officers; and established safeguards for protecting the assets of labor organizations. **C** is incorrect because The NLRA or Wagner Act takes into account only one side of this situation. The employer should also be proactive and exercise its right to clarify its position on the existence of unions in the workplace. **D** is incorrect because the Norris-LaGuardia Act, also known as the Anti-Injunction Bill, outlawed a specific kind of employment contract called yellow-dog contracts. Yellow-dog contracts are where employers make it a condition of employment that workers not join a union. Yellow-dog contracts have been determined as unenforceable in a court of law.

3. ☑ **D.** As the HR Director, you should prevent the supervisor from proceeding with a write-up. It is a direct violation of the National Labor Relations Act (NLRA) to prohibit a union from soliciting members in non-work areas. The break room is considered a non-work area.

   ☒ **A, B,** and **C** are incorrect. **A** is incorrect because the act that allows employers to vocalize their opposition to unions in a non-threatening manner is the Labor-Management Relations Act (LMRA). Also, prohibiting the distribution of union materials does not qualify as non-threatening. **B** is incorrect because this is not a provision of the LMRA. Also, the time employees are in the break room is not typically considered work hours. **C** is incorrect because a break room is considered a non-work area. The NLRA protects a union's right to solicit employees in non-work areas.

4. ☑ **C.** Even though verbal, this is potentially an example of a yellow-dog contract, which was deemed unenforceable by the Norris-LaGuardia Act. A yellow-dog contract is one in which an employer makes an offer of employment contingent upon the employee agreeing not to join a union.

    ☒ **A, B,** and **D** are incorrect. **A** is are incorrect because the Wagner Act, also known as National Labor Relations Act (NLRA), protects the rights of employees to form unions and collectively bargain for wages, benefits, hours, and other working conditions. **B** is incorrect because the Labor Management Relations Act (LMRA), also known as the Taft-Hartley Act, provides the employer with the right of employers to promote an anti-union message in the workplace as long as the employer is not threatening employees or bribing employees to discourage them from forming a union. **D** is incorrect because the Worker Adjustment and Retraining Notification Act (WARN) requires that employers provide notice 60 days in advance of covered plant closings during covered mass layoffs.

5. ☑ **A.** The Office of Labor-Management Standards (OLMS) provides oversight for the Labor-Management Relations Act (LMRA). Title IV of the LMRA establishes that union funds may not be used to support the candidacy of any candidate.

    ☒ **B, C,** and **D** are incorrect. **B** is incorrect because the National Labor Relations Board (NLRB) provides oversight for the National Labor Relations Act (NLRA). **C** is incorrect because the Department of Labor provides oversight in multiple areas, the most common area of oversight is the proper execution of the Fair Labor Standards Act (FLSA). **D** is incorrect because the Department of Justice (DOJ) would not be the entity most likely to be a first responder to a situation like this. At some point, the DOJ may be involved depending on the complexity of the violation.

6. ☑ **C.** A task force is formed to recommend solutions to a specific problem. Task forces are disbanded once the problem is solved.

    ☒ **A, B,** and **D** are incorrect. **A** is incorrect because employee-management committees are used to solve problems in a variety of areas and tend to be ongoing. **B** is incorrect because self-directed work teams are groups of employees who have a list of ongoing assignments they are responsible for. They assign tasks to each other and hold each other accountable. **D** is incorrect because committees may be ongoing or temporary and are formed to address ongoing issues such as planning the annual holiday party.

7. ☑ **A.** In a skip-level interview, an employee is interviewed by his or her manager's manager.

☒ **B, C, and D** are incorrect. **B** is incorrect because employee focus groups are a sampling of employees from various functional areas in a company that come together to provide input on employment matters. **C** is incorrect because employee surveys are used to gather information from large groups of people on a wide variety of topics. **D** is incorrect because exit interviews are surveys given when an employee is leaving the organization. It is likely that this is the data that HR has already provided to the CEO in this case. Because this information hasn't provided the answer he seeks regarding the reason for turnover, it would be most beneficial for the CEO to perform skip-level interviews.

8. ☑ **D.** A company intranet provides information to employees in real time. It is easily updated and available to anyone who logs into the company network. This would be the best choice of communicating a major change for a company operating on multiple continents.

☒ **A, B, and C** are incorrect. **A** is incorrect because a newsletter is static and would not be easily updated if there were a correction or update to the new processes. **B and C** are incorrect because neither an all-hands staff meeting nor a brown-bag lunch meeting are feasible for a company located in multiple countries.

9. ☑ **C.** Organizational climate focuses on how people feel about the organization. Even though this company professes to support an open culture where innovation is encouraged, the employees of the payroll department clearly don't feel as if this is the case based on the results of the exit interviews. The climate of a company relies heavily on how the leaders support employees.

☒ **A, B, and D** are incorrect. **A** is incorrect because organizational culture focuses on why people feel the way they do. This company seems to have the right structure in place so the issue has more to do with the fact that people feel a certain way about the company. A possible next step is to look at the way the direct supervisors in the payroll department manage the staff and provide leadership training to address any communication gaps between the company's stated values and the way those values are interpreted by those supervisors. **B and D** are incorrect because organizational development describes an intentional organization-wide planning effort to improve a company's efficiency.

10. ☑ **B.** The overall goal of an employee relations program is to maximize employee performance. The employment relationship affects all parts of an employee's life because employees spend a significant amount of time at work.

☒ **A, C, and D** are incorrect. Establishing employee dispute resolution techniques, increasing employee feedback, and communication to management are all excellent results that could result from having an effective employee relations program in place.

11. ☑ **B.** Flextime allows employees a window of time that they are to report to work and a window of time that is acceptable to leave. For this employee, this is the best option as the need to come in later than a standard start time occurs only sporadically throughout the month. Employers have to be sure to extend this option to employees in an equitable fashion as to avoid any embarrassing accusations of discrimination and to promote a positive employment relationship with all staff.

☒ **A, C, and D** are incorrect. Part-time work, job-sharing, and compressed workweeks are all alternate work schedules but don't best fit this employee's need. Part-time work and job sharing would reduce her overall hours unnecessarily. Working a compressed workweek may not satisfy all of the times she will need to report to work later than standard work hours.

12. ☑ **B.** The most effective way to generate more participation in this program would be to recognize the employees in a public forum, preferably with an incentive that they find valuable (for example, money or paid time off).

☒ **A, C, and D** are incorrect. A and C are incorrect because listing the employee names on the intranet or in a newsletter is a form of recognition but not likely to be as effective as public recognition with a meaningful incentive associated with the recognition. D is incorrect because a department-level staff meeting does not have the global impact the HR department hopes to generate.

13. ☑ **C.** Employee committees are formed to address various organizational concerns and include members from cross-functional departments. This promotes inclusion and diversity because it gives employees a platform for sharing differing opinions, expertise, and knowledge to meet an organizational initiative.

☒ **A, B, and D** are incorrect. A is incorrect because recognition events provide a platform for the company to acknowledge the accomplishments of employees in a number of different areas. This does not directly promote workplace inclusion. B and D are incorrect because work/life balance programs such as job-share impact employee engagement and retention by enabling employees to benefit from creative work schedules to assist them in managing their overall life outside of work.

14. ☑ **A.** Mutual trust between employees and management is the premise upon which a positive employee relations strategy is built. This trust is built over time and exists when employees believe that management is completely honest with them regarding the positives and negatives of the company's initiatives.

☒ **B, C, and D** are incorrect. B is incorrect because adhering to all laws and statutes related to employee relations is the barest minimum that a company can do. In order to build a positive and effective employee relations strategy, there has to be a commitment by the company to be deliberate and honest in its desire to create a fair and equitable company culture and climate. C is incorrect because mutual trust is built when employees believe that management is being completely honest with them. Only sharing the positive aspects of any initiative is disingenuous. D is incorrect because stating the company's non-union message does little to create positive employee relations without being coupled with an open door policy message, recognition opportunities, and other positive aspects of working for the company.

15. ☑ **D.** Even in times of economic downturn, employers who have positive employee relations programs in place where employees feel like they are treated with dignity and respect have more productive employees.

☒ **A, B, and C** are incorrect. Making changes to compensation or rewards, including recognition, doesn't ensure employee engagement. Employees still leave organizations for a number of intrinsic reasons, such as a poor relationship with a boss or because they feel underutilized.

16. ☑ **B.** To gain support for retention initiatives, it is critical that leadership understands how total turnover costs impact the bottom line. Turnover costs include not just recruitment expenses to replace the employee but also costs associated with training new employees and lost production time.

☒ **A, C, and D** are incorrect. A is incorrect because time-to-fill is a recruitment metric that may influence some managers to keep existing employees, but it is not the most effective metric to stir support for retention initiatives. C is incorrect because vacancy rate measures the percentage of all positions that are open for recruitment. D is incorrect because accession rate measures the rate of positions filled.

17. ☑ **D.** To prevent future turnover, the most effective step is to organize the data into meaningful categories such as career advancement, wage/benefits, supervision, and work/life balance. Then assess the top strengths and weaknesses and share that information with leadership.

☒ **A, B, and C** are incorrect. A is incorrect because leadership can learn from the past. Even though the data is from the past, it is still useful, particularly if the same supervisory staff is in still in place. B is incorrect because distributing spreadsheets all around without tying the data to meaningful information (also called "data dumping") is not an effective way to communicate what the organization is doing right and what it needs to improve in. Most leaders are busy and most likely do not have the time to read piles of spreadsheets, let alone turn them into actionable information. C is incorrect because tracking turnover numbers is not the same thing as information from exit interviews. Turnover reflects headcount changes; exit interviews reflect the opinions of exiting employees on factors that matter to them.

18. ☑ **A.** The stay interview is a proactive approach to finding out why good employees stay and what might make them leave an organization. The exit interview comes under criticism because the information is collected after the fact and it is too late to try to retain those employees. Many are adopting the stay interview method because it is proactive in curbing turnover depending on how the information is used.

☒ **B, C,** and **D** are incorrect. **B** is incorrect because turnover cost tracking is a tool used to measure the cost of replacing those who left an organization. **C** is incorrect because the exit interview surveys employees after they have decided to leave an organization. **D** is incorrect because the employee safety survey assesses how employees feel about one focused area, safety, and does not adequately measure all components that might affect if an employee stays with a company or not.

19. ☑ **B.** A key mistake made when conducting employee engagement surveys is not doing anything with the information. However, having managers create action plans responding to recommendations and communicate survey results to their own employees demonstrates leadership action and commitment. This action will encourage employees to participate in surveys.

☒ **A, C,** and **D** are incorrect. **A** is incorrect because tracking turnover to see if there is a correlation of impact from the survey would not necessarily encourage employees to participate in engagement surveys. **C** is incorrect because launching a communication campaign that doesn't address recommendations from a survey is meaningless (or all talk and no walk) in the eyes of employees. As such, this action will not necessarily increase employee participation in the survey process and may yield cynicism. **D** is incorrect because canceling future employee engagement surveys will ultimately prevent an organization from learning what motivates and concerns its employees.

20. ☑ **C.** Sodexo (an organization rated second in Diversity, Inc.'s "Top 50 Companies for Diversity") surveys cross-cultural mentorship participants twice a year to determine effectiveness. Questions are designed to measure engagement, performance, job satisfaction, and retention.

☒ **A, B,** and **D** are incorrect. **A** is incorrect because surveying applicants would determine if the reputation of the program is circulating outside the company. However, this does not adequately measure the effectiveness of the program. **B** is incorrect because surveying all employees to see if they would like to join the cross-cultural mentorship program is not practical and would not adequately measure program effectiveness. **D** is incorrect because while understanding leadership's perceptions on any initiative is important, this does not adequately measure program participants' engagement levels.

21. ☑ **A.** Identifying the need for a policy should be the first step of establishing policies. Some organizations make the mistake of creating a policy just to have one. Identifying a need for a policy is finding a gap in guidelines and expectations that threaten the organization's ability to achieve its objectives.

☒ **B, C,** and **D** are incorrect. **B** is incorrect because policies need to be developed before communicating them to employees. **C** is incorrect because determining policy content would come after determining if there is even a need for a policy. **D** is incorrect because updating and revising policies would come later, after the policies have been established. In fact, it is a good practice to periodically review policies to see if they have become obsolete or need to be updated.

22. ☑ **D.** Policies intended to clarify but maintain flexibility ideally use words such as "typically" or "may" and stay away from words such as "permanent," "only," and "always." The best phrase in this case is "typical behaviors in violation of this policy include but are not limited to:"

☒ **A, B, and C are incorrect. A** is incorrect because the word "permanent" is discouraged because it implies a long-term contractual employment agreement. **B** is incorrect because making promises within a policy does not permit flexibility. In addition, promising long-term employment has the same result as using the word "permanent": It implies a long-term employment contract. **C** is incorrect because making the promise that employees will only be terminated "for cause" prevents activities such as a reduction in force (layoff) without facing risk.

23. ☑ **B.** Giving employees the chance to ask questions is a great way to ensure they not only understand but also are engaged in applying the new policy. Having managers present and explain the new policy in department meetings is a way to facilitate the question and answer process of any new policy.

☒ **A, C, and D are incorrect. A** is incorrect because simply posting a policy on bulletin boards does not ensure employees will read the policy. **C** is incorrect because while e-mailing the policy may be an efficient way to distribute a new policy, it does not ensure that employees will read, understand, and correctly apply the new policy. **D** is incorrect because while it is true that new policies are required, a top-down approach with no means for interaction with the employees will not ensure an effective understanding of the new policy.

24. ☑ **C.** This is a good example of how a well-meaning policy can become obsolete or block the ability to achieve organizational objectives. In this case, the best answer is to revise the policy to allow job posting to occur internally and externally concurrently. This enables the company to maintain a commitment to internal employees while moving forward with searching for a qualified employee externally.

☒ **A, B, and D are incorrect. A** is incorrect because creating a time-to-fill metric doesn't immediately and adequately solve the problems that this internal job posting policy causes. **B** is incorrect because maintaining a status quo position on old or obsolete policies prevents an organization from achieving its objectives. **D** is incorrect because simply following an old policy doesn't correct a situation that is preventing timely recruitment of qualified talent.

25. ☑ **A.** The best proactive defense to any discrimination lawsuit is the implementation of a written disciplinary policy. It is critical to be able to demonstrate that the policy is being followed uniformly across the organization.

☒ **B, C, and D are incorrect. B** is incorrect because surveying exiting employees to see if they feel discriminated against is not proactive nor is it recommended.

C is incorrect because while training employees on cultural awareness and diversity is a good idea, it is not the best proactive strategy to preventing a lawsuit. D is incorrect because training leaders on diversity is not the best proactive strategy for minimizing the success of a lawsuit.

26. ☑ **A.** Most progressive disciplinary policies include provisions for verbal, written, and final warnings in the event of a policy violation. The best policies have guidance on typical steps but also allow flexibility based on circumstance.

 ☒ **B, C, and D are incorrect. B** is incorrect because meeting with people is part of the procedures around handling a policy violation complaint, but is not necessarily spelled out in a policy. **C** is incorrect because each violation typically requires some action even if it is just giving a verbal warning. **D** is incorrect because while there may be some language that speaks about the severity of a policy violation, it is not what is meant by a progressive disciplinary policy.

27. ☑ **B.** Conducting a thorough investigation is the best step. If anything, that will provide facts needed for any defense. Best case, you can resolve the issue and still correct any performance-related issues.

 ☒ **A, C, and D are incorrect. A** is incorrect because making a decision based on subjective input alone not only does not solve the issue but may create a bigger issue. **C** is incorrect because checking the supervisor's personnel record may not provide the information that an interview with both the supervisor and employee would reveal. **D** is incorrect because while it is a good idea to keep legal counsel in the loop of an escalating issue, it is best to conduct an investigation to gather the facts of the situation.

28. ☑ **D.** While going through a reduction in force is never pleasant, careful consideration of selection criteria is critical to minimize any disparate impact issues. The best selection criteria are those that can be clearly documented and are as objective as possible. Examples include job categories, prior disciplinary actions, seniority, and skill set.

 ☒ **A, B, and C are incorrect. A** is incorrect because simply selecting people for a reduction in force that have a record of complaining can set an organization up for whistleblower protection risks. **B** is incorrect because popularity is subjective at best. There are better selection criteria to use that would minimize risk. **C** is incorrect because you have to use caution around attendance as a selection criteria. Some attendance issues may be attributed to protected reasons such as family medical leave (FMLA) purposes. Using attendance as blanket-criteria for a reduction in force could lead to legal risk.

29. ☑ **C.** Among the first steps to take when a supervisor requests to terminate an employee is to review the personnel file for previous performance documentation. Additional steps include comparing this employee situation to written policies in place as well as checking for any protected status issues. Checking in with legal counsel before terminating an employee is also a good idea.

☒ **A, B,** and **D** are incorrect. **A** is incorrect because simply including an employee in a reduction in force does not resolve the performance issue but also causes risk. **B** is incorrect because giving the employee wrong information during the termination meeting not only causes legal risk but also damages the employer's reputation and credibility. **C** is incorrect because ignored performance issues tend to create more complex issues in the future. In addition, not taking corrective action impedes an organization's ability to compete in the marketplace for customers and skilled talent.

30. ☑ **A.** Some countries have lifetime-employment provisions, as in Indonesia. That means there is usually a government role in approving any termination decisions. In this case, the best step is to check local requirements and seek approval from the local Industrial Relations Board before moving forward with any employment terminations.
☒ **B, C,** and **D** are incorrect. **B** is incorrect because multinational organizations have both domestic and international obligations to recognize. **C** is incorrect because some countries have lifetime-employment provisions regardless of any "at-will" notifications or policies. **D** is incorrect because simply not moving forward on staffing change needs without considering all alternatives does not best serve the organization's objectives.

31. ☑ **A.** Loss of productivity will occur because current workers will have to train new or replacement workers.
☒ **B, C,** and **D** are incorrect because these are examples of financial costs that affect an organization's bottom line.

32. ☑ **B.** HR should contact the employee to find out if the absences are due to a protected leave such as FMLA, USERRA, or other state or federal leave requirement.
☒ **A, C,** and **D** are incorrect because these choices are not advisable in this situation.

33. ☑ **D.** Setting clear expectations will help prevent disciplinary actions because managers and employees will both have the same expectations. Expectations can be clarified in job descriptions.
☒ **A, B,** and **C** are incorrect because while these choices may possibly help prevent disciplinary problems, these choices are not the best option.

34. ☑ **C.** Open dialogue and problem solving will allow for two-way communication between manager and employee while enabling the manager to figure out what the performance issue is and to resolve it before it progresses any further.
☒ **A, B,** and **D** are incorrect because these choices are later steps in the progressive disciplinary process.

35. ☑ **B.** Because the offense is a severe violation, HR should move to termination.
☒ **A, C,** and **D** are incorrect because these choices don't address the severity of the situation.

36. ☑ **A.** Compulsory arbitration is one in which parties are required to accept arbitration, even if they don't want to.

☒ **B, C, and D are incorrect.** **B** is incorrect because facilitative mediation is a form of dispute resolution where a neutral third party helps each side come to a mutually beneficial agreement. **C** is incorrect because voluntary arbitration happens when all parties voluntarily agree to submit to an arbitration proceeding. In this case, it can be assumed that the agreement to go to arbitration was already predetermined by contract because the question states that the union and management agreed to engage in alternative dispute resolution in lieu of legal action for any labor dispute. **D** is incorrect because constructive confrontation is a type of mediation where the goal is to uncover and resolve the underlying conflicts that prevent parties from solving the core issue. The goal of constructive confrontation is to get parties to find effective ways to work together. Achieving agreement between all parties is not necessary.

37. ☑ **A.** During the fact-finding stage, the mediator may meet with parties separately to determine if each party has the same set of facts and that all issues are clarified.

☒ **B, C, and D are incorrect.** **B** is incorrect because during the negotiating stage, the parties are together and the mediator works to help them reach an agreement. **C** is incorrect because during the options stage, the parties are together and the mediator is sharing alternative solutions to the issues with both parties. **D** is incorrect because during the structure stage, the mediator is not meeting with anyone. The mediator is simply setting the parameters within which the mediation will happen—time, place, date, and attendees.

38. ☑ **A.** This is an example of a hot cargo contract. A hot cargo contract is a contract that the employer enters into with the union, at the request of the union: The employer agrees that its employees will not handle the products or materials of another employer, or that the employer itself will not deal with the other employer, whom the bargaining union considers unfair to organized labor. This is an unfair labor practice (ULP) on the part of the employer as defined by the National Labor Relations Act (NLRA).

☒ **B, C, and D are incorrect.** **B** is incorrect because featherbedding is a ULP on the part of the union where the union is requiring an employer to pay for services not rendered. For example, if an employer determines that, because of advances in technology, a position is no longer needed, then the union cannot force the employer to continue to employ someone in that position. **C** and **D** are incorrect because a yellow-dog or iron-clad contract is a contract where an employer requires an employer, as a condition of employment, to join a union. This was outlawed by the Norris-LaGuardia Act.

39. ☑ **D.** If the union tried to force this issue, it would be guilty of an unfair labor practice (ULP) known as featherbedding. Featherbedding is a labor union practice where the union requires the employer to pay for the performance of unnecessary work in order to protect the job of its member.

☒ **A, B,** and **C** are incorrect. **A** and **C** are incorrect because the school district has no obligation to retain a specific employee simply because they are a dues-paying member. **B** is incorrect because an iron-clad contract or yellow-dog contract is one that requires an employee to join a union as a condition of employment.

40. ☑ **C.** A secondary boycott is an attempt to stop people or companies from doing business with or for an employer that is engaged in a labor dispute with a union. This kind of boycott is an unfair labor practice (ULP).

☒ **A, B,** and **D** are incorrect. This is not an organizational or recognition strike. It can be inferred from the question that this union is recognized by the employer. It is true that this is an economic strike against Nationwide Appliances; however, by blocking the delivery drivers from making the delivery of refrigerators, the cashiers union has engaged in a secondary boycott against One Stop Delivery Services. This is a ULP that the employer can file with the National Labor Relations Board (NLRB) within six months of the incident.

41. ☑ **D.** Conducting a vulnerability assessment is a proactive strategy that provides an organization's leaders with insights into areas in which they are weak and susceptible to union organization attempts. A vulnerability assessment includes both internal and external insights that give an organization the ability to craft smart strategies to avoid union organizing.

☒ **A, B,** and **C** are incorrect. **A** is incorrect because implementing a retirement plan is not the best proactive action to take. In addition, giving benefits if you feel organizing is going on opens the organization to the charge of an unfair labor practice (ULP). **B** is incorrect because while giving everyone a pay raise may make everyone happy in the short term, it is not practical. In addition, union-organizing activity uses multiple platforms to convince employees to sign authorization cards, such as job security. There is a better proactive approach to take. **C** is incorrect because while trying to hire all employees with a positive attitude is noble, it is not an effective approach to union avoidance. This is particularly true when the work environment changes frequently, as do employee attitudes.

42. ☑ **A.** Time is of the essence when implementing effective avoidance strategies, particularly when rumors are circulating of offsite meetings. Leaders at all levels should be trained on union avoidance strategies as well as the expectation that they report union formation activities to HR in a timely manner.

☒ **B, C,** and **D** are incorrect. **B** is incorrect because terminating an employee suspected of union organizing activity is illegal and subject to charges being filed of unfair labor practice (ULP). This is true regardless of union contract or petition status. **C** is incorrect because offsite and off-duty meetings are considered protected activity. To avoid surveillance charges or other charges of unfair labor practices, it is best to not get involved or interfere with those meetings. There are better and legal steps an employer can take. **D** is incorrect because lack of action or complacency is sure to derail any union free organizational objectives.

43. ☑ **B.** Many employers communicate their position on unions, open communication, and transparency philosophies to new employees in the orientation process. Utilizing the new employee orientation is an effective way to ensure that new employees coming into the organization understand the overall philosophy.

☒ **A, C, and D are incorrect. A** is incorrect because while hiring employees with good communication and teamwork skills is a good practice, it is not necessarily an effective union avoidance strategy with new employees. **C** is incorrect because creating metrics to monitor an existing workplace culture is not a practice that is applied for new employees. **D** is incorrect because an employee engagement survey is used to measure attitudes, engagement, and satisfaction levels of existing employees and is not the best strategy for new employees.

44. ☑ **D.** Interest-based bargaining is characterized by harmony between both sides where neither side is trying to win a position but come up with an agreement that is amenable to both labor and management. There is more openness to explore alternatives that enhance the labor–management relationship.

☒ **A, B, and C are incorrect.** Positional, conjunctive, and distributive bargaining are characterized by opposing points of view and typically result in an impasse.

45. ☑ **B.** Coordinated bargaining, or multi-unit bargaining, refers to a type of bargaining where multiple bargaining units within a company negotiate simultaneously, typically to come to an agreement on mandatory subjects and allow all unions to work collectively on subjects that are mutually meaningful to their membership.

☒ **A, C, and D are incorrect. A** is incorrect because single employer bargaining occurs when a union meets with one employer to bargain. **C** is incorrect because parallel bargaining occurs when a union negotiates with a single employer and uses any gains from the prior negotiation to build on during negotiations with the next employer. **D** is incorrect because multi-employer bargaining occurs when a union negotiates with multiple employers at the same time.

46. ☑ **A.** Scheduling is typically a management right. It can be negotiated but that isn't in the best interest of the employer or the overall efficient operations of the business. As the HR leader, you should encourage management to do its best to leave this subject out of the collective bargaining agreement.

☒ **B, C, and D are incorrect** because job design is not an illegal or mandatory subject. It is permissible but does not have to be negotiated. It would be wise for management to do everything it can to avoid having scheduling or job design written into an agreement. Flexibility is needed in these areas to ensure that positions in the company support the company's current strategic direction.

47. ☑ **C.** An agency shop is one in which all employees pay dues whether or not they join the union. It is often called "fair share."

   ☒ **A, B,** and **D** are incorrect. **A** is incorrect because an open shop is one where employees do not have to be affiliated with the union to work. Employees are also not forced to pay union dues or a pay equivalent. **B** is incorrect because a union shop is one where all employees are required to join the union within a certain period specified by the contract. **D** is incorrect because a closed shop is one where an employee is required to join the union as a condition of employment. This is only legal in the construction industry.

48. ☑ **B.** The National Labor Relations Board (NLRB) may consider the company a successor employer. As a successor employer, the restaurant can make changes but the changes must be negotiated through the collective bargaining process. The NLRB considers the continuity in operations, types of products or services rendered, existing collective bargaining agreement, and the number of new employees gained from the acquisition when determining who it considers a successor employer.

   ☒ **A, C,** and **D** are incorrect because wages and hours are mandatory subjects. If the NLRB determines the company is a successor employer, then to make these types of changes, the new employer must negotiate with the union.

49. ☑ **A.** *Burlington Industries v. Ellerth* established that an employer can be held responsible for the unlawful acts of its employees. This is a legal concept known as *vicarious liability*.

   ☒ **B, C,** and **D** are incorrect. **B** and **C** are incorrect because the issue in both *Meritor Savings Bank v. Vinson and Harris v. Forklift Systems* is the existence of hostile work environment sexual harassment. **D** is incorrect because *Oncale v. Sundowner Offshore Services, Inc.* established the standard for same sex sexual harassment.

50. ☑ **C.** The Supreme Court decision in *Vance v. Ball State University* established that a person is a supervisor for the purposes of vicarious liability in cases of unlawful harassment under Title VII only if that person can take tangible employment actions against the accuser. The Supreme Court rejected the Equal Employment Opportunity Commission's (EEOC) guidance that a supervisor may be an individual who has authority to direct an employee's daily work activities. However, the employee still maintains the right to sue the company for being negligent in preventing the harassment.

   ☒ **A, B,** and **D** are incorrect. **A** is incorrect because the assumption that Jasmine did not report the incidents is irrelevant. Also, the scenario does not indicate that she did not report, only that the Sales Director claims no knowledge of a report. Jasmine could have reported directly to HR or some other supervisory authority. **B** is incorrect because the Ellerth and Faragher cases, taken together, established that whether or not an employer is vicariously liable depends on what happened to the plaintiff and if the harassment resulted in tangible employment actions being taken. **D** is incorrect because the EEOC guidance is only guidance, but Title VII did not define "supervisor" for the purposes of unlawful harassment.

51. ☑ **B.** Following the reservist's application for reemployment, the employer must reinstate her promptly.

☒ **A, C, and D** are incorrect. The Uniformed Services Employment and Reemployment Rights Act (USERRA) of 1994 requires employers of reservists who have been on active duty for 181 or more days to reemploy them promptly after completing their service.

52. ☑ **C.** A grievance process is a systematic and fair procedure for supervisors and employees to resolve complaints that arise. It typically includes timelines, what is eligible, and the decision-making process involved.

☒ **A, B, and D** are incorrect. A is incorrect because an open door policy refers to a communication philosophy indicating employees are free to voice their concerns to any level of management at any time. B is incorrect because while often supervisors mistake the grievance process as an HR-only procedure, it is a process that should be adopted wholeheartedly by the supervisors for it to be effective. D is incorrect because a team building process is an overbroad concept and it does not effectively reflect the grievance process.

53. ☑ **D.** Some labor groups and employers have realized benefits to joining forces and leveraging collective resources to accomplish objectives. This is known as a labor-management cooperative or agreement.

☒ **A, B, and C** are incorrect. A is incorrect because simply informing leadership of the new law's implications is tactical and would contribute significantly to the organization's objectives. B is incorrect because notifying the workforce of a potential layoff is premature and not effective in achieving organizational objectives. C is incorrect because by not taking any actions at all means to simply be reactionary, not proactive, in achieving organizational objectives.

54. ☑ **A.** An Action Plan Indicator (API) is a measure that shows if managers have communicated the survey results and involved employees in the improvement process. APIs are a measureable way to hold managers accountable.

☒ **B, C, and D** are incorrect. B is incorrect because not taking any actions to ensure results will produce disappointment at the next survey. C is incorrect because turnover information is reactive at best. There is a more proactive approach to ensure survey success. D is incorrect because creating a leadership development course on how to read survey results is not the best approach to ensure ongoing communication and to provide evidence that the employer took corrective action in areas indicated on the employee engagement surveys as needing improvement.

55. ☑ **B.** By their very nature, self-directed teams are empowered by and have a sense of interdependence among the team members. They all focus on a common goal. Self-directed teams are often used in organizations that thrive on having an innovative culture.

☒ **A, C,** and **D** are incorrect. **A** is incorrect because implementing an employee engagement survey alone is not what propels a company toward its innovation objectives. **C** is incorrect because while hiring employees who are innovative thinkers can be helpful, it really doesn't drive the current workforce toward a culture of innovation in the short term. **D** is incorrect because measuring employee performance alone does not instill a culture of innovation.

56. ☑ **B.** Involving employees in safety-related employee-management committees is an effective way to address issues in the workplace. Not only will management receive information from those closer to the issue, but employees will feel engaged and more likely to buy-in to any changes.

☒ **A, C,** and **D** are incorrect. **A** is incorrect because sending out a memo is not effective in garnering employee support in new initiatives. **C** is incorrect because creating metrics alone is not effective in engaging employees. An organization can throw numbers up on a wall but unless the employees are connected to the story it tells, it just becomes a meaningless piece of paper on the wall. **D** is incorrect because a top-down approach as this suggests is not necessarily effective in engaging the hearts and minds of employees.

57. ☑ **A.** Video conferencing is a low-cost solution enabling organizations to involve virtual employees in key decisions and projects.

☒ **B, C,** and **D** are incorrect. **B** is incorrect because sending memos of updates is an after-the-fact action and does not involve employees in the decision-making process. **C** is incorrect because, as in answer B, having supervisors send updates is an after-the-fact action and does not involve virtual employees in the decision-making process. **D** is incorrect because offsite employees are impacted by decisions made onsite. Employers should be cautioned about "out of sight, out of mind" sentiments as the virtual workforce can impact organizational objectives just as much as onsite employees.

58. ☑ **B.** Employers can share any information that is truthful, clear, and supported. An employer is covered by the concept of qualified privilege. Qualified privilege is a provision available under the law of libel and slander that allows a company to be immune from prosecution if the libelist of slanderous act is committed in the performance of a legal or moral duty and is free of malice and words uttered or statements written are done in good faith.

☒ **A, C,** and **D** are incorrect because even though these are all good strategies, they are very limited and do not allow the employer to give a meaningful reference. Choice D also is so generic that the supervisor responding to the reference check may overstate information that could potentially cause the company to be guilty of defamation, which is any communication that willfully damages an employee's reputation and prevents the employee from obtaining employment or other benefits.

59. ☑ **A.** Gina's supervisor may have created an implied contract with this statement. Employment-at-will, in the purest sense, means that the employer may terminate employment with or without notice and for good reason or no reason at all. The employee, in turn, may resign with or without reason and for good reason or no reason at all. By making the statement, "Keep up the good work and you'll have this job for life," Gina's supervisor may have invalidated the at-will doctrine.

☒ **B, C, and D are incorrect. B** is incorrect because a statutory exception exists if legislation changes the terms of the employment contract. **C** is incorrect because a public-policy exception exists when the application of the at-will doctrine conflicts with public policy. For example, an employee should not be discharged under the at-will doctrine if she refuses to commit perjury by lying to protect an employer under investigation for racketeering. **D** is incorrect because fraudulent misrepresentation exists when an employer entices an employee to work for the organization by presenting the company in a more stable condition than currently exists. For example, if someone accepts a position based on the employer telling him that he would be promoted to General Manager in one year while knowing that the company plans to close in three months, this is fraudulent misrepresentation.

60. ☑ **B.** A fingerprint-based criminal background check will likely reveal any convictions for violent crimes such as battery. The HR Director can then use this information to assist in determining whether or not to move forward with onboarding this candidate. The candidate must agree in writing prior to the background check being run, and the request can only be made after an offer of employment is extended.

☒ **A, C, and D are incorrect. A and C** are incorrect because a drug screen or motor vehicle records may or may not be relevant to performing this job effectively. However, in a business built on re-acclimating violent offenders into society, it is important to consider each potential new hire's criminal background as it relates to convictions for violent crimes. **D** is incorrect because this would occur after a person is already employed so it has no bearing on the initial employment decision and therefore does not prevent negligent hiring.

61. ☑ **A.** The first step in your approach should be to analyze why there is an increase in absenteeism and how much that has cost the corporation. The absenteeism policy can then be revised based on this data.

☒ **B, C, and D are incorrect. B and C** are incorrect because both choices assume that you know the cause of the absenteeism. **D** is incorrect because it is not a legal choice. If the employer allots a certain amount of paid time off (PTO), then it must be honored. The employer can't decide that an employee's absences are excessive and dock pay if her absences are in adherence with the current absenteeism policy.

62. ☑ **C.** Discussing the behavior with Sarah, while ensuring that words like insubordination are not used to characterize the behavior, is the best route. Calling out the exact action will help the employee identify exactly what the issue is and provide her with the opportunity to correct her behavior. Also, specific explanations are easier to defend if the employee follows up with legal action.

☒ **A, B,** and **D** are incorrect. All of these choices are over-reaching. Rolling eyes doesn't rise to the level of an immediate write up or termination. In addition, using words such as "bad attitude" is a characterization of the behavior, which is never advisable.

63. ☑ **D.** Clarifying the corrective action that could be taken if the performance improvement plan (PIP) is not met successfully will have the most impact on the behavior of such a chronic poor performer.

☒ **A, B,** and **C** are incorrect. These are all elements of a quality PIP but will likely do little to motivate or guide such a poor performer. However, being clear on the possible consequences for not successfully meeting the requirements of the PIP might.

64. ☑ **A.** Picketing in high numbers where other employees cannot physically enter the building would be considered an unfair labor practice.

☒ **B, C,** and **D** are incorrect because these choices are not examples of unfair labor practices.

65. ☑ **D.** An affected employee or union must file with one of the regional NLRB offices within six months after the alleged ULP was committed.

☒ **A, B,** and **C** are incorrect because they do not adhere to the time frame for filing an unfair labor practice.

66. ☑ **C.** If employees are organizing a campaign, an employer would want to try and persuade the employees not to form a union while taking caution to not inadvertently threaten or intimidate the employees.

☒ **A, B,** and **D** are incorrect. A and D are incorrect choices because these are examples of threats or promises and could be considered an unfair labor practice. B is incorrect because this would not be the first step in the process and could possibly happen later on or never.

67. ☑ **B.** Typically, negotiation of wage rates is considered an illegal bargaining subject for public sector employees.

☒ **A, C,** and **D** are incorrect choices because these choices reflect generally permitted bargaining subjects.

68. ☑ **A.** The primary goal of contract negotiation is to come up with a contract that will contribute to an ongoing constructive relationship that fosters effective resolution of issues.

☒ **B, C,** and **D** are incorrect because they are not the primary goal for contract negotiation.

69. ☑ **B.** After all three levels of management have worked on the grievance with no resolution, then a third-party outside arbitrator may be used.

☒ **A, C, and D** are incorrect because Felicia has already exhausted these options.

70. ☑ **C.** The employee should be suspended pending investigation. The company can choose to suspend with or without pay. The reason for the suspension is to allow the company to perform a thorough and fair investigation. Even if the employee is subsequently terminated, the time away from the job may protect others from an incident of potential workplace violence as well as protect the employer if the employee follows up with legal action.

☒ **A, B, and D** are incorrect. A and D are incorrect because a write-up is not a serious enough response given the facts presented in the question, which are that the employee is carrying a firearm, has recently had an altercation with a vendor, and is reported to have made threatening statements. **B** is incorrect because the company should move to the termination phase in this case but not an immediate termination. Tempers can flare and because the employee is armed, enraging him in this way may lead to unfortunate and unintended consequences.

71. ☑ **A.** This is an example of possible wrongful termination, also known as *retaliatory discharge*. When an employer terminates an employee in response to the employee doing something that is lawful or because they are a part of a protected class, the employee may have a wrongful termination case.

☒ **B, C, and D** are incorrect. B and D are incorrect because constructive discharge or constructive dismissal occurs when an employer makes a work environment so intolerable to an employee that they are essentially forced to quit. C is incorrect because a hostile work environment is one where the employee is repeatedly harassed thereby making the work environment intolerable.

72. ☑ **B.** HR's primary role is to ensure adequate documentation to support the termination and to coach the supervisor on how to conduct the termination meeting.

☒ **A, C, and D** are incorrect. A is incorrect because as much as possible the supervisor should conduct the termination meeting. The supervisor is most familiar with the employee's work and the issue(s) for which he is being terminated, and the supervisor has had the most interaction with the employee regarding improving performance. C and D are incorrect because returning company property and disabling access to company records are both shepherded by HR but are not HR's primary function in the termination phase.

73. ☑ **B.** Giving employees opportunities to exercise more authority in their jobs is an example of job enrichment.

☒ **A, C, and D** are incorrect because these choices are not the best example of job enrichment.

74. ☑ **A.** Reducing the absenteeism rate is a main advantage of allowing flextime for employees.

☒ **B, C,** and **D** are incorrect because these choices do not reflect the main advantage of flextime.

75. ☑ **C.** If employees participate in the decision-making process for the company, they are more likely to stay committed to the decision.

☒ **A, B,** and **D** are incorrect because although these choices may reflect an advantage, these would not be the main advantage.

76. ☑ **C.** It should first be determined who will conduct the investigation. Depending on the nature of the issue and the relationship of the HR department to the person being investigated, it may be necessary to engage a third party.

☒ **A, B,** and **D** are incorrect. These are all great elements of an investigation but wouldn't be the next thing you would do given the scenario presented.

77. ☑ **A.** HR should approach the employee who is allegedly being harassed to confirm whether or not harassment is taking place. If it is, the employee should immediately be protected by removing the harasser from direct interaction with him or her.

☒ **B, C,** and **D** are incorrect. **B** is incorrect because HR should act when the potential issue is brought to their attention, whether or not the employee being harassed reports the incidents themselves. They may be uncomfortable filing a complaint for a number of reasons. Regardless, HR would be negligent if it was suspected there was an issue and HR did nothing. **C** and **D** are incorrect because conducting an investigation and suspending the supervisor pending investigation are both steps HR should take, but they're not the best next step.

78. ☑ **B.** The supervisors should be counseled on the legal protections these employees have against retaliation. Retaliation claims with the Equal Employment Opportunity Commission (EEOC) are on the rise. Even in cases where the original claim is unfounded, employees have been successful with filing a subsequent retaliation claim.

☒ **A, C,** and **D** are incorrect. These are all great reminders, but the most immediate concern is for the supervisors not to succumb to the desire to penalize these employees for coming forward to report what they believed to be a problem in the first place.

79. ☑ **A.** Any misconduct that may result in termination should be investigated promptly and thoroughly.

☒ **B, C,** and **D** are incorrect because these choices are not the first step that HR should take without investigating first to see if the alleged misconduct actually occurred.

80. ☑ **D.** ADR will reduce the number of disputes that end up in court

☒ **A, B,** and **C** are incorrect because although these are valid choices, they are not the main advantage of using ADR.

CHAPTER 7

Risk Management

This functional area includes coverage of the following responsibilities and knowledge objectives.

Risk Management—Responsibilities Objectives

- **01** Ensure that workplace health, safety, security, and privacy activities are compliant with applicable federal laws and regulations.

- **02** Conduct a needs analysis to identify the organization's safety requirements.

- **03** Develop/select and implement/administer occupational injury and illness prevention programs (i.e., OSHA, workers' compensation) (PHR only).

- **04** Establish and administer a return-to-work process after illness or injury to ensure a safe workplace (for example: modified duty assignment, reasonable independent medical exam, accommodations).

- **05** Develop/select, implement, and evaluate plans and policies to protect employees and other individuals, and to minimize the organization's loss and liability (for example: emergency response, workplace violence, substance abuse).

- **06** Communicate and train the workforce on security plans and policies.

- **07** Develop, monitor, and test business continuity and disaster recovery plans.

- **08** Communicate and train the workforce on the business continuity and disaster recovery plans.

- **09** Develop policies and procedures to direct the appropriate use of electronic media and hardware (for example: e-mail, social media, and appropriate website access).

- **10** Develop and administer internal and external privacy policies (for example: identity theft, data protection, workplace monitoring).

Risk Management—Knowledge Objectives

- **61** Applicable federal laws and regulations related to workplace health, safety, security, and privacy (for example: OSHA, Drug-Free Workplace Act, ADA, HIPAA, Sarbanes-Oxley Act)

- **62** Occupational injury and illness prevention (safety) and compensation programs

- **63** Investigation procedures of workplace safety, health, and security enforcement agencies

- **64** Return to work procedures (for example: interactive dialog, job modification, accommodations)
- **65** Workplace safety risks (for example: trip hazards, blood-borne pathogens)
- **66** Workplace security risks (for example: theft, corporate espionage, sabotage)
- **67** Potential violent behavior and workplace violence conditions
- **68** General health and safety practices (for example: evacuation, hazard communication, ergonomic evaluations)
- **69** Organizational incident and emergency response plans
- **70** Internal investigation, monitoring, and surveillance techniques
- **71** Employer/employee rights related to substance abuse
- **72** Business continuity and disaster recovery plans (for example: data storage and backup, alternative work locations, procedures)
- **73** Data integrity techniques and technology (for example: data sharing, password usage, social engineering)
- **74** Technology and applications (for example: social media, monitoring software, biometrics)
- **75** Financial management practices (for example: procurement policies, credit card policies and guidelines, expense policies)

Balance is essential for a tightrope walker to successfully cross the wire. The same is true for the human resource professional in the area of risk management. The HR professional must balance the need for innovation, profitability, productivity, and competitive advantage with organizational and functional department risk management.

It is not an easy balancing act. However, with knowledge and experience, an HR professional can be just as successful as the tightrope walker. This section will test your knowledge in all the risk management responsibilities and core knowledge areas of the exam, covering items from applicable federal laws and regulations, to investigation procedures, to workplace safety and security risks, and much more.

Risk Management—Responsibilities Objectives

Objective 01 Ensure That Workplace Health, Safety, Security, and Privacy Activities Are Compliant with Applicable Federal Laws and Regulations

1. An employee is off the company's premises, cleaning the back access road leading to the company's building. The employee slips, falls, and injures his back. According to the Occupational Safety and Health Act (OSHA), this situation requires:

   A. All employees to be trained on safety protocols

   B. Recording on the OSHA 300 log

   C. The employee to seek medical attention

   D. The employee to be sent home

2. A manufacturing plant has decided to utilize a temporary agency to help staff forklift drivers for a short-term staffing need. The forklift drivers will be moving glass, boxes, and chemicals periodically. Which of the following steps will best meet OSHA's Hazardous Communication (HAZCOM) standards?

   A. The host company will provide generic hazard training, information concerning the categories of chemicals encountered, and site-specific information.

   B. The temporary agency will provide generic hazard training, information concerning the categories of chemicals encountered, and site-specific information.

   C. The temporary agency will provide generic hazard training, covering categories of chemicals encountered, and the host company will provide site-specific training.

   D. The host company will provide generic hazard training, covering categories of chemicals encountered, and the temporary agency will provide site-specific training.

3. A job candidate completes an application for a position available at a company. At the end of the application, the candidate is informed that the company may wish to run a background check. The applicant is informed of his rights and is provided an opportunity to request a copy of any background check results. The company is complying with which of the following federal laws?

   A. Privacy Act of 1974

   B. Freedom of Information Act of 1966

   C. Right to Financial Privacy Act of 1978

   D. Fair Credit Reporting Act of 1970

4. A retail business that operates 24 hours, 7 days a week, has adopted a workplace violence prevention program. The company created a policy of zero-tolerance for workplace violence. A reprisal-free reporting system has been set up to assure employees that no retaliation would take place if reporting a concern. The company also outlined a comprehensive security plan for its locations as well as established a relationship with local law enforcement representatives. In addition, the company's representatives conduct regular training sessions for all employees. This is an example of compliance under which of the following OSHA obligations?

   A. The General Duty Clause

   B. Code of Federal Regulations

   C. The Health and Safety Act

   D. Emergency Action Plans

5. An employee of a doctor's office often took a work laptop home. Information about patients is stored on the laptop for the employee's easy reference. While the employee was in a local grocery store, someone broke into his car and stole the laptop. Which federal law should the employer be concerned about?

   A. Federal Data Protection Act

   B. Sarbanes-Oxley Act of 2002

   C. Health Insurance Portability & Accountability Act

   D. Title 21 Code of Federal Regulations (21 CFR Part 11)

Objective 02   Conduct a Needs Analysis to Identify the Organization's Safety Requirements

6. A startup company that manufactures organic sunscreen products is looking to see what safety measures need to be put in place to ensure safety for all employees while on the job. The CEO has asked the HR Manager to conduct a needs analysis. What should the HR Manager do first in the needs assessment?

A. Propose solutions

B. Calculate costs

C. Gather data to identify needs

D. Choose and implement findings

7. When completing a needs analysis, the gap analysis showed that many of a technology company's computer stations are not ergonomically correct, especially the placement of the mouse and keyboard. What could be a serious consequence if an employee uses a non-ergonomic computer workstation for many years?

   A. The employee could develop serious neck and back problems and file a workers' compensation claim.

   B. HR could receive complaints about the workstations.

   C. The company may have to replace the computer workstation.

   D. The employee's productivity could decrease.

8. The HR Department has concluded a needs assessment for safety risks for its medical billing company where most employees are working on their computers for seven to eight hours per day. Now that HR knows that musculoskeletal disorders are a potential hazard, what is the best solution for preventing this potential hazard?

   A. Offer employees time mid-shift to rest.

   B. Have a compliant process in which employees feel comfortable letting management know if potential injuries arise.

   C. Involve senior management in the process.

   D. Provide training to employees on awareness of potential hazards.

9. When completing a risk assessment of a 200-person electrical engineering company's existing safety program, which of the following would be considered the biggest threat to having a successful safety program?

   A. Lack of funding

   B. Unskilled workers

   C. Training department deficiencies

   D. Lack of interest

Objective 03   Develop/Select and Implement/Administer Occupational Injury and Illness Prevention Programs (PHR only)

10. A mid-size manufacturing company has uncovered a potential occupational injury hazard. The level of smoke from the exhaust machinery may be causing unsafe levels within the building. What should the safety manager's first priority be to rectify this issue?

   A. Provide employees with masks.

   B. Install warning signs for persons with respiratory problems.

   C. Train employees about the problem and ways to reduce smoke.

   D. Design new ventilation system to reduce smoke to an acceptable level.

11. As the new HR Manager at an outpatient surgery center with employees who are exposed to potentially infectious material on a regular basis, what OSHA standard would be your top priority to implement?

   A. Process Safety Management

   B. Bloodborne Pathogens

   C. Emergency Exit Procedures

   D. Hazard Communication

12. Cyber Tronics, an electronics manufacturing plant has just received an onsite inspection from an OSHA officer, which was unannounced and unexpected. What steps can HR legally take if a violation is noted?

   A. Refuse OSHA officer access to new machinery.

   B. Tell the OSHA officer they must come back the following day.

   C. Allow the inspection and file a Notice of Contest within 15 days if an issue arises.

   D. Allow the inspection and file a Notice of Contest within 20 days.

Objective 04   Establish and Administer a Return-to-Work Process after Illness or Injury to Ensure a Safe Workplace

13. An employee has been injured on the job and the CEO asks the VP of HR to look into the return-to-work process and a possible modified duty assignment. The VP of HR requested that the employee obtain a return-to-work authorization from the doctor but the doctor's note simply states "light duty" work. What should the VP of HR do next?

A. Offer employee time off until she's ready to return to normal job functions.

B. Send the physician a lost work time report to clarify exactly which days have been missed from work.

C. Send the physician a detailed description of the accident so that the physician can form a medical opinion.

D. Send the physician a job description so the physician can form a medical opinion as to whether light duty work is appropriate.

14. An HR rep is reviewing a list of jobs to consider for an assembler employee who is returning to work after a repetitive motion injury resulting in a neck injury. Which of the following would be the best choice?

A. Performing quality checks on the products that the employee was previously assembling

B. Preparing paperwork for HR staff

C. Preparing mailing labels for the promotional materials

D. Answering phones for the front desk

15. The CEO of Club Pet, Inc. is questioning the HR department's proposal to create modified duty programs because of the extra administrative overhead these programs may cause. The CEO is requesting an explanation of the programs' value. What should HR highlight as the most important benefit?

A. Higher employee morale of all employees

B. Retention of valuable and trained employees, thus reducing the costs of re-hiring

C. A selling feature for the company for potential applicants

D. Workers' compensation rates may decrease

16. An employee is returning to work after a case of the shingles (a condition that results in painful lesions, stress, fatigue, depression, and skin sensitivity) and has not yet fully recovered. What would be the best example of a job accommodation an employer could provide?

A. Reduced work schedule and periodic rest breaks

B. Coworkers taking over the employee's tasks

C. A modified work station

D. A doctor on-call to help with pain

Objective 05   Develop/Select, Implement, and Evaluate Plans and Policies to Protect Employees and Other Individuals, and to Minimize the Organization's Loss and Liability

17. A fire alarm sounded in a building of approximately 500 employees. During the exit process, managers gave conflicting directions. Employees seemed confused as to what to do and where to go. Twenty minutes later, the entire building was vacated. What should immediately occur to minimize future liability?

    A. Create a process that accounts for all equipment, data, and other critical company property, and conduct training.

    B. Revise the evacuation plan, create a process that accounts for all employees and non-employees, and conduct training.

    C. Create a map of where everyone is located in the building so that a report can be handed to emergency personnel.

    D. Be prepared to provide medical assistance when necessary, learn CPR, and train key personnel in CPR.

18. Rumors have been circulating that one of the employees has been receiving threatening calls at work from her former abusive spouse. Which of the following is the best immediate action the employer should take to minimize liability?

    A. Because rumors are circulating at this point, calm employees down and educate them about expectations against spreading gossip in the workplace.

    B. Meet with leadership, develop a "violence in the workplace" policy, and get supervisors involved in training employees on the new policy.

    C. Interview the employee allegedly receiving calls, assess if there is a danger to her and others in the workplace, and take preventive steps.

    D. Establish an evacuation plan, train all employees on the new plan, conduct regular evacuation drills, and notify local authorities of the drills.

19. A supervisor reported that he just witnessed one of his employees staggering while walking. When he asked the employee if he was okay, the employee responded with slurred speech. The supervisor reported that he knows that this employee is a recovering alcoholic. What should be the best first step to take?

    A. Call a taxi and send the employee home until he feels better.

    B. Because the employee is violating policy, terminate his employment.

    C. Immediately ask the employee to submit to a drug test.

    D. Give the employee a rest period before he starts work.

20. A large retail establishment has a workplace violence policy protecting employees from harm. The policy clearly states employees should not under any circumstance engage in violent acts, including fighting. One night while on a break, an employee spotted a woman being attacked by a man in the parking lot. He asked the woman if she needed help and the attacker began hitting the employee. The employee fought back. What is the best course of action?

   A. Commend the employee for saving a customer's life and review the policy to add exceptions.

   B. Terminate the employee for violating company policy and post the policy for all employees.

   C. Provide the employee with a corrective action form and conduct training for all employees.

   D. Train all employees on expectations and safety procedures and provide self-defense techniques.

Objective 06   Communicate and Train the Workforce on Security Plans and Policies

21. An organization recently realized that a virus was launched in its computer system causing an overload on the server. The virus was tracked down to a common-use computer where an employee had downloaded what he thought was a document from a friend outside the company. What would be an effective course of action?

   A. Take the common-use computer away and restrict any e-mail use.

   B. Terminate the employee for downloading unauthorized documents.

   C. Continue on with the same practice because this virus was a one-time issue.

   D. Review and expand the policy and training to all front-line employees.

22. A multinational organization has locations across the globe. Reports are coming in of a possible outbreak of deadly protests in Egypt and other countries. What would be the best course of action that contributes significantly to a global workplace security plan?

   A. Implement global travel safety protocols for those employees potentially impacted by the protests.

   B. Wait to see if the protests subside and continue business activities as normal.

   C. Stay up-to-date on current events by watching the news and reading newspapers.

   D. Develop stress management training and require all managers to attend.

23. An organization conducts annual training on how to respond if a visitor should become combative and threatening to staff. One day an agitated visitor arrived on location and became combative and threatening to staff. The staff seemed uncertain about what to do. According to OSHA training guidelines, how would you improve the effectiveness of the annual training?

   A. Require mandatory retraining of situations involving combative visitors. Ensure supervisors and senior leaders are supportive of the retraining effort and make several retraining sessions available.

   B. Retrace steps through the training process. Ask key questions, such as whether objectives were clearly presented, whether the learning activity simulates the actual job, and whether employees are allowed to participate in the training process.

   C. Conduct a house-wide security training sessions. Invite the local law enforcement authorities to present training, and require all supervisors and managers to be supportive to ensure that staff attend training sessions.

   D. Interview the employees involved in this combative visitor incident. Consider corrective actions for the employees who did not respond appropriately during the incident, such as requiring the employees to attend training sessions.

Objective 07 Develop, Monitor, and Test Business Continuity and Disaster Recovery Plans

24. A Gulf Coast company located in Miami, Florida, is developing a disaster recovery plan in case of emergency. Which of the following would be an ideal part of the disaster recovery plan?

   A. Backing up all files electronically at an out-of-state location

   B. Storing records in a different room

   C. Storing records in a remote location, one hour from the Miami office

   D. Copying all hard copy files, so two copies are available

25. Your HR department has been tasked with formulating a disaster recovery plan. What is your first step?

   A. Inventory office equipment.

   B. Make an inventory of all jobs that would need to be relocated in order to keep the business running.

   C. Send files off-site for backup.

   D. Contact an insurance agent to inquire about necessary coverage.

26. What is the most important task the HR department can do to ensure a successful and effective business continuity plan?

A. Have insurance company contact information handy.

B. Create an employee phone tree.

C. Get executive sponsorship.

D. Test the plan prior to a disaster occurring.

Objective 08 Communicate and Train the Workforce on the Business Continuity and Disaster Recovery Plans

27. You are part of a multidisciplinary team to assess the effectiveness of the company's business continuity and recovery plan that has been in place for 10 years. A part of your role will be to assess the effectiveness of training on the business continuity and recovery plan. How would you assess the effectiveness of training?

   A. Interview all supervisors and find out how often training and drills occur.

   B. Review policies and check to see if training is based on old policies and practices.

   C. Attend training sessions, review all training materials, and check if the curriculum is up-to-date.

   D. Measure staff awareness by conducting surveys and interviews and observe reaction to drills.

28. An organization has had in place a business continuity and recovery plan for five years. Because nothing has happened in previous years requiring the use of the plan, there is a complacent attitude organization-wide. Most people laugh at the thought of training, shrug, and often say, "We have a plan and know where to grab the binder. What more do you want?" How would you solve this cultural dilemma?

   A. Report the negative behavior to supervisors.

   B. Test the plan involving employees in drills.

   C. Document the behavior in personnel files.

   D. Remind people of actual natural disasters.

29. Hurricane Katrina came ashore causing an underwater city to go without power and basic resources for weeks. An organization has kept data safely in a secondary site. However, employees could not travel to the site to access critical information. No one knew how to access the secondary site data in order to keep the business running. How would you prevent this type of issue in the future?

   A. Develop a business recovery plan and train employees.

   B. Develop a business continuity plan and train employees.

   C. Develop an information security plan and train employees.

   D. Develop a plan for travel in inclement weather and train employees.

Objective 09   Develop Policies and Procedures to Direct the Appropriate Use of Electronic Media and Hardware

30. Janice is an administrative assistant at a real estate company. She spends approximately 30 percent of her day browsing social media sites and shopping online. This has significantly impacted the quality and quantity of work she completes daily. When she started with the company, she signed a policy that prohibits surfing the Internet during work hours. What is HR's *best* next step? Her supervisor brings the concern to the HR Director and asks for guidance.

   A. HR should advise the supervisor to meet with Janice and review the Internet usage policy, adherence to it, and potential consequences.

   B. Janice should be terminated because she is in direct violation of a company policy.

   C. HR should provide training for all employees on the Internet Usage policy.

   D. HR should provide training for the supervisor regarding how to finesse a termination conversation.

31. There has been an increase in inappropriate websites being accessed from company computers in the past year. This has resulted in several worms and viruses circulating throughout the company network, which has cost thousands of dollars to repair. The IT Director would like to upgrade the firewall and install tracking software on all company computers. What should HR consider in this case?

   A. HR should advise IT to select and install the monitoring software.

   B. HR should restrict employee access to any company computer.

   C. HR should warn the IT Director that monitoring the websites employees visit directly violates the Electronic Communications Privacy Act.

   D. HR should develop an Appropriate Computer Use policy, train employees on the policy, and require employees to sign and acknowledge the new policy before IT installs the tracking software.

32. During new hire orientation, employees at a food and beverage distribution company sign an e-mail policy that states that all electronic activity done during the normal course of business may be monitored. From her company-assigned laptop, Michelle used her personal Gmail account to e-mail a friend details of her plan to start a similar company and forwarded a confidential client list to herself from her work e-mail to her Gmail account. The transmission of client lists to non-company e-mail addresses and the use of the company's electronic

devices for personal business is strictly prohibited per company policy, which was detailed in the e-mail policy Michelle signed at orientation. You are made aware of the series of electronic communications via a routine monthly communications report from the IT Department. As the HR Director, what is your best next step?

A. Nothing. Michelle has a reasonable expectation of privacy because she used her personal Gmail account.

B. Have a conference with Michelle regarding the e-mail policy signed at orientation and take the appropriate disciplinary action.

C. Nothing. Michelle has a reasonable expectation of privacy under the Electronic Communications and Privacy Act.

D. Terminate Michelle's employment immediately as this is a direct violation of company policy.

Objective 10   Develop and Administer Internal and External Privacy Policies

33. An employee of a national coffee reseller was recently denied a promotion. Since then, he has made several negative statements about the company culture, pay, and promotional opportunities via multiple social media websites. The Facilities Manager wants HR's support in discouraging this type of communication by other employees. As the HR Director, how would you address this concern?

A. Train supervisors on the provisions of the Electronic Communications and Privacy Act.

B. Develop a company privacy policy that clarifies what is expected of the employee in regards to social media.

C. Train staff on the provisions of the Privacy Act of 1974.

D. Develop a company privacy policy that details Internet use.

34. A hurricane caused flooding at Hopeful Healthcare's administrative offices. Several computer hard drives were destroyed, affecting the personal data of 400,000 patients. What is the *best* next step for the Chief Technology Officer?

A. Evaluate and modify the systems affected by the flood in order to reduce this risk in the future.

B. Store patient files on a virtual network.

C. Ensure that information-related policies are uniformly enforced across the company.

D. Hire a vendor to store backup files off-site.

35. The HR department has experienced significant turnover in the past five years. During that time, there have been six different HR Directors. With each change in leadership, department processes have been modified and the HR Specialists are no longer responding to external requests for employee information in a uniform manner. It has been reported that employee social security numbers and birth dates are sometimes provided over the phone. Which of the following is the *best* response the newest HR Director can provide in an attempt to resolve this issue?

    A. Implement and enforce a process for handling verbal and written employment verifications.

    B. Survey affected employees in an effort to identify the HR Specialists who are not using proper judgment in handling vital employee information and then counsel as needed.

    C. Implement and enforce a new employee confidentiality agreement.

    D. Only allow the HR Specialists to respond to requests for employee information made directly by the employee.

Risk Management—Knowledge Objectives

Objective 61 Applicable Federal Laws and Regulations Related to Workplace Health, Safety, Security, and Privacy

36. Which of the following would be considered a required recordable case according to the Occupational Safety and Health Administration (OSHA)?

    A. An employee used a small bandage to stop the bleeding from a paper cut.

    B. An employee went home from work early to recover from flu symptoms.

    C. An employee went to the doctor for back pains after lifting boxes in the office.

    D. An employee received aspirin from the employee health clinic for a headache.

Objective 62 Occupational Injury and Illness Prevention (Safety) and Compensation Programs

37. A company that is found to have a willful violation of safety and health standards is subject to a penalty of up to _____ per violation?

    A. $250, 000

    B. $70,000

    C. $7,000

    D. $100,000

Objective 63   Investigation Procedures of Workplace Safety, Health, and Security Enforcement Agencies

38. An inspection given by OSHA when a fatality, catastrophe, or complaint occurs would be what type of inspection?

    A. Incident inspection

    B. Violation inspection

    C. Programmed inspection

    D. Unprogrammed inspection

Objective 64   Return-to-Work Procedures

39. Farough wants to return to work as an Administrative Assistant two days after carpal tunnel surgery on her right hand. She is left-handed. The medical certification states that she can use her right hand in 14 days. If her employer agrees, which of the following return-to-work policies apply in this case?

    A. Reasonable accommodation

    B. Fit for duty exam

    C. Modified duty

    D. Interactive dialogue

Objective 65   Workplace Safety Risks

40. The OSHA Bloodborne Pathogens standard requires which of the following elements?

    A. Quarterly training for employees who may be exposed to blood-borne pathogens

    B. Vaccination for any employee who may be exposed to blood-borne pathogens

    C. Compensated time off for employees who are in treatment for illnesses resulting from blood-borne pathogen exposure in the normal course of work

    D. Written exposure control plan that explains how to prevent the spread of blood-borne pathogens

Objective 66   Workplace Security Risks

41. In which of the following instances is a non-disclosure agreement (NDA) most likely needed?

    A. A sales person uses a company-purchased calling list and then accepts a new job with a competitor.

    B. An IT company hires someone to develop proprietary software.

C. A former IBM employee opens an Internet café featuring only IBM products.

D. Ann Alese, a freelance artist, paints a portrait of the Madonna and signs it *"Alese – A Replica."*

Objective 67 Potential Violent Behavior and Workplace Violence Conditions

42. As it relates to workplace violence, court interpretation of OSHA's General Duty clause requires that employers do which of the following?

A. Provide employees with access to an Employee Assistance Program (EAP).

B. Provide training to supervisors on the topic of workplace violence.

C. Pay for ongoing private counseling for employees who are on leave due to stress.

D. Be aware of employees who exhibit possible signs of violent behaviors and take steps to prevent them from acting in a violent manner.

Objective 68 General Health and Safety Practices

43. Modifying, redesigning, or replacing a hand tool used in an employee's daily work with the intention of reducing the occurrence of musculoskeletal disorders represents which type of ergonomic control?

A. Engineering

B. Administrative

C. Workplace practices

D. Personal Protective Equipment

Objective 69 Organizational Incident and Emergency Response Plans

44. An emergency response plan may also include a standardized, on-scene, all-hazard incident management section. Which of the following best defines this concept?

A. Incident Command System

B. Emergency Triage Center

C. Incident Span of Control

D. Incident Command Center

Objective 70 Internal Investigation, Monitoring, and Surveillance Techniques

45. An organization wants to prevent the download of computer viruses and monitor employees' use of the Internet while on company time. Identify which of the following would be the best surveillance techniques?

    A. Supervisory monitoring system

    B. Computer monitoring system

    C. Audio/video monitoring system

    D. Call monitoring system

Objective 71 Employer/Employee Rights Related to Substance Abuse

46. Which of the following statements regarding an employee's rights related to substance abuse is correct?

    A. Individuals who currently use illegal drugs are protected by the Americans with Disabilities Act (ADA).

    B. If the results of a pre-employment drug screen reveal use of prescription drugs, the employer must treat this as confidential information.

    C. An alcoholic is a person not protected by the Americans with Disabilities Act (ADA).

    D. Employers are prohibited from using the results of a pre-employment drug screen to determine final hiring decisions.

Objective 72 Business Continuity and Disaster Recovery Plans

47. Ensuring computers and printers are available during a power outage is an example of what kind of plan?

    A. Succession Plan

    B. Strategic Plan

    C. Business Continuity Plan

    D. Evacuation Plan

Objective 73   Data Integrity Techniques and Technology

48. Which of the following will help a company minimize any negative impact to data integrity?

A. A policy that prohibits the sharing of passwords and the utilization of monitoring software that tracks and blocks the attempted download of phishing programs or malware

B. A policy that prohibits the use of social networking sites

C. A policy that prohibits the sharing of confidential information with competitors

D. A policy that prohibits sending unsolicited e-mails to outside vendors

Objective 74   Technology and Applications

49. A hospital has decided to use facial recognition technology to determine which employees are allowed to enter the maternity ward. Advocates state that the added security measures help families feel more secure. Without prior public notice, this collection of biometric data is a threat to what?

A. Employee privacy and identity theft

B. Hospital security procedures

C. Police investigation of unwelcomed hospital visitors

D. The hospital's customer service ratings

Objective 75   Financial Management Practices

50. Which of the following requires that a publicly traded company's employment offers consistently meet internal approval requirements, are consistent with established salary ranges, and that salary increases are documented and approved in accordance with internal policies?

A. Occupational Safety and Health Act

B. Equal Employment Opportunity Commission

C. Sarbanes-Oxley Act

D. Fair Labor Standards Act

1. B	18. C	35. A
2. C	19. C	36. C
3. D	20. A	37. B
4. A	21. D	38. D
5. C	22. A	39. C
6. C	23. B	40. D
7. A	24. A	41. B
8. D	25. B	42. D
9. A	26. D	43. A
10. D	27. D	44. A
11. B	28. B	45. B
12. C	29. B	46. B
13. D	30. A	47. C
14. A	31. D	48. A
15. B	32. B	49. A
16. A	33. B	50. C
17. B	34. A	

1. ☑ **B.** While training employees, providing medical assistance, and giving time off are good practices, they are not considered required practices under the Occupational Safety and Health Act (OSHA). In addition, this scenario describes the employee being off premises but conducting company business. Because the employee was conducting company business, the location is irrelevant. The employer is required to record this incident on the OSHA 300 log.

   ☒ **A, C, and D** are incorrect. **A** is incorrect because while training employees is a good practice, it is not a requirement upon an injury. **C** is incorrect because seeking medical attention is not a requirement. **D** is incorrect because sending the employee home is not a requirement.

2. ☑ **C.** The temporary agency is expected to provide generic hazard training and information concerning categories of chemicals employees may potentially encounter. Host companies would then be responsible for providing site-specific hazard training. OSHA sections 1910.1200(h)(1) and 1926.59 outline the employer's hazard communication standards.

   ☒ **A, B, and D** are incorrect. **A** is incorrect because both the host and temporary agency share hazard communication responsibilities. **B** is incorrect because, as in answer A, both the host and temporary agency share hazard communication responsibilities. **D** is incorrect because the host company is responsible for site-specific information while the temporary agency is responsible for general information.

3. ☑ **D.** The company is complying with the Fair Credit Reporting Act (FCRA) of 1970. The act was initially created to protect consumers from the disclosure of inaccurate information held by consumer reporting agencies. The act was later modified in 2003 to help address identity theft problems and make it easier for individuals to correct their credit information.

   ☒ **A, B, and C** are incorrect. **A** is incorrect because this law does not apply to job applicants. **B** is incorrect because the Freedom of Information Act is not applicable. **C** is incorrect because this does not apply to job applicants.

4. ☑ **A.** The General Duty Clause of OSHA requires an employer to do everything reasonably necessary to protect the life, safety, and health of employees. This includes the adoption of practices and processes reasonably adequate to create a safe and healthy workplace.

   ☒ **B, C, and D** are incorrect. **B** is incorrect because the Code of Federal Regulations does not apply in this situation. **C** is incorrect because the Health and Safety Act does not apply to this situation. **D** is incorrect because an emergency action plan is limited in scope and not an obligation necessarily under the General Duty Clause.

5. ☑ C. The Health Insurance Portability & Accountability Act is a privacy rule that regulates the security and confidentiality of patient information. The issue in this case is whether the employer did all it could to protect patient medical information.

☒ A, B, and D are incorrect. A is incorrect because the Federal Data Protection Act does protect consumer information but does not apply specifically to private medical information. B is incorrect because the Sarbanes-Oxley Act of 2002 does not apply to private medical information. D is incorrect because the Title 21 Code of Federal Regulations (21 CFR Part 11) does not apply to private patient medical information.

6. ☑ C. Gathering data is the first step in a needs assessment. Data can be collected through the use of surveys, observations, advisory groups, and interviews.

☒ A, B, and D are incorrect. A is incorrect because proposing solutions is the third step in a needs assessment process. B is incorrect because calculating costs is the fourth step in a needs assessment. D is incorrect because it is the fifth and final step of a needs assessment.

7. ☑ A. A potentially serious injury could result and also a costly workers' comp claim.

☒ B, C, and D are incorrect because although these choices may happen, they are not the most serious concern.

8. ☑ D. Providing awareness training to employees on potential hazards will help employees notice signs and symptoms earlier on.

☒ A, B, and C are incorrect because these solutions are possible but not the best solution.

9. ☑ A. Lack of funding will halt all aspects of a safety program's progress.

☒ B, C, and D are incorrect because although they are potential threats in a successful safety program, they are not the biggest threat.

10. ☑ D. The first priority is to eliminate the hazard completely. This could be done by installing a new ventilation system.

☒ A, B, and C are incorrect. All of these choices are possible actions to rectify the safety issue but they are of lesser priority when compared to eliminating the hazard completely.

11. ☑ B. The employer has an immediate requirement to keep employees safe from potentially infectious material. This would be the highest priority.

☒ A, C, and D are incorrect. A is incorrect because process safety management works to prevent releases of toxic, reactive, flammable chemicals. C and D are incorrect because although they are important standards to implement, they are not the most crucial in preventing possible injury as a result of possible needle sticks.

12. ☑ C. An employer has the right to file a notice of contest within 15 working days of citation.

☒ A, B, and D are incorrect. A is incorrect because OSHA officers are authorized to inspect all applicable machinery. B is incorrect because OSHA officers are authorized to enter without delay; however, the employer may refuse an inspection and require OSHA to provide a search warrant before requiring access. D is incorrect because the employer has the right to file a notice of contest within 15 days, not 20 days.

13. ☑ D. Providing the physician with the job description can help the doctor better understand the employee's job and therefore provide position-specific work restrictions for light duty.

☒ A, B, and C are incorrect because these would not help the doctor write proper work restrictions.

14. ☑ A. Quality checks of products provide the employee meaningful work and within the medical limitations.

☒ B, C, and D are incorrect because they are not part of an employee's normal job duties, and it is not meaningful compared to the previous job as an assembler.

15. ☑ B. Retaining qualified, trained, and valuable employees is of the utmost importance to an organization as rehiring costs can be a major burden for employers.

☒ A, C, and D are incorrect because these choices would not happen by creating a modified duty program.

16. ☑ A. Because of the fatigue, depression, stress, and pain caused by this illness, it can be accommodated with a reduced work schedule and additional break times to help the employee recuperate.

☒ B, C, and D are incorrect. B is incorrect because although a coworker may help the employee with a job accommodation, the employee is still responsible for completing the essential functions of the job. C is incorrect because this choice is not applicable in this situation. D is incorrect because most employers would not be able to afford to make such an accommodation.

17. ☑ B. The ideal step to minimize liability is to revise the evacuation plan. Create a process that accounts for all employees and non-employees, and conduct training on the plan. In addition, being able to account for all employees, non-employees, customers, and suppliers is a critical component as part of an evacuation plan. This will enable emergency personnel to assess whether or not they need to rescue individuals from a building. Ideal evacuation plans include an orderly process to exit the building and a designation area where a headcount can be taken.

☒ **A, C,** and **D** are incorrect. **A** is incorrect because the issue is with people exiting a building quickly and safely, not with the equipment. **C** is incorrect because having a map of where everyone sits is not an adequate approach to exiting the building safely. That said, having a headcount ready and knowing who may still be in the building is good information to hand to emergency personnel after exiting the building. **D** is incorrect because providing medical assistance is unrelated to the fact that people need to exit a building quickly, safely, and orderly in an emergency.

18. ☑ **C.** Under the General Duty Clause of OSHA, the employer is required to provide "place[s] of employment which are free from recognized hazards that are causing or are likely to cause death or serious physical harm to his employees" (General Duty Clause, Section 5(a)(1)). In this case, the employer is hearing rumors of a possible threat that may or may not come into the workplace. The best step is to investigate and determine whether or not there is a viable threat and take appropriate preventative steps.

☒ **A, B,** and **D** are incorrect. **A** is incorrect because just calming employees down alone does not effectively address a possible threat to safety in the workplace. **B** is incorrect because while the employer may wish to develop a "violence in the workplace" policy and train employees on the new policy as a good long-term practice, it doesn't address a possible eminent threat. **D** is incorrect because developing an evacuation plan is good for the long term but in the short term a threat needs to be assessed and dealt with immediately.

19. ☑ **C.** Individuals who are recovering alcoholics are protected under the Americans with Disabilities Act. However, the employer can ask employees to submit to a drug test if the employer has a reasonable suspicion that the employee is working under the influence of drugs or alcohol. If the employee refuses to take the drug test, the employer can take corrective steps to ensure a safe workplace. The best practice is to have a Drug and Alcohol Free Workplace policy that details what rises to the level of reasonable suspicion and what steps to take.

☒ **A, B,** and **D** are incorrect. **A** is incorrect because sending an employee home until he feels better not only delays solving the issue but also does not ensure a safe work environment in the future. **B** is incorrect because the employee is protected under the Americans with Disabilities Act. Terminating employment outright causes risk to the organization. **D** is incorrect because not only does this not address the issue but also exposes the employee and other employees to possible safety risks in the workplace. The best step is to balance the employee's rights under the Americans with Disabilities Act while ensuring a safe work environment.

20. ☑ **A.** This real-life scenario provides a perfect example of how liability extends beyond just the employee but also to non-employees, such as customers. Initially this employer terminated the employee who got involved in the altercation in the parking lot. The result was public outcry for punishing an employee for saving a customer's life and negative publicity for the company. The best course of action in this case is to commend the employee for saving someone's life but review the policy and consider exceptions that may apply that are aligned with the organization's overall objectives. Addressing what should happen if there is imminent danger to employees or non-employees is a good practice.

☒ **B, C, and D are incorrect.** B is incorrect because taking negative steps toward the employee who saved a customer's life can result in negative publicity and deter employees from watching out for the customer's best interest. C is incorrect because providing a corrective action plan and training does not secure the customer's safety in this case. D is incorrect because just providing self-defense techniques is short-sighted in terms of protecting the organization's liability.

21. ☑ **D.** The best course of action is to review and expand the policy to front-line employees. More often than not this will prevent disastrous cyber security issues that can result from an innocent download or click on a hyperlink.

☒ **A, B, and C are incorrect.** A is incorrect because in many cases a common use computer is an efficient way to provide house-wide computer access to better serve the customer. B is incorrect because this does not involve employees in the solution. C is incorrect because cyber attacks, hacking, and computer virus incidents are a common issue today. Without implementing proper precautions, the issue could occur repeatedly.

22. ☑ **A.** The best proactive step is to review, update, implement, and communicate global travel safety protocols immediately.

☒ **B, C, and D are incorrect.** B is incorrect because just waiting for updates is not a proactive step. Unrest in various countries is an unpredictable factor, and it is best to always take safety concerns seriously and act on them quickly. C is incorrect because simply staying up-to-date on the news is not proactive and effective in keeping employees safe. D is incorrect because while dealing with country unrest can be stressful, this alone is not an effective step in keeping employees safe.

23. ☑ **B.** According to OSHA training guidelines, you should consider retracing your steps through the training process. Ask key questions such as whether objectives were clearly presented, whether the learning activity simulated the actual job, whether employees were allowed to participate in the training process, and so on.

☒ **A, C, and D are incorrect.** A is incorrect because while an employer may require mandatory training as a good practice, this is not part of the OSHA requirements. C is incorrect because conducting house-wide security training sessions does not adequately address the ineffective training issue. D is incorrect because providing corrective actions in this case will not provide insights into improving training effectiveness and it will deter employees from expressing concerns.

24. ☑ **A.** Because natural disasters (hurricanes) are a possibility in that region, it is a necessary precaution to back up computer files electronically out of state and out of harm's way.

☒ **B, C,** and **D** are incorrect because these choices still leave the information vulnerable to natural disasters.

25. ☑ **B.** Taking inventory of all jobs needed for the business to operate is the most important and first thing HR should think about because without the proper staff, the business cannot operate.

☒ **A, C,** and **D** are incorrect because while these choices are applicable and needed during the process of disaster recovery planning, they are not the first step.

26. ☑ **D.** Testing the plan prior to a disaster actually occurring is the only way to ensure the proposed plan will actually work.

☒ **A, B,** and **C** are incorrect because while these choices are important to the success of the business continuity plan, they are not the most important to a successful plan.

27. ☑ **D.** The most effective way to assess business continuity training effectiveness is to check staff awareness. One sign of an ineffective training is a staff that lacks awareness of a business continuity and recovery plan.

☒ **A, B,** and **C** are incorrect. **A** is incorrect because interviewing supervisors to learn of drill frequency is not relevant to effective training. **B** is incorrect because reviewing policies is not an adequate step toward measuring training effectiveness. **C** is incorrect because while sitting in on training sessions is a good practice, it isn't the best way to measure training effectiveness.

28. ☑ **B.** Involving employees in drills that mirror realistic disasters is an effective way to correct complacency issues. In addition, disaster drills also show where there may be weaknesses in the business continuity and recovery plan.

☒ **A, C,** and **D** are incorrect. **A** is incorrect because reporting behaviors to the supervisor alone is not an adequate step for changing a culture of complacency. **C** is incorrect because simply documenting behaviors in the personnel file is not an effective step toward changing a culture of complacency. **D** is incorrect because reminding people of natural disasters alone is not an effective step toward changing a culture of complacency. The best course of action is to make disaster situations seem real through drills.

29. ☑ **B.** A business continuity plan is a set of documents, instructions, and procedures that identifies potential threats and provides direction on how to respond in ways that keep the business operating.

☒ **B, C,** and **D** are incorrect. **B** is incorrect because a business recovery plan includes procedures and guidelines in recovering business operations lost after a disaster. **C** is incorrect because an information security plan is an overbroad term that does not necessarily reflect a business continuity plan. **D** is incorrect because an inclement weather policy may be part of the larger business continuity plan.

30. ☑ **A.** HR should advise the supervisor to meet with Janice and review the Internet usage policy, adherence to it, and potential consequences.

☒ **B, C, and D are incorrect. B and D** are incorrect for similar reasons. While it is a best practice to continually provide supervisors with training on how to handle a conversation where an employee will be terminated, actually terminating Janice for this violation is drastic and results in lowering employee morale for the people still employed with the company. **C** is incorrect because it simply doesn't solve the issue presented.

31. ☑ **D.** Employees should be made aware of any policy that could violate their privacy before it is implemented.

☒ **A, B, and C are incorrect. A** is incorrect because HR should not encourage implementing this software before notifying the employee of the change and how it affects them. **B** is incorrect because restricting access to company computers is counterproductive. **C** is incorrect because the ECPA allows the monitoring of electronic communication by the employer when done during the normal course of business.

32. ☑ **B.** It would be appropriate to discuss these findings with the employee and engage in the disciplinary steps that are deemed appropriate per policy.

☒ **A, C, and D are incorrect. A** is incorrect because the e-mail use policy clarifies that any electronic communication made using the company's equipment can be reviewed. It is irrelevant that Michelle used her Gmail account. She transmitted this e-mail via the company laptop so a record of the content of the e-mail exists and was discovered during a routine review of all of the company's electronic communications. **C** is incorrect because there is no reasonable expectation of privacy under the ECPA. The bottom line is that Michelle used the company equipment to access her Gmail account and transmit this communication. Per the company's e-mail use policy, they are permitted to monitor. **D** is incorrect because it is advisable that the company closely review and evaluate Michelle's actions as they relate to the e-mail use policy before making any decision in regard to continued employment. Immediate termination may or may not be appropriate and cannot be determined until after an in-depth conference with Michelle and a review of all the facts pertinent to the investigation.

33. ☑ **B.** A good social media policy details what types of communication both on and off the job made via social media are acceptable. A company with a policy like this in place that was signed or acknowledged by employees helps to negate or discourage undesirable employee behavior with regard to social media.

☒ **A, C, and D are incorrect. A** is incorrect because ECPA makes no mention of social media. The act establishes that employers can monitor the creation of electronic communication prior to it being sent or after its receipt if it occurs during the course of business and employees have consented. **C** is incorrect because the Privacy Act of 1974 is not applicable in this scenario. It governs the collection and use of personally identifiable information. It provides that employees can request their records and have to be granted access to their records and given the opportunity to request a correction to those records. **D** is incorrect because an Internet use policy addresses how an employee accesses the Internet on company time.

34. ☑ **A.** The CTO should evaluate and modify the risk management systems in place for the hard drives in an effort to reduce or eliminate loss in the future.
☒ **B, C,** and **D** are incorrect. **C** is incorrect because simply enforcing policies won't address this situation. Policies should be enforced but there first needs to be a plan in place that includes a more secure way to store critical patient data. **B** and **D** are incorrect because while it may be a good idea to store backup files off-site or change the storage model so that hard drives are no longer needed (i.e., virtual network), without first assessing the risk in accordance with the organization's needs, the CTO would not know if off-site storage is a feasible or appropriate solution.

35. ☑ **A.** The newest HR Director should implement and ensure compliance with a process for responding to employment verification requests that are received either in written form or verbally. It is okay to respond to verbal verifications but in order to protect employees from potential identity theft, the information given out over the phone must be limited. Requests that are received in writing should be authorized by the employee, and it is a best practice that the written request originate from an established company on company letterhead.
☒ **B, C,** and **D** are incorrect. **B** and **C** are incorrect because simply reprimanding the offending HR Specialists or the signing of confidentiality agreements does nothing to rectify the issue. In both instances, the Specialists will be made aware of their error in judgment but because the situation, as stated, suggests that there are inconsistencies across the department in this area, it would be most effective to implement a process, train everyone on what the new process is, and enforce the new process consistently. **D** is incorrect because implementing a strict policy where the HR department only responds to employment verifications made directly by the employee, does not provide an appropriate level of customer service to the employee and makes daily operations cumbersome and ineffective. For example, an employee who is trying to qualify for a re-finance on a home loan may only need the employer to verbally verify for the bank their dates of employment and that they are indeed employed. If a policy such as D was in effect, the loan officer could not simply call HR and this would delay processing of the loan.

36. ☑ **C.** OSHA Standard 1904.7 considers a case to meet the general recording criteria if it involves a significant injury or illness diagnosed by a physician or other licensed healthcare professional, even when it does not result in death, days away from work, restricted work or job transfer, medical treatment beyond first aid, or loss of consciousness. An injury that is a result of something that happened on the job is a "reportable" event.

☒ A, B, and D are incorrect. A is incorrect because an employee receiving a small bandage for a paper cut is considered first-aid and not required to be recorded. B is incorrect because this act applies to workplace-related injury and illnesses. The flu or common cold is not generally included in this requirement. D is incorrect because the employee receiving aspirin for a headache is not considered an occupational injury or illness, and is not required to be recorded per OSHA requirements.

37. ☑ B. Up to $70, 000 per violation could apply if it is found that a company willfully violated safety and health standards (for example, knowingly locking exit doors).

☒ A, C, and D are incorrect. A is incorrect because $250,000 could apply if an employer is convicted in a criminal proceeding of a willful violation of a standard that resulted in an employee death. C is incorrect because this would apply when a serious violation is found that is likely to cause death or serious injury of which the employer should have been aware. D is incorrect because it does not apply to the fines in this question.

38. ☑ D. OSHA conducts two types of inspections. The "unprogrammed" inspection occurs when there is a fatality, catastrophe, or a complaint.

☒ A, B, and C are incorrect. A is incorrect because "incident inspection" is not an adequate term used to describe this type of OSHA inspection. B is incorrect because a violation inspection is not a relevant term. C is incorrect because a programmed inspection refers to a scheduled inspection by OSHA.

39. ☑ C. Modified duty is the best description of what is applicable because the accommodation would be temporary.

☒ A, B, and D are incorrect. A is incorrect because a reasonable accommodation is a permanent solution. Farough only requires an accommodation for a little less than two weeks. B is incorrect because a Fit for Duty exam is an appropriate and useful part of a return-to-work program but, in this case, it is already established that Farough can return to work shortly. The only question is how soon. D is incorrect because an interactive dialogue between the employee and the Return-to-Work Coordinator regarding the employee's fitness to return to work is something required by the American with Disabilities Act. However, carpal tunnel is not covered under ADA. It is a best practice for an employer to maintain an open dialogue with injured employees but it is not required in all cases.

40. ☑ D. The Bloodborne Pathogens standard requires employers to take measures to prevent exposure. This includes written documentation on how to take preventive measures, post-exposure evaluation requirements, reporting, and evaluation.

☒ A, B, and C are incorrect. Training, vaccinations, and paid time off are not requirements of the Occupational Safety and Health Act's (OSHA) Bloodborne Pathogens standard.

41. ☑ **B.** It would be in the best interest of the owners of an IT company to have a newly hired developer of a proprietary software sign a non-disclosure agreement. This will legally protect the company if the developer leaves and tries to work for a competitor or open his/her own business developing a similar software package.

☒ **A, C, and D are incorrect. A** is incorrect because the sales person is using a calling list that can be purchased from any company that sells lists for cold calling potential customers. **C** is incorrect because this former employee did not steal the Java Beans product and try to pass it off as her own. She is actually engaged in retailing Java Bean products. **D** is incorrect because Ann Alese is a freelance artist as opposed to a commissioned artist. She owns the copyright for the work she creates so it is unlikely that a non-disclosure agreement would be of any value.

42. ☑ **D.** Employers are required to maintain an awareness of potentially violent employees and take steps to prevent the violence from occurring.

☒ **A, B, and D are incorrect. A, B,** and **D** are incorrect for similar reasons. An EAP program is a great tool to assist employees who may be stressed and potentially violent; training for supervisors on recognizing and responding to threats of workplace violence is an excellent best practice; and providing counseling for employees who are on leave due to stress is an attractive benefit. However, none of these are OSHA General Duty Clause requirements.

43. ☑ **A.** Engineering controls include any ergonomic solution designed to fit the job to the person. They are preferred because they are a more permanent way to reduce ergonomic workplace hazards.

☒ **B, C, and D are incorrect. B** and **C** are incorrect: The terms can be used interchangeably and involve the establishment of efficient processes and procedures. An example would be establishing a job rotation so that workers rotate between different jobs that utilize different muscle groups. **D** is incorrect because a personal protective equipment control involves wearing protective equipment such as gloves to reduce or eliminate an ergonomic workplace hazard.

44. ☑ **A.** An incident command system (ICS) is a standardized on-scene, all-hazard incident management. This concept came about in the 1970s when several wildfires resulted in fatalities and millions in damages. Organizations have adopted the ICS concept as part of its incident plan as a way of systematically handling small or large incidents.

☒ **B, C, and D are incorrect. B** is incorrect because an emergency triage center does not adequately define the incident command system concept. **C** is incorrect because an incident span of control is not the definition of an incident command system. **D** is incorrect because an incident command center is only a part of the incident command system.

45. ☑ **B.** A computer monitoring system is a surveillance technique often used to monitor employees' use of the company computer. Employers use this method to also monitor productivity, and login and time worked information for telecommuting employees as well.

    ☒ **A, C,** and **D** are incorrect. **A** is incorrect because a supervisor cannot effectively monitor the use of a computer, particularly if it is a laptop that is taken home over the weekends. **C** is incorrect because an audio/video monitor tracks physical foot traffic or conversations in the workplace but does not adequately monitor computer use. **D** is incorrect because a call monitoring systems monitors phone usage and not necessarily computer use.

46. ☑ **B.** According to the ADA, if the results of a pre-employment drug screen reveal use of prescription drugs or other medical information, the employer must treat that information as confidential.

    ☒ **A, C,** and **D** are incorrect. **A** is incorrect because people who currently engage in the illegal use of drugs are specifically excluded from the definition of a "qualified individual with a disability" protected by the ADA when the employer takes action on the basis of their drug use. **C** is incorrect because alcoholism is considered a medical condition and protected under the ADA. **D** is incorrect because pre-employment job testing can only be done after an offer of employment is made, but the offer can be contingent upon a satisfactory drug screen, which means the employer can take action based on the results of the drug screen results.

47. ☑ **C.** A business continuity plan addresses how a company will perform normal processes in the event of a disaster.

    ☒ **A, B,** and **D** are incorrect. **A** is incorrect because a succession plan does not define a business continuity plan. **B** is incorrect because a strategic plan describes the overall direction of an organization. **D** is incorrect because an evacuation plan describes the exit strategy of a business and is part of an emergency response plan.

48. ☑ **A.** A policy that prohibits the sharing of passwords and the utilization of monitoring software that tracks and blocks the attempted download of phishing programs or malware.

    ☒ **B, C,** and **D** are incorrect. **B, C,** and **D** are incorrect for similar reasons. Protecting data integrity focuses on the corruption of company information assets. Examples include downloading malware or becoming a victim of a social engineer. Social networking sites, the potential release of copyright information, and sending e-mails from work have no effect on the corruption of electronically stored data.

49. ☑ **A.** Biometric screening can be a threat to employee privacy and result in identity theft because these measures allow the employer to collect a significant amount of demographic information and in the case of retinal scans, medical information as well. If the employer doesn't house this information in a secure and encrypted database, then an employee could have his or her information stolen and used by an enterprising hacker.

☒ **B, C,** and **D** are incorrect. **B** and **C** are incorrect for similar reasons. As long as employees are made aware of the new security procedures and the hospital management is cooperative with the police if there are unwelcomed visitors, there is no "threat." **D** is incorrect because the advocates of the new policy have indicated that this heightened level of security is desired by the residents of the maternity ward.

50. ☑ **C.** Section 404 of the Sarbanes-Oxley Act requires that public companies routinely review and test internal financial transaction controls (approval process). As a result, all salary offers, raises, or any other compensation must be documented and follow an established internal signature approval process.

☒ **A, B,** and **D** are incorrect. **A** is incorrect because the focus of the OSH Act is to protect employees from injury or illness. **B** is incorrect because the EEOC is the agency created by Title VII to promote equal opportunities in employment for protected classes. **D** is incorrect because the FLSA is a law that regulates employee status, overtime pay, child labor, minimum wage, record keeping, and other wage-related administrative issues.

About the CD-ROM

The CD-ROM included with this book comes with Total Tester customizable practice exam software with hundreds of practice exam questions for the PHR and SPHR exams, as well as a PDF copy of the book.

System Requirements

The software requires Windows XP or higher and 30MB of hard disk space for full installation, in addition to a current or prior major release of Chrome, Firefox, Internet Explorer, or Safari. To run, the screen resolution must be set to 1024 × 768 or higher. The PDF copy of the book requires Adobe Acrobat, Adobe Reader, or Adobe Digital Editions to view.

Total Tester Premium Practice Exam Software

Total Tester provides you with a simulation of the PHR and SPHR exams. The Total Tester Premium Test Engine includes all of the PHR and SPHR questions from the book, with more than 600 practice exam questions in total. You can create custom exams from selected exam knowledge areas. You can further customize the number of questions and time allowed.

The exams can be taken in either Practice Mode or Exam Mode. Practice Mode provides an assistance window with references to the *PHR/SPHR Professional in Human Resources Certification All-in-One Exam Guide*, an explanation of the answer, and the option to check your answer as you take the test. Exam Mode provides a simulation of the actual exam. The number of questions, the types of questions, and the time allowed are intended to be an accurate representation of the exam environment. Both Practice Mode and Exam Mode provide an overall grade and a grade broken down by knowledge area.

To take a test, launch the program and select PHR or SPHR from the Installed Question Packs list. You can then select Practice Mode, Exam Mode, or Custom Mode. After making your selection, click Start Exam to begin.

Installing and Running Total Tester
Premium Practice Exam Software

From the main screen you may install the Total Tester by clicking the Total Tester Practice Exams button. This will begin the installation process and place an icon on your desktop and in your Start menu. To run Total Tester, navigate to Start | (All) Programs | Total Seminars, or double-click the icon on your desktop.

To uninstall the Total Tester software, go to Start | Settings | Control Panel | Add/ Remove Programs (XP) or Programs And Features (Vista/7/8), and then select the Total Tester program. Select Remove, and Windows will completely uninstall the software.

PDF Copy of the Book

The entire contents of the book are provided in PDF on the CD-ROM. This file is viewable on your computer and many portable devices. Adobe's Acrobat Reader is required to view the file on your PC and has been included on the CD-ROM. You may also use Adobe Digital Editions to access your electronic book.

 NOTE For more information on Adobe Reader and to check for the most recent version of the software, visit Adobe's web site at www.adobe.com and search for the free Adobe Reader or look for Adobe Reader on the product page. Adobe Digital Editions can also be downloaded from the Adobe web site.

To view the electronic book on a portable device, copy the PDF file to your computer from the CD-ROM, and then copy the file to your portable device using a USB or other connection. Adobe does offer a mobile version of Adobe Reader, the Adobe Reader mobile app, which currently supports iOS and Android. For customers using Adobe Digital Editions and the iPad, you may have to download and install a separate reader program on your device. The Adobe web site has a list of recommended applications, and McGraw-Hill Education recommends the Bluefire Reader.

Technical Support

For questions regarding the Total Tester software or operation of the CD-ROM, visit www.totalsem.com or e-mail support@totalsem.com.

For questions regarding the PDF copy of the book, e-mail techsolutions@mhedu .com or visit http://mhp.softwareassist.com.

For questions regarding book content, please e-mail customer.service@mheducation .com. For customers outside the United States, e-mail international.cs@mheducation.com.

LICENSE AGREEMENT